The Theodicy of Peter Taylor Forsyth

The Theodicy of Peter Taylor Forsyth
A "Crucial" Justification of the Ways of God to Man

THENG HUAT LEOW

Foreword by Trevor A. Hart

◈PICKWICK *Publications* • Eugene, Oregon

THE THEODICY OF PETER TAYLOR FORSYTH
A "Crucial" Justification of the Ways of God to Man

Copyright © 2011 Theng Huat Leow. All rights reserved. Except for brief quotations in critical publications or reviews, no part of this book may be reproduced in any manner without prior written permission from the publisher. Write: Permissions, Wipf and Stock Publishers, 199 W. 8th Ave., Suite 3, Eugene, OR 97401.

Pickwick Publications
An Imprint of Wipf and Stock Publishers
199 W. 8th Ave., Suite 3
Eugene, OR 97401

www.wipfandstock.com

ISBN 13: 978-1-60899-435-9

Cataloguing-in-Publication data:

Leow, Theng Huat.

The theodicy of Peter Taylor Forsyth : a "crucial" justification of the ways of God to man / Theng Huat Leow ; foreword by Trevor A. Hart.

xviii + 268 p. ; 23 cm. Includes bibliographical references and index.

ISBN 13: 978-1-60899-435-9

1. Forsyth, Peter Taylor, 1848–1921. 2. Theology, Doctrinal — History — 20th century. 3. Theodicy. I. Hart, Trevor A. II. Title.

BX7260.F583 L45 2011

Manufactured in the U.S.A.

To

CHENG PING

Whose sacrifice made this work possible,
Whose companionship made it a joy, and
Whose love makes its contents more comprehensible to the author

Contents

Foreword by Trevor A. Hart / *ix*

Preface and Acknowledgments / *xiii*

Abbreviations / *xvi*

1. Introduction / 1
2. The Locus of the True Revelation of God and God's Self-Justification / 29
3. The First Outcome of God's Self-Justification: God Moves the World Inexorably Towards His Goal / 59
4. The Significance of the First Outcome of God's Self-Justification: The Teleological and Historical Natures of Forsyth's Theodicy / 98
5. The Second Outcome of God's Self-Justification: The Revelation of the Incomparable Suffering of God / 128
6. The Significance of the Second Outcome of God's Self-Justification: God as the Chief Sufferer and Giver and Christ as Our Model Of Faith / 153
7. Forsyth's View on the Origin of Evil / 179
8. The Significance of Forsyth's View on the Origin Of Evil / 214
9. Conclusion / 232

Bibliography / 241

Index / 263

Foreword

Peter Taylor Forsyth was born in Aberdeen in 1848, the son of a postman. Excelling in his undergraduate studies (in classical literature), after his graduation in 1869 he accepted a position as assistant to the university professor of Latin and, had a call to ordination not interrupted things, he might well have enjoyed a glittering career in the subject. Instead, he began his theological training, first in Göttingen at the feet of the great Liberal Protestant theologian Albrecht Ritschl (whose impact on Forsyth's outlook was immense, and in many respects survived the outward breach with "Ritschlianism" which marked his theological crisis and *volte-face* in the late 1880s) and then in London. During twenty-five years of pastoral ministry to Congregationalist churches in Bradford, London, Manchester, Leicester, and Cambridge, Forsyth acquired a reputation not just as a remarkable preacher, but as a speaker and a writer too, and one whose pen ranged with ease and authority across subjects and issues of wider public concern (art, culture, politics) as well as those of theology proper. Many of the greatest thinkers and artists of the nineteenth century came under his scrutiny—Hardy, Hegel, Ibsen, William James, Nietzsche, Schopenhauer, Tolstoy, Wagner, and Wordsworth to mention but a few—their abiding contribution and value being weighed in the light of Forsyth's own distinctive evangelical Christian vision. The result is a rich vein of theological reflection that takes the reader straight to the heart of Christian doctrine without ever leaving behind the shared experiences and concerns of the life we share as creatures in God's world. In 1901, by now an established star in the Congregational firmament, Forsyth was called to be Principal of Hackney College in London, a post he held until his death in 1921.

Like all authors, Forsyth is identifiably earthed in the particular concerns and debates of his own day; but like all great authors, what he has to say is rarely limited by such considerations. Additionally, he was remarkably prescient, the emphasis and focus of his major works regularly anticipating major theological developments in the decades following his death. To refer to him as a "Barthian before Barth," though (or even a "Moltmannian before Moltmann"), is to risk belittling Forsyth's own independent significance and contribution both as a prophet for the particular moment, and an enduring witness to the riches of the Christian theological heritage in a century and a culture which had already begun (and would continue) to lose sight of them. Through his immersion in the mind of Scripture and his rich intellectual engagement with the best of learning in a wide range of disciplines, Forsyth grasps that which abides in the human circumstance under God, and offers an account of it that is both passionate and profound. To revisit his writings even more than a century later is to be struck repeatedly by the freshness and the force of what he has to say, so much of which remains just as relevant to the church's life today as it ever was, once the appropriate adjustments to detail of time and place have been made.

The issue of the presence, nature, and extent of suffering in the world has haunted modern religious sensibility more acutely than it did our forebears in earlier centuries. The twentieth century in particular has been described as the most "brutal" yet in human history, and whether it is "man's inhumanity to man" in industrialized warfare, genocide, and acts of terror that is in view, or the enormity of innocent suffering in the wake of such "natural disasters" as famine, epidemic, earthquake, or flood, questions about "evil" and suffering and their place in the account that faith is called to give of God's character and of the world God has made gained a new prominence and a new urgency as that century opened. The relentless slaughter of so many men so quickly on the battle fields of the First World War came towards the end of Forsyth's career, and the enormity of its horrors and their impact on individual and national life alike drove him to his knees and thereafter at once to his writing desk. *The Justification of God* (1916) was to be one of Forsyth's finest works, though it drew identifiably upon much in his *oeuvre* that preceded it. Forsyth was heir to a tradition in Protestant theology which tended most naturally and easily to associate God and the things of God with the very best and most noble of human aspirations, capacities, achievements and experiences. By virtue of his relentless insistence on the centrality of the cross (and the atonement wrought there) to any theological reflection worthy of the epithet "Christian", though, Forsyth himself was able to identify God too (and perhaps more clearly and reliably) amidst the very worst and darkest that life has to offer, not just as one who exercises judgment on the sin and the sins of the world, but equally as one who, even as he allows that judgment to fall, stands squarely in solidarity with those who must bear its consequences. Forsyth's articulation of this fundamental theological insight draws eerily close at points to Moltmann's insistence some 60 years later (deemed a radical departure in its day) that the crucifixion, properly interpreted as an event in the Trinitarian life of God—viz. between the eternal Father and the incarnate Son— compels recognition that here God has penetrated the depths not just of our creaturely suffering, but of suffering as something of which God himself (as God) is capable. The Father suffers the death of his Son. For Forsyth, as for Moltmann, any "theodicy" of a properly Christian sort must both begin and end at this point, orientated throughout towards what occurs between Jesus and his Holy Father on Golgotha. In this respect, as in many others, while fundamentally a product of nineteenth century attitudes and assumptions, Forsyth's vision blazes a theological trail which his twentieth and twenty-first century successors might follow with confidence.

In this fine and judicious study of Forsyth's theodicy, Theng Huat Leow offers a first class introduction to the man and his work. Because everything in Forsyth's theological vision is held together not by any abstract "system" but by its relation to its theological centre of gravity in the cross (the heart of the "moral order" of creation as Forsyth has it), a treatment of his understanding of the core theme of God's righteousness necessarily ventures onto a wider "systematic theological" canvas. Thus, in this volume the reader will find reliable engagement with Forsyth's thinking about revelation, the atonement, the holiness of God, the incarnation, divine passibility, eschatology, and much else besides. The treatment is generous and appreciative, but critical nonetheless. The written style is clear and concise, and the provision of relevant intellectual context deftly and economically done. It was a great pleasure to supervise the research on which this book is based, and it gives me equal pleasure now to commend it to a wide readership.

Trevor A. Hart
Professor of Divinity
University of St Andrews

Preface and Acknowledgments

THIS MONOGRAPH IS A revised version of a doctoral thesis completed in 2009 at the University of St Andrews, United Kingdom. As is usually the case, the completion of such a project is a community effort, and grateful thanks are due to many.

I would, firstly, like to acknowledge God's masterful orchestration of the surprising series of events which enabled me to embark on my PhD studies, and his empowerment and guidance throughout its process. I also want to pay tribute to P. T. Forsyth, with whom I have spent a good part of the preceding few years of my life. I have found in him a reliable and insightful guide into the field of theology, one who has greatly expanded my grasp of this wonderful subject and strengthened my conviction to study, teach, preach and live it out for the rest of my life.

I mention next the Principal (Rev. Dr Ngoei Foong Nghian) and Deans (Profs. Tan Kim Huat and Roland Chia) of my alma mater, Trinity Theological College, Singapore. They have played a crucial role in facilitating my studies as part of the college's faculty-in-development programme. I further acknowledge the generous financial support provided for my studies by Trinity Theological College, the Brash Trust, and Wesley Methodist Church. Wesley is our home church in Singapore, and her senior pastor, Rev. Melvin Huang, and her pastoral team members Paul Satari and Andre De Winne have, in particular, been unstinting in their support. I would like to thank as well those relatives and friends who have contributed time, energy and money for our well-being. I am especially grateful to my parents, my parents-in-law, Siew Li and Melvin, and Cheng Ling for the immense sacrifices they have had to make to ensure that my family and I can stay in the UK with the peace of mind that everything is being well taken care of back home. The time they have spent here in St. Andrews helping us with the kids and the housework is also greatly appreciated.

I have, in the course of my studies, benefited greatly from the guidance offered by my supervisor, Rev. Prof. Trevor Hart. His insightful comments, always offered with generous doses of encouragement, have made this a much better piece of work. I also acknowledge the help I have received from Dr. Michael Partridge on matters concerning continental philosophy. Prof. Paul Moser of Loyola University Chicago has taken the trouble to upload a lot of useful material by Forsyth on his website, some of which were not readily available in the UK. One of the highlights during my time at St Andrews was the theology seminars, both the formal morning sessions and the occasional casual evening meeting. I would like to express my gratitude to both Prof. Alan Torrance and Dr. Steve Holmes for organising these scintillating events. The oral examination for my thesis turned out to be a pleasant as well as intellectually stimulating experience. I am grateful to my examiners, Prof. David Fergusson and Dr. Gavin Hopps, for their encouraging remarks and perceptive suggestions as to how my work could be further strengthened—most of which have been taken on board in this monograph. My fellow PhD student Jason Goroncy deserves special mention. I have enjoyed and benefited greatly from our long hours of discussion on Forsyth, and will always be grateful for his generous sharing of material on the Scottish theologian, some of which he had obtained at the considerable cost of time and money. Other fellow students whose friendship, insight and encouragement are deeply treasured include Darren Schmidt, Chris Chun, R. J. Matava, Chris Chandler, Dong Yoon Kim, Jeff Tippner, Aaron Kuecker, Pete Bellenger, Gerry Wheaton, Antonio Alvarez, and Luke Tallon. I would, in addition, like to acknowledge the kind permission of Blackwell Publishing to reproduce the content of my article entitled "'The Cruciality of the Cross': P. T. Forsyth's Understanding of the Atonement," which appears in *International Journal of Systematic Theology* 11.2 (2009) 190–207. Parts of this article appear in chapters 1 and 2 of this work.

My children, Natania, Benedict and Christina (the latter two born in Scotland), have been a great joy and delight to me, even though they have proven to be a handful at times. Their greatest contribution to my studies has been to keep me focused on "the moral as the real" (an axiom of Forsyth's). They move me frequently away from the realm of abstract thought in a peaceful environment to a noisy and messy world which constantly needs practical intervention to prevent it from spinning out of control. They impose on me, in other words, my profound moral obligations as a parent, and my work has been the better for it. Finally, I mention my wife, Cheng Ping. She has sacrificed more than anyone else in these three years of my studies, undergoing the transformation from a career woman to a full-time homemaker. I could not have completed this project without her competent management of the household and her love and encouragement. It is to her I dedicate this thesis.

Abbreviations

THE FULL DETAILS OF the works listed here are included in the bibliography. All the citations to Forsyth's works in our study will omit his name, unless it is necessary to include it in order to avoid confusion.

BOOKS BY FORSYTH AND ANTHOLOGIES AND COLLECTIONS OF FORSYTH'S WRITING

Authority	*The Principle of Authority in Relation to Certainty, Sanctity and Society: An Essay in the Philosophy of Experimental Religion*
Cruciality	*The Cruciality of the Cross*
Ethic	*The Christian Ethic of War*
Faith	*Faith, Freedom and the Future*
Father	*God the Holy Father*
Justification	*The Justification of God: Lectures for War-Time on a Christian Theodicy*
Life	*This Life and the Next: The Effect on This Life of Faith in Another*
Missions	*Missions in State and Church: Sermons and Addresses*
Parnassus	*Christ on Parnassus: Lectures on Art, Ethic, and Theology*
Person	*The Person and Place of Jesus Christ*

Positive Preaching	Positive Preaching and Modern Mind: The Lyman Beecher Lecture on Preaching, Yale University, 1907
Preaching of Jesus	The Preaching of Jesus and the Gospel of Christ
Recent Art	Religion in Recent Art: Expository Lectures on Rossetti, Burne Jones, Watts, Holman Hunt and Wagner
Revelation	Revelation Old and New: Sermons and Addresses
Sacraments	The Church and the Sacraments
Society	The Church, the Gospel and Society
Theology	Theology in Church and State
Work	The Work of Christ

1

Introduction

WHY FORSYTH'S THEODICY?

PETER TAYLOR FORSYTH BEGINS his great work, *The Justification of God: Lectures for War-Time on a Christian Theodicy*, by citing a warning he had received on including the term "theodicy" in the sub-title of this work. The appearance of such "an unfamiliar word," he was told, might "raise a certain prejudice in some minds."[1] "Theodicy" remains a complex word in our day because it is capable of assuming a variety of (related) meanings. Taken broadly, the term can "cover any theistic response to questions about how theism can be true in view of the existence of evils."[2] Within this broad definition, writers on the subject normally make a twofold distinction. "Defences" seek to show, on a purely logical basis, that the existence of evil is not incompatible with that of an all good and powerful God. "Theodicies" proper, on the other hand, propose actual reasons for the existence and even the prevalence of evil, ones which (in their view) preserve both the goodness and omnipotence of God.[3] In addition, "theodicies," understood broadly, can be classified according to the range of evils they purport to cover.[4] They can also be categorised according to whether they have a "theoretical" or "practical" emphasis.[5]

---

1. *Justification*, v.
2. Adams and Adams, "Introduction," in *Problem of Evil*, 3.
3. Ibid.; Van Inwagen, "Argument from Evil," 62; Tilley, "Use and Abuse of Theodicy," 306.
4. Trakakis, "Theodicy," 162–63.
5. Surin, *Theology and the Problem of Evil*, chap. 2.

How does Forsyth himself understand the task? He describes it according to the well-known lines of John Milton's *Paradise Lost*:

> To vindicate Eternal Providence,
> And justify the ways of God to man.[6]

To achieve this, Forsyth embarks on a "theodicy" proper rather than a "defence." He does not only seek to show that God's ways can be justified if a certain set of conditions were true. He also asserts, primarily on the basis of Christian revelation, that these conditions indeed pertain. This theodicy is not written in the abstract, but in response to a concrete situation—the outbreak of the First World War. At least in Britain, this War had, as E. R. Wickham points out:

> . . . raised the question of Providence, of the relation of God to History and of His character and very existence, in perhaps the most acute way that has ever happened, and certainly in the most public way. Not merely with religious men and serious thinkers, but quite literally with every Tom, Dick, and Harry.[7]

Forsyth indicates that he welcomes this challenge to the Christian faith posed by the War, because it has reoriented the focus of the people. They are now far less concerned with (what he considers) the less important questions pertaining to the relationship of science and rationality to the Christian faith. They are now obsessed with the key theme of Christianity, which is righteousness—even if the discussion pertains mainly to that of God's.[8] Forsyth sought to provide a response to this challenge to God's righteousness—it was, to him, an extremely worthwhile endeavour: "To justify God is the best and deepest way to fortify man."[9] In doing so, he deals with evil in a comprehensive manner, discussing both (as we shall see later) the phenomena of sin and suffering. His approach is, as he himself acknowledges, largely "practical" in nature, in the sense that it seeks to show what God has done and is doing about the evil in our world, rather than to try to reconcile the existence of God and evil on a purely intellectual or conceptual basis.[10]

---

6. *Justification*, v.
7. Wickham, *Church and People in an Industrial City*, 204.
8. *Justification*, vi; *Sacraments*, 307–8.
9. *Justification*, 7.
10. We will have much more to say about this "practical" versus "theoretical" distinc-

Our primary aim in this study is to describe the theodicy that Forsyth sets out. It has been recognised as making a significant contribution to its field. John Hick, for example, has characterised Forsyth's writings on theodicy as possessing "the eloquence and spiritual vision of a prophet," and credited him with bringing "teleological theodicy back to reality, both divine and human."[11] Kenneth Surin, on his part, sees Forsyth's theodicy providing a unique and valuable "full-blown thematisation" of the principle that God's work of atonement on the cross is his self-justification in the face of evil.[12] Others note the continuing relevance of Forsyth's theodicy in a world where the evils manifested during the Great War still abound.[13] Despite such positive assessments, there has not yet been a substantial full-length study of Forsyth's theodicy.[14] This project seeks to contribute to the filling of this lacuna. In doing so, we hope to advance the state of research into the thought of this remarkable Congregationalist theologian. Our focus will of course be on Forsyth's theodicy, but as it is intimately linked to many other areas of his thought, we trust that this purposive foray into the former will also yield insights into these other areas and heighten our appreciation of what Colin Gunton has called Forsyth's "integrating mind," which "[brings] together in an overall vision ... a wide range of intellectual, cultural and practical considerations."[15] We

---

tion in chapter 7. We will also argue there that Forsyth's theodicy encompasses key "theoretical" aspects as well.

11. Hick, *Evil and the God of Love* (1st ed.), 247–48. (The second edition of this work will simply be cited as *Evil and the God of Love*.)

12. Surin, *Problem of Evil*, 132.

13. Craston, " Grace of a Holy God," 60. For more general comments about the continuing relevance of Forsyth's works, see Hunter, *P.T. Forsyth*, 7; Gunton, "Foreword," in *Justice the True and Only Mercy*, xv; Hastings, *History of English Christianity 1920–1990*, 118; Huxtable, "P. T. Forsyth: 1848–1921," 75–76.

14. The closest thing we have to a full-length treatment are two doctoral dissertations which have dealt, in part, with Forsyth's theodicy. The first is Stephen J. Vicchio, "Problem of Evil," subsequently published as *The Voice from the Whirlwind*. This work comes across, however, as a general discussion on the subject of theodicy, with Forsyth's thought given only a limited airing. The second work is James T. D. Gardom, "Cross in Time and the Hidden Hand of God." While this thesis deals with Forsyth's writings in much greater detail, it is (as the author acknowledges in 7–10) more a work on the role of evil in Forsyth's epistemology than a description of Forsyth's theodicy. While it contains some good insights, it does not seem to have adequately set out the various aspects of Forsyth's justification of God.

15. Gunton, "Real as the Redemptive," 37.

also anticipate the possibility that our study might make some contribution to the task of Christian theodicy. While no theodicy can peel away all the mystery that surrounds the intractable problem of evil, we will consider how Forsyth's approach, treated in combination with insights from other thinkers, might advance discussion on the subject.

We should state at the outset that, because of the generally unsystematic nature of Forsyth's writings,[16] any attempt to set out his theodicy in a comprehensive and logically coherent manner soon finds that it has to go beyond mere description. As Trevor Hart puts it, "[Forsyth] himself refused the attempt to map the complex theological connections which lay tacit in his theological unconsciousness, thereby presenting any would-be commentator with the challenge of attempting to do so for him."[17] In our study, therefore, we will need to undertake three tasks in addition to simply setting out what Forsyth's writings say on the subject. We will have, firstly, to draw out the implications of these writings for his justification of God, something he does not always do for his readers. Only then will we be able to see clearly in what specific manner his writings seek to "justify the ways of God to man." Secondly, a competent study of Forsyth's theodicy will need to develop, on the basis of his writings, responses his theodicy could have made to the objections that have been raised against both it and others which share similar characteristics. Some of these objections have come to the fore only after Forsyth's time, such as the argument, which arose particularly strongly after the horrors of Auschwitz, that the exercise of theodicy itself is invalid and even immoral. Forsyth does not, of course, address objections such as these, but we will need to do so to support our contention that his theodicy retains contemporary significance. Finally, we will offer suggestions throughout our study as to how Forsyth's thought can be supplemented or revised in order for it to constitute a coherent and holistic response to the problem of evil. This will be necessary whenever we find him to be silent on or

---

16. There is general recognition of the fact that Forsyth was not a systematic theologian, in the sense that (as Alan Sell puts it), "he does not systematically ground arguments or pursue them wheresoever they lead; and there are loose ends in his work" ("P. T. Forsyth as Unsystematic Systematician," 134). Forsyth's describes his deliberate resistance to systematisation in passages like *Theology*, xv. Most commentators on his thought, however, see a deeper sense in which Forsyth's writings are systematic—in that everything radiates from the event of the Cross. We will elaborate on the centrality of the Cross to Forsyth's theology subsequently.

17. Hart, "Morality, Atonement, and the Death of Jesus," 17.

inconsistent in some key aspects of his justification of God. In these three tasks, we will be helped not only by the significant volume of secondary literature on Forsyth's thought, but also the insights of other prominent writers on theodicy, such as Fyodor Dostoyevsky, Albert Camus, Jürgen Moltmann, John Hick, Richard Bauckham, and Paul Fiddes.

We are aware that our attempt to set out in a fairly systematic fashion Forsyth's justification of God carries the danger, as J. K. Mozley puts it, of introducing into his position "an impression of logical coherence and orderly advance more formal than the writings themselves warrant."[18] We might easily distort Forsyth's views by prematurely resolving paradoxes he would rather hold,[19] or by making him affirm statements on points where he would rather be silent. We hope to minimise this possibility by making it quite clear throughout our study which statements represent Forsyth's express position, and which contain the inferences we draw from his writings and the suggestions we offer for supplementing or revising his position. We will also try to resist the temptation to force closure and consistency in areas where we find it quite clear that Forsyth is content to affirm the existence of a higher mystery which cannot be resolved through logical analysis. Finally, as we shall mention in chapter 2, most commentators on Forsyth recognise that there is a clear centre to his thought, in spite of the occasional nature of much of his writing. This is, of course, the Cross of Christ.[20] We will, in our study, consciously put the Cross at the centre of Forsyth's theodicy (as Forsyth himself does). With this "bed-rock"[21] in place, it is not likely that we will wander far from Forsyth's position, since the Cross is sure to pull us back to his central concerns.

It remains for us to offer an apology in this opening section. "The malady of quotation," according to Forsyth, "is very mischievous."[22] But, as with most others who write on Forsyth, we find it almost impossible to refrain from quoting him liberally in our study.[23] It is true, as numer-

18. Mozley, *Heart of the Gospel*, 72.

19. Forsyth's acceptance of the role of paradox in theology is brought forth by passages like *Faith*, 33–34.

20. The references will be given in chapter 2, together with an explanation of what the "Cross" connotes for Forsyth.

21. Mozley, *Heart of the Gospel*, 109.

22. *Courage of Faith*, 10.

23. Those who acknowledge the compulsion to quote Forsyth liberally include Duthie,

ous commentators have pointed out (some bitterly), that Forsyth's writing style is difficult and can at times obscure what he is trying to say.[24] Perhaps the most memorable observation is given by Howard Lawler: "[Forsyth] tortured language in an attempt to force it to yield greater secrets. Unfortunately the victim did not always survive."[25] In the bulk of the passages where language did survive, however, the effect of Forsyth's style is nothing short of incandescent. What Mozley has called "Forsyth on paper"[26] conveys the point he is making with such power to "stir the conscience and inflame the heart"[27] that any attempted paraphrase of it seems cold and limp by comparison. We will therefore, in many parts of our study, stand back and let Forsyth speak for himself. Robert McAfee Brown thinks that "the main function of books about Forsyth must be to whet the appetite of the reader so that he will be driven to read Forsyth himself."[28] If our medley of quotations helps to achieve this, it might not be so mischievous after all.

HOW WE WILL APPROACH OUR STUDY

The only work of Forsyth's specifically devoted to theodicy is *The Justification of God*. Although, for the reasons given in the next section, this will not be the only work we consult in the course of our study, we find all the major themes of Forsyth's theodicy contained there. They are, in fact, alluded to in this important passage:

> Is there any section of the Church that does not need to learn more deeply that the site of God's supreme revelation is not in the order of the world but in its crisis; that its nature is for the conscience not evolution but revolution; that it does not consecrate a natural ethic so much as redeem it; that by a new creation the Cross is both the foundation and the crisis of the whole moral world; that it was a

---

"Faith of P. T. Forsyth," 9; Gummer, "Peter Taylor Forsyth," 351; Meadly, "'Obscurity' of P. T. Forsyth," 315.

24. See, e.g., Shaw, "Theology of P. T. Forsyth," 358; Camfield, "Peter Taylor Forsyth," 9–10; Torrance, "Dominated by His Own Illustrations?" 59.

25. Lawler, "Universalism of P. T. Forsyth," 35.

26. Mozley, *Heart of the Gospel*, 71.

27. Duthie, "Faith of P. T. Forsyth," 9.

28. Brown, *P. T. Forsyth*, 7.

tragedy greater and more searching than any war; and that it is the creative source of the new morality, the new Humanity?[29]

As we see it, the starting point for a consideration of Forsyth's theodicy is the place where "God's supreme revelation" occurred—the crisis of the Cross. We will therefore begin our study proper in chapter 2 by examining Forsyth's appropriation of Luther's methodology of the *theologia crucis*. When our eyes are rightly focused on the Cross, we see that a momentous event has taken place there—what Forsyth calls "the self-justification of God." We will examine Forsyth's understanding of this key phrase, and how it forms, for him, the basis upon which all human attempts to justify God rest. This "self-justification of God" results in two outcomes which form the main thrusts of Forsyth's theodicy. The first is that God has solved the most fundamental problem with the world and is moving it inexorably towards its glorious goal. So, as the passage above mentions, the Cross functions as "the creative source of . . . the new Humanity" which is slowly being re-created in the history of the world. The second outcome is that the *theologia crucis* reveals to us that the Cross was, in fact, "a tragedy greater and more searching than any war," because on it God himself suffered the most in the battle against sin. These two outcomes, and their significance for Forsyth's theodicy, will be elaborated in chapters 3 to 6. In our final two chapters, we will explore the difficult issue of how Forsyth understood evil to have originated in our world and how this impacts his theodicy. Forsyth himself, given the "practical" nature of his theodicy, might not have seen this issue as particularly crucial for his justification of God. But, as we shall argue, these chapters are necessary to complete our study as they shed light on important areas of Forsyth's theodicy not expressly dealt with in the earlier parts of our study.

THE WORKS OF FORSYTH WHICH PERTAIN TO THE SUBJECT MATTER

We find it helpful, at the beginning of our study, to set out the range of Forsyth's works we will examine, given our subject matter. While our primary focus will, naturally, be on Forsyth's *The Justification of God*, the nature of theodicy is such that it cannot (and should not) be considered apart from the other branches of theology. This is especially so in the case of Forsyth, as his response to the problem of evil is particularly dependent

---

29. *Justification*, 105.

upon other aspects of his thought, most principally his doctrine of creation, Christology, soteriology, eschatology and epistemology. We will therefore, in this study, have to consider almost the entire corpus of Forsyth's works in order to obtain a well-rounded picture of his theodicy.

Forsyth, in ways not dissimilar to Karl Barth, underwent a famous "conversion" experience, in which he made a significant departure from the liberal theology prevalent in his day to a far more evangelical position. There are disagreements over the extent of this change in Forsyth,[30] but the generally accepted view is that the transformation in the man was a radical one, resulting in two clearly distinguishable stages of his thought.[31] Trevor Hart goes so far as to say that Forsyth's early sermon *Mercy the True and Only Justice* (possibly delivered in 1877) "is hardly recognisable as the work of the same man" when we take into account his mature writings.[32] Leslie McCurdy has done a careful study of the chronological development of Forsyth's thought in his writings, and concludes that his "conversion" experience probably took place over a period of time from the middle to late 1880s.[33] The commentators are generally agreed that by the time of the publication of the pamphlet *The Old Faith and the New* (1891) or, at the very latest, the article "Revelation and the Person of Christ" (1893), Forsyth had evidently crossed the "theological Rubicon,"[34]

---

30. See Wood, "Christ on Parnassus," 83–95 and the comments of Clyde Binfield in "Peter Taylor Forsyth: Pastor as Principal," 30 for the view that Forsyth remained very much a theological liberal throughout his life. Binfield, however, is not adverse to using the term "conversion" to describe the change in Forsyth which took place within the period 1878 to 1900: "Principal When Pastor: P.T. Forsyth, 1876–1901," 401.

31. See, e.g., Brown, *Prophet For Today*, 19; Hunter, *Per Crucem*, 17; McCurdy, *Attributes and Atonement*, 14. Note also Forsyth's well-known account of his own "conversion" in *Positive Preaching*, 192–93.

32. Hart, "Morality, Atonement," 17. The aspects in which the later Forsyth differs from the earlier promises to be illuminated by a close comparison of two articles he wrote on the poet John Milton—the second ("Milton's God and Milton's Satan," 450–65) being a revision of the first ("'Milton's Paradise Lost': Lecture by the Rev. P. T. Forsyth, MA," 4). From the revisions Forsyth made, we can obtain hints of where his thinking has changed. This, we suggest, might be a fruitful line of inquiry for those interested in pursuing the matter further.

33. McCurdy, *Attributes and Atonement*, 34–37. Robert McAfee Brown comes to a similar conclusion, suggesting that Forsyth gradually but profoundly deepened his theological views "in the years during and succeeding his pastorate at St. Thomas Square, London (1880–1885)" ("'Conversion' of P.T. Forsyth," 237).

34. This imagery was used by Hart, "Morality, Atonement," 17.

and the main structure and themes of his mature theology were clearly set out.[35]

The relevance of this discussion to our study is that it enables us to say at the outset that the theodicy we will examine is Forsyth's "mature theodicy," one primarily based upon his writings post-1891. Forsyth, to the best of our knowledge, did not write any work on theodicy in his earlier liberal period, but his very different treatment of key themes like the atonement then would mean that any theodicy he might have formulated during that period would probably look quite different from what was set out in *The Justification of God* and his other mature works. It is therefore important to issue this clarification. We will, in the course of our study, still make substantial references to Forsyth's pre-1891 writings, but this will mainly be in situations where we see them affirming a position consistent with Forsyth's mature thought. Also, while we remain open to the possibility of chronological development in Forsyth's thinking on theodicy post-1891, our research has, on the whole, borne out the consensus among Forsyth's commentators that his thinking was largely stable after his "conversion."[36] Robert McAfee Brown, for example, saw the outbreak of the First World War as a "grim and tragic vindication" of the themes Forsyth had sounded for the previous twenty years. To address the situation resulting from the War, therefore, the Congregationalist theologian did not have to come up with a fresh theology, but merely reiterated his consistent message in works like *The Justification of God*.[37] In our study, therefore, we will simply set out Forsyth's theodicy as a whole, without needing to distinguish the ideas associated with the various stages of a constantly evolving thought process.

In what follows, we will briefly set out Forsyth's view of reality and his understanding of evil, these being the key preliminary aspects of his thought with which we should familiarise ourselves before we discuss his theodicy proper.

35. See, e.g., Brown, *Prophet for Today*, 19 and "'Conversion' of P. T. Forsyth," 237; Rodgers, *Theology of P. T. Forsyth*, 7–8; Grant, *Free Churchmanship in England 1870–1940*, 229; Hart, "Morality, Atonement," 17; McCurdy, *Attributes and Atonement*, 14.

36. Brown, *Prophet for Today*, 19; Rodgers, *Theology of P. T. Forsyth*, 7–8; Hart, "Morality, Atonement," 17; McCurdy, *Attributes and Atonement*, 19. Mikolaski, "P. T. Forsyth," 324 and Hunter, *Per Crucem*, 17 also refer to the stability of Forsyth's thought, but they put the starting point for this at 1896, with the publication of *God the Holy Father*.

37. Brown, *Prophet for Today*, 131–32. See also the comment to a similar effect of Forsyth's one-time pupil H. F. Lovell Cocks in " Message of P. T. Forsyth," 215.

FORSYTH'S VIEW OF REALITY

The Moral as the Real

The notion that Forsyth saw "the moral as the real" has been explicated by commentators on his thought.[38] Hart has perhaps described this idea most clearly and succinctly:

> There is, according to Forsyth, a "moral order" which is just as surely woven into the fabric of God's creation as that other "order" which is investigated by the natural sciences. Indeed, in terms of the status of our knowledge, the moral must be said to be more ultimate and more reliable than either the physical or the intellectual.[39]

We will not enter here into a detailed analysis of this "moral order" envisaged by Forsyth or trace the provenance of his view of reality. Our aim is simply to highlight aspects of Forsyth's thought in this area to set the stage for our subsequent discussion of his theodicy, parts of which will only make sense when we understand the primacy Forsyth ascribes to the moral. To this end, we will look briefly at Forsyth's understanding of the source and nature of morality and how we human beings come into contact with it.

The Source and Nature of Morality

Forsyth follows Immanuel Kant in tracing the fundamental moral order of this world back to the notion of an absolute Being. He goes, however, much deeper than Kant in this aspect. Instead of limiting this Being to the role of an abstract supreme law-giver, Forsyth sees him as a personal God most supremely characterised by holiness. This holiness is the source of all morality. As he puts it, "The holy has no meaning apart from the conscience, majesty, and kingship of the righteous Father. Nor has the moral any ultimate meaning apart from the holy."[40] The moral order of the world, therefore, "reflects the nature of a holy God (without exhausting His being)."[41]

---

38. See, e.g., Rodgers, *Theology of P. T. Forsyth*, 269–73; Mozley, *Heart of the Gospel*, 73; Hart, "Morality, Atonement," 18–19; Gunton, " Real as the Redemptive," 58.

39. Hart, "Morality, Atonement," 18.

40. *Justification*, 118.

41. *Cruciality*, 28.

The emphasis on "the moral as the real" puts Forsyth, as Mozley correctly observes, firmly on the side of voluntarism in its struggle with intellectualism.[42] Forsyth himself states that while "the genius of natural thought is intellectual . . . the genius of Christianity is voluntarist; it is moral," and that "reality, therefore, is a kingdom of will, personality, and action."[43] He prefers to picture God as "an infinite spiritual power in essential action," rather than a being in a state of eternal repose.[44] As for human beings, Forsyth's voluntarism can be seen in the significant place he allocates to the operation of the human free will, which he understands largely in a "libertarian" sense, i.e., as the ability to choose which is not wholly determined by prior causes. Morality is, at one level, related to the right exercise of the will—the making of the right choices. So, for example, he writes in *The Principle of Authority*:

> Religion is thus at bottom a moral act in a mystic sphere. It begins in a choice between two conflicting values. We are religious because the divine comes as a contrast for our choice, and not as a continuity for our completion . . . It is . . . not a case of rational continuity as in Monistic Idealism, where we test the revelation or absorb it, but a case of moral preference, choice, and committal, in which the revelation tests and judges us.[45]

Forsyth's attribution of the source of morality to the holy God, however, serves as an important qualification to his voluntarism. He expressly repudiates the pragmatic voluntarism of his day which sees human consensus as the standard of true morality. Such a view leads ultimately to human self-worship, which represents the death of religion.[46] Forsyth also demonstrates a far deeper understanding of morality than mere behavioural compliance with a prescribed standard. Mozley again gives an accurate reading of Forsyth's position: while "no one was more intent on the moral character and leanings and issues of all true religion," equally "no one was less likely to substitute morality for religion."[47] Because "all the moral order is ruled from [God's] throne," morality, according to Forsyth,

---

42. Mozley, *Heart of the Gospel*, 73; and *Doctrine of the Atonement*, 182–83.
43. "Faith and Mind," 637, 640.
44. *Positive Preaching*, 207.
45. *Authority*, 172–73.
46. *Positive Preaching*, 228.
47. Mozley, "Preface," in Forsyth, *Sacraments*, ix.

cannot finally exist apart from the Christian faith.[48] Since the object of the Christian faith is a person, rather than a law, the moral as the real tells us that "the crisis of things is man's relation to the Holy."[49] True morality, therefore, is the farthest thing away from mere moralism. It is rather the "religious . . . habit of the moral soul's confidence and communion with a *holy* God."[50]

Correspondingly, when it comes to the notion of God's will, there is in Forsyth's writings the idea that this will is ultimately not to be seen as something detachable from God's personality. Because there is an "eternal unity of God's free will with His perfect nature," it is not the will of God *per se*, but rather the "holy God, a spiritually moral personality, self-determined and self-complete," which governs what the real is.[51] The moral order is therefore not external to God in the sense that it merely reflects what God thinks or wants. Rather, "He is His own kingdom," and the moral is derived from who God fundamentally is.[52] These ideas will have important implications when we come subsequently to discuss the relationship Forsyth envisages between God and our sinful world. Forsyth's voluntarism, for example, never goes so far as that of the seventeenth-century Presbyterian churchman Samuel Rutherford's, to say that God could have arbitrarily pardoned sin without the need for an atonement. Such a picture of God's will functioning so autonomously from who he is as the holy God (who therefore requires the punishment of sin) is completely alien to Forsyth's thought. As he puts it:

> Had God been but a King or a Judge, sitting beside a law He guarded but did not make, a law over Him, a law He was responsible to and for, the situation would have been simpler and slighter. He could then perhaps have found means, easy to a divine intelligence, to compromise with the law, or get round it. But God's holy law is His own holy nature, the principle of His own holy heart, the life action and norm of His moral personality, with no source or authority outside Himself, and no claim He could even wish to

---

48. *Rome, Reform, and Reaction*, 138.
49. Ibid., 229; "Veracity, Reality, and Regeneration," 206.
50. *Congregationalism and Reunion*, 22, 29 (emphasis in original).
51. *Positive Preaching*, 229; *Society*, 19.
52. *Justification*, 190.

ignore or evade. To tamper with it would have been to deny His own soul. He loves it as He must love Himself . . . [53]

Forsyth's insistence on the "eternal unity of God's free will with His perfect nature" not only enables him to avoid the extremes of voluntarism, it also secures his position from the opposite danger that the moral order, fundamental and real as it is, could in the end be seen as an independent power outside God, one able to effectively restrict his freedom. So, in response to a critic who accused him of "treating the holiness of God as though it were a power outside God, tying His hands," Forsyth replies simply that "what is meant by the holiness of God is the holy God."[54] To try to impersonalise the notion of "holiness" and then detach it from who God is is to attempt the ridiculous. God is bound to secure the moral order because he is true to himself, and for no other reason.

The Conscience as Our Contact with the Real

Our final brief comments in this section have to do with the issue of how Forsyth envisages we human beings come into contact with the real, i.e., through what means do the requirements of the moral order impinge upon us? Forsyth's answer is that this happens through the medium of human conscience. Our conscience is the "sense of responsibility" we owe towards what is morally right. When we breach our obligations to this understanding of what is right, our conscience accuses us with feelings of guilt.[55] It therefore seems to work against us, yet it is so integrally a part of who we are:

> We cannot get rid of this judge. He is not in our power. We cannot unmake him, though he be against ourselves . . . He is an incorporate part of our own being, our other self wedded to us for ever. What a strange thing we are—two, yet one! Two that cannot

---

53. *Preaching of Jesus*, 109. See also Forsyth's other statements to this end in *Work*, 112–13 and " Atonement in Modern Religious Thought," 56–57, 69.

54. *Work*, 131.

55. *Justification*, 13. We are speaking here of Forsyth's understanding of the role of the human conscience in the most general terms possible. McCurdy, *Attributes and Atonement*, 60–64 has written about how most of Forsyth's explication of the human conscience assumes the context of the Christianised West of his day, in which the notions of "God" and "Jesus Christ" would be familiar to the vast majority of the population. In such a context, McCurdy discovers, Forsyth is more precise in describing the sense of guilt we experience as a sense of transgression against this God or Christ.

agree—one that cannot be severed. Our enemy is of our essence, taken from under our very heart. We are one by being two. We are unhappy both because we are two and quarrel, and because we are one and cannot part. Neither of us can go out of the other's hearing. We may cease to attend much to each other, but we are always within call.[56]

Forsyth's anthropology gives pride of place to the human conscience. It is "the core of all life . . . the axis of all thought [and] the element of all final weal."[57] Forsyth clearly sees the possession of the conscience as the most fundamental aspect of what it means to be human. Hart has postulated that had Forsyth developed the neglected theme of the *imago Dei* in his writings, he would have founded it, not upon the human intellect, but the human conscience.[58] This is surely right, for if there is something which Forsyth sees both God and humans sharing in common, it is that both possess a conscience—in the sense of a requirement to conform to the holy.[59] The "conscience within the [human] conscience" is, in fact, "the conscience of God himself," judging us and requiring us to attain to his righteousness.[60] All this is entirely consistent with Forsyth's view of reality. If the moral is the real, then the aspect of our existence which connects us with this reality must be the most basic core of who we are.[61]

FORSYTH'S UNDERSTANDING OF EVIL

Distinction between Evil as Sin and Evil as Suffering

One of the key tasks before setting out any theodicy is to define clearly what is meant by the term "evil." Most basic works on theodicy divide "evil" into two categories for ease of discussion: "moral evil," which can be defined as that caused by human beings, and "natural evil," which is that apparently arising from causes other than human action or neglect.[62]

---

56. *Cruciality*, 63–64.
57. *Authority*, 107.
58. Hart, "Morality, Atonement," 19–20.
59. *Authority*, 58.
60. "Regeneration, Creation, and Miracle," 636.
61. For a more detailed discussion on Forsyth's view of the human conscience, especially the possibility of us attaining a "natural" knowledge of God through its functioning, see McCurdy, *Attributes and Atonement*, chap. 3.
62. See, e.g., Hick, *Evil and the God of Love*, 12; Whitney, *What Are They Saying About God and Evil?* 4–5; Surin, *Problem of Evil*, 60–61. Other categories which are less

Implicit in this distinction is the recognition that "evil" consists of both the elements of what might broadly be called sin and suffering. When we speak of "moral evil," for example, we do not merely refer to the suffering that human acts cause, but also the acts themselves if they were perpetuated with bad motives like greed, cruelty or contempt. These would, in a Christian context, be understood as sinful acts, and they are part of the problem of evil apart from their consequences.[63] The categories of "sin" and "suffering" therefore overlap with the distinction between "moral" and "natural" evils, in the sense that "moral evil" consists of both sin and the suffering perpetuated by it.

Forsyth, in his writings, does not draw any distinction between "moral" and "natural" evils. Such a distinction would, indeed, not be particularly useful in the context of his theodicy. He does, however, divide evil into the alternative two categories of "sin" and "suffering." Let us quote at length from a key passage in this regard:

> We have the question of evil as suffering and the question of evil as sin. They are distinct though closely connected. All sin is an ill, but all ill is not sin, nor is it caused by it. Suffering abounded in the animal world before man appeared with the moral freedom that makes sin possible. Pain came before sin, and, as it has no connection with freedom, it is non-moral. And in any theodicy, or justification of God, His treatment of the two is different, to our Christian faith at least. The power in Him can convert suffering to a sacrament, but it must destroy sin. It can transcend and sanctify suffering while the suffering remains, but sin it must abolish. The Cross of Christ can submerge suffering, and make it a means of salvation, but with sin it can make neither use nor terms; it can only make an end of it. God in Christ is capable of suffering and of transmuting sorrow; but of sin He is incapable, and His work is to destroy it. And, by a mystery hard to search, His conversion of the one is the same act as His destruction of the other. His transfiguration of suffering in the Cross is also His conquest of sin.[64]

This passage contains deep ideas which will take the whole of our study to unpack, and even then, not completely. It will suffice for the moment to

---

commonly used include "metaphysical evil" (Hick, *Evil and the God of Love*, 13–14) and "structural evil" (Ford, *Theology: A Very Short Introduction*, 67–71).

63. This point is made explicit in Stephen T. Davis, "Introduction," in *Encountering Evil*, 4.

64. *Justification*, 138–39.

note Forsyth's insistence that a distinction be drawn in a truly Christian theodicy between evil as sin and evil as suffering, because of the different ways they originate and relate to God. We will not, in our study, divide his treatment of sin and that of suffering into two distinct portions, since these two categories of evil remain, as Forsyth puts it, "closely connected." Nevertheless, we will have to constantly keep in mind Forsyth's drawing of this rather fundamental distinction between the two. We will also finally summarise our study by outlining separately his response to evil as sin and his response to evil as suffering.

Evil as Sin

The Nature and Severity of Sin

> Consider all the weakness and ignorance of men for which men have not themselves to blame, the weakness of our human condition, of the family, the genus man, of human nature, even where innocent. Consider the sins of circumstance, constitution, or even those which spring from short-sighted love . . . I say mercy to a poor finite creature like man when he had sinned was and is the truest and only justice.[65]

These are Forsyth's words. However, as the discerning reader will have guessed, they were words written prior to his evangelical "conversion," and represent a view of sin he would come to strongly repudiate. Sin, as Forsyth makes clear in his mature writings, cannot be seen as mere error, ignorance or weakness.[66] He also rejects what he calls the "Greek idea" of it as "infection with a moral microbe" and the "medieval idea" of it as "mere distance from God."[67] The correct noun to describe the nature of sin is rather that of a conscious and active *rebellion* on the part of human creatures.[68] We are not "runaways," "cowards," or "strayed children," but "rebels" and "mutineers."[69] Consistent with his view of reality (as outlined earlier), Forsyth understands our rebellion to be directed not ultimately at some abstract standard of right and wrong, but against the holy God

---

65. *Mercy the True and Only Justice*, 8–9.
66. "Ibsen's Treatment of Guilt," 119–20.
67. *Rome, Reform and Reaction*, 243.
68. See, e.g., *Justification*, 140; *Father*, 9; *Positive Preaching*, 233; *Christian Aspects of Evolution*, 22–23. A. M. Hunter makes a similar comment in *Per Crucem*, 57.
69. *Father*, 9; *Positive Preaching*, 233.

who is the true source of all morality. Sin is therefore not to be primarily defined as the contravention of a law, but the breaking of our relationship with the personal God. So "sin," ultimately, "is not a thing, it is a personal relation."[70] The defining event of sin, for Forsyth, occurred in our treatment of the Son of God during his earthly career. We demonstrate the full extent of our active hate of the holy God by rejecting his Christ and finally crucifying him.[71] This can be seen as paradigmatic of all our sinful acts—we deny the Saviour, "[strike] in the face God's holy love" and "put the Cross on Him again" each time we sin.[72]

What are the consequences of this human rebellion for God himself? Because sin is that which seeks to undermine the moral reality underpinning this world, and this moral reality is in turn derived from the most fundamental nature of God as holy, Forsyth sees that sin threatens the very life of God. Forsyth does not shy away from passages like the following:

> God is fundamentally affected by sin. He is stung and to the core. It does not simply try Him, It challenges His whole place in the moral world. It puts Him on His trial as God. It is, in its nature, an assault on His life. Its total object is to unseat Him. It has no part whatever in His purpose. It hates and kills Him. It is His total negation and death. It is not His other but An other.[73]

Forsyth makes the somewhat shocking assertion that if sin has its way in the end, God would die.[74] In fact, God can be said to have been constantly "dying" in the sense that every act of sin committed so far "reduces His headship" and limits him in a way that is not self-determined.[75] To save himself, therefore, God has to respond to this challenge posed by sin. He must fight it to the finish—"there is no compromise possible" because "die sin must or God."[76]

---

70. "The Preaching of Jesus and the Gospel of Christ.," 300. Forsyth demonstrates his aversion to the metaphysical description of sin as non-being in his critique against R. J. Campbell's "New Theology." He insists that sin must be understood first and foremost in moral categories: "God, Sin, and the Atonement," 670.

71. *Missions*, 56–57.

72. *Preaching of Jesus*, 3.

73. *Positive Preaching*, 252.

74. *Justification*, 151–52; *Positive Preaching*, 38, 104, 235.

75. *Justification*, 152.

76. *Missions*, 71; *Justification*, 151.

Sin Given a Personality

Another interesting aspect of Forsyth's writings on sin is their allusion to the notion that it possesses a separate personality from that of the human sinner. We already see hints of this in the passages above describing sin as the arch enemy of God which threatens his life. Such talk of God and sin fighting to the finish and so on does seem to portray sin as a kind of independent foe of God, apart from any human involvement. This kind of image is reinforced when we note Forsyth's tendency to describe human beings and their sin as two separate entities. He speaks, for example, about "an eternal damnation of sin which sears it out of the sinner,"[77] and how God's anger is fundamentally directed towards our sin, and only derivatively towards us as we identify ourselves with it.[78] This tendency is perhaps seen most clearly in Forsyth's repeated insistence that, in his atoning work, Christ was "made sin" for us rather than made a sinner.[79] The fuller implications of this idea will be explored subsequently, but we observe here that one of the reasons for Forsyth's insistence on this distinction is that it allows for his belief that it is sin which God has to judge, rather than the sinner. God's judgement therefore fell upon Christ because, having been made sin, he becomes the proper recipient of this judgement. As he puts it, "God made Him sin, treated Him as if He were sin; He did not view Him as sinful . . . God lovingly treated Him as human sin, and with His consent judged sinful sin in Him and on Him."[80] This notion that it is sin which is the prime target of God's judgement does seem to attribute to it a personality of sorts, since it does not appear to make sense to describe an insensible and non-animate object as the recipient of judgement. These passages, read as a whole, appear to allocate to sin the role of the third key "person" in the scheme of things, besides God and human beings.

The Christian tradition has, of course, provided an avenue for viewing evil in personal terms—in the form of Satan or the devil. Forsyth

---

77. *Authority*, 120.

78. *Work*, 241. See also "Atonement in Modern Religious Thought," 58–59.

79. See, e.g., *Work*, 83, 150–51, 160; *Positive Preaching*, 124.

80. *Work*, 150–51. Forsyth could possibly have been influenced here by the tendency of his one-time mentor James Baldwin Brown to distinguish between the sin and the sinner when describing Christ's atoning work. See the latter's *The Divine Treatment of Sin*, 199–200 and *The Doctrine of Annihilation in the Light of the Gospel of Love*, 116–17, 123–4. Baldwin Brown's position is also set out in Geoffrey Rowell, *Hell and the Victorians*, 202.

does use this personal name for evil in his writings, particularly when he speaks of the War. So, if Britain should fail to engage Germany in combat, it would be equivalent to "[giving] everything up to the devil, and [seeing] the world overrun by his angels."[81] This is because the War should be seen ultimately as a struggle between "the prince of this world and the Lord its Righteousness."[82] We suggest, however, that Forsyth uses the terms Satan, the devil and the "prince of this world" in a different sense from much of the tradition. Satan is, for Forsyth, not literally a fallen angel, a creature of God who first fell into sin and then incited humans to follow suit. Forsyth uses this term, rather, as a hypostatising of sin itself. It is the name he gives to the reality of sin viewed as a personality.[83] We know this, firstly, through Forsyth's tendency to speak of "Satan" and "sin" interchangeably, especially when he writes concerning the atonement. He sees, for example, the Cross as the place where Christ "judged and executed the sinful principle," an act which he equates to "the destroying of the prince of this world."[84] We also note Forsyth's specific reference to "the power of evil gathered and personified" in the form of a "world-spirit" at the Cross,[85] reinforcing the notion that Satan is, for him, sin (as rebellion against God) personified rather than an actual creature at the forefront of this rebellion.

Why did Forsyth see a need to postulate sin as a personality? He might have done so for rhetorical reasons. As Richard Floyd points out, "personification is often a preacher's way of bringing home an abstract idea,"[86] and Forsyth the preacher must have known that there is no better way to convey the reality of sin than by picturing it in the form of a person with a will and purpose. Forsyth, however, makes it quite clear that the personality of sin is, for him, more than a mere metaphor. He indicates, firstly, that this is the manner in which sin is portrayed in the Gospels.

---

81. *Ethic*, 23.

82. Ibid., 106. See also passages like *Ethic*, 40, 109, 150; *Roots of a World-Commonwealth*, 17.

83. This idea arose in the course of my conversations on this topic with my friend Jason Goroncy. The obvious exceptions to this rule are when Forsyth speaks of "Satan" in contexts where the meaning of this term has been fixed by another source, as, for example, is the case in his article "Milton's God and Milton's Satan."

84. *Person*, 265. See also *Society*, 10.

85. *Missions*, 60–61.

86. This is mentioned in Floyd's unpublished thesis entitled "Criticisms of P. T. Forsyth," 28; cited in David Wilkinson, "'We Preach Jesus Christ and Him Crucified,'" 203.

These narratives describe Christ's belief that the evil he was struggling with was essentially personal in nature. They vividly portray "a triumphal procession of Christ through a host of demons; or it is as he were cutting a way through such a bodyguard in the kingdom of Satan to reach and dethrone their King upon the Cross."[87] Now Forsyth's understanding of the kenosis that the incarnate Christ underwent would imply that not all of Christ's beliefs are necessarily accurate (this is a point we will consider in more detail later). He insists, however, that Christ's belief about the devil is "on a totally different footing from His views about the date of a Psalm," because the former has to do with the main thrust of his ministry.[88] Therefore:

> Our modern experience is against a personal Satan. But Christ's was the other way. And if we must choose here between Christ and the modern mind, surely He who really redeemed from evil must know whether the reality He fought was chiefly a principle or a person.[89]

Although Forsyth is not equally explicit about this, another source of inspiration for his seeing sin as a personality could be the writings of his much admired apostle Paul. Paul, in passages like Rom 7:13–25, portrays human beings as "victims" of sin as well as its "villains" (to use Tom Smail's terms).[90] Or, as Alan Lewis puts it, Paul engages in a kind of "hypostatising of evil" by refusing to be fully identified with sin and postulating it as "an outside power which has invaded and occupied his inner territory, holding him in thrall as Pharaoh did the Hebrew captives yearning for deliverance."[91] Forsyth is certainly familiar with this Pauline tendency to hypostatise sin.[92] He might have been describing something to the same

---

87. "Christ's Person and His Cross," 19.

88. *Society*, 105.

89. *Missions*, 10. A similar reading of the Gospels is offered by John Tulloch in his Croall Lectures, published as *Christian Doctrine of Sin*, 102–11. There, Tulloch understands the Gospels to teach "an active Power or Principle of evil outside of man, and exercising influence over him," one depicted by names like "Satan" and "the Devil" (104–5).

90. Smail, *Once and for All*, 52–57.

91. Lewis, *Between Cross and Resurrection*, 424. Lyonnet and Sabourin, *Sin, Redemption, and Sacrifice*, 54–55 note that Paul's use of *hamartia* to designate personified sin recurs forty times from Rom 5:12—8:10.

92. He notes Otto Pfleiderer's description of it in his review of the latter's work: *Pfleiderer's View of St Paul's Doctrine*, 12.

effect when he uses the language of "incarnation" to describe sin's domination of us:

> There is an incarnation of the evil one as well as of the Holy One; though its king has neither the moral power nor the spiritual courage to appear as a historic person. For he cannot reduce himself to such limitation, nor empty himself to the form of a servant. He only acts in avatars and not incarnation, or he suborns picked servants full of the unholy ghost, or societies of culture which are the habitations of cruelty.[93]

The suggestion here seems to be that the evil personality "incarnates" itself in the lives of human beings and human societies. Our individual and corporate rebellion against God can therefore be seen as the manifestation of the evil personality in our lives. Maintaining the "victim-villain" tension, however, Forsyth never allows this evil "incarnation" to be used as an excuse to exculpate us from our own guilt in such rebellion. The reason for this is probably because we have a choice in this matter, and have willingly allowed this "incarnation" of the evil personality to take place in our lives. We are therefore not innocent victims of the heavenly war, but "rebels taken with weapons in our hands."[94]

On a more philosophical level, Forsyth could well have been influenced by the suggestion of James Galloway, made in his work *The Philosophy of Religion*, that moral evil, which arose initially from the wrong exercise of human free will, can subsequently:

> ... [develop] into a power in society which influences modes of thought and habits of life, and leaves its impress on institutions. Hence sin comes to function as a collective force, maintaining itself from generation to generation, and offering a constant resistance to the progress of the good. Proteus-like it takes new forms in the course of the struggle with advancing culture.[95]

Galloway's view is premised upon his understanding that sin develops only within a social system. Due to the "living and organic character of society, moral evil cannot be restricted to a particular point or points, but always tends to diffuse itself through the system, much in the way that a

---

93. *Sacraments*, 98.
94. *Positive Preaching*, 38.
95. Galloway, *Philosophy of Religion*, 520–21. This work is cited in the bibliography of *Justification*.

disease affects the condition of the whole body."[96] We further suggest that Forsyth's tendency to attribute a corporate personality to abstract entities like humanity,[97] society,[98] the nation[99] and the Church[100] might also have led him to postulate such a personality for sin. Under the influence (which Forsyth expressly names) of forces as diverse as the teachings of the Oxford Movement and the psychological theories of Wilhelm Wundt and Henri Bergson, and inspired by doctrines like that of the Trinity (with its assertion of "the personal Godhead's relation to its inner Trinity of persons") and Christ's teachings on the corporate nature of guilt and judgement,[101] Forsyth postulates that the entities mentioned above have "a corporate personality, a common will, which does not come into existence just by pooling wills." This is because "a race of growing persons cannot really cohere in anything which is just put together, or whose nature is lower than indivisible personality."[102] Forsyth, we suggest, approaches sin in a like manner. It is not merely the sum of our individual wills rebelling against God. Our individual defiance somehow coalesces into an indivisible corporate personality which both enslaves us and seeks the death of God. This, Forsyth insists, resonates well with the church's experience of sin. When she struggles with vast movements like "Mammonism," "Paganism," and "Naturalism," and when she observes the forces that pushed Europe towards the Great War, she should be driven to a belief "in a kingdom of evil very active and very intimate," which is an "organised power of disorganisation" seeking to wreck "the organisation of the holy."[103] After all, such organised rebellion is far beyond the ability of any individual or group to plan and carry out—it is, rather, the "super-individual" personality[104] of sin which directs the operations of this rival Kingdom to God's. Finally, we see Forsyth's voluntarism as possibly another driving force for his attribution of a personality to sin. Since the moral is the real,

96. Ibid., 520.
97. *Theology*, 120.
98. "Cross of Christ as the Moral Principle of Society," 13–14.
99. *Ethic*, 162.
100. *Theology*, 150. A. E. Garvie adds that Forsyth often also personifies the Cross itself: "Placarding the Cross," 343.
101. *Theology*, 119–21, 153–60.
102. "Cross of Christ as the Moral Principle of Society," 13–14.
103. *Sacraments*, 98–99, 114. See also *Justification*, 25.
104. Forsyth uses this phrase in *Theology*, 155.

and the will takes pride of place, the deepest account of something, for Forsyth, must surely be that which describes it in personal and voluntarist terms. Any account of sin falling short of this therefore fails to adequately portray the nature of God's enemy and the depth of his struggle with it: "We lower the whole level and tension of the conflict if we discard a war in heaven and think of God's antagonist as only human, or a principle. The Lord has a controversy not with His people only but with a rival king and strategy."[105]

To summarise, therefore, Forsyth certainly views his "personification" of sin as far more than a mere metaphor. To describe sin as a personality is, for Forsyth, perhaps the most accurate way to portray the reality of its nature and effect. Yet, as we have suggested above, Forsyth is also careful to step back from attributing to sin the status of a real ontological being. We cannot point to any creature, even angelic ones, and say that this is sin itself.[106] Forsyth's aversion to dualism (which we will examine more closely later) also forecloses any attempt to postulate a non-created being eternally vying for supremacy with God. Sin, for Forsyth, is therefore a kind of personality without a concrete existence in the form of a being. We are unable to say much more beyond this, for Forsyth, with his reluctance (perhaps imbibed from his teacher Ritschl) to delve too deeply into metaphysical discussions, does not provide more details of his understanding of sin as a personality.

The Knowledge of Sin

Forsyth's view on the nature and severity of sin was one not shared by the majority of his contemporaries. He observes that "no feature in the moral physiognomy of the day is more marked than the decay or absence of sin."[107] He was also perceptive enough to realise that this "dullness to sin,"[108] while appearing on the surface to boost the dignity of man, ultimately dilutes the greatness of the human soul. This is because:

---

105. *Sacraments*, 98.

106. We therefore think that Forsyth would have agreed with the view of Röhser, who saw the Pauline "hypostatisation" of sin as a step stronger than merely seeing the personality of sin as metaphor, but one which falls short of attributing to sin the status of a real ontological being. Röhser's view is described by E. P Sanders in "Sin, Sinners" (New Testament)," in David Noel Freedman, *Anchor Bible Dictionary*, vol. 6, 45–46.

107. "Preaching of Jesus," 288.

108. Ibid., 291.

> Everything that enhances the native purity of man, that extenuates his sin, that diminishes his guilt, and sets over him but a kind father, really belittles his greatness. Man can only have huge guilt because capable of great things (Matt. vi. 23). It is a tremendous power to be capable of sin against God.[109]

We mentioned earlier that the defining moment of sin, for Forsyth, was the crucifixion of the Son of God. It therefore follows that he traces the widespread ignorance of the severity of sin in his day to the then prevailing tendency to downplay the significance of the Cross.[110] Forsyth sees, for reasons we would go into later, that the most complete revelation of God's holiness took place at the historical event of Calvary. In the same way, the fullest exposure of the nature and severity of what opposes this holiness (i.e., sin) occurred there as well. The starting point for this affirmation is the notion that only God knows the full extent of sin: "Only the absolutely holy can measure sin or judge it."[111] In dealing with sin on the Cross, Forsyth postulates, God knew what he had to do to ensure its destruction. He had to bring sin "to a moral head" and incite it to "do its very worst," so that he could deal with it "as a unity" and "at a centre."[112] This God does by revealing his absolute holiness in the person of the incarnate Son:

> The appearance of good often has its first effect in aggravating the energy of evil. The revelation in sanctity is at the same time a revelation of sin; and the growth of one accentuates the antagonism of the other. The one forces the other to show itself plainly, to throw off its mask, to put forth all its wicked resource. Grace enters to develop sin into transgression, to bring sin to the surface and make it overt. Then comes the encounter, and the prince of the world is judged.[113]

From this, it follows that the mode of Christ's death was of vital importance to Forsyth. If Christ had died through natural causes or by accident, the atonement would not have been effected. It had to be "a death of moral violence" brought about by the wickedness of human beings, as only this

---

109. *Missions*, 32.
110. This tendency is mentioned in *Society*, 18; "Preaching of Jesus," 300.
111. *Justification*, 26.
112. *Cruciality*, 22, 58; *Work*, 133.
113. *Christian Aspects of Evolution*, 24.

demonstrated the culmination of sin and its rage against the holy.[114] Now this idea that it was necessary to bring sin to its head certainly has important implications for Forsyth's view of the atonement, and they shall be mentioned subsequently when we explore this topic. For the present, we note that Forsyth sees the crucifixion of God's Son as that one point where sin manifests itself most fully, such that he can resort to the singular and call it "the world's one sin."[115] Forsyth utilises almost the whole range of superlatives available in his arsenal to describe this "one sin" revealed at the Cross:

> We must realize sin distinguished, subtle, cosmic; sin so universal that it needs a Church truly catholic to cope with it. Think of great sin, of world-sin, sin in the grand style, sin Machiavelian, national, warlike, sin past thinking of, and you must turn to the Cross . . . The death of Christ is a revelation of sin such as we do not get from his life alone, of sin more deadly and desperate than arises from the mere neglect or dislike of his person. It was a revelation not of the common sins of the common man, but of high-placed sin—of illustrious sin, imposing, even dazzling, sin, of distinguished perdition and unsuspected ruin; the sin of a fine fearless godlessness abetted by earnest ecclesiastics, scholars, jurists, by party politicians, popular leaders, sentimental preachers, deserting disciples, and betrayers who kept all the commandments perhaps from their youth up, by spiritual wickedness in high and reputable places.[116]

For Forsyth, therefore, to discover the true nature and severity of sin, we must "turn to the Cross" and nowhere else.

The converse also holds true. We not only come to know what evil truly is through the highest manifestation of the good (in the form of the holy, on the Cross), but also come to know the good through evil, at least on an empirical level.[117] The reason Forsyth gives for this is that we tend to depreciate the significance of what happened at the Cross without an appreciation of the true severity of evil. We do not realise the true nature of God's holiness and the extent to which God would go to maintain and extend it throughout his creation. We do not, in Forsyth's words, "experi-

---

114. *Cruciality*, 86, 93.
115. *Preaching*, 247.
116. "Christ's Person and His Cross," 20–21.
117. "Ibsen's Treatment of Guilt," 122.

ence the Gospel as God's utmost with man's worst."[118] He can therefore write that "we do not believe enough in Christ because we do not believe enough in Satan."[119] In Forsyth's mind, therefore, there exists a reciprocal relationship between our understanding of good and evil: "That is how we must see the deadliest sin to realize the saving Cross. It is how the saving Cross, as the compendious Acts of Christ's national universal person, opens our eyes to the perspective of sin."[120]

Evil as Suffering

Forsyth's comments on the nature of suffering are far briefer than those on sin. The first thing to note is that when Forsyth purports to deal with the issue of "suffering" in his theodicy, he is referring quite exclusively to human suffering. While he occasionally acknowledges the reality of animal suffering,[121] he does not appear to have dealt with it in any significant way, either in *The Justification of God* or his other works. Also, Forsyth does not seem to have explicated the meaning of the term "suffering" in any detail, probably because he does not see any confusion over it in his day, unlike "sin." He does, however, demonstrate a keen eye in seeing that the nature of suffering varies from era to era. The modern struggle, he observes, is not so much with death, as with pain. The nature of pain itself has also changed to become more psychological and emotional rather than physical—"more in the nature of care, fear or despair."[122] A large part of such despair arises from what Forsyth calls "nineteenth-century weariness."[123] In an early pamphlet entitled *The Weariness in Modern Life*, he elaborates that such weariness is largely spiritual (rather than physical or mental) in nature, and arises, quite paradoxically, from the phenomenal growth of our knowledge about the world. This progress in scientific understanding has not been accompanied by a growth in our spiritual awareness, such that "people are unfamiliar with their souls, and therefore to a certain extent uncertain of them, afraid of them." What is more, the advent of scientific criticism has stopped "the supply of food" which had

---

118. *Society*, 99. Forsyth even quotes the skeptic David Friedrich Strauss with approval: "No Satan, no Redemption": "Some Effects of the War on Belief," 18.

119. *Sacraments*, 120.

120. "Christ's Person and His Cross," 21.

121. E.g., in *Justification*, 138.

122. *Father*, 48.

123. *Recent Art*, 60.

previously fed our souls.[124] Forsyth is probably referring here to the rise of movements like Higher Criticism of the Bible and Darwinian evolution which impacted the Christian faith in Britain so severely during his time. The result of all this was that:

> Man, in his noblest and most distinctive part, has been reduced to insignificance, as compared with the huge expansion given to our conception of the outward world . . . Knowledge has outgrown the power to use it. The best part of us is threatened with smothering. We know all about the order of the world. We know, and declare we can know, nothing about the soul of the world.[125]

Forsyth continues:

> The chart never was so clear, but the compass is overboard. We see more than our forefathers, but we are not so sure of our way, because we believe less . . . Our sympathy is absorbed in the abyss of our knowledge. We are in a state of spiritual exhaustion. No wonder we feel weary.[126]

This astute reading of the people's mood reflected the social, religious and political upheaval Victorian society was then undergoing.[127] The subsequent rise of the Great War did, of course, refocus the minds of the people on physical and emotional suffering, as well as death. However, as we have noted earlier, the War also aggravated the spiritual emptiness described by Forsyth, as the religious faith of the people underwent a further devastation, with new questions relating to theodicy arising in addition to those posed by science.[128]

We would also re-emphasise here the point made earlier that Forsyth draws a rather strong distinction between sin and suffering, such that the latter is not necessarily antithetical to God's holiness in the way that sin is. Suffering can be used by God for his purposes.[129] This point is made

124. *Weariness in Modern Life*, 6–7.

125. Ibid., 7.

126. Ibid., 9.

127. Brief summaries of such upheaval and their effects can be found in Griffith, *Theology of P. T. Forsyth*, 21; Brown, *Prophet for Today*, 14–16; Williams, "P. T. Forsyth: Holy Love and the Cross of Christ," 114–16; Camfield, "Peter Taylor Forsyth," 4–5.

128. Wickham, *Church and People*, 204–6.

129. In this, Forsyth follows a distinction drawn by some of his contemporaries, e.g., Fraser, *Philosophy of Theism*, 154, 161; Fairbairn, *Philosophy of the Christian Religion*, 151, 159, 167; Galloway, *Philosophy of Religion*, 526–30.

especially strongly in an article, reproduced from Forsyth's pencil notes, entitled "Suffering."[130] There Forsyth praises the value of suffering in moulding us towards God's holiness. The visitation of suffering can therefore be one of great mercy.[131] Forsyth also mentions, in another work, that our prayers should operate on the higher level than merely petitioning for the removal of pain. We should instead ask God to make a "sacrament" of our suffering, letting it drive us closer towards him, resulting finally in "a true Eucharist and giving of thanks."[132]

CONCLUSION

We have, in this introductory chapter, explained the scope of our study and the purpose for undertaking it. We have also considered briefly Forsyth's view of reality and his understanding of evil. Having dealt with these preliminary issues, we are now ready to examine Forsyth's theodicy. According to the outline given above, we will begin by looking at Forsyth's appropriation of the *theologia crucis* and his understanding of that crucial term the "self-justification of God."

---

130. In *Revelation*, 90–92. This article consists entirely of Forsyth's statements in point form, made in preparation for a sermon. Its tenor is therefore disjointed and confusing. But it is sufficiently clear to support the assertions made in this section.

131. Ibid., 90–91.

132. *Soul of Prayer*, 43.

2

The Locus of the True Revelation of God and God's Self-Justification

THE LOCUS OF THE TRUE REVELATION OF GOD: FORSYTH'S *THEOLOGIA CRUCIS*

The Cross as the Centre of Forsyth's Theology

IN OUR EARLIER DISCUSSION on the task of presenting Forsyth's theology in a systematic manner, we noted that, notwithstanding the obscurity in writing style and inconsistency in details we sometimes find in his writings, there is a clear core which holds his thought together. Forsyth himself proclaims the Cross to be the "true and magnetic North" which guides all his thinking,[1] and the commentators are inclined to agree. Mozley is frequently quoted for his apt imagery of Forsyth's thought as resting on the circumference of a circle, where every point has a straight line back to the centre, which is the Cross of Christ.[2] Hart, on his part, notes the impressive breadth of topics covered by Forsyth's pen, including the doctrine of God, Christian ethics, the sacraments and the state of the society, and concludes that Forsyth wrote everything "*sub specie crucis.*"[3]

---

1. *Positive Preaching*, vii. Forsyth does not explicitly state here that the "true and magnetic North" refers to the Cross, but that is clearly implied when we read what he writes in *Positive Preaching* as a whole.

2. Mozley, *Doctrine of the Atonement*, 182. See also Mozley's comments to a similar end in *Heart of the Gospel*, 109; and "Preface," in Forsyth, *Sacraments*, viii, ix.

3. Hart, "Morality, Atonement," 16. See also similar comments by Sell, "P. T. Forsyth as Unsystematic Systematician," 145; Hunter, "P. T. Forsyth Neutestamentler," 103; Robert McAfee Brown, "P. T. Forsyth," 145.

Now the term "Cross" can be interpreted in a variety of ways, and Sell has perceptively pointed out that Forsyth uses the expression to refer to a "constellation of ideas, including the actual Cross of Calvary, the cross eternally in the heart of God, the lamb slain from the foundation of the world, the Son's voluntary, obedient, juristic, victorious work," amongst others.[4] If we were to summarise this range of ideas, we can say that the "Cross," for Forsyth, refers to the historic event at Calvary and its significance, both for God and creation. This will be the meaning we intend whenever we use this term in our study.

Forsyth's Appropriation of the Theologia Crucis

There are many implications to be teased out from the idea that the Cross is central to Forsyth's theology. The most important one, upon which all the others rest, is the observation that Forsyth appropriates the concept of *theologia crucis* in the sense that it was first expounded by the Reformer Martin Luther. Forsyth, in other words, views the Cross as the epistemic lens through which we come to see God and his work most clearly, because that is the point at which God reveals himself most completely.[5] "*Crux probat omnia*," says Luther, and Forsyth could not agree more.

Forsyth affirms this methodology of *theologia crucis* throughout the entire corpus of his works. He insists, in varying ways, that "the site of revelation . . . [is] in Christ and His Cross."[6] While he does not dismiss the idea of natural revelation altogether, he sees that all we can take away from there is a suggestion or hint of God, one wholly inadequate for the purposes of our redemption.[7] The initiative for knowing God can therefore never rest with us. We do not try to find him in our world through our preferred means, but must allow him to reveal himself to us in the Cross, the only place where we "possess [God] securely and finally."[8] We

---

4. Sell, "P. T. Forsyth as Unsystematic Systematician," 121–22. See 135 for a further "cluster of convictions" which Sell sees Forsyth expressing through his use of the term "Cross."

5. Expositions of Luther's *theologia crucis* can be found in von Loewenich, *Luther's Theology of the Cross*; McGrath, *Luther's Theology of the Cross*; Moltmann, *Crucified God*, 207–14.

6. *Justification*, 9, 78–79, 172; *Missions*, 216; "Preacher and the Publicist," 11.

7. *Justification*, 54; *Revelation*, 14–16. See "Revelation and the Person of Christ," in *Faith and Criticism*, 99–103 for Forsyth's sustained critique of natural revelation.

8. *Revelation*, 20; *Justification*, 54.

do so because the Cross was an act which "corresponds to its own total ethical nature in the spiritual world" and "into which a whole divine life was put."[9] It was, in other words, a supremely moral act, executed by God, which accurately reflects who he as the holy is.[10] While we will examine the nature of this act more closely in the second part of this chapter, we note here that Forsyth sees this act as so basic that his assertion that the moral is the real finds its origin and paradigm there. For him, Christianity is ethical "because of its faith in the supreme and all-inclusive ethical act of God in the Redeemer."[11] Gunton, in an astute comparison between the conceptions of "morality" held by Kant and Forsyth, can therefore write that "while Kant's morality finally becomes a rational and paradoxically anthropocentric system, everything requiring assessment at the bar of human reason, Forsyth submits everything to the judgement of God made known on the cross of Christ."[12] More specifically for our purposes, Forsyth sees the *theologia crucis* as the key to his justification of God. "There is," he writes, "no theodicy for the world except in a theology of the Cross."[13] We will see subsequently how this is so. Let us, however, first look at an example of Forsyth's *theologia crucis* in action.

An Example: Forsyth's View of God's Election

Forsyth's *theologia crucis* permeates his entire theology (as it should), and we can cite numerous instances of its operation.[14] We choose, in this section, to consider Forsyth's understanding of the doctrine of election as an example of how he appropriates the *theologia crucis*, since this doctrine features prominently in Forsyth's scheme of theodicy.

The traditional Calvinistic notion of God's election was no longer popular during Forsyth's time. Few saw it as credible, and "nineteenth-

---

9. *Positive Preaching*, 230.

10. McCurdy has a section in his book entitled "A Christological Definition of Holiness" which explicates this idea in greater detail: *Attributes and Atonement*, 156–58.

11. *Rome, Reform and Reaction*, 239.

12. Gunton, "Real as the Redemptive," 57.

13. *Justification*, 124. Mozley comments that "the referring of the justification of God to the Cross of Christ as to its one proper *locus revelationis* is a very striking instance of Dr. Forsyth's theological insight and power of subtle combination": *Heart of the Gospel*, 113.

14. An excellent summary of how the various aspects of Forsyth's theology are affected by the *theologia crucis* is given in Wood, "Christ on Parnassus," 83–84.

century sensitivities" were generally troubled by the moral implications of the idea that God had from eternity decreed a significant section of the world's population to reprobation.[15] Forsyth appreciated the validity of these objections to the idea of election. But, while he saw that the doctrine itself had to be reformed, he was unwilling to jettison it altogether. It was, to him, the "most mighty of all [dogmas] for personal faith,"[16] and too much would be sacrificed if we were to completely abandon it. One aspect of it which Forsyth was eager to retain was the theocentric nature of the doctrine, found in the fact that it was more eager to uphold God's freedom than that of the human creature.[17] We will have occasion subsequently to discuss the significance of Forsyth's theocentric approach to doctrine, but let us now focus on how Forsyth re-conceptualises the notion of election in the light of his *theologia crucis*.

Forsyth begins by affirming the traditional Calvinistic position that election is the foundation of our certainty in God as it is the "eternal divine act which is the ground of every historic act of His in Christ and kingdom."[18] But he then questions the conventional starting point for the doctrine, which is the God who in his absolute freedom decrees salvation and reprobation to different segments of the human population. For Forsyth, such a view of God is untenable, because it is derived from speculation arising from our observation of the world.[19] We perceive the existence of two classes of people, those who respond to the Gospel and those who do not, and then seek to explain this phenomenon by developing a corresponding notion of God and his dealings with the world. This, to Forsyth, is a clear instance of naturalistic epistemology,[20] the illegitimate *theologia gloriae* which leads invariably to a distorted understanding of deity. The correct starting point for understanding the doctrine of election is rather that of Christ. Forsyth justifies this by pointing out that the object of God's election is depicted in the Bible as first and foremost

---

15. Brown, *Prophet for Today*, 14; Horrocks, *Laws of the Spiritual Order*, 126.
16. *Faith*, 310.
17. *Authority*, 255.
18. Ibid., 346.
19. Ibid., 358.
20. Ibid., 357.

Christ. He is the "Captain of the elect." Election can therefore never be comprehended apart from who Christ is and what he did.[21]

What are the implications of understanding God's election in the light of Christ and his work? Forsyth insists that, through Christ's work on the Cross, we see that that the content of God's election is salvation. And salvation can only reveal "the principle of salvation;" it says nothing at all about reprobation.[22] For Forsyth, therefore, understanding God's election through the *theologia crucis* means that we know only that election expresses the goodness of God and his loving purposes for the world, as evidenced in his saving of it. We do not derive any knowledge at all about the source of evil in our world, beyond the fact that it has something to do with the "mystery of human freedom."[23] We therefore fall into serious error when we try to make the doctrine of election do too much, i.e., to explain the source of both good and evil. This leads to the postulation of "two causes in this act, two wills [and] two gods."[24] Forsyth therefore rejects the traditional formulation of double predestination. The *theologia crucis* tells us that election is solely one to life.

Throughout the whole discussion, we see Forsyth's methodology holding firm. It is only through the Cross that we understand what election means: "The centre of majesty has passed, since Calvin, from the decrees of God to His Act, to the foregone establishment in Christ's Cross of a moral Kingdom without end, which is the key and goal of history."[25] This, for Forsyth, is an issue on which there can be no compromise or mediating position. If we do not put Christ and his Cross at the forefront of our epistemology, we invariably debase him. The traditional Calvinistic doctrine of election, with its starting point in God's eternal decrees, views Christ as a mere instrument for carrying them out. He has no greater status than an "engine" of God who executes God's will.[26] It is bound to make Christ superfluous once the decrees have been executed and the end is reached.[27]

21. Ibid., 353.
22. Ibid., 359.
23. Ibid., 357.
24. Ibid., 358.
25. *Faith*, 277. The title of the section of the book in which this passage appears is "The New Calvinism – I." Forsyth is eager to develop a new Calvinism for his time.
26. *Authority*, 358.
27. Ibid., 353.

Forsyth's Theologia Crucis *and the "Self-Justification" of God*

So Forsyth attributes prime epistemic value to the event of the Cross. It is able to tell us truths about the person and work of God. It can do so because a primary event took place there—the "self-justification" of God.[28] This is *the* key concept in Forsyth's theodicy, and much of the rest of our study will be spent unpacking its meaning and implications. But already the perceptive reader might raise a protest. Forsyth, in his theodicy, should be seeking to justify God to human beings. Why is he focusing so much of his energies on the notion of God's self-justification? Forsyth provides a ready answer:

> God's demand on man takes the lead of man's demand on God. And both are overruled by God's demand on God, God's meeting His own demand. Only God's justification of man gives the secret of man's justification of God. The justification at the root of all other is God's self-justification.[29]

It is God's self-justification which provides the basis for the human attempt to justify God. Forsyth therefore sees his task in theodicy as showing that such self-justification did take place on the Cross, and that the human justification of God follows quite naturally from this. We will now attempt to explicate this complex notion of Forsyth's.

THE CROSS AS GOD'S SELF-JUSTIFICATION

Introduction

The Oxford English Dictionary gives the following as one of the definitions of the term "justification": "The action of justifying or showing something to be just, right, or proper; vindication of oneself or another; exculpation."[30] As his daughter Jessie Andrews testifies, Forsyth possessed in abundance "that *Sprachgefühl*—that deep sense of word-values—which is born in every Celt."[31] This is demonstrated in the way he taps into the rich vein of meaning inherent in the word "justification," in order to provide the content for his key phrase "God's self-justification." We see

---

28. "The Cross of Christ ... is God's only self-justification in such a world": *Justification*, 32.

29. Ibid., 35.

30. "Justification," *The Oxford English Dictionary*.

31. Jessie Forsyth Andrews, "Memoir," in Forsyth, *Work*, xxvi.

Forsyth employing this phrase in two main senses. There is, firstly, the idea of "God's self-justification" as God vindicating himself and his holiness against the challenge of sin.[32] When used in this first sense, "God's self-justification" refers to the event of the atonement.[33] This is because Forsyth sees the main significance of Christ's atoning work on the Cross as the victory and fulfilment of God's holiness against the threat of sin. There is, besides this, the notion, more closely related to theodicy, of "God's self-justification" as God showing himself to be righteous and good in spite of the existence of evil in our world.[34] "God's self-justification" is, in this sense, God's own engagement in theodicy. We will examine in turn each sense of the phrase.

"God's Self-Justification" as God Vindicating His Holiness against Sin

Forsyth's Understanding of the Atonement

There is, among the commentators on Forsyth's theology, the lingering critique regarding the vagueness and incompleteness of his writings on the atonement. Even such an ardent admirer as A. M. Hunter found himself having to say that Forsyth's exposition of the subject "often lack lucidity."[35] Another strong supporter, that one-time student of Forsyth's Sydney Cave, laments his mentor's failure to write systematically on the subject, adding that "I have long felt that one of the greatest books on the Atonement would have been the book Forsyth might have written but did not write."[36] As we shall see later, one of the main points of difficulty commentators find in Forsyth's description of the atonement concerns his insistence that it is, amongst other things, a penal act.

Because the atonement lies at the heart of Forsyth's theodicy, and a proper understanding of it is basic to appreciating his justification of God, we find it necessary to offer here our exposition of Forsyth's un-

---

32. *Authority*, 7; *Faith*, 276. Commentators have also noted Forsyth's use of this phrase in this first sense: see, e.g., Rodgers, *Theology of P. T. Forsyth*, 58; Mikolaski, "P. T. Forsyth," 320.

33. Gunton interprets Forsyth's phrase likewise in *Actuality of the Atonement*, 106.

34. See *Justification*, 122–25 for a sustained use of the phrase in this second sense.

35. Hunter, "P. T. Forsyth Neutestamentler," 103.

36. Cave, "Dr. P. T. Forsyth: The Man and His Writings," 117. For other comments to a similar end, see Mozley, "Forsyth—the Theologian," 110 and *Heart of the Gospel*, 83; Sykes, "Theology through History," 233; Bradley, *P. T. Forsyth: The Man and His Work*, 139–40; Camfield, "Peter Taylor Forsyth," 6.

derstanding of this doctrine, one that hopefully goes some way towards dispelling the charge that it is vague and incomplete. This will provide us with the foundation we require for our subsequent discussion of Forsyth's theodicy. In the interest of space, however, we will seek, as far as possible, not to replicate the valuable work already done in this field, and focus our attention on answering the key questions raised by the secondary literature.

We will also seek to be deliberate, when setting out Forsyth's understanding of the atonement, in mentioning the impact Christ's resurrection has upon it. Such emphasis is necessary as a corrective to the view of some commentators that Forsyth sought to explicate the atonement without significant reference to the resurrection.[37] Forsyth himself has admittedly given support for this view with his frequent assertion that the Cross is a "finished work" in its own right, and that the resurrection which followed was merely "God's seal upon it" and God's way of publishing aboard its achievements.[38] There are other parts of his writings, however, which (in apparent violation of such assertion) describe the resurrection as integral to what God achieved in the atonement. We will highlight these aspects of Forsyth's writings to argue that Forsyth's ostensible disparaging of the significance of the resurrection for the atonement might not represent his last word on the matter.

Forsyth notes that, in the history of the Church, three main "theories of the atonement" have been developed to explain the event at Calvary. These view the work of Christ respectively as a victory over evil, the act which satisfies God and his demand, and that which regenerates human beings.[39] While Forsyth does not agree with all the details of these three theories in the ways they have historically been expounded, he sees that the themes behind these theories accurately describe what happened at the Cross:

> The work of Christ was thus in the same act triumphant on evil, satisfying to the heart of God, and creative to the conscience of man by virtue of His solidarity with God on the one side, and on the other with the race. He subdued Satan, rejoiced the Father, and

---

37. See, e.g., Bradley, *Man and His Work*, 166, 270; Thompson, "Was Forsyth Really a Barthian before Barth?" 254–55.

38. *Society*, 18; *Preaching of Jesus*, 17; *Missions*, 13; *Positive Preaching*, 184, 189, 246.

39. *Work*, 199.

set up in humanity the Kingdom, all in one supreme and consummate act of His own.[40]

In expositing his own view of the atonement, therefore, Forsyth incorporates what he sees to be the key themes behind these three theories. It would therefore be convenient for us to set out Forsyth's view under the three headings of the Cross as satisfaction, victory and regeneration.

The Cross as Satisfaction

The controlling idea in Forsyth's understanding of the Cross as satisfaction is that, in the context where God's holiness is being compromised by sin, only an adequate response of holiness "from the side of the culprit world" would be able to satisfy the demands of this holiness.[41] Precisely such a response was given on the Cross, when Christ confessed the holiness and righteousness of God's judgement upon sin. Because of Forsyth's insistence that Christ on the Cross was "made sin," this judgement was at the same time one inflicted upon Christ himself. Christ's confession on the Cross was therefore one of the righteousness of God's judgement upon him. As Forsyth puts it, "[Christ] lifted up His face unto God and said, 'Thou art holy in all Thy judgements, even in this judgement which turns not aside even from Me, but strikes the sinful spot if even I stand on it.'"[42] Such a confession satisfies the "wounded holiness" of God.[43]

Forsyth's affirmation of the traditional view that Christ is both fully God and fully human (although the particular form this affirmation takes is rather different from that expressed in the Chalcedonian formula) is relevant here. It is important to affirm Christ's divinity because of Forsyth's assertion that the atonement is essentially gracious in nature. Christ's identity as God tells us that the atonement stems wholly from the initiative of God, and that it was God who paid the greatest price in effecting it. "The atonement," Forsyth insists, "did not procure grace, it flowed from

---

40. Ibid., 224.
41. *Justification*, 172.
42. *Work*, 150. Although Forsyth depicts Christ's confession here using the form of direct speech, he explains (at *Work*, 149) that he does not base such confession upon anything Christ actually uttered, whether on the Cross or before. Christ's confession was rather manifested through the way in which the incarnate Son lived and died. We will have more to say about this in chapter 5.
43. The phrase "wounded holiness" was used by Forsyth in *Work*, 126.

grace."[44] This is why God's vindication of himself and his holiness is a "*self*-justification," because it was one provided by none other than God himself. Forsyth would insist equally strongly, however, that Christ has to be fully human, because this fulfils the need for the confession of God's holiness to come from the world, the context in which it was violated.

In setting out this view of the atonement as the satisfying of God's demand, Forsyth is eager to disabuse us of the notion that Christ's suffering on the Cross was valuable as the bearing of an equivalent penalty to what the world deserved for its sinful rebellion against God.[45] The purpose of Christ's suffering was in no way to "exhaust" the judgement of God by bearing the full brunt of it.[46] Rather, Christ's suffering was valuable as the context in which his confession of God's rightful judgement was made. Christ's confession was adequately holy because it was made "amid conditions of pain, death, and judgement."[47] To understand why, we have to look again at Forsyth's Christology. His reliance upon the notion of kenosis led him to the view that Christ on the Cross did not fully understand the purpose for his suffering and death and the significance it would have for God and the world.[48] Christ knew enough to understand that he was somehow bearing the penalty of sin in his experiences, but he could not see in its entirety the glorious outcome it would have for God and the world. Christ's confession was therefore holy because it was made through the "obedience of faith,"[49] one exercised amidst a tremendous

---

44. *Cruciality*, 41. Sell sees this as "the most important sentence in the whole of twentieth-century theology": *Nonconformist Theology in the Twentieth Century*, 172.

45. See, e.g., *Cruciality*, 41; *Work*, 126.

46. Forsyth is partially motivated here by the desire to avoid the trap set by Socinus in his writings against the satisfaction views of the atonement. If an equivalent penalty has been paid on the Cross, God's forgiveness does not then arise out of grace, but obligation. Forsyth stresses, conversely, that even God's acceptance of the holiness of Christ's confession as adequate for atonement is essentially gracious in nature: "Atonement in Modern Religious Thought," 61–62.

47. *Work*, 205–6.

48. *Father*, 21–22; *Sacraments*, 256. We will elaborate upon Forsyth's kenotic Christology in a subsequent chapter.

49. Forsyth uses the term "obedience of faith" in places like *Congregationalism and Reunion*, 38; *Authority*, 67, 324. Forsyth sees no ultimate difference in meaning between the terms "obedience" and "faith." He approves of Ritschl's characterisation of faith as obedience, and speaks of "the obedience which faith itself is, which is the natural feature and seal of faith" (*Revelation*, 69).

personal cost. Such obedient faith accepts without question "the will and Judgement of God" as "the holiest thing in all the world."[50]

For Forsyth, therefore, one major outcome of the atonement is "the perfect satisfaction the Holy finds in the Holy, and the delight of the Father in a Son with whom He is always well pleased. That holiness of the Son of God is the complete reparation to the holiness of God the Father."[51] It is also at this point when consideration of the resurrection becomes relevant. In a passage where Forsyth reflects upon how ministers of Christ constantly undergo the experience of "death" and "resurrection" in Christ, he writes:

> We are one with the Christ, not only on His Cross, but in His resurrection. Think, brethren, of the resurrection power and calm, of that awful final peace, that infinite satisfaction in the eternal thing eternally achieved, which filled His soul when He had emerged from death, when man's worst had been done, and God's best had been won for ever and for all.[52]

The term "satisfaction" is mentioned here, and in the context it refers to the satisfaction Christ felt after the resurrection, "when he had emerged from death." In this sense, the resurrection is crucial to the satisfactory aspect of the atonement, because the satisfaction of the Son of God (as the second member of the Trinity) cannot be left out in postulating the complete satisfaction of God. Moreover, even if we were to restrict our consideration to the satisfaction of the Father, it is difficult to envisage Forsyth seeing the Father gaining any lasting satisfaction from Christ's confession of his holiness upon the Cross if Christ had remained permanently under the dominion of death, given Forsyth's constant assertions about the Father's love for his Son.[53] Indeed, the Father's basic identity

---

50. *Work*, 163. This idea that Jesus exercised "faith" is a contentious one in Forsyth's writings, one which has to be carefully expounded. This we will attempt in a later chapter. It is also interesting to note Forsyth's express acknowledgement that Kant's maxim that "supreme action is doing right for right's sake alone" was influential in his insistence that Christ's confession was made without him knowing the full significance of that act: "Christ and the Christian Principle," 142(fn).

51. *Justification*, 174.

52. *Revelation*, 124.

53. See, e.g., *Person*, 273; *Work*, 147–48.

as Father would itself have been fatally compromised if the Son had remained permanently dead.[54]

The Cross as Victory

Forsyth, as T. Hywel Hughes points out, puts great emphasis on the notion of the Cross as the victory of God over sin.[55] While he clearly rejects certain aspects of the patristic doctrine of *Christus Victor*,[56] he does see God "judging and executing the evil power" on the Cross.[57] It is in this context that he relies most heavily upon the penal idea. We discuss, therefore, Forsyth's use of the penal concept here under the "victory" heading rather than "satisfaction" (where it would more traditionally belong). Forsyth, however, would want to make an important distinction here. What happened on the Cross "was not a penal satisfaction holy and atoning, but a holy substitutionary atonement with a penal element."[58] This somewhat obscure statement might be clarified if we state in greater detail what Forsyth denies and what he affirms. He denies that Christ was punished by God, especially in the manner set out in what he sees as the standard view of Protestant Orthodoxy. Christ, Forsyth insists, did not deflect God's anger from us sinners upon himself, and should not be seen as a sort of third party who procured grace from God to human beings as a result of his substitutionary sacrifice.[59] The wrath of God could never fall upon his beloved Son.[60] The atonement is therefore not "a penal satisfaction" of God. Yet, at the same time, Forsyth affirms that Christ's suffering on the Cross had "a penal element." He took the curse and the judgement of sin, which by right did not belong to him as a sinless person.[61] This attempt by Forsyth to draw such a distinction has attracted its share of criticism.

---

54. As alluded to in *Father*, 91.

55. Hughes, "Dr. Forsyth's View of the Atonement," 34. Hughes also mentions that the warm reception which the victory motif set out in Gustav Aúlen's *Christus Victor* received in Great Britain might be attributable to the influence of Forsyth's teaching.

56. For example, the notion that God had to deal with the rights that Satan had won over humans: *Work*, 231–32.

57. *Society*, 24.

58. Ibid., 26.

59. *Cruciality*, 40–41.

60. *Work*, 147–48. We will examine Forsyth's qualifications to this statement in a later chapter.

61. Ibid., 159.

Both Sell and Hughes, for example, point out that Forsyth has failed to explain clearly how this distinction is logically to be made.[62] Mozley, on his part, makes the more general criticism that Forsyth's retention of the penal idea is the "real obscurity" in his writings on the atonement. For him, it is not clear at all what Forsyth means by statements like "God judged sin upon Christ's head."[63] We will attempt, in this section, to explicate Forsyth's understanding of the penal element in the atonement in a way which hopefully provides an answer to these criticisms. It is here that we must give some consideration to Forsyth's appropriation of Hegel.

Forsyth's relationship with Hegel is an ambivalent one. Often, he issues bitter criticism of the philosopher's ideas, mostly for their tendency to undermine notions of the personality and the will (and therefore the moral).[64] In other parts of his writings, however, Forsyth lauds the achievement of Hegel in rescuing Christianity from the older rationalism,[65] and acknowledges the debt his thinking owes to the philosopher.[66] Stanley Russell calls Hegel the "ongoing temptation [for Forsyth] with whom there was an intellectual affinity of spirit." Forsyth saw that the Christian gospel cannot (and should not) be confined to the philosopher's system, but he "never abandoned the hope that the gospel could take over the system and make it serviceable to its needs."[67] Russell himself points out one sense in which Forsyth's notion of the atonement is reliant upon Hegel's *Philosophy of Right*, in particular the idea that any upset in the moral balance of society was to be redressed by meting out appropriate punishment on the offender.[68] We propose here that Forsyth's view of the atonement is Hegelian in a possibly more fundamental sense when he sets out his view of the Cross as victory.

The key to understanding in what sense Forsyth sees the atonement to be "penal" lies, we suggest, in explicating his cryptic phrase that Christ

---

62. Sell, "P. T. Forsyth as Unsystematic Systematician," 121; Hughes, "Dr. Forsyth's View of the Atonement," 37. Hughes goes so far as to conclude that there is "no way out" for Forsyth except to abandon the penal idea altogether.

63. Mozley, *Doctrine of the Atonement*, 189. See also Shaw, "Theology of P. T. Forsyth," 368 for criticisms of a similar nature.

64. See, e.g., *Authority*, 178–79.

65. *Person*, 219.

66. *Positive Preaching*, 195.

67. Russell, "Spoiling the Egyptians," 236.

68. Ibid., 224–29.

was "made sin" (rather than a sinner) on the Cross. There is an important passage in *The Justification of God* which alludes to what this means:

> All sin inflicts a death on God. It is a *diminutio capitis*. It reduces His headship. It imposes on Him a limitation which is quite unlike all His other determinations in that it is not self-determined, and is therefore absolutely intolerable. If His self-determining power were not capable of a determination mightier than the alien one from sin, sin would conquer, and death would reign. But the meaning of the Incarnation is that God was capable, in His self-emptying in Christ, of a self-limitation, i.e., a self-mastery of holy surrender, whose moral effect was more than equal to the foreign invasion by sin. He died unto sin, as man dies by it . . . His holiness so dies as to inflict on sin a death which it has not power to repel . . . God so died as to be the death of death. He commands His Own negation—even when it pierces as deep within Himself as His Son. He surmounts the last, the most limiting, phase of finitude—evil. He could so identify Himself with sin and death, His absolute antitheses, that He conquered and abolished both, in an act which brings to a point the constant victory of His moral being.[69]

There is a footnote to this section which tells us that "this line of thought is pursued with fine and deep suggestion in Hegel's *Religionsphilosophie*, ii, 249ff. Only some caution is required."[70] Forsyth does not state the precise edition of Hegel's *Lectures on the Philosophy of Religion* he is referring to here. We can infer, however, from the volume and page reference given, that Forsyth probably has in mind the 1840 edition.[71] The relevant section is one where Hegel describes "the true Other" to God as the Son.[72] Bernard Reardon summarises this section well:

> The whole realm of differentiation [from God] may be broadly designed the Kingdom of the Son, on the theological principle that he is not only God's agent in creation but contains within himself the archetypes of all created things. The Son therefore is

---

69. *Justification*, 152–53.

70. Ibid., 153.

71. Hegel, *Vorlesungen über die Philosophie der Religion*. See Reardon, *Hegel's Philosophy of Religion*, 123–24 for details about the various editions of Hegel's *Lectures*, both in the original German and their English translations. To these should be added the 1987 edition.

72. Hegel, *Vorlesungen über die Philosophie der Religion*, vol. 2, 249. The equivalent section begins at vol. 3, 35. Subsequent references will be to this 1895 English translation.

to be thought as free personality existing for himself and in clear distinction from the Father's own being.[73]

Hegel postulates "an act of going out on the part of God into finitude" in and through his Son.[74] Now finitude, as Reardon points out, is for Hegel the true source of evil. In the drive of finite things to assert their finitude and to remain estranged from the infinite, they are in a state of evil.[75] Hegel's idea here is therefore that the Son of God, in his incarnation, assumes the nature of the antithesis of God (i.e., evil as finitude). This antithesis would, however, subsequently be negated by eventual reconciliation with the infinite. This is likely to be the "line of thought" in Hegel which Forsyth refers to in his footnote, one he finds useful in explicating what happened at the Cross. It gives expression to Forsyth's conviction that God in Christ underwent such a radical self-limitation that he "could so identify Himself with sin and death, His absolute antitheses." Reading this passage together with Forsyth's assertion that sin is primarily to be conceived of as a personality in opposition to God, we can infer that what he means by Christ being "made sin" is that Christ on the Cross assumed the status of this arch enemy (or antithesis) of God.[76] While the exact mechanics of how this takes place are unclear, this act of Christ being made sin seems to be connected with the notion we saw in the previous chapter of sin being brought "to a moral head" at the Cross so that God could deal with it "as a unity" and "at a centre." This unified centre of sin was located nowhere else than in Christ himself, with the result that sin in its entirely was dealt with in one fell swoop of judgement upon Christ, resulting in its death and God's victory over it. Forsyth therefore also utilises here Hegel's

---

73. Reardon, *Hegel's Philosophy of Religion*, 68.

74. Hegel, *Lectures on the Philosophy of Religion*, 38.

75. Reardon, *Hegel's Philosophy of Religion*, 69. See also Hegel, *Lectures on the Philosophy of Religion*, 71.

76. This understanding of Christ being "made sin" (2 Cor 5:21) does not seem to fall readily into the ways this verse has traditionally been interpreted. It differs from the traditional Reformed understanding that it refers to God imputing our guilt as sinners to Christ (McCormack, *For Us and for Our Salvation*, 19–20). It also implicitly rejects the traditional Roman Catholic view that the phrase refers to Christ being rendered a "sin-offering" (Weinandy, *In the Likeness of Sinful Flesh*, 80–81). The third possibility, as pointed out by Lyonnet and Sabourin, *Sin, Redemption, and Sacrifice*, 250–51, is to understand it as referring to the event of the Son assuming human nature. This Forsyth does not embrace as well.

idea that the Son's complete identification with God's antithesis leads finally to the negation of such antithesis.

Forsyth in his footnote, however, also urges "caution" in the appropriation of Hegel's thought. One possible need for such caution stems from Hegel's vastly different conception of evil from that of Forsyth's. For the latter, as we have seen, the true antithesis of God is not merely finitude *per se*, but an active personality which seeks to impose finitude on God and therefore to kill him. The free self-determination of God which Forsyth speaks about thus not merely leads to the identification of God with finitude, but also with "the last, the most limiting, phase of finitude—evil."[77] This fundamentally different view of evil also leads Forsyth to part company with Hegel in the latter's reliance on his notion of "sublation" (*aufheben*), in which the antithesis is envisaged to be both destroyed and preserved in a higher synthesis. Evil, for Forsyth, is not a relatively neutral concept like finitude. It is not something integral to the nature of God's other and which therefore has to be taken up and synthesised in a reconciliation. It is instead to be seen almost as a third "other" in the scheme of things, besides God and human beings.[78] For there to be true reconciliation between the latter two parties, sin has to be totally destroyed with no element of preservation whatsoever. That is why Forsyth insists on the "death" of sin in the passage quoted above.[79] Such cautious appropriation of Hegel serves as a good illustration of how Forsyth tries to commandeer philosophy to the service of the gospel without allowing it to unduly dictate the way in which the gospel is to be understood. George Hall is therefore right in observing that Forsyth utilises Hegel's "positivity of negation" in his description of what happened at the Cross, but one which is "set now in a framework at odds with Hegel's own."[80]

We suggest, further, that it would be consistent with Forsyth's approach thus far to postulate that it was Christ's act on the Cross of confessing the holiness of God's judgement which played a decisive role in the negation of sin. Christ being "made sin," in the sense Forsyth understands it, enables us to treat his response of acceptance, praise and the

77. The term "evil" is used here in the sense of sin rather than suffering.

78. This is perhaps why Forsyth refers to sin as "An other" to God rather than "His other" in the passage we quoted earlier from *Positive Preaching*, 252.

79. See also Forsyth's assertion that sin is "outside the range of reconcilable things" in *Positive Preaching*, 161–62.

80. Hall, "Tragedy in the Theology of P. T. Forsyth," 95.

The Locus of the True Revelation of God and God's Self-Justification

justification of God for his judgement as the response *made by sin to its judgement*. Such a response of worship would subvert totally the nature of sin as opposition to God's holiness, resulting in its negation and death. It is therefore possible, we think, to see the obedient confession of Christ on the Cross as constituting in itself an integral part of God's judgement on sin. Although Forsyth does not describe the effect of Christ's confession in exactly this way, there are several allusions in his writings to the idea that this confession played an integral role in the destruction of sin. For example, in a passage from *The Work of Christ*, Forsyth writes that Christ's acknowledgement of God's holiness "must place itself as if it were active sin under the reaction of the Divine holiness,"[81] suggesting that Christ's acknowledgement was made from the *locus standi* of sin. He also notes how Christ "did enter the sphere of sin's penalty and the horror of sin's curse," and did this in order that "from the very midst and depth of it, His confession and praise of God's holiness might rise like a spring of fresh water at the bottom of the bitter sea, and sweeten all."[82] This imagery suggests that Christ's confession of God's holiness was made while he was bearing the penalty in his identity as sin, and that such confession transformed the nature of the depths to which he had sunk. Similarly, in *Positive Preaching and the Modern Mind*, Forsyth appears to draw a link between Christ's confession of God's holiness and the destruction of sin:

> In His Cross He confessed and satisfied the holiness of God in a way so intimate, so absolute, that it was also the radical exposure of sin in all its sinfulness, and thus it became its destruction. If the sinless could not confess sin, He exposed it. He could, and did, confess the holiness which throws sin into complete exposure and ruin.[83]

There are two powerful ironies involved here. Sin, as we saw earlier, is that implacable foe of God which seeks his death. God in Christ, however, won his victory over sin precisely by dying, and therefore completing the negation of God's antithesis. So, "there are victories that are defeats. In the victory of sin, sin received its deathblow. Sin left its sting in Christ, but it

---

81. *Work*, 189.
82. Ibid., 148.
83. *Positive Preaching*, 172. See also Forsyth's statements to a similar end in *Missions*, 17; *Recent Art*, 186; "Paradox of Christ," 130.

cost sin its life."[84] Secondly, although Christ won his victory by identifying himself so closely with sin that he can be said to be "made sin" and to receive judgement and even to confess on its behalf, it took a sinless Christ to effect the triumph, since it was only one who was not under sin's power who could master it and subvert it to act in a way ultimately fatal to itself.[85]

Having explored the possible meaning and significance of Christ being "made sin," we are now in a position to consider whether Forsyth's attempt to draw a distinction between Christ being punished by God and him undergoing a penal suffering can be comprehensibly maintained. We begin by looking at Hart's promising suggestion:

> Christ's death may be described as *penal* because it relates directly to that which we could only experience as punishment—namely, the consequence of our sin in its collision with God's holy nature. But God did *not* punish Christ on the cross. It is only a sense of personal guilt which transforms the experience of that which is the consequence of human sin into punishment, and Christ, in experiencing death, knew no such guilt.[86]

Hart's point is to base the distinction on a matter of perspective. We sinners experience the judgement of sin as punishment, but Christ, because of his sinlessness, did not. Yet the term "penal" could be utilised to describe his experiences because of their substitutionary nature—he took our deserved punishment. We would agree with the thrust of this argument that the distinction boils down to an issue of perspective.[87] In

---

84. *Missions*, 61. There is therefore the sense here, akin to the patristic *Christus Victor* theories, of sin being tricked into its destruction. It responded to the incitement of God's holiness by bringing itself to a head on the Cross in order to win its victory over God through killing the Son of God, little knowing that this same act would lead to its defeat. Forsyth did give guarded approval to the patristic idea of the fooling of Satan in *Justification*, 214. This observation also goes some way towards refuting Justyn Terry's criticism that Forsyth fails to explicate the necessity of Christ's death with regard to the overcoming of sin, leading to the possibility that "the judgement of God could have been fulfilled in Christ had he been rescued from the cross before he died" (*Justifying Judgement of God*, 91–92, 98). It is rather the case that Forsyth sees both the confession and the death of Christ as essential to the final overcoming of sin.

85. This idea is alluded to in *Work*, 223.

86. Hart, "Morality, Atonement," 31.

87. We therefore disagree with Terry's suggestion that the essential way to differentiate between "penalty" and "punishment" in Forsyth's writings on the atonement is simply to see that the former "[carries] less of a sense of something inflicted on an involuntary victim" than the latter (Terry, *Justifying Judgement*, 84).

the light of our earlier discussion, however, we would vary the perspectives involved here. Christ's suffering and death may be termed "penal" because, from sin's (more so than the sinners') perspective, what Christ experienced was sin's punishment for its opposition to God. Christ was, after all, made sin (rather than a sinner), and we recall our earlier observation that it is sin (rather than us sinners) which constitutes the primary target for God's judgement. It is at the same time true to say that God did not punish Christ, because, from the Father's (and not so much Christ's) perspective, the wrath which fell upon Christ was directed solely at the sin to which he had been made, and not at his beloved Son. We say this because when Forsyth speaks of the absence of punishment on Christ, it is usually from the viewpoint of the Father.[88] Moreover, Forsyth did say that Christ on the Cross bore "a sense of the sinner's relation to the personal vis-à-vis of an angry God,"[89] making it difficult to assert that Christ felt absolutely no penal element at all in his suffering and death on the Cross.

One further issue we have to consider is whether such a view of the atonement, with its insistence that Christ primarily bore the punishment of sin (rather than the sinner) undermines its substitutionary nature in any way. On this, Forsyth is firm that there is a real sense in which Christ took the punishment we deserved.[90] One way to explain this would be to recall the point made earlier that sin, although a personality in its own right, seeks to "incarnate" itself in human individuals and societies. This did happen, with the result that "sin is graven in . . . It goes into the tissue of the spiritual being."[91] We can infer from this that our close identification with sin (in terms of our willing participation in its rebellion against God) would mean that any punishment meted out upon it would inevitably inflict us as well. What Christ did, then, was to somehow concentrate sin in his person and then receive its punishment with a holy confession. This is "an eternal damnation of sin which sears it out of the sinner,"[92] one which enables us to escape the punishing wrath of God. An advantage

---

88. See, e.g., *Work*, 83.

89. Ibid., 243.

90. Ibid., 159; "Foolishness of Preaching," 153. Forsyth, however, prefers the term "representation" to "substitution" to describe Christ's work on the Cross, for reasons which will be given in the next section.

91. *Work*, 84.

92. *Authority*, 120.

of this way of describing Christ's substitutionary death is that it helps to explain Forsyth's insistence that the atonement did not change God's feelings towards us, but only God's treatment of us. "God," Forsyth maintains, "never ceased to love us" even when we were sinners, and needed no placation.[93] He could not, however, treat the world according to the love he feels because we were so closely identified with his arch enemy sin. The killing of this foe through Christ's work on the Cross enabled God to restore communion with the world and to exercise his kindness to it.[94]

We turn finally to give brief consideration to how the resurrection of Christ impacts on Forsyth's understanding of the Cross as victory. In a passage from *The Cruciality of the Cross*, he writes that "when Christ died at sin's hands it meant that sin was death to the holiness of God, and both could not live in the same world. When he rose it meant that what was to live and rule in the world was the holy God."[95] We get the impression here that, if Christ had not risen from the dead, the most we can assert from the encounter at the Cross is that both God (in Christ) and sin died. Christ's resurrection, however, means that the holy God lives and rules as a result of the conflict. This must surely be integral to the comprehensiveness of God's victory at the Cross.

The Cross as Regeneration

We arrive at the third and final aspect of Forsyth's view of the atonement. The first thing to note about Forsyth's exposition of the Cross as regeneration is that it is far removed from the merely exemplary notions of the atonement prevalent during his time. As Forsyth would insist, the regenerative effect of Christ's work is created by the act on the Cross rather than exemplified or modelled by it.[96]

---

93. *Work*, 105, 109.

94. In a similar fashion, this argument supports McCurdy's carefully argued thesis that Forsyth does not envisage a "strife of attributes" in God (between his love and holiness), one which is resolved by the atonement. See *Attributes and Atonement*, chap. 7. There is therefore, *contra* Lawler, "The Universalism of P. T. Forsyth," 57, no "lingering uneasiness" on Forsyth's part "with the substitutionary penal element in a moralized theology."

95. *Cruciality*, 101–2.

96. *Work*, 212. For this reason, Forsyth rejects also the Grotian theory of the atonement, which falls short "by treating the Cross as a warning that that order cannot be tampered with rather than as the crucial establishment of the holy Kingdom" (*Preaching of Jesus*, 111).

How is such an effect created? To answer this, we have to return to Christ's confession of God's holiness at the Cross. Forsyth, in addition to all the other significance he attributes to this momentous act, sees it as a proleptic confession by the "new penitent Humanity" whom Christ both creates and represents before God.[97] Christ's confession on the Cross, in his capacity as a true human being, has "such a moral effect" that it changes us subjectively, in the course of time, from rebellious sinners to repentant persons, who will ourselves come to participate in his confession and acknowledgement of God's holiness.[98] It is in this context that Forsyth expresses his wariness in using the term "substitution" to express the work of Christ, preferring instead the idea of representation.[99] J. I. Packer has criticised Forsyth on this point, saying that before Christ's death can be representative, it must be substitutionary.[100] This seems to be a misunderstanding of Forsyth's use of these terms. Forsyth, as we have seen earlier, does not deny the substitutionary nature of Christ's death. While affirming the *concept*, however, he is cautious about the use of the *term*, because of its connotation (arising from its employment in Protestant Orthodoxy) that the atonement was achieved "over our heads" and that our sanctification is not an integral aspect of it.[101] Forsyth would like to affirm the opposite: "We are justified only as we are incorporated (not clothed) in the perfect righteousness of Christ, our Regenerator . . . It is this being in Christ for our justification that makes justification necessarily work out to sanctification, and forgiveness one with eternal life."[102] He found

---

97. *Work*, 192–93.

98. Ibid., 191–92; *Justification*, 174–75. Taking into account what we concluded in the previous section, we can perhaps say that Christ represents both sin and the "new penitent Humanity" upon the Cross. The mode of representation for both need not be envisaged as fundamentally different—but the effect of Christ's confession on one is the very opposite of the other because of the difference in nature between sin as the implacable foe of God and human beings as persons created for communion with God.

99. *Work*, 182.

100. Packer, "What Did the Cross Achieve?" 22–24.

101. *Work*, 182. I. H. Marshall also recognises that "representation" for Forsyth contains the idea of "substitution and more" ("Theology of the Atonement," 58). See also Gunton's comments on how substitution and representation should be seen as correlative, rather than opposing, concepts (*Actuality of the Atonement*, 166–67).

102. Ibid., 215.

in "representation" the term which could possibly be used to express this fullness of meaning.[103]

There is therefore the sense in Forsyth's understanding of the atonement that it is both completed and began in the historic event of the Cross.[104] It is completed in the sense that Christ's confession satisfied the demand of God's holiness, and also that God achieved victory over sin.[105] But, from another perspective, the atonement only started the process of the sanctification of all creation—a process whose completion is integral to the satisfaction of God and his victory over sin. Mozley captures well this paradoxical flavour in Forsyth's writings on the atonement when he writes of him that "no one was more sure that Christ's work was a finished work. No one had a keener eye for its prolongation in the new creation of which Christ was the Head."[106]

But how exactly does the "finished work" relate to "its prolongation in the new creation"? We look to Hart again for an apt summary of Forsyth's position:

> What [Forsyth] seems to be insisting here . . . is that in Christ something happens in the historical sphere which yet has meaning and value discernible only when we cast our gaze beyond that sphere; that Jesus' saving activity, rooted as it is in history, was not confined to the theatre of the human story, but, supremely at the point of the cross, has its deepest meaning only within the telling of God's story. Something happened there which, whatever its impact on humans, and whatever its historical consequences, had decisive consequences for God himself, "establishing the kingdom" in the very life of God which is the moral order, bringing the Holy to an effective self-realisation which must subsequently work itself out more widely in the historical realm. What we have here, then, is something akin to the eschatological tension between the "already" and the "not yet" of the New Testament theology of the kingdom, in which the "already" is understood as referring to an adjustment made within the very nature or life of God, and the "not yet" to its eventual actualisation in the human sphere.[107]

---

103. Although he himself recognised that it was still inadequate in some respects for this purpose: *Work*, 210.

104. *Positive Preaching*, 238.

105. Forsyth cites with approval the Reformation understanding of the "finished work" of Christ on the Cross (*Person*, 23).

106. Mozley, *Heart of the Gospel*, 86.

107. Hart, "Morality, Atonement," 25–26.

This observation is supported by Forsyth's constant insistence that there is another eternal world or reality, "not far from any one of us," in which "God's name is [already] perfectly hallowed" and his Kingdom perfectly established. This was achieved, of course, at the Cross, that "point of space and time which was the critical node of Eternity itself."[108] The perfect situation in this other world invades ours and in the course of time actualises its victory in our history[109]—a movement which Forsyth has described using the patristic notion of *perichoresis*, with the qualification that it is the "eternal" world which exercises its creative influence on ours, rather than the other way around.[110] It is in this context that Forsyth makes his most significant mention of the work of the Holy Spirit. The Spirit, for Forsyth, is most fundamentally the Spirit of the Cross—a Spirit whose ministry lies in bringing to historical realisation the eternal work of the crucified Christ, which was itself carried out in history.[111] "What is eternity," Forsyth asks, quoting Ritschl, "but the power of the spirit over time?"[112] The work of the Spirit, therefore, can be understood as "the procession of an eternal act," since it is the way in which Christ's work of reconciliation on the Cross "[covers] the whole of history and [enters] each soul."[113] This aspect of Forsyth's thought will be considered further in the next chapter.

108. "Congregationalism and the Principle of Liberty," 517.

109. *Justification*, 156–57, 168; *Society*, 21.

110. *Preaching of Jesus*, 83. Forsyth uses the term *perichoresis* in the context of denoting the relationship between the objective and subjective poles of God's salvation—I have extrapolated it to refer to the relationship between the "eternal" world and ours. Another imagery Forsyth uses is that of "the waves of the infinite sea . . . always making advances to our earthly shore" ("Christ at the Gate," 180).

111. In saying this, we show our preference for the understanding of Forsyth's pneumatology offered by Thompson, "Was Forsyth Really a Barthian before Barth?" 243; McCurdy, *Attributes and Atonement*, 232; and Sykes, "P. T. Forsyth on the Church," 13–14 over the minority opinion advanced by Russell, "Spoiling the Egyptians," 232–34, which postulates that "as Forsyth saw it the Holy Spirit must primarily be viewed in relation to the work of Spirit in nature, rather than in the light of being the eschatological, sanctifying gift, who draws a world back from its fallenness into completion." Our view is that Russell adopts an overly Hegelian reading of the passages he quotes on Forsyth's understanding of the Spirit, and fails to give sufficient emphasis to Forsyth's express repudiation of the notion that the work of the Spirit can be understood apart from its organic link to that of Christ on the Cross: e.g., in *Revelation*, 53; *Society*, 114; *Preaching of Jesus*, 80.

112. *Christian Aspects of Evolution*, 28.

113. "Does the Church Prolong the Incarnation?" 207; *Work*, 130. So, even in pneumatology, we see Forsyth's *theologia crucis* holding firm. Gunton's pithy formula that "as Christology universalises, the direction of pneumatology is to particularise" is apt as a summary of Forsyth's view here: Gunton, "Church on Earth," 61.

We conclude this section, as we did the previous two, by considering the significance of Christ's resurrection for the aspect of the atonement set out here. We begin with Forsyth's observation that, historically, it was the resurrection which founded the Church. This event declared to the world God's view that redemption was completed in the Cross. Without it, none of us would have certainty about what the outcome of Christ's sacrifice was, and the Church would consequently not have come into being.[114] While such a description of the resurrection still views it more as an event which published the results of the atonement than one which contributed to its realisation, we can infer from it the indispensability of the resurrection for the success of the regenerative aspect of the atonement. If the resurrection had not taken place, and no Church had come into existence because no one could stand firmly in the faith of what God has done on the Cross, it would be difficult to see how the regeneration Forsyth envisages could ever take place. Forsyth, however, goes further than this in other parts of his writings, and allocates to the resurrection an organic role in the regenerative aspect of the atonement. He writes about how "we rise because He rose; and we rise not like Him but in Him,"[115] and:

> We are the beneficiaries of His conquest by union with Him. We are not so much conquerors by His side or in His wake; we are members of Him and His moral victory. Every soul saved is regenerate by the Resurrection (1 Peter i. 3). That is the source of the Spirit of our regeneration—its point of real origin.[116]

It is difficult to envisage a more prominent role for the resurrection in bringing about the regenerative aspect of the atonement than this. Forsyth extends his reliance on the notion of us being *en Christo* from the Cross to the resurrection. As we are in union with Christ, the possibility of any human being rising to newness of life depends on Christ himself so rising. Forsyth therefore says in consequence that Christ's resurrection is the real source and origin of "the Spirit of our regeneration."

Conclusion

We have explored Forsyth's understanding of "God's self-justification" in the first sense, i.e., God vindicating himself and his holiness against the

---

114. *Positive Preaching*, 189. See also *Father*, 91–92.
115. *Justification*, 229.
116. Ibid., 230.

challenge of sin. This is equivalent to Forsyth's understanding of the atonement, and we have tried to set out this understanding in a way which, we hope, renders it both concrete and systematic.

It will be apparent from the above description that Forsyth's first view of "God's self-justification" is difficult to classify under any one of the traditional theories of the atonement. This is also evidenced by the varying ways in which the secondary literature has attempted to do so.[117] This difficulty probably stems from Forsyth's somewhat original exposition of the traditional themes of the atonement, as well as the manner in which the various aspects of his understanding of this event integrate into one another. Forsyth himself explains some ways in which such integration happens. God's victory over sin and his redemption of sinners is necessarily "the obverse of His regenerating and sanctifying effect on us," since "to deliver us from evil is not simply to take us out of hell, it is to take us into heaven" (showing the relationship between victory and regeneration). Similarly, the regenerating effect of the Cross cannot be seen in isolation from that of the satisfaction of God, since such regeneration is the "condition" of God's satisfaction[118] (showing the relationship between satisfaction and regeneration). We would add, from our discussion, that satisfaction and victory are also integrally related to each other, in that it is the same act of Christ's confession which brings satisfaction to God as well as contributes to the destruction of sin. Forsyth himself sees the key thread running through all three aspects as "the perfect obedience of holy love which [Christ] offered amidst the conditions of sin, death and judgement."[119] This perfect obedience and its resulting confession of God's holiness was, as we have seen, the basis for God's satisfaction, his victory over sin and his regenerating work on his creation.[120]

---

117. See, e.g., Mozley, *Doctrine of the Atonement*, 73–74 (Under the "Substitute" heading); Gunton, *Actuality of the Atonement*, 106–9 ("Satisfaction"); Hughes, "Dr. Forsyth's View of the Atonement," 34 ("Victory"); Sykes, "Theology through History," 234 ("Sacrifice").

118. *Work*, 202.

119. Ibid., 201.

120. We therefore judge to be too hasty Terry's conclusion that Forsyth's "attempt to unite the different aspects of the atonement under the perfect obedience of Christ does not succeed": Terry, *Justifying Judgement*, 105. There is also the sense in which Irenaeus' view of the atonement as recapitulation is incorporated into Forsyth's approach to the subject. This will be more apparent when we elaborate, in chapter 5, on Forsyth's understanding of the life of Christ and its relation to his death on the cross.

From a broader perspective, Forsyth's view of the atonement is also integrative in other ways. Firstly, he never allows what are commonly known as the "objective" and "subjective" aspects of the atonement to conflict with each other, seeking instead to integrate them into a seamless whole. In fact, Forsyth sees the subjective effect of the atonement to be so grounded in its objective pole that the more we emphasise the latter, "so much the more it becomes our subjective possession."[121] Secondly, despite the occasional criticism that Forsyth gives inadequate emphasis to Christ's humanity,[122] he seems to have sufficiently asserted the reality of the two natures of Christ and the indispensability of each in the atoning act. We note, thirdly, how Forsyth's exposition of the atonement accounts for the overcoming of sin both as a personality in its own right and as that human trait of rebellion against God. The former has been conspicuously absent from most major theories of the atonement since the patristic emphasis on *Christus Victor*, and Forsyth's treatment of the subject can be seen as an attempt to recapture this ancient aspect of harmartiology and render it comprehensible to the modern mind. Forsyth's view of the atonement can therefore be said to offer a holistic view of sin, and consequently a holistic account of its eradication from creation. Fourthly, Forsyth's view could form the basis for a reconciliation between (what Smail calls) the concepts of "punitive justice" and "restorative justice" in the atonement. Forsyth's doctrine of the atonement certainly has a strong punitive element, but it is against sin, rather than Christ, and it leads finally to the restoration of our right relationship with God.[123] Finally, Forsyth demonstrates in this writings an integration of philosophy and theology, but one done in a way whereby the latter provides the overarching framework in which the former can be commandeered to explicate certain aspects of it where appropriate.

---

121. *Preaching of Jesus*, 81–82.

122. See, e.g., Bradley, *Man and His Work*, 270–71; Griffith-Jones, "Dr. Forsyth on the Atonement," 315.

123. Smail, *Once and for All*, 93–99. Smail does acknowledge that Forsyth's view is integrative of these two concepts, but did not elaborate on how this is so. He would, we suggest, have been better placed to do so had he given more consideration to Forsyth's rather unique harmartiology.

"God's Self-Justification" as God Vindicating His Righteousness in Spite of the Existence of Evil

When Forsyth writes specifically on the topic of theodicy, he gives the phrase "God's self-justification" a slightly different slant from that discussed above. He uses it to refer to God vindicating his righteousness in spite of the existence of evil in our world. "God's self-justification," in these contexts, is to be understood as God's own participation in the exercise of theodicy. It is the defence he sets up for himself against the accusation that he is not good because evil exists in his creation. We see Forsyth using the phrase in this fashion in passages like the following where he speaks of the questions which arise in the human mind whenever the world faces significant crises (like the Great War):

> Questions then come home about the connection of evil and suffering, sin and sorrow, grief and goodness. Then it is that the desire for a teleology quickens and deepens into the passion for a theodicy. Has the teleology a moral end? Is God's goodness secure? The teleology of things is congested into a crisis which demands that revelation be *the self-justification of God*. Is the great end not only there but is it just, and does it justify the dreadful means? Our quest for a divine plan becomes a concern for the divine justice.[124]

But how does God go about defending his righteousness and goodness in the face of such prevalent evil in our world? He does so through the Cross—"the supreme theodicy is atonement."[125] We note from this that, for Forsyth, the first and second aspects of "God's self-justification" are intimately related.[126] Mozley, that astute commentator on Forsyth, is

---

124. *Justification*, 122 (emphasis ours). See also 123–25 for Forsyth's sustained use of the phrase "God's self-justification" in this sense. He summarises his position on 125: "The only final theodicy is that self-justification of God which was fundamental to His justification of man."

125. Ibid., 175.

126. Smail appreciates how Forsyth (whom he calls "the prince of theologians") joins the themes of atonement and theodicy, but goes on to say that "for the systematic working out of these insights we have however to wait until after the Second World War, for those German theologians whose most accessible representative is Jürgen Moltmann in *The Crucified God*" (*Once and for All*, 45). We hope to show, in the chapters that follow, that Smail need not have waited so long—there is already present in the writings of "the prince of theologians" a "systematic working out" of the integration between atonement and theodicy. It is, in fact, a working out which anticipates some of the ideas for which Moltmann would become well-known.

right in understanding his theodicy as "an extension of the doctrine of the atonement."[127] We see two senses in which this is so. Firstly, Forsyth draws out the implications of the atonement for the exercise of theodicy. What happened on the Cross, in his view, not only justifies us to God. It also justifies God to us. The message of the Cross is therefore not one solely concerned with soteriology—it has everything to do with theodicy as well. We will, in the rest of our study, consider how, for Forsyth, the Cross as atonement justifies God.

The second sense in which Forsyth's theodicy is "an extension of the doctrine of the atonement" can be seen as we look at some important questions he poses:

> Can God so secure His righteousness that the unrighteous world shall be His praise? Can He get such a world to call Him, from the heart of its evil, guilt, and misery, and under the ban of His judgement, yet holy, wise and good? That would be the supreme theodicy, the last justification of God, uttered in silent action by a Humanity that forgets its own fate in entire concern for His righteousness and glory.[128]

So did God manage to get our world to acknowledge his holiness, wisdom and goodness in the midst of its evil, guilt and misery? Forsyth has no doubt about the answer:

> But that is what we have in Christ's atoning Cross. There we have the one perfect, silent and practical confession of God's righteousness, which is the one rightness for what we have come to be, the one right attitude of the world's conscience to God's. In Him Humanity justifies God and praises Him in its nadir; and that is the great theodicy.[129]

We have seen how, for Forsyth, Christ's confession of the holiness of God's judgement upon sin on the Cross constitutes the key event of the atonement. The passage above tells us that Forsyth sees another layer present in this confession made by Christ—it is at the same time one which affirms that God is in the right in spite of the evils present in the world. It is, in other words, a confession of theodicy.[130] Moreover, this confession

---

127. Mozley, "Forsyth—the Theologian," 110.
128. *Justification*, 174.
129. Ibid.
130. See also *Sacraments*, 306 for Forsyth's assertion that the work of Christ answered

was made, not by a detached observer of the horrors of sin and suffering, but the most tragic victim in world history of such horrors—the Son of God who had "become sin" and was bearing its judgement upon the Cross. Such praise of God's goodness and holiness from the midst of the deepest despair is, Forsyth suggests, the acme of the justification of God.[131] But that is just Christ's confession—how does that constitute the world's response to God? The answer has already been given in our section "The Cross as Regeneration." Forsyth sees that Christ's confession on the Cross will inevitably impact human beings subjectively, since all of us were "in Christ" when such confession was made. Christ's justification of God on the Cross will, in other words, be followed and complemented by the world's justification of God—the acknowledgement by the world that God is "holy, wise and good" in spite of the evils we experience. It is to this which Forsyth refers when he speaks about the completion of theodicy. This will take place in that final state of affairs when creation, after a long period of groaning and travailing, finally utters in perfect harmony "[God's] self-justification after all for having made it."[132]

Forsyth therefore sees a reciprocal relationship between the atonement and theodicy. The atonement enables theodicy in the sense that it gives us the resources to engage in this exercise, and guarantees, through the representative nature of Christ's confession on the Cross, that it will bear fruit, most comprehensively in the *eschaton*. Conversely, theodicy functions as one of God's aims in the atonement, such that God's final satisfaction will not be attained unless and until its exercise is completed and all come to justify God's goodness. This idea is conveyed in an interesting passage where Forsyth implicitly engages with the famous first question of the Westminster Shorter Catechism (i.e., "What is the chief end of man?"). In addition to our chief end being to glorify and enjoy God, Forsyth tellingly adds that we were made to "justify" God. This, indeed, is the "supreme object of life" for all human beings.[133] God's intended *eschaton* therefore cannot be arrived at apart from the fulfilment of theodicy. Forsyth's engagement in this discipline can therefore be described not

---

both the questions "How shall man be just with God?" and "How shall God seem just with man?" The latter is expressly labeled by Forsyth as one concerning theodicy.

131. *Cruciality*, 102.
132. *Faith*, 272.
133. Ibid. See also *Justification*, 23–24 for a similar idea.

only as one based upon God's self-justification, but also, more profoundly, as his contribution towards the realisation of such self-justification.

We conclude this section with some brief comments, as before, on the impact of Christ's resurrection on Forsyth's understanding of God's self-justification set out here. Forsyth establishes the "cruciality" of the resurrection for God's exercise of theodicy in this manner:

> If the Cross was a mere martyrdom, and ended all, it really upset all. It did not overcome the world. It solved nothing. Nay, it aggravated everything. It deepened the problem. The best of men met the worst of fates and succumbed, and God said nothing and did nothing. No solemn shock of judgment justified Christ or confounded His slayers. His faith was the great illusion. Nay, the Cross alone is no solution without the solution for the Cross itself, the Resurrection, and all its train beyond Christ's death. The solution of life is death shown practically as a victory over death of every kind.[134]

In Forsyth's view, therefore, the event of the crucifixion, if it had not been followed by the resurrection, would not have functioned as a justification of God at all. It would, in fact, be the death of theodicy, since "the best of men met the worst of fates and succumbed, and God said nothing and did nothing." But because the resurrection, as "the solution for the Cross," did take place, we gain the confidence that God will take action to right all wrongs and vindicate all undeserving victims of evil. We will then have the basis to confess God's righteousness in the end.

Two Outcomes of the Self-Justification of God

We have examined in this chapter how, for Forsyth, the cross as atonement justifies God. We will proceed, in the next part of our study, to look at two outcomes of the atonement and their significance for Forsyth's theodicy. They form, indeed, the two main thrusts of Forsyth's justification of God. We turn now to look at the first such outcome, which is that God is, through his self-justification, moving the world inexorably towards its glorious goal.

---

134. *Justification*, 224.

3

The First Outcome of God's Self-Justification

God Moves the World Inexorably towards His Goal

INTRODUCTION

WE HAVE SEEN IN the previous chapter how Forsyth's notion of God's self-justification possesses both its objective and subjective aspects. In that historic event of Christ's crucifixion, the demand of God's holiness was satisfied, the most basic problem of sin and guilt was dealt with in God's comprehensive victory, and God's righteousness was fully vindicated in spite of the existence of evil in this world. We also noted, however, that Forsyth saw the need for this perfect state of affairs already attained in the "eternal" realm to fully permeate our world in the course of its history in order for God's self-justification to be truly complete. This was to be the work of the third member of the Trinity—the "Spirit of the Cross," who brings to full subjective realisation all that was objectively achieved by the crucified and risen Christ. That this work will eventually be completed is not in doubt. The world, for Forsyth, has been fundamentally "reconstituted" in the light of Calvary,[1] and is inexorably moving towards the *telos* God has determined for it:

> The righteousness swift and complete in the Cross is the same righteousness which is slowly making the kingdoms of the natural world into the righteous Kingdoms of a holy God. All history in its deep long meaning, in its slow substantial meaning, is Christ coming into His own. It is the self-exposition, the self-effectuation, of the Redeemer.[2]

---

1. *Justification*, 124.
2. *Ethic*, 118–19.

The comment has been made that, in comparison with his exposition of what happened at the Cross, Forsyth "does not develop to an equivalent extent . . . how this reconciliation is subjectively appropriated."[3] Justyn Terry adds the charge that:

> For Forsyth, the work of salvation is so concentrated into the cross of Christ that he is in danger of suggesting that all that remains thereafter is to appreciate the new state into which we have been transferred. So complete is the work of Christ that our repentance and life of faith are less a joining to Christ and participation in his work than a recognition of what is already the case. The role remaining to the Holy Spirit is thus essentially the educative one of bringing home to the individual and society what is already true.[4]

We hope, through this chapter, to show that these comments are quite fundamentally mistaken. In our reading of Forsyth, we find him elaborating in quite substantial detail how Christ's work on the Cross is to be subjectively realised in our world, and in a way which goes far deeper than the mere transmission of an epistemological "appreciation" of our "new state." As mentioned in our previous chapter, such elaboration forms what we see to be the first main thrust of Forsyth's theodicy. This chapter will set out these thoughts of Forsyth's, and will be followed by the next which examines their significance for his justification of God. Before looking at how Forsyth describes the movement of the world towards God's goal, however, it would be helpful to first understand what Forsyth envisages this goal to be, so that we know to what kind of end state he sees everything to be moving.

THE GOAL OF HUMANITY AND THE REST OF CREATION

The Goal of Humanity

While Forsyth paints the final state of affairs with a variety of descriptions, the primary one he utilises is that of the human soul perfected in holiness. Since the root problem of the world is human sin and guilt, it follows quite naturally that the glorious end of the world should be based on the complete hallowing of the human soul. True to his understanding of holiness as residing in a personal God, however, Forsyth does not see

---

3. Russell, "Spoiling the Egyptians," 225–26.
4. Terry, *Justifying Judgement*, 102.

such human perfection in holiness primarily as the attainment of some abstract standard of righteousness or morality. It is, rather, our participation in God's holiness—as he puts it, "we are holy with the holiness of God."[5] Perfected human beings participate fully in this divine holiness by entering into a state of union with God.[6]

True to Forsyth's voluntarism, however, the union between God and humans he envisages is not of a substantial or intellectual kind, but one of the will. It is "a unity of moral soul."[7] Our fully sanctified human consciences will be "wedded" with God's conscience,[8] and our unified consciences will move our wills in the same direction. The term which Forsyth prefers to describe such union with God is "communion"—the reciprocal fellowship which two moral persons enjoy with each other.[9] This communal understanding of human perfection ties in well with Forsyth's vision that humanity will, in the *telos*, come subjectively to participate in the perfect *response* of holiness to God which Christ made on the Cross. We should add that there is also a strong inter-human communal element in Forsyth's vision of the end-state. When the intractable problem of human egoism has been overcome by the completed process of sanctification, true human unity will be achieved.[10] Persons will have so much to give each other that we can be said to "mutually interpenetrate" one another. This takes place without any of us losing our individuality, which, after all, is the basis for us having something unique to offer to other persons.[11] In this glorified state, Forsyth envisages that the eradication of evil as sin will be accompanied by the cessation of evil as suffering. While suffering arose in this world before sin did (a point we will consider in a later chapter), the final destruction of sin "carries with it also the end of pain."[12]

---

5. "Christ Our Sanctification," 733.

6. This is why Forsyth prefers to say that "God is our Salvation" rather than "God is our Saviour." He does not save or perfect us for something external to himself. Rather, he has willed that "He should Himself be our perfection and our life" (ibid).

7. *Justification*, 74; *Monism*, 16.

8. *Justification*, 172.

9. *Life*, 56; *Work*, 69; *Authority*, 202–3.

10. *Justification*, 13–14, 110.

11. *Life*, 94–95.

12. *Justification*, 140.

The Goal of the Rest of Creation

There has been, in the secondary literature, a rather sustained critique of Forsyth to the effect that he has explicated an overly negative view of creation. One strand of this critique focuses on Forsyth's apparent disparaging of creation in its material sense. Rodgers, for example, questions if Forsyth "really [reflects] the Biblical appreciation and joy in the earthly blessings of the Lord."[13] It is clear from the context that by "earthly," Rodgers refers to the notion of physicality or materiality. Jeremy Begbie notes in some detail how Forsyth portrays matter in an unduly negative light in the latter's *Christ on Parnassus*. There, Begbie claims, the material nature of artistic works is seen almost as a hindrance to their ability to convey spiritual truths.[14] There are certainly grounds for these comments in Forsyth's writings, as he does demonstrate, in several places, an almost Gnostic tendency to downplay the material creation in favour of a deeper spiritual reality.

We suggest, however, that these critiques should be tempered by a reminder that, for Forsyth, "the moral is the real." This dictates, to him, that the deepest reality of creation is not its materiality but its sphere of morality.[15] Forsyth gives a lengthy defence of his downplaying of created materiality on this basis in *Christ on Parnassus*. It is worth quoting him in some detail:

> The real world is not what Nature gives, but what conscience gives. A man is a real man, not as he lives with Nature, but as he lives with his conscience, lives centrally with his conscience . . . But in Nature there is no conscience. A living conscience, therefore, worshipping Nature confronts something lower than himself in dignity and reality. He loves and pursues with energy something without moral urgency or even ideal. If he spend himself wholly on this he is losing his soul, in the ethical sense of the phrase. He may be full of soul, as the saying is, but he is bestowing his moral self upon something not moral, or not yet moral; and surely that is

---

13. Rodgers, *Theology of P. T. Forsyth*, 264.

14. Begbie, "Ambivalent Rainbow," 212–18.

15. This observation also goes some way towards responding to Daniel Hardy's critique (found in "Created and Redeemed Sociality," 40) that Forsyth neglects the notion of a "created sociality." Forsyth's emphasis on "the moral as the real" surely presupposes such a "sociality" on the part of human beings, since the bulk of the content of morality has to do with our relationships with other human beings, with the rest of creation and with God.

> throwing his soul's reality away... Where does the moral soul and self find the moral reality for which it craves? Where can it find it but in God, and God's supreme, eternal, moral action? A person can only rest in a person, a soul in a soul. Nature and soul are alike unreal till they are settled on that rock.[16]

Forsyth sees a fatal danger with an over-preoccupation with the material aspects of Nature. It turns us away from the deepest reality of this world, and can easily lead to the dead end of idolatry—the worship of Nature itself.[17] This does no favours to either human beings (the worshippers) or Nature (the worshipped). We are moral beings and are made for nothing less than communion with the supreme moral being, who is God. We cheat ourselves of this destiny if we remain contented with our focus on Nature. The greatness of Nature herself is also paradoxically compromised when we see her as an end instead of a means to the moral being behind her:

> Even Nature deserves the artist's greatest. She is so great that we cannot continue to do her justice if we are incapable of the greatest passion. We must worship a moral power above and within her ... we are not fair or adequate to great Nature herself if we come to her witless of the moral passion behind her which sets man above her; if we do not realise that morality is the nature of things.[18]

These observations lead us to make two comments. Firstly, it appears that Forsyth's apparent disparagement of material creation could be motivated by a tendency he sees among the practitioners of the arts to focus upon such materiality as an end in itself, and therefore miss out on the deepest aspect of reality. One can perhaps fault Forsyth for phrasing his statements in an unnecessarily extreme fashion, but it is not uncommon for persons battling an entrenched position to over-emphasise the opposing stance. Secondly, we echo Gunton's observation that Forsyth's emphasis on "The Real as the Redemptive" (which is a more focused way of stating that the moral is the real) leads him to "shape a theology of nature in the light of redemption."[19] Gunton notes how Forsyth manages to escape the characteristic weakness of Western theology which sees the

---

16. *Parnassus*, 272–73.
17. Ibid., 274.
18. Ibid.
19. Gunton, "Real as the Redemptive," 51.

salvation of human beings as one which takes them out of the created order.[20] Forsyth is indeed very critical of any "sectarian" conception of salvation which understands it as "the proceeds from a good sale of the wreck of creation."[21] He notes the prevalence of such "sectarian" tendencies in his own Free Churches, and tries to persuade them that:

> The object of the Gospel is no longer to save a group out of the world, but to save the world itself. That is felt to have been its original purpose. Souls, sects, and Churches are saved in a universal, a racial, salvation. The world is no longer an area from which the Church is gathered, a broad soil from which a small barn is filled. It is the raw material for the Kingdom, it is the Kingdom in the making. The actual world is not only the workshop of God. It is His Building in process.[22]

In another passage, Forsyth disputes the notion that it is "the whole of Christ's work to create a kingdom of souls whose moral elevation should transcend all the ills that flesh is heir to, and lose in elation the sense of them."[23] Instead, in the regeneration of human beings, creation itself is also regenerated—it is "created more creatively."[24] One only has to look at the language used by Forsyth in these passages (e.g., raw material, Building, flesh) to infer that he sees the renewal of creation to encompass all its aspects—material and moral. For Forsyth, therefore, the "sphere of nature," with all its materiality, receives from the Cross "a consecration from God's will and purpose."[25] As mentioned in the previous chapter, such consecration is, in fact, vital to the completion of God's self-justification. The fulfilment of theodicy is, we recall, "the concent of a creation uttering His self-justification after all for having made it." The converse also holds true—theodicy, for Forsyth, is "incomplete" while "the groan-

---

20. Ibid. It is interesting that Gunton cites a passage from Forsyth (*Authority*, 206) where the latter is probably criticising Ritschl for his idea that the redemption of human beings involves the "beating down" of Nature. This challenges Rodgers' assumption (in *Theology of P.T. Forsyth*, 264) that Forsyth's apparent low view of creation can be traced to the lingering influence of Ritschl.

21. *Justification*, 207.
22. *Sacraments*, 125–26.
23. *Faith*, 272.
24. *Justification*, 207.
25. *Parnassus*, 84.

ing of creation is not stilled."²⁶ From the perspective of the goal of creation, therefore, we are led quite far away from the notion that created materiality is an obstacle to the realisation of spiritual reality. It is in fact an indispensable aspect of the fulfilment of the most significant aspect of such reality—the self-justification of God. We infer from Forsyth's writings, however, that created materiality can perform this role to perfection only in the *eschaton*, when the presence of sin is totally eradicated from the world and we are no longer tempted to worship matter as an end in itself. It is therefore perhaps more accurate to say that, in all his disparaging remarks on material creation, it is sin (and its distorting effects) which Forsyth is really attacking, rather than matter itself.

The main point of our participation in this discussion on Forsyth's doctrine of creation is to argue that Forsyth, from the perspective of redemption and the *telos*, has a high view of creation in all its aspects, including its materiality. God's salvation, in addition to perfecting human holiness, involves the holistic renewal of the rest of creation, such that it participates in the justification of God in the *eschaton*.

Forsyth's "Christian Universalism"

We have seen Forsyth's assertion that God's goal for both human beings and the rest of creation will be a glorious one. We now have to grapple with the thorny issue of what Forsyth's understanding of the extent of such a goal is when it comes to the former. Will all of humanity reach this *telos*, or might some fall short? This is not an easy question to answer, because there are strands in Forsyth's writings which seem to affirm both positions. We will, in this section, attempt to synthesise Forsyth's statements in a way which makes the best sense of them. We begin by observing that Forsyth, in many places, affirms the salvation of the entire human race—what he calls "Christian universalism."²⁷ We see the impetus for this affirmation arising from Forsyth's understanding of the atonement. For the efficacy and completeness of Christ's work on the Cross to be realised, the human race as a whole must be saved. The need for satisfaction for God's "wounded holiness," for one, "can only be met by a personal holiness upon the scale of the [human] race, upon the universal scale of the sinful

---

26. *Faith*, 272.
27. "Christianity and Nationality," 397.

race."[28] Anything less would be insufficient. What Christ presented to God on the Cross was therefore "not the perfect obedience of a saintly unit of the race," but "a perfect racial obedience."[29] We recall the point made in the previous chapter that Forsyth sees Christ's confession on the Cross as a proleptic confession by the "new penitent Humanity" whom Christ both creates and represents before God. What Forsyth makes clear here is that this "new penitent Humanity" refers to the entire human race, and not merely a section (however large) of it. Similarly, Forsyth argues that God's victory over sin achieved on the Cross would be less than comprehensive if his salvation fails to reach any segment of the human race. The "permanence of evil," in terms of the endless existence of persons in hell, means nothing less than that God is "foiled and the Cross of Christ of none effect."[30] The doctrine of "conditional immortality," promoted by prominent Congregationalists like Edward White and R. W. Dale,[31] is for Forsyth also not a viable theological option. When God's holiness is resisted, Forsyth insists:

> . . . the resistance is not simply to be overborne and erased; it must be converted and recovered, else the Holy is less than universal, infinite, and absolute. The unholy must be restored to holiness. It is unmade but to be remade. And there is none but the Holy creative enough to do this. And He must—by the necessity of His holiness . . . As holy He deals with His broken law in the Act which heals the broken soul.[32]

The "miserable doctrine of annihilation" teaches, in contrast, that "there is a way of getting rid of sin other than by conversion," but the solution it suggests is "not curing but killing." It is, in effect, "to confess that a section of the human race has been successful in withstanding the power of the cross of Christ and must be exterminated in order that the cross may have imperial and universal sway."[33] Such an outcome is no victory for God's holiness at all.

28. *Work*, 126.
29. Ibid., 129.
30. "'Bible Doctrine of Hell and the Unseen,'" 4.
31. See Rowell, *Hell and the Victorians*, 182–83, 188, 203–4 for the positions of White and Dale.
32. *Justification*, 65.
33. "Bible Doctrine of Hell and the Unseen," 4. Other statements of Forsyth's explicitly or implicitly rejecting annihilism include *Ethic*, 80; *Justification*, 74; "Preaching

We can therefore say that universalism serves, for Forsyth, the purpose of securing what he understands to be the "objective" aspect of the atonement. We saw earlier how Forsyth criticises Protestant Orthodoxy for over-emphasising this objective aspect at the expense of the subjective appropriation of what Christ has done on the Cross. He is also astute enough to see, on the other hand, a dangerous trend in the Protestantism of his day which moves in the opposite direction. There is a "deadly kind of subjectivity" which views the purpose of the Cross merely as that which allows for the conversion of individuals or groups of people.[34] This sees salvation taking place "by private bargain," with each person coming to God individually and getting a personal discharge from his sin.[35] Such a subjective over-emphasis on the atonement "[reduces] it to God's dealing with a mass of individuals," and fails to understand that "it changes a whole race's relation to God."[36] This rootedness of Forsyth's "Christian universalism" in the "objective" aspect of the atonement also means that it possesses a firmly theocentric basis. The entire human race will be saved, not primarily because of any inherent human value or right, but because this outcome constitutes a vital component of God's self-justification.[37] As Forsyth puts it, "mankind was redeemed in the Cross not for its own sake but for the sake of the Holiness of God, for the sake of His Holy One, for Christ's sake."[38] Or more succinctly, "the Christian ground for immortality [and we might add, universalism] is that the Lord hath need of him."[39]

What we have set out above seems to make it obvious that Forsyth is a committed universalist, in the sense that he is certain of the salvation of the whole human race. Such salvation will occur because it is the result of God's atoning work on the Cross, and is in turn necessary for the completion of such work. Forsyth, however, makes our assessment of his position

---

of Jesus [VII]," 298. Rowell, *Hell and the Victorians*, 201–2; and Pitt, *Church, Ministry, and Sacraments*, 265 also see Forsyth denying this doctrine, the former suggesting that Forsyth was following in the footsteps of his mentor James Baldwin Brown in doing so.

34. *Work*, 93–94.

35. Ibid., 117.

36. Ibid., 96; *Cruciality*, 18.

37. It is true that Forsyth does at one point attribute his universalism to "the unspeakable value of a [human] soul" (*Authority*, 354). But it is clear from the context that any value that the human soul possesses is derived from its relationship with God and what its perfection means to God. Cf. Lawler, "Universalism of P. T. Forsyth," 4.

38. *Authority*, 364.

39. *Life*, 38.

a lot more difficult by throwing in the occasional "dissenting passage," in which he seems to leave open the issue of whether every single human being that ever existed will be redeemed. From our observation, these "dissenting passages" fall into two major categories. The first involves a questioning of whether the notion of the "human race" must necessarily include every single human person. So, for example, Forsyth urges, "And do not go away with the hasty conclusion that the salvation of the race must necessarily mean the salvation at last of every soul in it. You have first to settle the question whether every soul ever born is required for the unity of the race as a whole."[40] The second category of such passages seems to leave open the question of the salvation of all due to the ability of humans to ultimately reject it. So, for example:

> There is plenty of punishment that hardens and hardens. That is why we are obliged to leave such questions as universal restoration unsolved. Even when we recognise the absolute power of God's salvation, we also recognise that it is in the power of the human soul to harden itself until it become shrunk into such a tough and irreducible mass as it seems the very grace of God could do nothing with. Certainly there are people here, in this life, who become so tough in their sin that the grace of God is in vain.[41]

This is premised, of course, on what we saw in chapter 2 concerning Forsyth's insistence that the salvation of human beings must never be achieved "over their heads." Anyone who is to be saved must subjectively come to trust in Christ as his Redeemer, and finally participate in the confession of God's holiness and goodness at the *eschaton*. Moreover, the premium Forsyth allocates to the functioning of human free will in his voluntarist scheme means therefore that no one, not even God, can coerce a true saving faith out of any individual. "Salvation and coercion," Forsyth insists, "will not go together."[42]

How should we understand these "dissenting passages"? We begin by echoing Howard Lawler's observation that Forsyth has, in none of these passages, denied the possibility of a universal salvation of human beings.[43] The *eschaton* might still see the redemption of every single human being

---

40. *Revelation*, 35. A similar question is raised in *Missions*, 241.
41. *Work*, 161.
42. *Missions*, 22.
43. Lawler, "Universalism of P. T. Forsyth," 102.

that ever existed in the history of our world. In fact, from Forsyth's writings on the topic of individual eschatology, we gain the impression that this outcome is, for him, virtually a certainty. God has, Forsyth seems to suggest, a way in the afterlife to redeem every human soul without violating their freedom. We will now set out the relevant portions of Forsyth's writings in this area.

We saw in chapter 2 that Forsyth fundamentally redefines the Calvinistic doctrine of election according to his *theologia crucis*. He also proposes other modifications to the traditional doctrine in his writings on personal eschatology. He contests the idea that a person's spiritual state at the point of his physical death irrevocably fixes his status either as God's elect or reprobate. For Forsyth, the process of election lasts long beyond the human lifetime into eternity (understood as time without end). We will let him describe this process in his own words:

> One elect succeeds another, and each lives for all in rising cycles. From the non-elect in one stage comes the elect for the next. And so on, in an ascending series of elects, till the whole human lump is refined, till all are brought in—the worst and most intractable last, since freedom may not be forced. There is all eternity to do it in. Here time is no longer. The ungathered fruit of one age yields seed for the next . . . And so the elective process goes on—the elite serving the submerged in every cycle—till we all come to the fullness and quality of the universal and eternal Christ.[44]

So Forsyth envisages a post-death existence for human beings in which they dwell in an intermediate state with the continued opportunity to exercise their free will. In spite of his Protestant heritage, Forsyth does not hesitate to call this intermediate state "Purgatory."[45] (However, as we shall see, the manner in which Forsyth understands this term differs in significant ways from the traditional Roman Catholic conception of it.) This is a state of existence in which God's moral discipline of the human soul continues after death, in what is probably a more vigorous fashion.[46] This discipline takes place in "stages" and "cycles,"[47] but it is unclear how

---

44. *Justification*, 166.

45. *Life*, 42.

46. Ibid., 13 mentions that the "sordid trivialities" which take up so much of our time in this life will not occupy us in the next—the focus there is on the "moral discipline" of the soul.

47. Ibid.

literally Forsyth intends such terms. He may have pictured our post-death existence as consisting of clearly distinct phases in which we pass from one to the next sequentially. There also seems to be no set time limit within which this post-death phase is to operate before we finally arrive at the glorious *eschaton* when the "whole human lump" would be in a position to reply to God's holiness with an adequately holy response of its own. There is "all of eternity to do it in." We also see that, inherent in this purgatorial state, for those who pass from this life as non-Christians, is the opportunity to embrace the Christian faith.[48] As the above passage suggests, Forsyth takes seriously the Biblical notion that God's election is a selection not to privilege, but to service and sacrifice. The elect are always chosen to serve the non-elect by bringing them into God's Kingdom, and this is true both of this life, and every "cycle" of the post-death existence. This ministry of the elect is facilitated in these cycles by a "congenial spiritual climate" for Christian conversion.[49] Souls in the afterlife enjoy the "great leisure of Eternity," and have the time and space to remember and reflect upon their experiences in their previous life.[50] Further clues concerning the post-death environment are given when Forsyth addresses what must have been a hot topic of his day: the fate of the non-Christian soldiers who gave their lives in the Great War in the attempt to resist (what Forsyth sees as) the evil of German aggression.[51] Here, Forsyth puts forth the idea that the sacrifices made by these dead would render them receptive to the post-death invitation of the "wondrous Christ," whom they will meet.[52] Forsyth is quick to emphasise that their noble manner of death does not by itself save them. However, such death has great moral value and may constitute the "first step to a new life" for these persons.[53] We learn from this that there is, for Forsyth, a significant sense of continuity between this life and the next. One's manner of living it and even leaving it has

48. In this Forsyth follows the trend in nineteenth-century British theology of envisaging a post-mortem opportunity for repentance: Powys, "Nineteenth and Twentieth Century Debates About Hell and Universalism," 109.

49. *Life*, 117.

50. Ibid., 118.

51. That this must be a "hot topic" among the Christians of Forsyth's day is supported by Thomas Langford's observation that "the majority of men in service [during the Great War] were estranged from the church and highly critical of its practice" (*In Search of Foundations*, 257).

52. *Justification*, 157–58.

53. *Life*, 41–43.

major post-death implications on how one responds to Christ and on the processes of moral discipline one has to undergo. "Our life beyond," as Forsyth puts it, "is in a moral relation of causality with this . . . We take with us the character we make."[54]

We see, therefore, that Forsyth seeks, in his writings on the afterlife, to reconcile the notions of God's sovereignty (phrased in terms of his election) and human free will, one neatly encapsulated in his statement that "we are all predestined in love to life sooner or later, *if we will*."[55] The mechanisms which Forsyth relies upon to reconcile these seemingly contradictory notions are environment and time. With a conducive environment for conversion and given sufficient time, Forsyth expects that all will freely come to embrace the gospel, even the "worst and most intractable." He makes the additional point that God has a basis for his confidence that all will eventually come to respond to him because we were all created in Christ and for Christ.[56] This anticipates in some ways John Hick's argument that we can be certain of a universalist outcome because human beings are not ultimately neutral in relation to God's saving efforts. As Hick writes: "Since man has been created by God for God, and is basically oriented towards him, there is no final opposition between God's saving will and our human nature acting in freedom."[57]

How do these writings on personal eschatology fit with Forsyth's "dissenting passages"? Which qualifies the other? We suggest that the best approach is to read the "dissenting passages" as effective qualifications to all of Forsyth's assertions of universal salvation, even those he makes in his writings on the afterlife. The notion of the human free will is so fundamental a concept in Forsyth's entire theology that we should see him seeking to maintain its integrity even at the expense of injecting an element of unsettling uncertainty into his eschatology.[58] So, while Forsyth (because

54. Ibid., 113.
55. Ibid., 13 (emphasis in original).
56. "Christ and the Christian Principle," 150; *Pulpit and the Age*, 11.
57. Hick, *Death and Eternal Life*, 254.
58. We are fortified in this conclusion by the observation that most commentators on Forsyth hold back from proclaiming him as an out-and-out universalist: e.g., Mozley, *Heart of the Gospel*, 104; Rodgers, *Theology of P. T. Forsyth*, 67; Pitt, *Church, Ministry, and Sacraments*, 151–53; Sell, "What Has P. T. Forsyth to Do with Mercersburg?" 181, 207–8. One exception might be A. E. Garvie, "Cross-Centred Theology," 326. It might also be relevant that some contemporaries of Forsyth held back from dogmatically affirming "the larger hope" because of the reality of human freedom, e.g., Bruce, *Apologetics; or,*

of his notion of the afterlife) definitely sees the salvation of every human being as a virtually certain outcome, he takes too seriously the reality of human freedom to be able to assert that it must be inevitable. This brings him in line with the view of some contemporary theologians who have argued convincingly that there is no way for one to postulate universal salvation as a certainty while consistently upholding the reality of human free will. David Fergusson, for example, writes:

> Universalism appears to be committed to a theology that is as deterministic and destructive of human freedom as the doctrine of double predestination in hyper-Calvinism. In particular, it does not allow any human being the freedom to finally say "no" to God. Yet without this possibility can we really be said to have the freedom finally to say "yes" to God?[59]

His comments are partly based upon Grace Jantzen's observation (made specifically against Hick's position) that a dogmatic assertion of universalism, even one premised upon "humanity's created bias towards God," ultimately "robs the idea of choice of all significance." Our decisions for or against God in the interim do not matter at all in the end because all of us will finally be brought to the same position.[60] R. R. Cook adds the observation that the human will can actually become more, rather than less, intransigent as time goes by, as repeated sinning makes it more and more difficult for one to repent.[61] A conducive environment and time without limit, even coupled with our inherent bias towards God, might therefore still be insufficient to guarantee universal salvation, as long as the freedom to sin continues.[62]

Christianity Defensively Stated, 68–69; Fraser, *Philosophy of Theism*, 266; Baldwin Brown, *Doctrine of Annihilation*, 128–30. Baldwin Brown especially exercised a profound influence on Forsyth's thinking.

59. Fergusson, "Will the Love of God Finally Triumph?" 199.

60. Jantzen, "Do We Need Immortality?" 39–40.

61. Cook, "Is Universalism an Implication of the Notion of Post-Mortem Evangelism?" 407.

62. See also Trevor Hart's criticism of John A. T. Robinson's certainty of a universal salvation in "Universalism: Two Distinct Types," 30–32. In addition to the points made here, some have tried to rely upon the notion of God's foreknowledge to affirm the certainty of universalism and yet uphold human freedom. The argument is that God would have refrained from creating any human being whom he foreknew would remain intransigent throughout eternity. This presumes that God possesses "middle knowledge." Forsyth does speak about God knowing that he possesses the resources within himself to

To summarise, therefore, Forsyth's "Christian universalism" appears to assert that the whole human race will be saved as a result of God's atoning work, because Christ represented this race before the Father in his holy confession on the Cross. This "race," however, might ultimately not consist of all the human beings that ever lived in the history of the world. There remains (to use Barth's term) the "impossible possibility" that some might exercise their free will to reject God's salvation even throughout eternity. We will, in the next chapter, consider how we might try to make sense of these assertions, and the impact this has on Forsyth's theodicy. Now, however, having looked at the end state envisaged by Forsyth for both human beings and the rest of creation, we turn to consider Forsyth's description of the movement of our world towards this end.

FORSYTH'S NOTION OF THE "CRUCIAL EVOLUTION" OF THE WORLD

Its Difference from the Modern Evolutionary Notions of Progress

The prevailing mood in Europe, from the middle of the eighteenth century to the First World War, was one of optimism. In Britain, in particular, Darwinian evolutionary theory had combined with "the air of satisfaction and optimism" prevalent during the expansive Victorian and Edwardian periods to produce the widespread belief that "progress is the meaning of history."[63] When the First World War arose, a conflict "in which more than thirty-seven million human beings were slaughtered or maimed,"[64] the outcome was an acute and public questioning of God's goodness, and even of his existence.[65] Forsyth, ever the astute observer of his society, comments that the loss of faith many experienced in light of the War was,

---

overcome sin when he created the world (e.g., in *Justification*, 125), but this is some way off from the claims made here. This proposal is also not without its set of problems—see Van Holten, "Hell and the Goodness of God," 50–51 for a critique. The validity of the concept of "middle knowledge" has also been questioned: e.g., in Adams, "Middle Knowledge and the Problem of Evil," 110–25.

63. Hick, *Evil and the God of Love* (1st ed.), 242; Newbigin, *The Gospel in a Pluralist Society*, 112. Examples of such optimism can be found in Martineau, *Study of Religion*, vol. 2, 128–38; Drummond, *Lowell Lectures on the Ascent of Man*, 429–37; Campbell, *New Theology*, 60–63.

64. Hick, *Evil and the God of Love* (1st ed.), 243.

65. Wickham, *Church and People*, 204; Griffith-Jones, *Challenge of Christianity to a World at War*, xii.

at the bottom, an epistemic matter. Seduced by a relatively long period of peace, rise in living standards and advances in science, the arts and other areas, the people of the Christian West in Forsyth's day had began to see such conditions as the norm for their existence.[66] They also started to tie the notion of God's goodness to the maintenance of their well-being and progress—God is good only if things continue to go well. These people "draw their belief from God's treatment of them or their time."[67] Forsyth attributes this phenomenon in his day to such influences as the scientific mindset,[68] pragmatism,[69] the notion of biological evolution[70] and even "Chalcedonism" in the Church[71] (which is Forsyth's shorthand for an overly intellectual conception of the Christian faith). But, whatever the causes, Forsyth sees this as another clear instance of how the *theologia gloriae* has led us to misconstrue the person and work of God. What the people of Forsyth's day were doing was to try to understand how God is like by looking at the events and processes of the world. It was therefore of little surprise that the War and the anarchy which resulted should throw their faith into disarray.[72] Such failure of the *theologia gloriae* is finely summed up in Forsyth's quote of Tennyson:

> I found Him in the flowering of the fields,
> I found Him in the shining of the stars,
> But in His ways with men I found Him not.[73]

The Cross was completely neglected as the epistemic lens through which to view God. Sadly, even the Church was guilty of such omission. Forsyth observes that she, like the rest of society, has fundamentally based her understanding of God's goodness on what happens in nature, and utilised the Cross only in remedial fashion, to "console or stay us when the scheme fails and hopes come to grief."[74] Such an approach is

---

66. *Justification*, 162.
67. Ibid., 201.
68. Ibid., 78.
69. Ibid., 91.
70. *Person*, 145; *Christian Aspects of Evolution*, 33.
71. *Justification*, 90.
72. Ibid., 17, 75. Moltmann is another thinker who finds the roots of "metaphysical atheism" to lie in its appropriation of the *theologia gloriae*: *Crucified God*, 219.
73. *Preaching of Jesus*, 84.
74. *Justification*, 77.

unable to cope with a disaster the magnitude of the War, with the result that the Church was as puzzled as the rest of society about the events that had descended upon them.

Forsyth proceeds to demonstrate what a weak foundation the modern assumption of continued progress rests upon. Rodgers accurately sees Forsyth focusing his attack on the twin movements of historicism and idealism, both of which were prevalent in his day.[75] With regard to the former, Forsyth seeks to undermine its methodological soundness. The mere study of history does not give us a standard by which we can measure what progress is.[76] Nor is the attempt to inductively extrapolate history towards its end legitimate, for the simple reason that we do not know how much of history there is yet to come, and therefore cannot know for sure if we have experienced a sufficient span of time to be able to accurately track its development.[77] All attempts to induce trends are thus necessarily subjective. The subjective nature of this exercise allows it to be influenced, often unconsciously, by the personal ideals of the historian. These are usually "intuitive ideas, like freedom, culture or spirituality, whose assumed value really begs the question."[78] Such subjectivity has also led to a selective consideration of historical events and processes, with the result that their grimmer aspects, like wars and the competitive struggle for money and other ills which raging capitalism brings,[79] are frequently left out of the historian's calculations. In Forsyth's poetical rendering:

> You saw the long expanding series broadening to the perfect day. You saw it foreshortened in the long perspective, peak rising on peak, each successively catching the ascending sun. The dark valleys, antres vast, and deserts horrible, you did not see. They were crumpled in the tract of time, and folded away from sight. The roaring rivers and thunders, the convulsions and voices, the awful conflicts latent in nature's ascent and man's—you could pass these over in the sweep of your glance. They were subterranean to your calm purview. You never lived through one of these cosmic wars. So you easily framed to yourself a long panorama of rising

---

75. Rodgers, *Theology of P. T. Forsyth*, 75–76.
76. *Justification*, 10.
77. Ibid., 41; *Positive Preaching*, 154–55.
78. *Authority*, 200–201.
79. *Justification*, 10.

evolution, and that steady crescendo became your standard of expectation.[80]

Any fair attempt to extrapolate the lines of history will therefore find that they are "neither straight, nor on any calculable curve, [but] labyrinthine."[81] There is ultimately no "unitary and beneficient plan of operations" to be found by studying the course of history on its own.[82] Once the historical basis for the notion of continued progress is undermined, the ground from underneath the forms of idealism which postulate a glorious future for the world is also taken away. As Forsyth pointedly asks, "If a sure past do not promise a reign of love, is there more hope from a conjectural future?"[83] There is no guarantee, or even any reliable indication, that the expectations of idealism will in the end materialise.

In the midst of these assaults on historicism and idealism, however, Forsyth makes it clear that he is too faithful to the Christian tradition to jettison the concept that the world is indeed moving towards a glorious end. He is aware, after all, that the belief in the idea of progress owes its origin not ultimately to secular optimism, but the ancient faiths of Judaism and Christianity, which had challenged and vanquished the then prevailing cyclical view of history.[84] He would insist, however, that if we choose to appropriate the notion of a *telos* (one introduced to the world at large by Christianity), we should also embrace what Christianity has to say about what the end is like and how the world moves towards it. And about this Christianity speaks, not through the process of world history *per se*, but at a specific point in time in this history. As Forsyth asks:

> If the course of history promise little by induction, is there a point of history which does more by insight; which at once exhibits a goal both of God's purpose and man's progress, and has power to make that goal realise itself, power to make it, while goal, at the same time the active ground of the historic career? If we have no self-projected goal which is more than an ideal, have we one given, descending from God, to be within us the final principle and deep dynamic of human growth?[85]

80. Ibid., 163–64.
81. Ibid., 41.
82. Ibid., 10.
83. Ibid., 11.
84. Ibid., 141–42; *Christian Aspects of Evolution*, 37.
85. *Justification*, 11.

He responds with a resounding yes to these questions:

> There can only be one source of such knowledge. It is the final account God gives of Himself . . . God's account of Himself, of His way with man, and of the purpose He infuses into history, His account of His will, on the scale and depth of the great convulsive judgments, is in Christ and His Cross, or it is nowhere.[86]

We will, for convenience, call this movement of the world, as apprehended by the *theologia crucis*, its "crucial evolution" (this is not a term Forsyth himself uses). As the above passages suggest, a key difference between this and those notions of progress disputed by Forsyth lies in what they view to be the cause of the movement of the world. The latter, taking their inspiration from Hegelianism, locate the source of the world's progress in an immanent process within this world, one which will somehow lead to "a grand consummation" of all things.[87] "Crucial evolution," on the other hand, does not place its faith in the notion of the process itself, but in an *act* which originates, empowers and superintends the process.[88] This act of the Cross is at once part of world history and also "planted from heaven" to be the seed of the growth of the Kingdom of God on earth.[89] The Christian story, therefore, can be understood as "the evolution of a new creation pouring from a historic point."[90] This difference in the attribution of the source of the world's movement leads to an equally varied outcome as far as the goal of this movement is concerned. The modern ideas of progress are ultimately unable to formulate any such goal with certainty, because the Darwinian notion of biological evolution upon which they have placed such heavy reliance is unable to postulate a final end.[91] For "crucial evolution," on the other hand, "the goal and the ground are one,"[92] and the Cross gives us both, in the way we have exposited earlier.

---

86. Ibid., 31.

87. *Positive Preaching*, 150; *Work*, 73–74; *Authority*, 178–79.

88. *Positive Preaching*, 229. Forsyth stresses that it is only "acts" which are revelatory, because they are performed by a moral personality, and they demonstrate his will and conscience. A "process," on the other hand, if taken by itself, can easily be treated as impersonal, leading to the conclusion that there is really "nothing moral in it" (*Work*, 67–68).

89. *Christian Aspects of Evolution*, 13.

90. "Reality of God," 610.

91. *Positive Preaching*, 169–70; *Christian Aspects of Evolution*, 8–9.

92. *Authority*, 37.

Forsyth, therefore, has in principle no objection to the idea of evolutionary progress, so long as it takes its proper place within the overarching framework of the Christian gospel: "The evolutionary idea is certainly compatible with Christianity, but not so long as it claims to be the supreme idea, to which Christianity must be shaped. Evolution is within Christianity, but Christianity is not within evolution."[93] It is, we suggest, in this larger context which the various debates about Forsyth's reliance upon the Hegelian dialectic should be conducted. Some commentators have noted how Forsyth, in spite of all his harsh criticisms of Hegel, "[puts] on Hegelian spectacles when it [comes] to trying to discern patterns within history."[94] So, whether it is in the fields of the history of art,[95] British Christianity[96] or Western society,[97] Forsyth describes their movements in the categories of the Hegelian dialectic, seeing how one stage of development sows the seed for its opposing tendency, and how the resulting conflict produces the next level of advance. Looking at these writings on their own, it is easy to come to the conclusion, as Ralph Wood does, that Forsyth is in fact a "true Hegelian," and should therefore be viewed more as a "triumphalist" Liberal than one who is in a genuine revolt against theological liberalism.[98] From the larger perspective we presented, however, it is rather more accurate to say that Forsyth's "Hegelian spectacles" are calibrated to the "degree" of the act of Christ on the Cross, since it is this act which both propels and allows us to perceive such a dialectical movement of history. Hegel's dialectic is, in other words, utilised merely as a possible mode of describing the effects of the primary act of the Cross in some areas of history,[99] rather than as a complete system of

---

93. *Person*, 10.

94. Russell, "Spoiling the Egyptians," 221.

95. Wood, "Christ on Parnassus," 85; Begbie, "Ambivalent Rainbow," 214–15.

96. Russell, "Spoiling the Egyptians," 221.

97. Clements, "P. T. Forsyth," 153; Thompson, "Was Forsyth Really a Barthian before Barth?" 251.

98. Wood, "Christ on Parnassus," 86, 91–93.

99. There is the possible objection that Forsyth's appropriation of the Hegelian dialectic cannot be viewed as a description of the effects of the Cross since he uses this dialectic to account for the movement of pre-Christian history as well as history after Calvary. This can be easily met with the idea that the Cross has chronologically retrospective as well as prospective effect on world history. Forsyth does not seem to have explicitly asserted this, but it follows naturally from his statements (considered in the previous chapter) that the Cross is an event in eternity as well as time. It has perfectly reconstituted

philosophy which accounts for the how, where and why of the movement of the world. Forsyth's appropriation of Hegel here therefore follows the pattern established in his use of the same philosopher's thinking to explicate the atonement—it is the use of Hegel in a framework very much opposed to his own, and therefore can be described as the commandeering of his philosophy to the service of the gospel. We therefore find Forsyth's claim to be promoting the "teleological interest of Redemption" taught by positive Christianity rather than the "cosmological interest of evolution" advanced by liberal theology[100] to be justified.

The Need for Faith

One question remains from our discussion above. If the world is indeed proceeding along the lines of a "crucial evolution" towards its glorious *telos* because of what God has done in the act of the Cross, how are we to perceive this movement? The way of the *theologia gloriae*, as we have seen, is closed, and we are not able to trace the path of such evolution by observing the course of history and trying to induce its trends through our supposedly neutral human reasoning. The alternative Forsyth presents is one he draws yet again from Luther: we are able to perceive the "crucial evolution" of the world only through the eyes of faith.[101] Forsyth also follows Luther closely in his understanding of what this "faith" is. It is "personal trust in the personal God in Christ, the personal response to, and appropriation of, God's own personal and eternal act of pardoning and redeeming grace in Christ."[102] This stress on the personal nature of faith leads Forsyth to distinguish it from a trust placed upon concepts like the Church, Christianity, or any "system of creed or conduct"[103]—it is faith in the person of God which is key. Yet, as the definition given above also suggests, it is not a kind of abstract personal trust devoid of content. "Christian faith always carries implicit in it Christian belief," which, for

---

the eternal realm which in turn impinges upon world history. It would not be unreasonable to postulate that this eternal realm would be able to invade and transform world history past, present and future. A. E. Garvie, in a different context, also affirms the need for Forsyth's theology to postulate the retrospective effect of the Cross ("Placarding the Cross," 349).

100. *Positive Preaching*, 164.
101. *Christian Aspects of Evolution*, 9; *Authority*, 372, 401.
102. *Gospel and Authority*, 125.
103. *Father*, 89; *Rome, Reform and Reaction*, 61–62.

Forsyth, can be summarised in the work of Christ on the Cross to redeem us.[104] Forsyth also insists that faith is much more than "a single act" of committal which we only make once in our lives. It is rather a "life act"—something fundamentally absorbed within our wills and weaved into our everyday experience.[105] Finally, we note a tendency in Forsyth's writings to contrast faith with sight. Faith is exercised most supremely when we trust in spite of what we see and experience.[106] But it is also true that our experience can confirm our faith, and "the more [faith] knows the stronger it grows in trust of the power that overcomes."[107] The order of priority is the all-important thing: Faith "is *realised* by experience, it proceeds in experience, but it does not proceed *from* experience."[108]

Having seen what Forsyth understands by "faith," we now explore in greater detail his idea that the "crucial evolution" of this world can only be grasped by it. We detect, in his writings, two strands of meaning to this assertion, each closely related to the other. The first is that faith in God and his work on the Cross gives us the certainty that this "crucial evolution" is taking place even though we cannot tell how particular events which seem to go against such evolution fit into this trend. God "does not let us pierce with our theoretic reason the deep method and long strategy of His saving Will with the whole world."[109] Therefore:

> We have no vision of a moral harmony that submerges misery and evil, and spreads to order all, but we trust One who has not vision only but command; and we have absolute ground for trusting Him in Jesus Christ the Agent, and not but the seer, of the world reconciliation. Not only can God solve the world, He has solved it, in His own practical way of solution, by saving it—by an act done, and not a proof led, nor a scheme shown. His wisdom none can trace, and His ways are past finding out; but His work finds us; and His grace, His victory, and His goal become sure.[110]

---

104. *Faith*, 219–20.
105. *Ethic*, 178; Forsyth, *Authority*, 101; "Faith and Experience," 416.
106. *Recent Art*, 104–5; "Faith and Experience," 415.
107. *Recent Art*, 110.
108. *Father*, 108 (emphasis in original).
109. *Justification*, 140.
110. Ibid., 158. See Rodgers, *Theology of P. T. Forsyth*, 78 for a similar observation.

Forsyth is under no illusion that such an exercise of faith is easy.[111] Indeed, he questions the authenticity of the "faith" of those who have not experienced any real tragedy,[112] and therefore cannot be said to have undergone what Luther understood as the positive experience of *Anfechtung*. The notion that faith should be viewed as a form of escapism or a way to generate false courage is therefore absurd. Rather, it takes supreme courage to believe in God's victory over a troubled world like ours.[113]

The second strand of meaning to Forsyth's contention that faith allows us to grasp the "crucial evolution" of this world rests on the idea that, having appropriated by faith the work of Christ on the Cross, we are given the lens to interpret certain events in our world as integral elements of such evolution. There is a pattern established by the Cross which characterises God's dealings with the world, and looking at world history through this pattern allows us to perceive realities which a straightforward application of the *theologia gloriae* will not reveal.[114] We will, in the next section, describe what this pattern is and how Forsyth interprets historical events in its light. An important point to note before we move there is that this second strand of meaning is closely related to the first. Forsyth insists that, in spite of the revelation given us through the Cross, we still only see the underside of the "tissue of history." There is a complete design clearly discernable on the upperside, but only God the Weaver sees it unobtrusively from this angle. At best, we are given the opportunity to look up "beyond the edge of the canopy, to see in a glass what the Weaver sees always." We observe then:

> . . . condensed and reflected, as in a concave mirror in the heavens, the large lines of the scheme and even the denouement. We see there, in a small but finished form, the purpose which on the seamy side of the fabric is but in blurred and uncouth shape. We see not yet all things working out the Kingdom, but we see Jesus.[115]

---

111. *Justification*, 162.

112. Ibid., 98–99. Forsyth also speaks about the "tonic element in doubt" which leads, after struggle, to genuine faith (*Recent Art*, 47).

113. *Justification*, 232; *Cruciality*, 79.

114. Forsyth therefore follows Luther is seeing the *theologia crucis* as a means to determine God's work, not only on the Cross, but in all of history. See Tomlin, "Theology of the Cross," 65, 70 for a succinct description of Luther's position.

115. *Ethic*, 166.

Such imperfect seeing means that there will always be a need to exercise faith in the first sense. Because of our inability to trace with complete certainty the role which historical events play in the "crucial evolution" of the world, we will always need to trust that God's power is inexorably moving things towards their intended goal, even when this does not seem to be the case.

GOD'S JUDGEMENT AS THE PATTERN IN WHICH GOD MOVES THE WORLD TOWARDS HIS GOAL

The Idea of Judgement in Forsyth's Thought

In his article "P. T. Forsyth: The Prophet of Judgement," A. F. Simpson notes that, in spite of the revival of interest in Forsyth's teachings during that time (the early 1950s), there was virtually no attention given to his doctrine of judgement. This was surprising given the prominence this idea has in Forsyth's thought.[116] We observe that little in this regard has changed since Simpson wrote his article. We hope to correct this imbalance of attention to some extent with our present section focusing on Forsyth's concept of judgement.

"Judgement," for Forsyth, is the inevitable reaction of God's holiness to the sin which opposes it. Such reaction seeks the destruction of sin and the full reinstatement of God's holiness wherever it has been compromised.[117] As we have already seen, the primary arena of God's judgement upon the sin of the world is the Cross. It was there that sin was destroyed and God's holiness found satisfaction. In addition, the judgement which took place there provides the irreversible impetus for the movement of the world towards the consummation of God's holiness. Forsyth can therefore say that everything else that happens from the time of the Cross, even the last judgement at the *eschaton*, is but the working out of the details of this primary act of judgement.[118]

The main way in which Forsyth sees this primary act of judgement being worked out in the history of this world is via, what we might call for convenience, "secondary acts of judgement" (this is not a term Forsyth himself uses). The most prominent example Forsyth gives of such judge-

---

116. Simpson, "P. T. Forsyth: The Prophet of Judgement," 148.

117. *Ethic*, 52. Bradley, *Man and His Work*, 127, and Rodgers, *Theology of P. T. Forsyth*, 48 make similar observations.

118. *Justification*, 191; *Work*, 160.

ment is the Great War.[119] These secondary acts of judgement constitute the "intra-worldly action of Christ's Cross" and are a key part of God's strategy for moving the world towards God's crucial goal.[120] As mentioned in the previous section, the proper way in which we come to interpret historical events as constituting these secondary acts of judgement is via the *theologia crucis*. Secondary acts of judgement can be identified as such because they operate under a similar pattern and towards a similar purpose to that established by the Cross. In Forsyth's vivid imagery, they are the "flashes of lightning" which follow upon the Light which has come into our dark world.[121] The "ruling principle" for interpreting all instances of secondary judgement is therefore the Cross.[122] Based on this "ruling principle" and other comments made by Forsyth, we can describe some of the more important characteristics of God's secondary acts of judgement.

Key Characteristics of God's Secondary Acts of Judgement

Their Main Purpose is the Actual Final Establishment of God's Holiness

Just as the event of the Cross, for Forsyth, took place primarily for the satisfaction of God's holiness and its victory over sin, God's acts of secondary judgement have the main purpose of "completing" that victory by "the actual final establishment of righteousness upon the wreck of sin."[123] Secondary judgement, in other words, serves the fulfilment of the subjective realisation in the history of this world of what has been objectively achieved at Calvary. Forsyth boldly asserts that this aim takes priority over the extent of any creaturely suffering and death which might be needed in order to establish such holiness. This, again, is akin to what happened on the Cross, where God the Father allowed his Son to undergo incomparable suffering and death in order to satisfy his holiness.[124] We gather

---

119. Although he laments that few of his contemporaries see it as such: "Preacher and the Publicist," 7–8. One contemporary writer who did view the War in terms of God's judgement was Forsyth's fellow Nonconformist W. Whitaker. See his article "Is Our Faith Shaken?" 141–42.

120. *Justification*, 188–89.

121. *Sacraments*, 97.

122. *Ethic*, 120.

123. *Missions*, 52.

124. *Ethic*, 170; *Work*, 126; *Justification*, 180, 202–3. Forsyth's view of the suffering of God on the Cross is a topic on which we will elaborate in a later chapter.

from this that the magnitude of a disaster which befalls human beings is *per se* no bar to it being interpreted as an act of God's secondary judgement. Forsyth, as we have mentioned, sees the War as a clear instance of such an act, in spite of the fact that it resulted in an unimaginable scale of human suffering and death.

The good news for human beings is that the Cross also tells us that God has chosen to establish in actuality his holiness in a way which does not destroy and condemn us as the servants of sin. On the contrary, God, in his grace, has linked the victory and satisfaction of his holiness to the redemption of human beings and the establishment of our communion with him.[125] This was why he sent Christ to perform his representative role of bearing the judgement of sin on our behalf. We are therefore assured that God's secondary judgement also works towards our redemption—it is "judgement unto salvation."[126] It follows from this that God's secondary acts of judgment have nothing to do with justice at all, in the sense of God pouring out his wrath on human beings and terrorising them for the sake of retribution.[127] They are purposive rather than vindictive. They serve the purpose of reminding a forgetful world that there is a holy God who reigns over all things and who is bringing all things to his end. So, out of his grace, "God can spare us no judgment which is needful to *hallow* His love, and lift it from the fondness of a blind parent to the power which moves to His end the earth, the heavens, and all the stars."[128] The alternative open to God, as Forsyth sees it, is to leave the world wallowing in its sin and misconception of the nature of God and of reality. This would be the really cruel course of (in)action, because it would signal that God has given up on his determination to move the world towards his appointed end. Indeed, according to Forsyth, the absence of secondary judgement when the situation calls for it would lead to a stronger demand for the justification of God's goodness than the fact of their occurrence.[129] Speaking again of the War (and also the labour unrest in England at that

---

125. Rodgers, *Theology of P. T. Forsyth*, 48

126. *Positive Preaching*, 214; "Christ at the Gate," 180.

127. Bradley, *Man and His Work*, 122. See also *Ethic*, 147; *Work*, 135–36; Simpson, "Prophet of Judgement," 153. We might add that the only sense of retribution there is in secondary judgement is one which is present in the primary—the continual retribution upon sin, as it seeks to make actual its destruction on the Cross.

128. *Justification*, 118 (emphasis in original).

129. Ibid., 186.

time), Forsyth judges that "so far from destroying faith, faith might well shake if no such judgement came on a loveless world."[130]

The two assumptions underlying such assertions are, firstly, that human beings, left on our own in the context of our world, do not naturally move towards God and his purposes. Events therefore need to occur which stir us to repentance and movement in the right direction. This is entirely consistent with our earlier description of Forsyth's view of sinful humanity as being in an active state of rebellion against God. The second assumption which Forsyth makes is that the way in which God moves the world towards his end is not via coercion, i.e., he does not override the free will possessed by his human creatures. Judgement is "the only kind of pressure possible between the Free and the free"[131]—it is the mode of relation which God adopts in order to lead free wills in his direction without violating their integrity.[132]

It also follows from this that the events which constitute secondary acts of judgement must necessarily be those which disrupt the ordinary course of our lives in order to facilitate our reflection over the way in which we and our societies have been living. The development of "spiritual personality" takes place most productively through "the creative discipline of life, and especially its tragedies."[133] We should therefore expect to find in the history of our world not a smooth sequence of development as envisaged by modern notions of progress, but a series of "catastrophes and crises." This again adheres to the pattern set by the Cross, an event which Forsyth views as the "crisis of all crises."[134] It is best to allow Forsyth to put this across in his own way:

> Beyond the steady conflict of the struggle for existence the course of history gets into tangles and knots at particular periods. Seasons of calm and beauty discharge themselves in thunderstorms, which clear the moral air and open space for new energies and new peri-

---

130. "Veracity, Reality, and Regeneration," 202.

131. *Authority*, 159.

132. Some of Forsyth's contemporaries have relied upon other bases to assert that God is able to move the world to its *telos* in spite of the reality of human freedom. William James' famous chess analogy is a favoured illustration. See, e.g., Galloway, *Philosophy of Religion*, 556–58; Adeney, *Faith-to-Day*, 40–43.

133. *Justification*, 74.

134. Ibid., 185. Forsyth notes that "crisis" in Greek stands for "judgement" and sees an intimate relationship between the two (*Positive Preaching*, 204).

ods. There are harvests which are the end of an age. Good and evil work together till their intrinsic antipathy refuses any longer to be compressed; then there is an explosion which changes the face of things. There comes a day of the Lord, and a new world . . . These Armageddons are repeated in history, issuing in waves, as it were, from the central and absolute crisis of the Cross. And what we look down on from God's right hand is a great wager and waver of battle, a winning campaign of many swaying battles, progress by judgement, a rising scale of crises, working out in historic detail to an actual kingdom of God, with its strategic centre and eternal crisis in the death of Christ. The Scripture idea of history is not a stream of evolution but a series of judgments. It is an idea more revolutionary in its nature than evolutionary.[135]

Such statements recall the observation we made earlier about Forsyth's appropriation of the Hegelian dialectic to describe the manner in which he sees some areas of history to be developing. We can infer here that Forsyth might have adopted this dialectic (with its notion of a clash between a thesis and its antithesis) because it was a ready tool at hand to describe his idea of evolution by crisis—an idea which Forsyth derives not from Hegel, but from what he understood to have happened on the Cross. This reinforces our conclusion that Forsyth appropriates Hegel at the junctures where he could be of service in explicating a particular aspect of Forsyth's "crucial" framework.

They Arise Both from Moral Necessity and the Decisions of a Personal God

We enter next into the consideration of how Forsyth envisages instances of secondary judgement to arise. Forsyth, in some places, describes these instances of judgement occurring as a moral necessity, in the sense that they are an inevitable result of where the particular combination of sin prevalent then was leading the people. For example, he remarks that it would indeed be surprising if the mixture present during his time of "an egoist civilisation, an individualist salvation, and a non-moral theology in a world which belongs by right to the kingdom of conscience and God" did not explode into the Great War.[136] On an individual level too, the expected occurrence of a "headache after a debauch" and "paralysis after

---

135. *Christian Aspects of Evolution*, 24.
136. *Justification*, 97.

years of debauch" constitute instances of secondary judgement.[137] From this perspective, therefore, Forsyth sees acts of secondary judgement operating in a rather impersonal fashion, in the manner of "an automatic release when the cup of iniquity was filled."[138]

Such a perspective is, however, balanced by Forsyth's other assertion that acts of secondary judgement should be viewed as the outcome of the decisions of a personal God. Judgement, from what we see on the Cross, is ultimately "an adjustment between persons—God's and man's. It is not between a soul and a law."[139] Forsyth is concerned that if we lose this personal element in the idea of God's secondary judgement, we yield too much ground to the Hegelian exaltation of the process over act (as Schiller did in postulating his thesis that "*Die Weltgeschichte ist das Weltgericht*"). This renders the person of God finally superfluous because the moral order then appears to be "detachable from Him" and operational on its own power.[140] Secondary judgement, in this case, may still teach us the distinction between right and wrong, but the lack of a personal God standing behind it implies that it is merely retributive rather than purposeful in nature.[141] To counter this, Forsyth insists that God is never a deistical spectator of our world, but one who actively "takes a hand in the game" in judging the world towards his goal.[142] This second perspective allows Forsyth to see certain events as acts of secondary judgement even though they do not arise as the moral consequences of sins committed by their recipients. So, for example, Forsyth tells a story in *The Cruciality of the Cross* about a faithful Christian missionary to the North American Indians who saw his wife and children killed in front of him, and who was then "harried in bonds across the prairie." Forsyth's response was to praise this missionary for being able to "[call] just the judgement of God which he feels but has not himself earned."[143] (We will comment further

---

137. *Ethic*, 73.
138. *Justification*, 185.
139. Ibid., 187.
140. Ibid., 210–12.
141. Ibid., 203–5.
142. *Ethic*, 31. Forsyth might have been inspired by Joseph Butler's attempt, in his writings against Deism, to obliterate the distinction between God's acts and those of "nature" (see the latter's *Analogy of Religion to the Constitution and Course of Nature*, 123–24).
143. *Cruciality*, 102. Forsyth seems therefore to have departed significantly from his

on this difficult passage [and others in a similar vein] later.) We echo, in concluding this section, Gunton's observation that Forsyth sees the reality of both an immanent justice in the processes of our world (after the manner of the Greek tragedians) and the "sovereign freedom of God" which stands behind and governs these processes.[144] We suggest that Forsyth is able to hold these two notions together because of his position that the moral reality of this world is ultimately derived from the holiness of the personal God.

They Are More Likely to Fall on God's People

Another aspect of Forsyth's understanding of secondary judgment is that God's people, like Israel in the Old Testament, are not immune from it.[145] In fact, these acts of judgement are more likely to fall "on the Church and its faith, rather than on the world and its no faith."[146] This makes sense if we remember that, for Forsyth, secondary judgement serves the purpose of reminding people of the reign of a holy God. Since Christians are those who already subscribe (at least nominally) to the Christian concept of God and his holiness, they are the ones best placed to discern the right lessons from these acts of judgement. We can also infer that "judgement begins at the house of God"[147] because the wrongs committed by God's people issue the strongest call for it.[148] God surely expects his people to be those most in tune with his holiness. The Church is the "trustee of the moral principle of Redemption"[149] and has the responsibility of being the community through which the Spirit works to bring about the actualisation of the effects of the Cross.[150] If she is unable to play this role because she herself is mired in sin and misconception, she must first be judged. It

---

early attempt to dissociate God from the operation of the laws he has instituted for the world, which he made in *Old Faith and the New*, 13 (fn).

144. Gunton, *Actuality of the Atonement*, 108–9.

145. *Justification*, 186.

146. Ibid., 186–87. A. B. Bruce mentions a similar idea in his *Providential Order of the World*, 186–87.

147. *Ethic*, 156; "Conversion of the 'Good,'" 769.

148. This is alluded to in *Positive Preaching*, 252: "The greater the love the greater the guilt. And the closer the love the greater the reaction against the sin, the greater the wrath."

149. *Society*, 6.

150. *Charter of the Church*, 61.

is probably to this end that Forsyth speaks approvingly of the maxims that "the greater the light the greater the perdition,"[151] and "the worst antagonism may be where there is most in common."[152]

They Can Be Effected by Human Agency

Forsyth also affirms that God's secondary judgement can be carried out by human agents: "If God has committed all judgement to the incarnate Son He has committed some to the men in whom the Son works, and works more than even they know."[153] These human agents, as the last quotation suggests, may either be aware or unaware of their role in relation to God. For those whom Forsyth calls "men of faith," their duty is to be so in tune with the will of Christ as to be able to discern whether he is calling them to undertake a certain task as the carrying out of God's judgement.[154] It is, according to Forsyth, "sceptical humility" to assert that God's people can never be certain whether a particular course of action fulfils this requirement. He argues that ordinary human conscience, even in its ruins, can discern much of what is right and wrong,[155] implying that consciences which have been redeemed by Christ should be even more equipped to carry out such evaluation. God is, however, not restricted to using only his people as his agents. As Forsyth somewhat pointedly asks:

> Did [God] not use Assyria on Israel? I have spoken of A.D. 70; did He not use Rome against Jerusalem in A.D. 70? Was there no connection between the rejection of Christ and the destruction of Zion? Did Christ, as the providence of His own Kingdom, not summon then the legions it did not suit Him to ask for to avert the Cross?[156]

God can therefore also use those who are not part of his people to carry out his secondary judgement. These people are used by God without any inkling on their part as to this larger reason behind their actions.[157] In fact, as the example of Rome against Jerusalem in 70 AD tells us, God's

---

151. *Justification*, 132–33.
152. *Ethic*, 156.
153. Ibid., 82.
154. Ibid., 54–55, 186.
155. Ibid., 74.
156. Ibid., 87.
157. *Justification*, 214.

sovereignty extends here to the point where he is able to mobilise sin against sin. He sets what Forsyth sees as the lesser evil of Rome against the greater evil of Israel, using one sin to destroy another.[158] This notion is also clearly brought forth in this passage:

> So God, moving in His mysterious way, and mocking by His ironic subtlety both the clever devilry of the wicked and the merely stalwart ethic of the pedantic impossibles, sets sin against sin, plays one sin off against another, and by one brings another to naught. God's will is done when sin with the sin uppermost is destroyed by sin with the sin in hand.[159]

We may pause here to consider these somewhat surprising remarks of Forsyth's. Did we not observe in our first chapter that, while Forsyth understood that God could utilise suffering for his redemptive purposes, he is in such opposition to sin that with it he "can make neither use nor terms; [he] can only make an end of it"?[160] Is there an inconsistency here, one which might undermine Forsyth's assertion of the absolute antagonism between God and sin, turning it possibly into something akin to the Hegelian notion of conflict in which both opposing parties actually cooperate to bring about a higher synthesis? Perhaps concerned that his readers might reach such a conclusion, Forsyth insists that "God is not the less holy because in His government of the world He employs sin against sin."[161] We agree with this assertion for three reasons. Firstly, there is no insinuation here that God ordains the sin he uses. As we shall see more clearly in chapter 7, Forsyth is strongly adverse to the idea that God could actively will sin in order to achieve his purposes. The picture here is therefore one of God utilising a sin which has come about through human willing in order to attain his goals. So God did not ordain Rome to destroy Jerusalem—that was Rome's decision, but God used it for the purposes of his judgement against Israel. Secondly, Forsyth suggests that God could use sin in the manner described only post-Calvary. It is only after that great conflict on the Cross which resulted in God's victory that God holds sin "in the hollow of His hand" and can "suborn" it for his

---

158. *Ethic*, 156. Another notable example Forsyth cites is that of the French Revolution, where God used the crimes perpetuated by the revolt to abolish the "prior and Satanic situation" (*Ethic*, 29).

159. Ibid., 29.

160. *Justification*, 139.

161. *Ethic*, 30.

purposes.[162] This does not undermine at all the notion that God and sin were indeed at one point engaged in a life and death struggle. It merely affirms the authority of the victor to deal with the vanquished in the way he likes once the conflict is resolved.[163] Thirdly, the only purpose which Forsyth envisages God has for his use of sin is its eradication.[164] The picture Forsyth paints is therefore not that of God using sin as a willing and cooperative ally in furtherance of a common cause. It is more akin to one in which God manages to trick sin into unintentionally acting against its own interest (note his phrases like "plays off one sin against another, and by one brings another to naught"). Such a "use" of sin surely does not compromise the fundamental antagonism between the two parties. We also suggest that Forsyth might have derived this understanding of the "deception of sin" in God's secondary judgement from the pattern set by the Cross, where Forsyth saw sin being similarly deceived into manifesting itself fully at Calvary, leading to its destruction.[165] "Satan's last chagrin is his contribution to God's kingdom,"[166] and that is as true of the rest of history as it was on the Cross.

The arguments of Forsyth in this section are found mainly in his book *The Christian Ethic of War*. The occasion which prompted this work was the response of pacifism among some segments of the British population to the First World War. Forsyth attacks such an ethic in a somewhat aggressive manner, asserting that a nation can be used by God to carry out his judgement upon another which has seriously violated his standards of righteousness. It is quite clear that Forsyth intends to restrict his argument for the use of human agency in divine judgement to the case of nation states. He sees a unique role played by such entities in God's scheme of things. Nations are, according to him, moral entities like human beings, possessing moral obligations to each other and to God. The

---

162. *Justification*, 154, 160.

163. The problem of how God's defeat of sin at the Calvary can account for God's use of sin chronologically prior to that event can, we suggest, be resolved if we understand Forsyth's event of the Cross to have retrospective effect. See our earlier comments on this point in our discussion of Forsyth's notion of the world's "crucial evolution."

164. *Ethic*, 28, 42–43; *Positive Preaching*, 162.

165. Mark Corner comes to a similar conclusion concerning Forsyth's understanding of how God uses sin in "'Umbilical Cord,'" 130–32. He mentions, for example, at p.130 that, for Forsyth, "even where good is drawn out of evil, [evil] retains its sheerly unredeemable quality."

166. *Justification*, 214.

duty of nations is, however, not to repent and exercise faith in God, since they are unable to enter the personal dimension involved in such acts. It is instead to promote the righteousness of God's Kingdom through the resources which God has given to it. Any attempt to fulfil this duty vis-à-vis another nation which has abandoned the way of righteousness renders a nation an agent of God's judgement.[167] An argument such as this cannot be easily transferred to the realm of human individuals or groups. Forsyth makes this clear by stating expressly that the moral sanction for the use of force should rest only in the hands of nations and not its sub-units, whether groups or individuals.[168]

They Encompass a Wide Scope of Events

A key consideration in this chapter concerns what Forsyth envisages to be the scope of God's secondary judgement. To what events in this world does the concept apply? Forsyth certainly seems to understand the notion of secondary judgement very widely. In the first place, as we have seen, Forsyth's position is that most, if not all, of the "natural" consequences of sin constitutes such judgement. Moreover, he sees such "natural" consequences going beyond the cause and effect idea of a "headache after a debauch."[169] One other important consequence of sin which God's judgement inflicts is the "bite" of our conscience—that sense of guilt pressing on "our small souls with a pressure from the reservoir of all the high wickedness of the world."[170] Forsyth describes this sense of guilt thus:

> It is true, when the conscience begins to act we often find no more than a vague sense of imperfection before the Christian standard, or a dim disquiet. But that is not all. We find also an inner schism and a real sense of retribution, however vague, when conscience does bite. The curse comes home . . . It is the judgment of being found out, whether by self or society. And the torment of being found out by yourself, and carrying about in yourself a living fraud, a moral corpse, can become to some as great as the exposure to the world. What comes home is the nemesis of guilt in the course of life, not in the judgment outside life. It comes home either in visible tragedy or in inward desiccation and calm despair. The sense

---

167. *Ethic*, 35, 104, 162; Rodgers, *Theology of P. T. Forsyth*, 72–73.
168. *Ethic*, 81.
169. Ibid., 73.
170. *Justification*, 25.

of guilt is still there, it is often more active than we are allowed to know. And it cannot be escaped. It is very actual.[171]

Therefore, even when God's secondary judgement is apparently absent because we seem to have escaped the consequences of our wrongdoing, such judgement is ironically being carried out as "its tarrying works upon us more than its coming. It enlists our imagination as its ally. It broods evasive, provoking, potent."[172] The dread of judgement is itself judgement.

Secondly, we see a wide scope to Forsyth's notion of secondary judgement because it encompasses sufferings experienced not only by evildoers, but also those whose lives are relatively committed to doing God's will, and who consequently appear to have little or no need to undergo such judgement. These acts of judgement therefore go beyond the "natural" consequences of sin—they can be, to the human eye, unexpected and even undeserved occurrences of tragedy. We have already seen Forsyth's interpretation of the calamity which overtook the faithful Christian missionary to the North American Indians. Another notable instance of such tragedy is the illness experienced by that devoted servant of God R. W. Dale at the end of his life.[173] Judgement, Forsyth observes, strikes also "men whose passion did not need to be overruled for the Kingdom of Heaven, but was purely and wholly engrossed with it."[174] Such an "anomaly" can be accounted for if we remember that God's acts of secondary judgement are characterised by purposive grace and not retribution. However holy and faithful a Christian is, there will always be room for spiritual growth, and these instances of secondary judgement are God's gracious prompting for such growth. Forsyth saw Dale as one who appropriated such judgement in the correct spirit, for the latter could testify that "it never came home to him before as it did with his extreme pain that Christ was not only his Saviour but his King, who had the right to exact anything and everything from him at His silent discretion."[175] We note that even here Forsyth's *theologia crucis* is operative. Secondary judgement on dedicated persons of God need not surprise us when we see "the gigantic, and ironic paradox of the Cross, which crushes the best to raise both them and the world."[176]

171. *Positive Preaching*, 102–3.
172. *Justification*, 213.
173. *Authority*, 373.
174. *Justification*, 215.
175. *Authority*, 373.
176. *Justification*, 215.

For the purposes of determining what Forsyth sees as the scope of God's secondary judgement, it is also instructive to examine his interpretation of the events of the Great War. Certainly he saw that Germany's conduct had violated all standards of righteousness expected of nations and had rightly called forth God's judgement upon her in terms of the conflict. But what about the suffering inflicted by Germany upon the people of other nations, whether those she conquered or were fighting against? Were these instances of God's secondary judgement as well? How far does the concept extend? Forsyth, while generally promoting a theocentric perspective on world affairs, was not above having a strong sense of nationalism. Britain had already, according to him, twice saved liberty and justice for the world in God's name—once against the Spanish Armada and once more against Napoleon. Forsyth saw the Great War as yet another call from God on his country to serve His Kingdom.[177] Due to this strong sense that his nation was in the right in this war, he was unsparing of his critique of the German nation, even suggesting at one point that her people have left the realm of humanity and now posed an outside threat as a "vermin to the race."[178] All these would seem to suggest that Forsyth saw the judgement of God proceeding only in one direction as far as the War was concerned—towards Germany, and not her opponents (who were the agents of God's purposes). However, at the close of *The Christian Ethic of War*, when Forsyth contemplates what the situation would be like after the War ends, he shows that he has not forgotten the larger picture demanded by the theocentric perspective he is so passionate about. There, he abandons all parochialism, which he might have demonstrated only in order to meet what he saw as the need of the hour—to undermine the perceived deadly influence of pacifism and arouse his people to fight for righteousness on behalf of God's Kingdom. He rises then to sublime heights as he postulates that Britain, after she has won the victory, should realise upon careful reflection that the chastisement of the War was also meant for her. Sin was a common characteristic of both sides of the conflict, and the wickedness of Germany was merely representative of that of the whole Western civilisation, which had abandoned the God of its heritage. The correct reading of the War was therefore to see its horrors as the terrible chastening called forth by the sins of Christian Europe as a

---

177. *Ethic*, 6–7.
178. Ibid., 10.

whole.[179] These comments on the War reinforce our observation that the scope of God's secondary judgement is, for Forsyth, very wide indeed.

Nevertheless, to these observations on the wide scope of God's secondary judgement, we must add the qualification that Forsyth (to the best of our knowledge) never proclaimed that every single instance of suffering that has ever been experienced in world history can rightfully be attributed to these acts of judgement. As we mentioned in our opening chapter, Forsyth's theodicy was written specifically to address the situation of the Great War. Most of his statements on the notion of God's secondary judgement were made in this context. He does not go further to suggest that what happened during this terrible time can or should be extrapolated into a universal rule accounting for all cases of suffering throughout world history. Indeed, when we look at Forsyth's view of the origin of evil in chapters 7 and 8, we shall suggest that Forsyth postulates other possible reasons for suffering, ones founded upon the conditions in which the first human beings found themselves.

They Always Arrive—in This Life or the Next

The final key characteristic of God's acts of secondary judgement we will consider is that they are unfailing, in the sense that all sin which hinders the world towards attaining its *telos* will ultimately be judged, until it is repented of. If God appears to be silent at any particular points in history, it does not represent the failure of judgement, but its storing up. He "always arrives," even though the journey might be "in long orbits, out of sight and sound." Forsyth explains that any unrepented sin missed out by the chastening effect of God's judgement would mean that the unholy lingers on in the *eschaton*.[180] This surely cannot be, given Forsyth's anticipation of the perfection of holiness in creation at the end. One should therefore not put too much premium on quiet times when all seems to go well. God's secondary judgement still broods over our world so long as it does not attribute to him his rightful status.[181]

---

179. Ibid., 195–96. Forsyth makes the same critical self-evaluation of the state of his country in *Justification*, 102–3; "Some Effects of the War," 17. Forsyth's Nonconformist compatriot E. Griffith-Jones was another who showed commendable courage in pointing out Britian's guilt in the events leading up to the War, while the War was still raging: *Challenge of Christianity to a World at War*, 14–15, 25–27, 40–41, 79.

180. *Justification*, 216.

181. Ibid., 213.

We might at this point raise two sets of objections. The first is to question the tardiness of God in carrying out his secondary judgement. Would not his purpose of reminding the world of its accountability to his holiness be achieved far more easily if every violation of it were quickly and obviously accompanied by its needed judgement? Forsyth has two responses to this objection. The first is to reiterate the point we had seen earlier that, from the perspective of the guilty conscience, the "brooding" of God's judgement is judgement itself. Secondly, in his appropriately titled article "The Slowness of God," Forsyth argues that to require God's "thunder of judgement [to follow] fast on the flash of sin" is to demand that God lower himself to act in accordance with our human passion and wisdom. In opposition to our human desire for immediate judgement, God exercises his mercy and patience. If he were moved by passion in the same way as we are, the earth would long have been "swept clean." Moreover, God's wisdom dictates that it is ultimately more effective to have his judgements "slow, circuitous [and] lingering" than otherwise. He enacts his strategy based on his complete grasp of the whole picture, both in terms of space (he seeks to "bring everything home") and time (he plans how his successive acts of judgement complement each other). Our limited perspective does not allow us to judge the rightness of this strategy. Our task is to trust that the mode and timing of God's judgement are the most appropriate for his purposes.[182]

The second objection seems an even more obvious one. It is, in our experience, simply not true that God's secondary judgement "always arrives." We all know of cases where those terribly guilty of sin and who need God's chastisement most pass from this world without experiencing such secondary judgement to an appropriate extent. They seem to die contented, with the assured sense that they have escaped the consequences of their wrongdoing. Some have their consciences so seared that even the accusing voice in this region ceases to trouble them. Forsyth's answer to this is simple: these evildoers do not "cheat judgement by dying."[183] It is here that a consideration of Forsyth's notion of the afterlife becomes relevant again. We noted earlier that, for him, God's moral discipline of the human soul continues beyond this life into the next. God's secondary judgement therefore operates beyond physical death. The purpose of such

---

182. "Slowness of God," 219–20.
183. *Life*, 19.

secondary judgement in this post-death realm remains the sanctification of human souls—Forsyth's idea of "purgatory" has a refining, rather than retributory, function. Such a view of personal eschatology allows Forsyth to assert meaningfully that God's secondary judgement "always arrives." In fact, he makes it clear that his whole doctrine of secondary judgement rests in a significant way upon this understanding of personal eschatology. If death were indeed to determine the state of a human soul forever, he would have responded to the War in a very different way. Instead of viewing it as an occasion for Britain to enact her role as God's agent in judgement upon Germany, he would have argued that it was impossible for any nation to "morally go to war," for that would lead to millions dying and many of them entering "eternal torment."[184] That God's sanctifying judgement continues beyond death, however, means that what happens in this world does not have the last say on the state of a soul. All judgement is therefore "saving judgement,"[185] even the judgement that leads to death.

CONCLUSION

We have given, in this chapter, a description of what Forsyth sees as the first major outcome of God's self-justification as far as his theodicy is concerned—God moving the world inexorably towards the goal set by the Cross. We have looked at Forsyth's understanding of the end-state of both humanity and the rest of creation, his idea of the "crucial evolution" of this world and how we can perceive it, and his thesis that God's key strategy for effecting such evolution of the world is via judgement. This chapter, in other words, can be seen as an outline of Forsyth's understanding of the workings of God's providence in the history of our world (and beyond).[186] We will proceed in the next chapter to consider the significance of this first major outcome of God's self-justification for Forsyth's theodicy.

184. Ibid.

185. *Justification*, 197.

186. An explanation of "providence" offered by Forsyth's Nonconformist contemporary E. Griffith-Jones seems to describe Forsyth's understanding of this doctrine particularly well: ". . . we are to consider God as the Personal Ruler and Guide of His universe, related to all as Creator and Sustainer, and holding a special relation to men as free moral agents; but ever and always actively and efficiently directly all forces, and wills, and events to that 'Divine far-off event to which the whole creations moves'" (*Challenge of Christianity to a World at War*, 4).

4

The Significance of the First Outcome of God's Self-Justification

The Teleological and Historical Natures of Forsyth's Theodicy

THE TELEOLOGICAL NATURE OF FORSYTH'S THEODICY

Introduction

WE HAVE SEEN IN the previous chapter that the first outcome of God's self-justification is an essentially teleological one—the world is being inexorably superintended by God's Spirit towards a glorious end as a result of what happened at the Cross. Forsyth sees this outcome providing a theodicy: the "teleology of the world with a divine destiny for it in righteousness . . . must be (amongst other things) a theodicy."[1] His reasoning here is simple: In order to arrive at the glorious *telos* of the world, the human race must undergo the sufferings it has and will experience in the history of this world. One significant source of such sufferings and how they are necessary for the attainment of the *telos* will be considered in chapters 7 and 8, when we examine Forsyth's view of the origin of evil. The other significant source is, of course, God's acts of secondary judgement. They represent the key strategy God utilises to move the world towards its goal, one which inevitably results in human suffering. The teleological aspect of Forsyth's theodicy argues that all these instances of suffering are justified in the light of their role in bringing about the glorious end. The key questions, as Forsyth puts it, are:

1. *Justification*, 98.

> To what do all things work together? They ask what is it all worth at last, what is to be the end of earth's long historic day. Is it sheer oblivion or another morning? Has history a destiny worth all its awful cost? Do all its large lines converge on anything, its throbbing sorrows, its soaring aspirations, its tragedies sordid or sublime, its dreadful conflicts, its splendid achievements, its miserable failures, its broken hearts and mined civilisations, its conquests over nature and its collapses into it—do they all curve in some vast trend and draw together to a due close? Is it an end that can never make them worth while? Do they all work together for good and love? What does man mean?[2]

The answers to these pressing questions have already been given unequivocally in Christ's Cross, "the goal and justification of all the devious, dreadful ways of earth."[3] This goal serves indeed as justification—it renders, in Forsyth's mind, all the suffering undergone in order to attain it seem worthwhile. This will be the case not only from God's perspective, but all creation, when it arrives at the *eschaton*, will call God "holy whatever has come and gone, and [own] that it was worth all it endured to serve with such praise." Forsyth even goes so far as to say that creation at that point would willingly "go through it again at the Father's will."[4] Such uncategorical assertion that "the end will justify the means"[5] places Forsyth's justification of God firmly within the camp of what John Hick has called "teleological theodicies."[6] Tom Smail's statement (which in turn is adapted from Julian of Norwich) can therefore serve as an apt summary of this aspect of Forsyth's thought: "All shall be well, and all manner of things shall be well, but only because Jesus has died for the world and risen again."[7]

As the standard works on theodicy tell us, however, important objections have been raised against "teleological theodicies" and the manner in which they seek to justify God in the face of evil. We will, in this chapter, consider five of the more significant of these objections, particularly in

---

2. Ibid., 225.
3. Ibid., 202.
4. Ibid., 129.
5. Ibid., 67.
6. Hick, *Evil and the God of Love* (1st ed.), 242.
7. Smail, *Once and for All*, 174. Smail's statement is made in the context of his discussion on the atonement.

relation to the suffering arising from God's acts of secondary judgement. (We will supplement the comments here with further observations in Chapter 8 after we have considered the other significant source of evil Forsyth postulates.) We will also construct the plausible responses Forsyth might have given to these objections, and consider if his theodicy is able to withstand the challenges posed by them.

Are the Means Necessary and Appropriate to Achieve the End in Question?

One significant question "teleological theodicies" have to answer is whether the means involved (with their consequential suffering) are necessary and appropriate to achieve the end in question. If they cause far more suffering than is required for attaining the goal, the viability of the theodicy under consideration is clearly undermined. We have already seen why, given Forsyth's assumptions of sinful humanity, the reality of human free will and how we consequently need to be "woken up" into repentance, the means of God's secondary judgement must necessarily involve some measure of suffering most of the time.[8] It is unfortunate, however, that Forsyth did not proceed, in his writings, to demonstrate in a systematic fashion that God's acts of secondary judgement are indeed necessary and appropriate, in the sense that they do not result in more suffering than is needed.

We can infer, however, from Forsyth's constant insistence that the purpose of secondary judgement is reformative (rather than retributive) in nature, that he holds the assumption that God would not inflict any more suffering upon the recipients of his judgement than is necessary to move them towards repentance and holiness. Forsyth also compares, at one point, God's acts of judgement to the surgical pains necessary for the restoration of health.[9] This surely carries the implication that God will not undertake any procedure which does not contribute to the healing of the patient. Moreover, in describing the actions which human agents of God's judgement are entitled to carry out in pursuit of secondary judgement, Forsyth is careful to emphasise that the goal of judgement must

---

8. Eleonore Stump sees the notion that evil might be useful in turning our wills towards God as obvious, given what we know of human psychology and experience ("Problem of Evil," 408–10).

9. *Work*, 135–36.

determine the means undertaken. So, for example, in the case of the War, it would be wrong for British soldiers to kill their German counterparts if the "strong superman" of Germany could be bound and his evil checked with lesser means.[10] It is relevant too to remind ourselves that Forsyth's view of personal eschatology allows him to see that even those acts of secondary judgement which result in the death of their recipients are not necessarily excessive. These acts of judgement might not be fruitless as there is the strong likelihood that their recipients would be able to learn the intended lessons in the next life. Contra Nietzsche, therefore, what kills me can, for Forsyth, make me stronger.

These general affirmations of the necessity and appropriateness of God's secondary judgement must be supplemented by two further observations. Firstly, we note that Forsyth does not hold the simplistic view that God's acts of secondary judgement are appropriate in the sense that they always lead immediately to their intended effect. The judgement of God will "sift and part." Some will respond with faith and appropriate the right lessons, while others will sink deeper in their doubt and even hatred of God.[11] This happens because of the reality of human free will. God can bring about acts of judgement, but he will not dictate how we respond to them.[12] Therefore, in Forsyth's scheme of things, the fact that a particular act of judgement does not lead immediately to its intended result does not *per se* render it inappropriate.

Our second observation is that Forsyth realistically acknowledges that acts of secondary judgement may have indiscriminate effects. He recognises, for example, that there were many "good, godly, and gentle spirits in Israel" in 70 AD, but that did not stop Christ from issuing his sentence of destruction upon the land.[13] These "gentle spirits" did not live in a way which necessitated the calling forth of God's secondary judgement in the form it was administered, but they suffered and even died as a result of it. We arrive therefore at the problem of "innocent suffering" in pursuit of God's goal for the world. This leads us inevitably to Fyodor Dostoyevsky's *The Brothers Karamazov*, a text which, in Richard Bauckham's estima-

10. *Ethic*, 7, 9.

11. *Justification*, 5–6, 176.

12. This idea is alluded to in passages like *Congregationalism and Reunion*, 12; *Preaching of Jesus*, 94–95, 119–20; "Majesty and Mercy," 307 which speak of the slowness of moral progress due to the reality of creaturely freedom.

13. *Ethic*, 22.

tion, has "attained virtually scriptural status in modern discussions on theodicy."[14] Ivan Karamazov's challenge to his brother Alyosha is well-known, but it is worth repeating here:

> Tell me yourself directly, I challenge you—reply: imagine that you yourself are erecting the edifice of human fortune with the goal of, at the finale, making people happy, of at last giving them peace and quiet, but that in order to do it it would be necessary and unavoidable to torture to death only one tiny creature, that same little child that beat its breast with its little fist, and on its unavenged tears to found the edifice, would you agree to be the architect on those conditions, tell me and tell me truly?[15]

Bauckham observes accurately that "Ivan Karamazov's argument is essentially one against any eschatological theodicy of the kind which justifies suffering as the price to be paid for the achievement of some eschatological purpose of God in the future, when it will be seen to have been worth the price." Bauckham goes on to elaborate that the key problem Ivan identifies for such theodicies is the presence of "innocent and senseless suffering," especially that of children. Such suffering, according to Bauckham, cannot be justified as "either due to the child's own fault or serving as the child's own ultimate good." The only way it can be explained in a teleological scheme of things is that it is for "someone *else*'s benefit." This violates our sense of justice. Bauckham therefore summarises that "in the name of justice, [Ivan] *rebels* against the God who can only be justified by calling injustice just."[16]

How would Forsyth have responded to such a formidable objection? The first argument we can construct from his writings is that such instances of suffering are not necessarily unjust because these "innocent" victims share in the sinful condition of a larger whole to which they belong. Here we return to Forsyth's notion of the "corporate personality" which we first encountered in chapter 1. At the most general level, Forsyth holds an anthropology which sees that what truly unites all human beings is the human conscience.[17] This makes sense when we remember that, for him,

---

14. Bauckham, *Theology of Jürgen Moltmann*, 72.

15. Dostoyevsky, *Brothers Karamazov*, 321.

16. Bauckham, *Theology of Jürgen Moltmann*, 72–74 (all emphases in original). Albert Camus comes to a similar conclusion in *The Rebel*, 50: Ivan pleads "for justice which he ranks above divinity."

17. "Christianity and Nationality," 397; *Work*, 122–23.

it is the conscience which connects human beings to the deepest reality of the moral realm, and which therefore constitutes the most fundamental core of what it means to be human. Forsyth then proceeds to describe this human conscience as a single corporate entity, rather than discrete units individually possessed by us.[18] He also sees that sin has infected this corporate conscience, so the "whole race" is embroiled in guilt.[19] God's wrath is therefore a "racial and solidary" one in which we all share.[20] Forsyth's *theologia crucis* proves relevant here as well. We do not, according to him, determine the depth of our involvement in sin by looking at the wrong we individually have done. We look instead at what sin has done to Christ on the Cross, and then realise that we share in this sin.[21] Forsyth moves from this general attribution of sinfulness to the human race to postulate that nations and societies might also function as corporate personalities which manifest particular forms or combinations of sinful acts. Based on the same reasoning, the citizens of these nations and members of these societies share in the "solidary guilt" of the larger entity, regardless of whether they have individually committed these sins.[22] God's secondary judgement therefore falls on the nation or society "as a collective unit with a solidary policy and ideal."[23] Forsyth quotes Augustine from his *City of God* on this point: "Both good and bad endure one scourge, not because they are guilty of one disordered life, but because they do both too much affect this transitory life; not in like measure but both together."[24] It is therefore no accident that in his works on the War like *The Justification of God* and *The Christian Ethic of War*, Forsyth constantly speaks of the sin of the German nation, Western civilisation and the human race, and hardly makes any reference to individual sin. There is probably, in his view, no one who can rightfully claim to be exempted from secondary judgement.

---

18. *Justification*, 194.

19. *Authority*, 404. Williams, "Holy Love and the Cross of Christ," 118–19 and Hunter, *Per Crucem*, 58 make similar observations about Forsyth's harmatiology.

20. *Work*, 241.

21. *Society*, 115.

22. *Theology*, 157–58.

23. "Conversion of the 'Good,'" 760. Forsyth cites in this article the practice of Christ, who "judged in wholes and saved in wholes" (768).

24. *Justification*, 104.

All of us are rightful recipients of it by virtue of the fact that we belong to a larger entity whose attitudes and actions call for it.[25]

If this first response proves difficult for those of us living in an age of individualism to accept, Forsyth does present another. He stresses the flip side of this corporate guilt, which is universal redemption.[26] Everyone, whether "innocent" or deserving recipients of secondary judgement, will participate in the glorious *eschaton*. Forsyth paraphrases Rom 11:32 to make his point: "All were shut up unto judgement that mercy might be on all."[27] It is in this context that Forsyth makes one of his rare references to the notion of "compensation"—the joys of the end will be more than sufficient recompense for any "innocent" suffering undergone.[28] In discussing this, he does not shy away from the intractable problem of the suffering and death of children. Forsyth recognises what a huge challenge to the Christian faith such occurrences are: "Undeserved sorrow and the death of the innocent are common things enough, and for the most part depressing enough, shaking to its roots the faith of those who would otherwise not find it hard to believe."[29] Christianity, however, provides an answer to this challenge. In a commentary on Holman Hunt's painting "The Triumph of the Innocents" (which depicts the infant Jesus smiling at the sight of the children, now glorified, who were murdered in Herod's massacre at Bethlehem), Forsyth writes:

> And, while I am speaking of the children, is it not an exquisite touch of fancy, that happy wonder of the child who, with all his looking, cannot find on his new flesh the wound that slew him, though the shirt is rent still? The world can tear but the garment of the soul. And there may be some childish spirits beginning the

---

25. This would probably be Forsyth's response to Nick Trakakis' creative re-interpretation of the thrust of Ivan's argument in his article "Theodicy," 178–79. Trakakis argues there that Ivan's point is that even though "we [accept] that everyone must suffer in order with their suffering to purchase eternal harmony, it is terribly wrong to subject children to this scheme . . . This is not so much an attack on some extravagant form of utilitarianism, but a criticism leveled against those who cannot see the inviolable sanctity of childhood." Forsyth's anthropology and harmatiology would dictate that there is no such thing as "the inviolable sanctity of childhood"—all, regardless of age, are part of the humanity which is embroiled in sin.

26. With the qualifications set out in the previous chapter.

27. "Conversion of the 'Good,'" 768.

28. *Life*, 29.

29. *Recent Art*, 179.

life beyond, who are actually disappointed at the loss of an earthly grievance, and puzzled, nay, unsettled, to find how shallow the most poignant and fatal of their old troubles were.[30]

This, then, is the notion of compensation put in a pictorial form—one which expresses the belief that the "most poignant and fatal" of our "old troubles" reveal themselves to be shallow compared to the glory of the life to come. We may infer, therefore, that Forsyth would probably have agreed with Elder Zosima's consolation to the woman who had lost her two-year old son, quoting the words of "a great saint of antiquity":

> Do you not know . . . how daring such infants are before the throne of God? There are none more daring than they in all the Kingdom of Heaven: "You gave us life, O Lord," they say to God, "yet no sooner had we beheld it than You took it away from us again." And with such daring do they ask and demand that the Lord immediately accords them the rank of angels. . . . Therefore let me tell you also, mother, that your infant too of a certainty now stands before the throne of the Lord, rejoicing and merry, and saying his prayers for you.[31]

This idea of a recompense for "innocent suffering" seeks to answer Ivan Karamazov's objection (as interpreted by Bauckham) on two counts. Firstly, it argues that no injustice results from such suffering because the compensation received by these victims is more than adequate to make up for the terrible experiences they have gone through. (The rejoinder has, of course, been raised that no such adequate compensation is possible—this will be discussed in the next section.) The second thrust of this idea is to challenge the assertion that "innocent suffering" can only be for "someone *else's* benefit."[32] Forsyth's contention that God's acts of secondary judgement are necessary to move the world as a whole towards the glorious

---

30. Ibid., 177.
31. Dostoyevsky, *Brothers Karamazov*, 69.
32. Responses along a similar (although not identical) line to Ivan's challenge have been made by contemporary philosophers of religion like Stump, "Problem of Evil," 410–12 and "Second-Person Accounts and the Problem of Evil," 97; Adams, *Horrendous Evils and the Goodness of God*, 29–31, 156. Forsyth's refusal to affirm a utilitarian theodicy in which individuals suffer for the sake of a larger good in which they do not share might evidence the influence of Kant, who has dictated that no human being should be viewed as a means rather than an end—see McKenzie, "Kantian Theodicy," 240. Forsyth therefore, in our view, successfully sidesteps Trakakis' critique of theodicies which violate Kant's categorical imperative (in "Theodicy," 182 [fn]).

eschaton means that they can be dispensed with (and "innocent" suffering avoided) only at the expense of the entire human race forgoing its participation in this end. In Forsyth's scheme of things, such an outcome would be heavily detrimental to every human being concerned, whether they would have experienced these acts of secondary judgement as deserving or "innocent" recipients. It is therefore in everyone's interest that such secondary judgement be carried out. Looking at things from this larger perspective makes it inaccurate to say that the "innocent" victims of secondary judgement suffer only for the benefit of others.[33]

We see, therefore, that although Forsyth did not set out systematically to show that God's acts of secondary judgement are necessary and appropriate, there appears to be adequate resources in his writings to defend the argument that they are so. It is, of course, impossible to arrive at any objective proof of this point. We cannot, for example, tell from our human perspective whether a lower level of discipline than a world war would have sufficed to achieve God's aim of waking Europe up to its neglect of God and his ways. This is where Forsyth's constant stress on our need for faith can be utilised to bolster his position. We saw in the previous chapter Forsyth's insistence that, because we only see imperfectly in this world, there will always be a need to trust that God is moving all things towards his goal. Such faith in the purposefulness of God's activity in the world must surely encompass the faith that God will not inflict any suffering which is not intended to contribute towards this movement. It is, therefore, ultimately faith in God's character and his dealings with the world as revealed by the Cross which gives us the assurance that God's means of secondary judgement are always necessary and appropriate to the end he has in mind.

Can the Ends Ever Justify the Means?

We follow the last objection with an even more fundamental one, i.e., the argument that history has shown us that the "means" involved are

---

33. A hint of these two responses might, in fact, be present in Book VI of *Brothers Karamazov*, a section which, in Dostoyevsky's own understanding, was intended to provide an answer to Ivan's atheism. (Dostoyevsky's comments to this effect are cited in Sutherland, *Atheism and the Rejection of God*, 82–83.) See, e.g., 392–93 of the novel, where Zosima and his mysterious visitor Mikhail speak affirmatively of the idea that "each person [is] guilty for all creatures and all things, as well as his own sins," and where they look forward to the time when "human solitariness" (in the sense of trying to find life's completeness solely within oneself) will end.

so terrible that no end could possibly justify them.³⁴ Such an objection is frequently made in the light of the horror of the Second World War, especially that involved in the Third Reich's systematically implemented genocide of the Jews.³⁵ Dorothy Sölle summarises well the viewpoint of these opponents of teleological theodicies when she claims that "no heaven can rectify Auschwitz."³⁶ The approach of these writers frequently involve citing instances of immense suffering resulting from great human cruelty,³⁷ and then arguing that no imaginable final outcome could justify or compensate for such suffering. These writers resist what they see as the mistake of treating suffering in an abstract way, discussing it as a mere theoretical concept.³⁸ The correct approach, as Kenneth Surin puts it, is "to engage with the sheer particularity, the racial contingency, of human evil." To achieve this, "[theodicy] must necessarily be articulated from the standpoint of the victims themselves. A theodicy is not worth heeding if it does not allow the screams of our society to be heard."³⁹ Such a "victim-centred" approach to theodicy is starkly illustrated by Irving Greenberg's recounting of the shocking testimony of a Polish guard at the Nuremberg War Crimes Tribunal. This guard told the Tribunal in vivid detail how the Nazis in the concentration camps threw children alive

---

34. Besides this, there is also the argument made on the principle that some acts (like killing the innocent) are intrinsically wrong, and the consequences they lead to are irrelevant in determining whether they are justified: Phillips, *Concept of Prayer*, 92–94. Under Forsyth's scheme of thought, however, such a strict application of deontological ethical reasoning to God's acts of judgement simply does not make sense, for what is moral is derived from God's holiness. Since, as Forsyth sees it, the theodicy that is revealed by the Cross is a teleologically-based one, there remains little room for the deontological labeling of acts as intrinsically right or wrong.

35. Davis, "Introduction," in *Encountering Evil*, 6 and Roth, "Silence of God," 408–9 both note how the Holocaust has become the paradigmatic instance of evil in modern-day discussions on theodicy. Bauckham goes so far as to propose that the challenge of theodicy in the modern age be reduced to one word: "Auschwitz" (*Theology of Jürgen Moltmann*, 71).

36. Sölle, *Suffering*, 149.

37. Marcel Sarot sees "two clusters of examples which are especially popular": Ivan Karamazov's horrifying stories and the suffering of the inmates at Auschwitz ("Auschwitz, Morality and the Suffering of God," 135).

38. See, e.g., Surin, *Problem of Evil*, 36–37; Wollaston, "'Starting All over Again,'" 459. See also the references to the dangers of "abstraction" in Camus, *The Plague*, 73–77, 90ff., 140ff.

39. Surin, *Problem of Evil*, 52.

into the crematorium furnaces.[40] Greenberg proposes that "no statement, theological or otherwise, should be made that would not be credible in the presence of the burning children."[41] Surin's response to this challenge is to acknowledge that:

> No attempted justification of God on the part of human beings can aspire to meet this test; indeed, the very thought that it is possible for someone to say, with the sufferings of these children in mind, that God is justified, is a blasphemy. This episode can only prompt penance and conversion; it cannot motivate a theodicy, even one which takes the form of an atonement.[42]

The reference to the inadequacy even of a theodicy founded upon the atonement renders Surin's remarks a direct challenge to Forsyth's justification of God. Surin does, in fact, explicitly dispute Forsyth's idea of an eschatological recompense for all the "innocent" victims of suffering. He also questions Forsyth's claim that "the moral enormity of the cross outweighs that of any other deed of human malevolence," saying that Forsyth might have written otherwise had he lived to see the evil which occurred in the Nazi concentration camps.[43] Such a statement implies that Forsyth's teleological theodicy proves inadequate when confronted with some of the worst cases of evil history has seen. Is Surin right?

Eleonore Stump has expressed her view about discussing the topic of Auschwitz in the context of formulating a theodicy:

> Nazi atrocities against the Jews were so great an evil that there is something disgusting and reprehensible about unemotional discussions of the goods which might constitute a morally sufficient reason for God to have allowed it. And since we are all members of the species which perpetrated that evil, since we are in some sense siblings of the evildoers, perhaps the only seemly response is one like Job's (cf. Job 40:4–5 and 42:2–3): silence in the face of something beyond our capacities to understand, in recognition of our unworthiness to judge.[44]

---

40. Greenberg, "Cloud of Smoke, Pillar of Fire," 9–10.

41. Ibid., 23. See also Wollaston's observation that "it is now commonplace to insist that only those who were 'there' can know, that is, to ascribe epistemological and ethical primacy to the responses of those who were 'there', the victims and the survivors" ("Possibility and Plausibility of Divine Abusiveness," 4).

42. Surin, *Problem of Evil*, 147.

43. Ibid., 136.

44. Stump, "Suffering for Redemption," 434.

We share many of these sentiments. Like Stump, however, we will proceed to discuss this topic, for the reason that it represents (as Surin has pointed out) the acid test for Forsyth's teleological theodicy. Our assumption here is, of course, that the suffering and death experienced by the Jews in this terrible event are not to be construed as God's secondary judgement imposed upon them for their chastisement.[45] They are seen here rather as the "innocent" victims of such judgement, in the sense set out in the previous section.

Turning to Surin's challenge, our initial response is to say that he assumes a level of naiveté concerning evil on Forsyth's part which is difficult to sustain. While Forsyth certainly did not live to see the horrors of Auschwitz, he did encounter human atrocities that go quite to the depths. For example, in an early sermon where Forsyth appealed to his congregation for funds for the victims of the Turkish suppression of the Bulgarian uprising in 1876, he said that he had "forced" himself, "with pity, with anger, with tears, and ... suppressed maledictions," to read the entire sequence of letters published in the *London Daily News* on that event.[46] He then invites his congregation to picture themselves in the midst of the aftermath of the massacre:

> ... they cry in fifties, "We are starving, we are starving." ... See the men fighting, suffering, as only a people choosing between death and freedom can. See the women crying for food for themselves and children, or with that silence of life more pathetic than death bearing about a speechless shame which is no shame but sacrifice, or recurring, with shuddering and pallor, to the memory of their impaled children, and their headless brothers, fathers, and sons.[47]

While atrocities such as these do not, in important senses, rival Auschwitz in the magnitude of horror,[48] Forsyth's familiarity with such perverse acts

---

45. Interestingly, however, this is the interpretation given by some of the victims of the Holocaust to their own suffering: Wollaston, "Divine Abusiveness," 4–5.

46. One of the dispatches sent by J. A. MacGahan to the *London Daily News* can be read online at: http://www.attackingthedevil.co.uk/related/macgahan.php (accessed: January 1, 2009).

47. "Turkish Atrocities," 4.

48. Robert Willis argues for the discontinuity between Auschwitz and other cases of evil because the former "is distinguished by being the first instance of a situation in which the full bureaucratic and technological apparatus of the state was mobilized for the primary purpose of extermination," and the qualitatively and quantitatively "larger measure of Christian complicity in its occurrence" ("Confessing God after Auschwitz," 271–76.

of human cruelty must mean that it would take a lot to show that his theodicy could be taken by surprise with the magnitude of human sin and suffering. Surin does not appear to have discharged this burden of proof.[49] All he seems to have done was to assume *a priori* the rightness of his notion that no end can ever justify the means in the light of the horror of the Holocaust, and then evaluate Forsyth's theodicy on the basis of this assumption. He does not appear to have explored the possibility that there could be arguments in Forsyth's works which contest this fundamental assumption. On our part, we see Forsyth making an important challenge to this whole notion of a "victim-centred" approach to theodicy with his insistence on the need to appropriate the movement of history through faith via the lens of the *theologia crucis*. Everything boils down to a matter of perspective. Forsyth would not be surprised at all, we think, to hear the claim that the evils of this world are so terrible that we can envisage no end which could serve as a justification for them. He would, in fact, say that such a limitation on the part of the human eye and mind accords well with his assertion that it is futile for us to try to derive true knowledge about the person and work of God from our observation of the world and the movement of its history. Forsyth's rejection of what he sees as the *theologia gloriae* would therefore respectfully suggest that the victims of suffering, while they are in the midst of such suffering, are not in the best position to evaluate issues like whether the end will justify the suffering they are currently experiencing. A far more reliable answer to this question comes from appropriating God's revelation, through the Cross, of what the end will be like. We see then, by faith, that all the redeemed, whether "innocent" or deserving recipients of secondary judgement, will acknowledge that these acts of judgement meted out to keep the human race as a whole on track towards this end are worth the suffering endured. All creation will then, in other words, participate fully in Christ's confession on the Cross of God's holiness and goodness. In what is therefore an ironic twist, we can say that Forsyth's approach to theodicy is also fun-

---

49. Also going against Surin's contention are the numerous comments found in the secondary literature concerning the uncanny relevance Forsyth's writings have for the situation arising from the Second World War. See, e.g., Cocks, "Message of P. T. Forsyth," 214; Gummer, "Contemporary Theologian," 249; Lambert, "Great Theologian and His Greatest Book: *The Work of Christ*," 244. Perhaps the most telling comment is that made by D. R. Davis that the best book written on the Second World War was written during the First. He was referring to Forsyth's *Justification*. (This comment is cited in Miller, "P. T. Forsyth: The Man," 3.)

damentally a concrete (as opposed to abstract) "victim-centred" one. It is one which unquestioningly relies upon the perspective of the person he sees as the victim of the greatest evil this world has ever seen—Jesus Christ on the Cross:

> Christ stills all challenge since He made none, but, in an utter darkness beyond all our eclipse, perfectly glorified the Holy Father. If He, the great one conscience of the world, who had the best right and the most occasion in all the world to complain of God for the world's treatment of Him—if He hallowed and glorified God's name with joy instead (Matt. xi. 25–27; Luke xxiii. 46), there is no moral anomaly that cannot be turned, and is not by long orbits being turned, to the honour of God's holy love, and the joy of His crushed and common millions.[50]

This particular historic event of Christ's confession on the Cross is our guarantee that the end will surely justify the means, no matter how terrible they might seem to us.

We have, so far, conducted the discussion of whether the end can ever justify the means mainly from the perspective of the human sufferers, both now and in the *eschaton*. To complete the discussion, we need to point out that what has been called the "relentless theocentricism" in Forsyth's theodicy[51] leads him to view the debate from an even higher level than what we have already considered. Forsyth's constant insistence on the priority of God's interest over that of human beings means that he is able to affirm that the end justifies the means simply because this end

---

50. *Justification*, 127–28. Surin's argument that Forsyth would have changed his position that the evil seen at the Cross outweighs all other acts of "human malevolence" had he lived to see Auschwitz cannot stand, because it ignores the fact that Forsyth's sees the sin committed against Christ on the Cross as essentially differing in kind rather than in quantity. As we have seen, the sin at Calvary was sin bringing itself to a head and hurling itself with all its might at the Son of God. This fact alone seals its primacy among all other acts of human sin in the history of the world. Also, to rely on the perspective of a victim such as Christ, who has obviously not gone through all the horrors of Auschwitz, is not unfairly reductionistic. As C. S. Lewis points out in *Problem of Pain*, 116–17, all suffering is personal to the sufferer. There is therefore no one who actually experiences in sum all the suffering of the Holocaust, and who in so doing gains a better right to speak on this matter compared to other victims of (what Marilyn McCord Adams calls) "horrendous suffering." In fact, as we shall see in the next chapter, Forsyth goes further to assert that Christ's experience on the Cross was the epitome of human suffering, thus conferring upon him the highest authority of all to represent the victim's viewpoint.

51. MacKinnon, "Teleology and Redemption," 107.

is the self-satisfaction of God and his holiness. The significance of this end for God, as we have seen in the previous chapter, justifies any magnitude of human suffering necessary to attain it. To debate the question of whether the ends can ever justify the means by citing one terrible episode of human suffering after another is, therefore, for Forsyth, missing the main point. God, and not man, is the "Arch-Egoist,"[52] to whom the worth of everything must ultimately be referenced.

Such thoroughgoing theocentricism has, quite naturally perhaps, drawn criticism. Hughes complains that "the God of Forsyth seems to be more concerned with Himself, with His holiness, His judgement, His satisfaction, than with the sinner," in violation of the Gospel emphasis on God's love for the latter.[53] A more careful reading of Forsyth reveals, however, that there is no conflict in his mind between God's concern for his own holiness and his love for sinners.[54] It is the former which leads to the latter, and the sinner's welfare is only secured if God's interest is given priority:

> Man is only saved by God's holiness, and not from it, not in spite of it. He is saved by the tragic action of a holy God, by the honour done by God in Christ to His own holy name and purpose . . . He is true to false man because first true to His own nature and promise. His justification of man is only possible by a practical justification of Himself. We should be more sure of man's salvation if we sought first God's righteousness—as He Himself does—if we were more concerned to secure His Kingdom than man's weal. There is nothing so good and wholesome for man as the Kingdom of God and its holiness, which Christ sought first, and won. Nothing else assures man's destiny, or realises all that it is in him to be. The great and final assurance we need is that God will save, must save, has saved His own holy purpose, gospel, and glory; and that history is the action of that salvation, surely however obscurely, irresistibly however slowly. With that Faith we are sure of man's Future. And only so. Man could never come to himself till God came to His own. If we first hallow God's name, as Christ did first, as God in Christ did, we are delivered from all evil, and all things are ours.[55]

---

52. *Life*, 30.

53. Hughes, "Dr. Forsyth's View of the Atonement," 37.

54. Similar observations are made by Sell, "P. T. Forsyth as Unsystematic Systematician," 111–12 and Griffith, *Theology of P. T. Forsyth*, 26.

55. *Justification*, 126–27.

In the final outcome, therefore, there will not be two differing verdicts on whether the end is worth the suffering undergone. God and human beings will both affirm that it is so, and on both the premises that God's self-satisfaction and human joy are perfected in this end. The "egoism of God" is, without doubt, "the blessing of the world," because "it is the egoism of the sacrificial God of the Cross, lifted up to draw all men unto Him."[56]

The alternative, as Forsyth sees it, to such a theocentric starting point is an anthropocentric focus, one where "man picks up all the egoism [which] God discards."[57] The human being now stands in the centre, and "everything [comes] to turn on man's welfare instead of God's worship."[58] The result of this, as Forsyth so accurately sees, is that "as with man we begin, with man we really end."[59] We see clear traces of such an anthropocentricism embedded within the claim that, given the experiences we have undergone, the end can never justify the means. Such an evaluation is, from start to end, one made by human beings. It is therefore one which fails ultimately to transcend our limited human perspective.[60] The simple questions posed by Alister McGrath still seek a satisfactory answer:

> Some say that nothing can ever be adequate recompense for the suffering in this world. But how do they know? Have they spoken to anyone who has suffered and subsequently been raised to glory? Have they been through this experience themselves?[61]

---

56. *Life*, 34–36. Another important aspect of Forsyth's affirmation that man's interest is best secured by putting God's at the priority is the idea that neglect of God's holiness and righteousness will inevitably lead to a devaluation of the human soul, to the point that "men will be more easily treated as tools in a great concern, or as pawns in a great game" (*Society*, 29). These thoughts echo Ivan Karamazov's foreboding that "everything is permitted" once we remove God from the scene. See Camus, *The Rebel*, 50–56 and Bauckham, *Theology of Jürgen Moltmann*, 75–80 for excellent commentaries on this pregnant statement of Ivan's.

57. *Life*, 31.

58. *Justification*, 18.

59. Ibid., 19.

60. The interpretation offered by Sutherland of the crux of Ivan Karamazov's rebellion is interesting in this regard. Sutherland suggests that Ivan's atheism is paradoxically founded upon a deliberate acknowledgement of "a finite God . . . the god who is the invention of a Euclidean mind, and of whom one *can only* think and talk in anthropomorphic terms. The setting of such a conception . . . is the speculations of the Russian boys passing the time of day over a pint of beer" (*Atheism and the Rejection of God*, 36). Ivan, on this reading, is a victim of a restricted anthropocentric perspective.

61. McGrath, *Bridge-Building*, 144.

Will the Theodicy Lead Ironically to Greater Suffering?

Another common objection raised against teleological theodicies is that they might conceivably reduce the stimulus for us to resist sin and alleviate suffering. Such theodicies, after all, see a purposive nature to evil, and this might lead to a reluctance on the part of human beings to intervene in situations of evil out of a concern that such intervention might go against God's will and undermine the pedagogical value of these situations.[62] Forsyth's insistence that we in this world, at best, see God's plan only dimly, might go some way towards answering this objection. Because we do not know the exact mechanics of God's secondary judgement, it would be presumptuous on our part to defy the clear Biblical commands to resist sin and alleviate suffering on the basis that we are aiding the realisation of God's strategy for a particular stage of our history. Moreover, Forsyth's theodicy envisages, as we have argued, instances of sin and evil which do not fall under the rubric of secondary judgement. Therefore, our role, as Britain's was during the War, should be to use the resources we have been given to do what is right from the perspective urged upon us by our human conscience informed by the Gospel, and to leave it to God to work out the intricacies of his plans for the world.[63]

In any case, to say that something happens because it is "God's will" is, for Forsyth, hardly a conclusive argument against human intervention. In a section entitled "The Insistency of Prayer" in his treatise *The Soul of Prayer*, Forsyth enters into a compelling discussion about the relationship between God's will and ours. He affirms that occurrences of poverty, disease and death could well be in line with God's will. However, our correct response in such situations is not passive submission to an inevitable fate, but active resistance with prayer and other practical measures. "To struggle with Him is one way of doing His will. To resist is one way of saying, 'Thy will be done.'"[64] It can therefore, for Forsyth, be God's will for us to resist his will. Such a profound understanding of the relationship between God's will and ours certainly leaves no room for the simplistic excuse that we should not resist sin and alleviate suffering for fear that it might go against God's will.

---

62. See, e.g., McGrath, *Christian Theology*, 292–93; Bauckham, *Theology of Jürgen Moltmann*, 82; Farley, *Tragic Vision and Divine Compassion*, 22; Camus, *The Plague*, 106, with examples in 111.

63. A similar response to this objection is given by Stump, "Problem of Evil," 412–43.

64. *Soul of Prayer*, 88–90.

Another aspect of Forsyth's writings on judgement which could conceivably be exploited to result in greater suffering is his affirmation that humans can play the role of the agents of God's secondary judgement. By postulating that God's people are able to discern if a particular course of action open to them constitutes an execution of God's judgement, Forsyth has placed what might be seen as a terrifying responsibility in their hands. It is true that Forsyth does not leave us devoid of guidelines as to which actions constitute God's judgement and how we are to carry them out. He mentions, for example, that careful consideration should be given to the ends of an action in evaluating its rightness,[65] and urges that judgement, if it is to be carried out, must be done with the minimum affliction of suffering needed to achieve the objective of promoting God's righteousness.[66] He also rejects the notion that Christianity can be spread by war, and limits the use of force to the resisting of wrong rather than the doing of good.[67] Moreover, with the severe decline of Christianity in the West, there might not be many countries left which are willing to acknowledge themselves as "Christian nations." Forsyth's insistence that only such nations can intentionally act as God's agents of judgement therefore makes the issue a moot one for all but perhaps a few countries in our world today.[68] Yet, because a superpower like America remains possibly one of these few countries, and its readiness to go to war has recently been exemplified in its campaigns in Afghanistan and Iraq, this question remains one which deeply affects our world today. Any abuse of Forsyth's idea that Christian states can serve as human agents of God's judgement can lead to immense suffering and distort Forsyth's theodicy as one which promotes suffering rather than explains it.

It is in this regard that the attitude manifested by Forsyth in his capacity as a citizen of a country he believes to be acting on God's behalf in the War might prove crucial. As we commented earlier, in spite of numerous "nationalistic" assertions on his part, he ultimately shows a loyalty to God's kingdom that far exceeds any obligations he feels towards his na-

---

65. *Ethic*, 9.
66. Ibid., 7, 9, 76.
67. Ibid., 87.
68. We should reckon, however, with Philip Jenkins' suggestion that a "new wave of Christian states, in which political life is inextricably bound up with religious belief," might arise in the near future in segments of the global South (*Next Christendom*, 142).

tion.⁶⁹ This loyalty led him to say that if Britain had entered into the War for reasons of "exploitation and aggrandisement," he would have opposed it with all his might.⁷⁰ He calls himself one of those "who are ready to turn even on their own land if ever it yield itself as the servant of public wickedness, and if it should rise up, in the name of whatever culture, to defy the humane kingdom of the righteous God of the nations."⁷¹ That these are not empty words is shown in two instances when Forsyth did protest against the actions of his country. When Prime Minister Disraeli decided not to intervene to stop the Turkish atrocities in Bulgaria in 1876, on the ground that "our duty at this critical moment is to maintain the empire of England," Forsyth thunders in a sermon against the self-centredness of such a policy. He sets out the correct perspective on things:

> ... there is a higher unity than the nation, there is the race; and there are higher duties than patriotism. In front of the patriot comes the Redeemer. The Saviour of society is more than the deliverer of a people, and the plain interest of a nation must sometimes yield to the claims of the race at large. That I take to be the chief message of Christianity to the nations of the world to-day.⁷²

The second instance is one where Forsyth protested not against a failure to intervene, but against a war Britain fought which he felt was not morally justified. When told of the justification given by the Church authorities for the second Anglo-Afghan war (1878–1880), i.e., that it would be a means of introducing the Gospel to Afghanistan, Forsyth decried such reasoning as akin to "cooking God's meat over hell fire."⁷³ Forsyth's ultimate loyalty to God and his kingdom led him to an attitude of deep self-reflection and awareness of where he and his people stood vis-à-vis the holy God. It is ultimately this higher loyalty that might serve as the most effective resistance against the temptation to abuse the possibility that we might serve as God's agents. Any Christian nation which purports to take this responsibility upon herself will, if she is true to Forsyth's spirit, do it with the sole purpose of serving God's kingdom, and consequently

---

69. Anything less would, in fact, render Forsyth ironically guilty of the sin of nation-worship, an attitude for which he harshly criticises the Germans (in, e.g., *Ethic*, 34–35).

70. *Roots of a World-Commonwealth*, 6–7.

71. Ibid., 20.

72. "Turkish Atrocities," 4.

73. *Charter of the Church*, 89. Forsyth speaks further of this war in *Missions*, 117. See also Forsyth's praise for the patriotism demonstrated by missionaries for the Kingdom of God—one which far transcends their loyalty to their nation (*Missions*, 36, 192).

demonstrate the lack of any triumphalism. She will also keep in mind his firm assertion that God's agents can themselves be judged in the course of carrying out judgement on others, and avoid identifying her cause too closely with God's. She will, in fact, carry out such judgement with much fear and trembling, being aware of her own sinfulness and the possibility that she herself is sharing in the judgement she is inflicting. Again, in his non-systematic and occasional fashion, it does seem that Forsyth has established an adequate reply to the charge that his teleological theodicy might ironically lead to greater suffering.

What If Not All Attain to the Glorious End?

In the previous chapter, we have discussed the thorny issue of Forsyth's "Christian universalism," and concluded that his numerous assertions that the whole human race will be saved by Christ's atoning work on the Cross are effectively qualified by two provisos. They are, firstly, that this "race" might not include every single person that ever lived in the history of our world, and that we are "obliged to leave such questions as universal restoration unsolved" because the human free will might ultimately persist in its rebellion against God. (These provisos can be seen as the flip side of each other, as those who might not be included in the "race" to be redeemed are those who exercise their free will to persist indefinitely in their sin.) These provisos, as we have seen, have important implications for Forsyth's understanding of the atonement. If just one human being excludes himself from the glorious *eschaton*, can we say that God's satisfaction and victory are complete? What about the efficacy of Christ's representation there of the entire human race before God? More pertinent for our study, we have to ask whether the self-justification of God in the second sense (i.e., the vindication by God of his righteousness in spite of the existence of evil in our world) can, in this case, be said to be fulfilled. We mentioned in chapter 2 that Forsyth envisages the completion of theodicy to reside in the acknowledgement by all creation in the *eschaton* that God is "holy, wise and good" in spite of the evil we experience. If some, or even one, creature does not participate in such acknowledgement, is God's theodicy complete?

There is, unfortunately, nothing we find in Forsyth's writings which directly addresses these questions. We are forced then to try to glean insights from some possibly relevant statements of his. We want to consider if we can make sense of the notion that, while the race is redeemed in Christ, it might not consist of every human being that ever lived. T. F. Torrance, on his part, would suggest that we do not have to. The attempt to use "this-worldly logico-causal" analysis to map the relationship between Christ's atonement and our salvation is, for him, an invalid exercise.[74] Forsyth himself, in a critique of the brand of universalism promoted by R. J. Campbell and his "New Theology," disdains the easy way in which Campbell arrived at the conclusion of salvation for all. He had, in Forsyth's view, settled "the most awful of moral problems—the eternal destiny of moral beings" as if it were a simple mathematical issue, drawing logical conclusions concerning the relationship between the finite and the infinite. Forsyth yearns for competent moral reasoning in this area, and alludes to the point that he would be comfortable if this led to an "inconsistent" position, noting that "there are many deeply exercised Christians who find it hard to do justice consistently to all the moral realities by which the destiny of men is determined."[75] So Forsyth himself might also not see the need to resolve this conundrum in a logical way, and think it sufficient to accept the paradoxical state of affairs as presented to us by the moral realities of sin and human freedom. The completion of God's self-justification in both senses, we think he would say, is inevitable. God will not be thwarted. If this completion should include the fact of some not saved, it is completion nonetheless—only we do not understand how.

If such agnosticism proves unsatisfactory, and we try to push deeper, we do find in one of Forsyth's sermons a suggestive remark we can expand on to try make some sense of the matter. He asks the question of his congregation, "Can a man sin himself into final ruin?" His answer is:

> If ever he do it will not be because he has sinned himself outside the pale of mercy, but because he has sinned himself beyond the moral possibility of repentance; because Faust has gone on and on till he became a Mephistopheles himself, denial became his nature, and evil became his element and his good.[76]

---

74. Torrance, "Atonement. The Singularity of Christ and the Finality of the Cross," 245–48.

75. "God, Sin, and the Atonement," 670. Campbell's position is stated succinctly in his work *The New Theology*, 214.

76. This section of Forsyth's sermon is set out in Porritt, "Leading Churches and Preachers," 717.

If he exists, the person who is ultimately not saved even after an eternity of opportunities to repent has, as the passage above suggests, identified himself so intimately with sin that he can be said to have "[become] a Mephistopheles himself." What this could imply is that this person undergoes a transformation—as a result of his long career of rebellion against God, he becomes identified more with sin (or Satan) than with the human race.[77] Some support for this idea might be derived from Forsyth's voluntarism, which might allow for the possibility of someone making the ontological leap from being Faust to becoming Mephistopheles if his will and actions come to flow so unerringly with that of sin (speaking here of it as a personality). In such a case, it might not be too ridiculous or arbitrary to exclude him from the ambit of the human race which Christ represents on the Cross, and to re-classify him together with the sin which is to be destroyed. His exclusion from the glorious *eschaton* would therefore not compromise the notion that the whole human race arrives there safely. Such a "solution" though, would still not be entirely satisfactory, as there remains something artificial and contrived about the notion that a human being can effectively cease to be one. Moreover, Forsyth's mention in the above quotation that it is not possible for a person to "[sin] himself outside the pale of [God's] mercy" implies that God still seeks the redemption of the one who has become Mephistopheles, and that consequently he remains human *coram Deo*, since God (in Forsyth's scheme) has no mercy whatsoever on sin. We might therefore conclude our evaluation by saying that Forsyth's refusal (or, perhaps more accurately, inability) to affirm universalism without his provisos leave important questions unanswered. This appears to be one point where his teleological theodicy does not seem to have a satisfactory reply to the objection raised against it.[78]

Should There Be No Place Given to Retributive Judgement At All?

In our discussion of Forsyth's understanding of the atonement, we saw that there is indeed a strong penal or retributive element in Forsyth's view of judgement. With regard to sin, judgement is strictly retributive

---

77. Lewis, *Problem of Pain*, 127–28 contains a similar idea that what is finally cast into hell are the "remains" of a man rather than a human being itself. Such a creature is "already a loose congeries of mutually antagonistic sins rather than a sinner."

78. Lawler raises the additional difficulty of Forsyth's neglect to include Satan in his universalistic scheme ("Universalism of P. T. Forsyth," 125 [fn]). We do not see this as an issue because, as we have mentioned in chapter 1, we see Forsyth using the term "Satan" to refer to sin personified, rather than a created being.

in nature—it seeks only to destroy and not rehabilitate. With regard to human beings as the willing agents of sin, however, Forsyth's firm assertion is that judgement takes on a purely reformative function. An argument, however, can be raised that retributive justice for human sinners should constitute an essential component of a satisfactory theodicy.[79] This is especially so when we consider particularly heinous acts of human sin. We return to *The Brothers Karamazov* for a pointed presentation of the problem. It is difficult to read of the horrific instances of the torture and killing of children recounted by Ivan, and not wish for some kind of retributive consequences upon the perpetuators of these crimes. We would recoil, together with him, from the idea that the mother will embrace the torturer of her child in the *eschaton*,[80] if the torturer had not already received at least a measure of the just deserts for his act and been transformed through this into a different person. In a similar vein, Samuel Cox notes that the main opposition to the earlier editions of his *Salvator Mundi* (which proposed an essentially reformative view of God's punishment in the afterlife) rested on the fear that he had undermined too greatly the retributive element in punishment.[81] We saw earlier that Forsyth does address (in our opinion, adequately) the issue of compensatory justice for the "innocent" victims of suffering. He does not, however, seem to have dealt with the subject of retributive justice for the "guilty" perpetuators of suffering in as comprehensive a manner. This does seem a serious omission, especially given Forsyth's emphasis on "the moral as the real." He surely has to provide some kind of answer to the human longing for retributive justice, which forms an important facet of what many would perceive to be a moral outcome. Such longing might also receive Biblical justification from verses like Rom 17:12–21, which exhorts us not to avenge ourselves on the basis that it is the Lord who will repay.

We suggest, therefore, that Forsyth's theodicy would be strengthened if he could retain a retributive component in his view of God's secondary judgement. It is, in our view, possible to introduce such a component into his thought without upsetting the basic structure of his theodicy. It must, however, be done carefully. To swing to the other extreme and see the main function of secondary judgement as retributive for human sinners

---

79. Such an argument has been made by, e.g., Lewis in his *Problem of Pain*, 122–24.
80. Dostoyevsky, *Brothers Karamazov*, 320.
81. Cox, *Salvator Mundi*, 225–26.

The Significance of the First Outcome of God's Self-Justification 121

would go against Forsyth's insistence that "mere retribution . . . is morally stupefying."[82] It would also, more fundamentally, undermine his position that the representative work of Christ on the Cross had borne the retributive effects of sin on our behalf. We propose to distinguish, then, between what we might call "pure retribution" and "the retributive aspects of secondary judgement." The former involves meting out on the sinner what he truly deserves, meaning that (as we suggested earlier) he would be destroyed together with the sin he had chosen to identify himself with, and consequently fail to arrive at the *telos*. Such "pure retribution" would no longer take place in the light of Christ's substitutory (or representative) work on the Cross on our behalf. This still leaves room, however, for the functioning of "the retributive aspects of secondary judgement." This refers to the presence of a retributive element embedded within the concept of reformative judgement, one which does not ultimately compromise the rehabilitative aim of such judgement. Cox has tried to introduce an idea akin to this in his response to his critics. He maintains that "the punishment of the unrighteous [is] at once retributive and remedial."[83] Among the points he makes in this regard are two which might prove useful for modifying Forsyth's theodicy.

The first is the assertion that, as a general rule, the means of reformation become more painful the more we have turned away from God.[84] There is, therefore, rooted within reformative judgement a principle akin to that of just deserts. We see that such an idea can be easily received into Forsyth's thought, because of his own frequent reliance on the "natural" moral consequences of sin to characterise the nature of secondary judgement. We can therefore say that there is an implicit notion of "justice" in Forsyth's view of secondary judgement, in that it understands sin to incur, as a general rule, painful consequences to a degree roughly corresponding to its severity.[85] It would also be consistent with the emphasis Forsyth places on the functioning of the moral order to introduce the idea that the quantum of pain needed for the refining process is (again as a general

---

82. *Revelation*, 91.
83. Cox, *Salvator Mundi*, 205.
84. Ibid., 93–94, 212–13.
85. We must remember, however, that this "justice," for Forsyth, does not always operate according to a fixed formula of cause and effect. There remains, as we saw earlier, a personal element to secondary judgement which transcends the operation of the moral order and defies any mechanical rendering of it.

rule) broadly proportional to the depth of sin into which we have sunk. Presumably, the more profound our wickedness, the more it would take (in terms of painful experiences) to strip us of our self-confidence and turn us to God. Further, Stephen Travis mentions the idea that:

> ... part of the reformation of the offender involves him learning to respect the moral order which God has instituted in the world (and hence learning to respect God's holiness). That this lesson is needed is shown by his prior behaviour—performed perhaps with the implicit belief that the requirements of the moral order will never catch up with him. Proportionate suffering is therefore an integral part of reformation.[86]

The second potentially constructive idea of Cox's is the notion that there exists a powerful retributive element in the growing knowledge of one's sin.[87] An integral part of the sanctification process envisaged by both Cox and Forsyth is that we will, in this life or the next, slowly become aware of the full magnitude of our sin and its effect on God and our fellow human beings. The sense of sorrow and remorse we would then feel can be viewed as an aspect of retribution for these sins. Moreover, the impact upon us of this sense would, conceivably, be in proportion to the severity of our sins, and hence the notion of just deserts is again retained. We see hints of such an idea present in Forsyth's writings when he speaks of the pain we will experience when we realise the true significance of what we have done against an absolutely holy and loving God. In an early sermon, Forsyth speaks of such realisation as "the knowledge that will fill the cup of your remorse." Such remorse is so terrible that we will come to see that "the pains of love are more awful than the stings of force and hate, and the chastisement of the Lord more dreadful than any torments of Satan."[88] Forsyth speaks of the same theme in a much later work, *The Justification of God*—this time in terms of the "self-judgement" we all have to undergo: "And at the last must there not be some great crisis of self-judgement, when we all see Him as He is, and see ourselves as His grace sees us?"[89]

To return to *The Brothers Karamazov*, we can therefore say that Forsyth's idea of judgement, as modified, allows for the possibility that the

---

86. Travis, *Christ and the Judgement of God*, 4.
87. Cox, *Salvator Mundi*, 93–94, 155, 213.
88. "The Bible Doctrine of Hell and the Unseen," 4.
89. *Justification*, 188.

general (who in Ivan's story sent his hounds to tear up a hapless young boy in front of his mother) would experience an unimaginably painful rehabilitative process, an aspect of which consists of the full realisation of the impact his act has had upon God and his victims. This realisation would bring, in Hick's words, "utter revulsion against his own cruelty and a deep shame and sorrow at the memory of it."[90] If he were indeed to embrace the child's mother in the *eschaton*, he would not be doing so without having first received these retributive-cum-reformative punishments for his act. These refinements to Forsyth's thought, we suggest, might go some way towards satisfying the sense of justice our conscience demands. This is a sense which certainly needs to be refined in the light of the atonement, in that it would be wrong for us to demand "pure retribution" for anyone, seeing how we ourselves are also saved from such retribution by the grace shown on the Cross. But we suggest that the longing for the retributive aspects of essentially reformative judgement to be carried out might not be misplaced. It stems, after all, from the moral order instituted by God, and looks to the functioning of the same order for its realisation.

THE HISTORICAL NATURE OF FORSYTH'S THEODICY

Having looked at the teleological nature of Forsyth's theodicy, we turn now to consider (far more briefly) the other major significance of the first outcome of God's self-justification, which is that it imparts a strong historical character to this theodicy. Forsyth likes to point out that the justification of God he is offering is a practical one. Theodicy, to him, is ultimately not a theoretical problem to be solved by adducing arguments and proofs. It is, instead, one founded upon "a historic self-justification of God" and followed by the outworking of this event in world history.[91] Therefore, the end, when it comes, is not some totally alien sphere which crashes into ours and obliterates (and therefore renders worthless) all that has gone all before. It is, rather, one brought into existence by the concrete historical events which we experience, both good and bad:

> Thus [God] makes a new world—so new that there is no difference greater than between the new humanity and the old. Yet He makes it out of the old. The old is not swept away as by total deluge, and a

---

90. Hick, *Death and Eternal Life*, 165. Hick, however, rejects any notion that this constitutes "divine punishment."

91. *Justification*, 98.

new race suddenly created on the earth. The new humanity grows from old history. Revolution is interwoven with evolution.[92]

Forsyth sees this emphasis on the historical nature of his theodicy serving as a much needed corrective to the trend in Christianity, since Protestant Orthodoxy, to reduce it to a private matter divorced from "public history and social affairs."[93] The result of this is to make "Evangelicalism a byword of national impotence," and erase any relevance God might have to the life we share with others in our community.[94] In the meantime, secular notions of progress have seized the opportunity to claim the ground of history yielded by Christianity. This is all the more painful for Forsyth as he sees these notions of progress having no firm basis, and inevitably frustrating the expectations they generate. Forsyth thus sees a need for the Christian faith to reclaim history as "the prize of the Cross,"[95] and to give Christians a secure hope for the future of our world, one that would not be unhinged even by tragedies like the War.[96] Forsyth's approach, in this sense, can be seen as diametrically opposite to that other response to the War offered by twentieth-century German dialectical theology, which (as Bauckham observes) took refuge in the "theological flight from history." For them "the First World War established that history was no place in which to look for theological meaning and the historical future no proper object of Christian hope."[97] Forsyth saw, conversely, the War as the sign of God's continued care of and involvement in human history. His emphasis on the "historical future" as the ground for hope foreshadows in some aspects the later "theology of hope" movement. Forsyth's ambition for history is, in fact, no less than Moltmann's, and the latter's statement

---

92. "Paradox of Christ," 113. Forsyth's desire to protect the integrity of history also extends to the history of individuals, as evidenced by his treatment of the topic of personal eschatology. We see this in the intimate connection he posits between this life and the next, such that the judgements we have to undergo and the rewards we obtain after we die are intricately linked to our moral choices and experiences in this life. In fact, as we have seen, Forsyth's desire to give integrity to our choices in the here and now leads him to retract from an unqualified assertion of universalism, an outcome crucial in so many respects to the rest of his theology. He gives credence to the power of the human soul to harden itself so greatly in this life that the knot might not be undone even in eternity.

93. *Justification*, 192, 206–7; *Life*, 88.

94. *Justification*, 207; *Life*, 88.

95. *Justification*, 190.

96. Ibid., 54.

97. Bauckham, "Theology after Hiroshima," 588.

accurately describes the high stakes Forsyth invests into history in order to gain returns for his theodicy:

> At the deepest level the question of world history is the question of righteousness. And this question extends out into transcendence . . . If the question of theodicy can be understood as a question of the righteousness of God in the history of the suffering of the world, then all understanding and presentation of world history must be seen within the horizon of the question of theodicy.[98]

In trying to foster his notion of true Christian hope, we see Forsyth having to navigate a careful course between two dominant streams of thought in his time. While he remains greatly indebted to various figures in Protestant Orthodoxy and modern thinkers like Kant and Schleiermacher, he seeks to overcome the tendency of these scholars to turn the Christian faith inward towards the believer. In doing so, he finds an occasional ally in Hegel, but makes it clear that he rejects the fundamental immanentism in this philosopher's thinking, which destroys the personalism and voluntarism at the heart of Forsyth's theology. The narrow path he finally settled upon was the way of the Cross as the source and goal of all world history. Because this Cross is, at the same time, both a concrete historical act and an event in the eternal realm which transcends history, Forsyth sees that there is nothing in history which can defeat its sovereign reign. Therefore, although our hope is one in the purposefulness and progress of history, it is paradoxically immune from anything history might throw at us:

> We are not dependent on the course of events for a belief in God, or His salvation, or our destiny. The great transaction is done. And if the path of its realisation among men be through desert, hill, sea, or earthquake which casts the hills into the sea, that does not destroy the soul's rest, patience, or power, its work, sacrifice, or worship. Faith is fixed on God's eternal saving Act for history, sure beyond the reach of any catastrophe that history may show.[99]

Forsyth also sees a practical utility in such true Christian hope, in that it can alleviate a great deal of mental and emotional suffering in times of crises. So, while he recognises that "there is a calm which is a mere matter of temperament," he urges us to secure the more valuable "peace which

---

98. Moltmann, *Crucified God*, 175.
99. *Ethic*, 125.

is that of faith."¹⁰⁰ Even when faced with unbearable situations of suffering, we have the resources to "call in the health and beauty of a more innocent world to redress the balance of grief and guilt in this."¹⁰¹ Moreover, while the world reacts with shock and lament to God's acts of secondary judgement, those who have hope respond with joy, as the Psalmist did in a passage so incomprehensible to modern minds:

> Let the heavens rejoice, let the earth be glad;
> let the sea resound, and all that is in it;
> let the fields be jubilant, and everything in them.
> Then all the trees of the forest will sing for joy;
> they will sing before the LORD, for he comes,
> he comes to judge the earth.
> He will judge the world in righteousness
> and the peoples in his truth. (Ps 96:11–13)¹⁰²

We rejected the suggestion given earlier that Forsyth's theodicy might ironically lead to greater suffering. We see now that it has, conversely, the potential to alleviate much anguish if its tenets are appropriated by faith into our lives. This mention of faith brings us aptly to the conclusion of this chapter.

CONCLUSION

We have considered here what we see to be the two main significances of the first outcome of God's self-justification for Forsyth's theodicy. Firstly, it renders this theodicy a teleological one, in which the claim is made that the glorious end to which everything is moving justifies the suffering we undergo in order to attain this end. Secondly, this first outcome imparts a strong historical character to this theodicy, in the sense that it is in and through world history that God's justification of himself is being realised. The main facet of evil addressed by these two aspects of Forsyth's theodicy is clearly human suffering. Forsyth attempts to justify such suffering on the basis of its purpose, and to say that such purpose is being worked out not in some esoteric realm divorced from our world, but in our everyday lives and experience. In doing so, Forsyth seeks to give hope and

---

100. *Society*, 13.
101. *Recent Art*, 207–8.
102. *Justification*, 184, 197.

The Significance of the First Outcome of God's Self-Justification

joy to those whose lives and experiences have led them down the path of suffering.

Forsyth would insist that the key to appropriating these two aspects of his theodicy is faith. Indeed, the notion that the end justifies the means is, as Albert Camus points out, a terrifying one if this end is fixed and the means implemented by the wrong hands.[103] The person "in charge" is therefore key. We must believe that God has indeed fixed a goal for the world through the Cross. We must trust in his power to move it there and in his love and wisdom to do so in a way that does not inflict more suffering than necessary. We must, moreover, have faith that God will render this end a just one for both the "innocent" victims and the "guilty" perpetuators of suffering. We are called to believe all these even when "it all seems very slow, and justice seems for periods even turned backwards."[104] We have no other alternative, as Camus accurately points out:

> "Come down from the cross and we shall believe in you," their police agents already cry on Golgotha. But He does not come down and, even, at the most tortured moment of His agony, he protests to God at having been abandoned. There are thus no other proofs but faith and the mystery that the rebels reject and the Grand Inquisitors scoff at.[105]

But we might still ask: Does God fully understand what he requires of us? Does he realise how difficult it is to trust him when we witness or experience terrible suffering? Forsyth will come to these questions in the next chapter.

---

103. Camus observes that this was what happened when the Nazis appropriated Nietzsche's assertion that the end justifies the means: *The Rebel*, 68.

104. *Justification*, 124.

105. Camus, *The Rebel*, 55–56.

5

The Second Outcome of God's Self-Justification

The Revelation of the Incomparable Suffering of God

INTRODUCTION

Having set out what we see to be Forsyth's position on the first major outcome of God's self-justification and its significance for his theodicy, we move on, in this chapter and the next, to do the same for the second major outcome. Forsyth's basic idea here is that, through God's act of self-justification on the Cross, we gain knowledge of the incomparable suffering of God in his battle against sin. This suffering of God envisaged by Forsyth is, in Smail's term, a "two-fold" one. As Smail elaborates, "On the cross there is a two-fold sacrifice; on the one hand the costly self-offering of the Son to the Father on behalf of humanity, and on the other the self-offering of the Father in the giving of his Son to save the world."[1] We will describe Forsyth's views on the suffering of the Son and that of the Father in turn. Both rely heavily upon Forsyth's kenotic Christology.[2] While this is not the place to describe this Christology in any significant detail, it would facilitate our subsequent discussion to set out its broad contours.

---

1. Smail, *Once and for All*, 128–29. (Smail is not specifically describing Forsyth's views here.)

2. In postulating such a Christology, Forsyth followed the path many of his contemporaries took from the late nineteenth century onwards. See Dawe, *Form of a Servant*, 127–31 for a fine summary of the development of kenotic Christology in Britain during that time, beginning with A. B. Bruce's Cunningham Lectures, *Humiliation of Christ*, in 1876.

Forsyth saw that the second member of the Trinity made a "premundane renunciation" which involved emptying himself of "the form, the glory, the immunity of Godhead."³ This "great eternal act of Christ in heaven and Godhead, before and beyond history" was the foundation of the incarnation of the Son in history.⁴ Forsyth is careful to emphasise that this divine self-emptying does not involve the extinguishing of the divine attributes and self-consciousness in the incarnate Christ. He prefers to understand *kenosis* in terms of "two modes of being," God and human. In becoming man, God gave up his divine mode of being and took on a human, finite mode of being. In the context of the latter, the divine attributes take on a different form. Omniscience, for example, changes from being "an intuitive and simultaneous knowledge of all things" (as is its manifestation in the eternal realm) to "a discursive and successive knowledge," where actual knowing only arises through the human process of growing in understanding. "The stress," Forsyth insists, "falls on the mode of existence of these qualities, and not on their presence or absence."⁵

Forsyth is eager to complement this self-emptying of the Son with the opposite concept of a *plerosis*. Having made his "premundane renunciation" and come into the world as a result of it, Christ, throughout his earthly career, grew, through a process of intense moral struggle, towards regaining the divine form of the attributes and consciousness he had "emptied" himself of. This process culminated in "the cross, resurrection, and glory," when Christ reconquered the divine mode of being.⁶ Forsyth insists that this process of growth proceeds not in opposition to, but in parallel with, the kenotic movement, which also continues throughout Christ's earthly career and reaches its depths in the Cross.⁷ These two movements of "the diminuendo of Kenosis" and "the crescendo of a vaster Plerosis"⁸ form the basis for Forsyth's reconceptualisation of Christology. Rather than trying to conceive of Christ according to the metaphysical formulas of old, Forsyth prefers what he calls the "metaphysic of faith."⁹ This sees Christ as the "node" at which the two movements, understood

---

3. *Person*, 318; *Father*, 41.
4. *Father*, 38.
5. *Person*, 295–96, 307–8.
6. Ibid., 308, 330, 349.
7. Ibid., 232, 311.
8. Ibid., 311.
9. Ibid., 356.

generally as that from God to humanity and vice versa, meet in reconciled calmness.¹⁰ Forsyth also calls this a "metaphysic of the ethic," which sees the simultaneous culmination of these two movements in "God's supreme moral act of redemption and in man's supreme moral act of faith," both of which are realised in the one person of Christ on the Cross.¹¹

Forsyth hints that a major reason for his postulation of a kenotic Christology was the desire to take seriously the life of the historical Jesus in the light of his belief in the pre-existence of Christ.¹² The epistemological route he took to arrive at this Christology was, true to his *theologia crucis*, via Calvary. He explicitly rejects the Hegelian approach to *kenosis* and its viewing of Christ's life, death and resurrection as mere illustrations of a more fundamental philosophical process, in which the Infinite goes into the finite before resuming its former status.¹³ Forsyth also declines, implicitly, to follow the lead of other British kenoticists like Charles Gore, who saw the incarnation itself as the focal point at which we come to understand Christ's self-emptying.¹⁴ In an article significantly entitled "The Divine Self-Emptying," Forsyth writes, "The centre of the Incarnation is where Christ placed the focus of His work—not at the beginning of His life, but at its end; not in the manger, but in the cross. The key to the Incarnation is not in the cradle, but in the cross. The light on Bethlehem falls from Calvary."¹⁵ This is so because it is only in the Cross that we see the "historic consummation" of the two movements of *kenosis* and *plerosis*, since it is there that Christ reached both "the nadir of that self-limitation which flowed from the supramundane self-emptying of the Son" and "the zenith of that moral exaltation which had been mounting throughout the long sacrifice of his earthly life."¹⁶ The Cross must therefore form the epistemological key for understanding the nature of the incarnation and of Christ's person.¹⁷

10. Ibid., 338, 346.

11. Ibid., 356.

12. Ibid., 289, 294. In this, Forsyth falls in line with the other kenoticists of his time who attempted "to mediate [the] new historical accent on Christ's humanity with the confessions of the past" (Thompson, "Nineteenth-Century Kenotic Christology," 77).

13. *Father*, 36–37.

14. Gore's views on the epistemological significance of the incarnation are well summarised in his work *Dissertations on Subjects Connected with the Incarnation*, 172.

15. *Father*, 40.

16. *Person*, 232.

17. Ibid.; *Father*, 40.

We conclude here our all too brief summary of Forsyth's kenotic Christology. We will subsequently elaborate on some of the aspects mentioned here where they prove relevant to the specific aspect of God's suffering under discussion. We move on now to consider the various aspects of Forsyth's understanding of the suffering of God the Son. We should make the preliminary clarification that, according to the terms of Forsyth's kenotic Christology, any reference in the following discussion to the suffering of the incarnate Christ must carry the implication that it was the Son, as the second member of the Trinity, who suffered. This, for Forsyth, connotes divine suffering, since the patristic strategy of defending God's impassibility by postulating a human suffering in the Son which does not touch his divine nature[18] is alien to Forsyth's scheme of thought, which rejects the substantial metaphysics of traditional Christology. It was, for Forsyth, the Son who underwent a self-emptying to exist under the human mode of being. All his experiences under this mode of being, including suffering, are therefore his own, and they touch him as the divine person he is.[19]

THE SUFFERING OF THE SON

The Suffering of Christ in His Growth towards the Cross

The Growth of the Incarnate Christ

Forsyth writes approvingly of the idea of God's immutability. "What is of Godhead," he insists, "does not grow: it is from Eternity to Eternity . . . The growth of a divine personality in Eternity is a much more impossible thing than the co-existence of three."[20] From what we mentioned earlier, however, we know that statements such as these are qualified by his assertions as to the reality of the growth of the incarnate Christ as he undergoes the process of *plerosis*. The way Forsyth reconciles these two seemingly opposing positions is, of course, to say that the attribute

---

18. See Weinandy, *Does God Suffer?* chapter 8 for a comprehensive description and defense of this position.

19. In this sense, Forsyth's Christology, *contra* Dawe, *Form of a Servant*, 140–41, probably has more affinity with the Alexandrian model than the Antiochene one. Forsyth has also offered a critique of Antiochene Christology in "Faith, Metaphysic, and Incarnation," 715–16. We would agree with Dawe, however, that Forsyth's Christology ultimately does not fall neatly under any of these two categories.

20. *Person*, 284.

of immutability manifests itself in different ways according to the "mode of being" in which it functions. This argument can, however, only work if there is some basic conceptual correspondence between the growth Jesus experienced and God's eternal immutability. Forsyth postulates such a correspondence by proposing an "active" notion of immutability, one which involves movement. So, God's "changeless nature is not stock-stiff and apart. It has an absolute mobility. It has in it the power and secret of all change, all out-going, without going out of Himself."[21] This "divine mobility" is an "uncaused self-contained vitality" and a "changeless change" in God.[22] We get a hint that these cryptic phrases are intended to describe the eternal movements the members of the Trinity make towards one another when Forsyth writes that one key aspect of this mobility is the eternal going out of the Father to the Son.[23] Forsyth sees this divine mobility assuming the characteristic of ordinary human growth once set in the context of time and space. We grow, in fact, as humans because God implants in us his eternal movement as part of the bestowal upon us of his image.[24] The divine mobility which the Son enjoys in eternity is, therefore, "translated into human growth" under the finite mode of being.[25] Consequently, the concept of growth, far from being incompatible with the idea of God's immutability, lies within it and is demanded by it.[26]

So Jesus grew. Forsyth mentions that this involves a development of his consciousness, both in the "natural" sense (as he grew to know more and more of the world in which he lived) and the "spiritual" sense (as he slowly grasped the fact of his fundamental identity as God's Son). There was also growth in his personality, as he came to interpret his experiences more accurately and exercise his will more resolutely.[27] However, in answering the question as to how we are primarily to conceive of Jesus' growth, Forsyth writes that he "developed as Redeemer. He grew in his

---

21. Ibid., 342.

22. Ibid., 338.

23. Moreover, because all creation is in the Son and comes into being through the Son, this "Son-ward advance" is also "the ground of God's movement towards human beings" (ibid., 338, 342–43).

24. Ibid., 336.

25. Ibid., 339.

26. Ibid., 308.

27. Ibid., 121–22.

vocation rather than in his position, more even than in character."[28] We therefore find moral development in the incarnate Christ, but it is not merely ethical growth in the abstract, but "the deepening mastery of a moral vocation . . . [and] the dynamic development of a Redeemer."[29] He became, in other words, progressively more suited and ready to carry out his redeeming work as he grew, until he finally made his redemptively efficacious confession on the Cross.

This Growth Involves Suffering

What is involved in this development of Jesus as Redeemer? In what aspects must he grow so that he can perform this vocation perfectly? Forsyth has no doubt about the answer: He needed to learn obedience to God.[30] This makes sense when we recall the point made in Chapter 2 that Christ's confession to God on the Cross was an adequately holy response to God's holiness because it was made in the obedience of faith. Forsyth is strongly insistent that Jesus had never at any point before his death realised the full significance his suffering and death on the Cross would have for both God and his creation.[31] His confession of God's holiness on the Cross was therefore made not for the sake of the glorious consequences of this act, but due to "His perfect committal to the will of God,"[32] i.e., on the strength of his obedience to the Father's will. Growing in obedience is therefore the essential developmental path which Christ the Redeemer must take, in preparation for that ultimate act of redemptive obedience on the Cross.

How then did Jesus grow in obedience? Forsyth, relying on the authority of passages like Hebrews 2:10 and 5:8, tells us that Jesus learnt obedience "by the things he suffered."[33] This idea of growth through suffering resonates well with Forsyth's insistence on the indispensability of the "moral process" for building up a person's character. This process necessarily involves the soul's experience of "moral conflict," probably a reference to its painful struggle with the temptation to go against God's

---

28. Ibid., 126. Forsyth does not explicitly mention here that this is the "primary" way we are to conceive of Christ's growth, but this sense is conveyed through the context.

29. Ibid.

30. Ibid., 121, 126.

31. *Father*, 20–21; *Sacraments*, 256.

32. *Preaching of Jesus*, 20.

33. *Person*, 121, 126.

will.³⁴ Now Forsyth is not afraid to say that even God cannot truncate this "moral process"—not even he can "create a character full-blown" at the onset of its existence.³⁵ So, if the incarnate Christ were to grow in any meaningful sense, he could have no special dispensation from the need to undergo this process.³⁶ If he overcame temptation, it was not due to any extraordinary powers on his part, but a resolute exercise of his will in faithfulness to God.³⁷ Forsyth wants to dispel the notion that Jesus' sinlessness was "of that natural, sweet, poised, remote, and aesthetic type." It was rather a sinlessness that was won through "agony," because it involved undergoing one moral crisis after another, vanquishing a series of "crosses" in succession.³⁸

Those familiar with Forsyth's Christology will know that he is firmly committed to the traditional Western position of *non posse peccare*. Christ could not have sinned—he had a "foregone immunity" in this respect.³⁹ Does this not threaten to undermine all we have said in the preceding paragraph? Were Jesus' struggles with temptations merely a show, since his victory over them was already foreordained? Forsyth's answer is a resolute "no." The key, for him, is that the incarnate Christ, as a result of his *kenosis*, did not know of his immunity to sin.⁴⁰ He did not know there was only one possible outcome of victory. Subjectively speaking, therefore, he faced temptation like the rest of us, having to struggle to make the decision to remain faithful to God.

Except for one particular aspect (which we will cover below), Forsyth does not enter into significant detail about the temptations Jesus experienced and the agony he underwent in order to overcome them. Perhaps he did not want to enter into unnecessary psychological speculation about the state of Jesus' mind, especially when such find little support from the Gospel narratives.⁴¹ We are therefore left with Forsyth's quite elaborate

34. *Recent Art*, 197(fn); *Work*, 183.
35. *Recent Art*, 197(fn).
36. *Person*, 341.
37. *Work*, 183.
38. *Revelation*, 128–29; *Justification*, 227–28.
39. *Person*, 301.
40. Ibid., 301, 342.
41. Forsyth shows an aversion to an overly speculative analysis of Jesus' "inner life" in his critique of Wilhelm Herrmann: "Inner Life of Christ," 154; "Man and the Message," 4–5. Forsyth does affirm that it is possible to understand some aspects of Jesus' "inner

description of what he probably sees as the most significant aspect of the suffering Jesus went through prior to the Cross: his struggle with the Father's will for him to die at Calvary.

Christ's Struggle in His Journey to the Cross

In Forsyth's account of Jesus' life, he asserts that Jesus "did not start with the Cross in a clear programme."[42] Jesus was not aware initially of his final destiny at Calvary. When the vague concept first dawned upon him that God might have had willed his life to go "the bitter way," he was plagued by "spiritual uncertainty," which brought pain to him in an emotional, and possibly even a physical, sense.[43] This uncertainty would, in fact, linger until close to the end of his life. His desperate plea at Gethsemane that "if it be possible" showed that even then he hoped the Father might have an alternative path for him.[44]

What was the cause of the pain Jesus felt? To trace the answer, we need to examine how Forsyth tries to re-enact the thoughts and motivations of Jesus on his way to the Cross. Forsyth participates, in other words, in his own reconstruction of the "historical Jesus," albeit in a more modest way than those attempted by many of his contemporaries.[45] Forsyth, in this project, relies heavily upon the work of the great New Testament scholar Albert Schweitzer. Schweitzer's landmark study *The Quest of the Historical Jesus* had been translated into English in 1910,[46] and Forsyth acknowledges his indebtedness to this work by citing it approvingly in his

---

life", but only through his relation to the Cross—the *theologia crucis* again!: "Inner Life," 156, 160; "Faith and Mind," 641. We will subsequently see how Forsyth elaborates upon these aspects.

42. "Inner Life," 162.

43. *Recent Art*, 194–95.

44. *Person*, 341; "Inner Life," 162.

45. Although modest, Forsyth's reconstruction of the "historical Jesus" is, as we shall see, sufficiently comprehensive to challenge Garvie's somewhat surprising comment that Forsyth neglected almost completely the first-century Jewish context of Jesus' life and death, and that "he depreciated any attempt to understand the inner life of Jesus, especially His relation as Son to God as Father" ("Placarding the Cross," 350–52). Garvie has also made another critique (in "Cross-Centred Theology," 329) that Forsyth was inconsistent in his depiction of Jesus' consciousness as to the necessity of his death. We also hope to demonstrate here that this is misplaced.

46. Schweitzer, *Quest of the Historical Jesus*.

all-too-rare footnotes.[47] In line with Schweitzer's analysis, Forsyth suggests that Jesus' original ministry was focused upon calling his people, the Jews of his time, to a radical repentance, in the light of his belief that God's kingdom was imminent.[48] The hope was to bring forth a "national repentance," in which (to use Schweitzer's phrases) the "host of penitents" would "wring" the Kingdom from God. This would, in Jesus' understanding, lead in turn to a situation of great crisis, the details of which were predicted by Jesus in his apocalyptic discourses. This Jesus understood as an essential preliminary to the coming of the Kingdom.[49] Jesus also saw himself as the promised Messianic King who has come to reign, as an earthly political ruler, over the coming Kingdom.[50] Because Jesus had not yet, at this stage of his ministry, sensed clearly the call to the Cross, his appeal to Israel was *bona fide*—he put all his heart into it and genuinely hoped for success.[51] The eventual result was, however, dismal failure. His compatriots failed to respond to him or his disciples in a sufficiently significant way to generate the crisis that would usher in the Kingdom.[52]

Forsyth continues to follow Schweitzer in seeing that Jesus, now deeply impatient for the Kingdom, planned to stir up the required crisis by other means. He would push events so that they hurl quickly to his death.[53] From this point of the narrative, however, Forsyth quietly departs from the German scholar, and re-constructs Jesus' motivations in his own distinct manner. Instead of postulating, as Schweitzer did, that Jesus now viewed his death as his substitutionary bearing on behalf of his people of the tribulations that would precede the Kingdom (and therefore necessary),[54] Forsyth frames it more in terms of Jesus offering his death as

---

47. See, e.g., *Work*, 163(fn); *Preaching of Jesus*, 41(fn). This is not to say that Forsyth, with his mastery of German, could not have read the original edition when it was published in 1906. Hunter mentions the influence of Schweitzer upon Forsyth in Hunter, "P. T. Forsyth Neutestamentler," 103.

48. *Preaching of Jesus*, 5.

49. Ibid., 48. This account of Forsyth's view is supplemented by details from Schweitzer, *Quest of the Historical Jesus*, 355–56, 360–62, a move we consider justified given Forsyth's explicit acknowledgement that he is following this part of Schweitzer's thesis here.

50. *Ethic*, 152–53.

51. "Inner Life," 162; *Preaching of Jesus*, 5.

52. *Preaching of Jesus*, 5, 48–49.

53. Ibid., 41.

54. Schweitzer, *Quest of the Historical Jesus*, 387–89.

one option in a final critical choice he presents to his people.[55] Jesus saw that if the Jewish nation were, even at this late stage, to accept his claim of Messianic Kingship, he would proceed to reign over it. A "shocked and saved Israel" would then be at the "head of God's Kingdom in the world."[56] If the nation, on the other hand, were to continue to reject Jesus' claim and finally kill him, God's great judgement would fall upon her and she would be destroyed.[57] This was, in Jesus' understanding, a decisive juncture for Israel—she had to make the choice "unto national salvation or damnation."[58] Forsyth proceeds to say that Jesus subsequently realised the decision the Jews would inevitably make. They would reject and kill him. This meant that Jesus' death would usher in the Kingdom of God for the entire world, but with ethnic Israel not at its head and not even participating in its glory. Forsyth understood Jesus' parable of the wicked tenants as making this point. The Kingdom will be "transferred . . . from national to universal hands . . . over Israel's corpse."[59] It was probably at this juncture that Jesus' awareness that it might be the Father's will for him to go to the Cross, which must have been growing throughout this time, developed into a firm conviction:

> Already He had seen death to be *inevitable* from without, from the temper of His foes. He *could* not escape it. Now it is carried home to Him, how *necessary* it was from within, from His Father. He *must* not escape it. His work required it. It was in God's will. The will of the Pharisees becomes to Him, by a sure mystery and miracle, the will of God. Both willed His death.[60]

---

55. "Conversion of the 'Good,'" 767.

56. *Preaching of Jesus*, 52.

57. Ibid., 49–50.

58. Ibid., 49. There is the interesting issue of whether this was an objectively real choice, apart from Jesus' perception of the matter. Could the Cross really have been averted if Israel had chosen otherwise? Forsyth's probable answer is that, given the context of our world, the crucifixion of Jesus was "quite inevitable" (*Work*, 108).

59. *Preaching of Jesus*, 49. It is unclear how Forsyth intends to reconcile his assertion that Jesus, in his earthly career, did not understand the full significance of his death on the Cross with his statement here that Jesus knew his death would usher in the Kingdom all over the world. Perhaps one way to do so would be to say that Jesus' notion of this Kingdom is a vague one, and he did not possess detailed knowledge of the glorious *eschaton* his death would lead to. He would also, under this suggestion, not know its full significance for God in terms of the satisfaction of his holiness.

60. *Missions*, 4–5 (emphases in original).

In obedience to this call, Jesus set his face resolutely towards Calvary, although (as we saw) he kept hoping, even up to Gethsemane, that the Father might have an alternative course for him.

This account provides the context for understanding the possible reasons for the agony Jesus felt in his journey to the Cross. We might suppose that, to the extent that Jesus foresaw it, at least part of this agony must have arisen due to the dread of the suffering which the Cross would involve (the details of which will be given in the next section). His sorrow at being constantly rejected by the people he sought all his life to minister to must also have been significant.[61] Forsyth himself emphasises one struggle which proved particularly agonising for Jesus—that which resulted in the sacrifice of the vocational goal he had set for his own life, which was to attain to "the power and glory of a brilliant worldly career" of being the Messianic King of Israel.[62] In *Religion in Recent Art*, Forsyth mentions that Jesus pursued his "false and selfish thoughts of Messiahship" out of his "self-will" and "worthy Egoism," possibly suggesting that Jesus might have sought to reign as ethnic Israel's Messianic King out of a sense of personal ambition.[63] In his later works, however, Forsyth clarifies that the temptation Jesus faced was far more subtle than simply that of personal aggrandisement:

> He saw the kingdoms of the world, and the glory of them. It was not their pagan splendour, but the glory they might yield to God, if Messiah put out His latent powers and became their literal King. He flushed to anticipate the scene. He saw His own Puritan race keen for a lead. He saw empire wide open to such powers as His, where He might serve God on a royal scale, and make Him an offering of a conquered world.[64]

The idea of the Cross, when it came upon Jesus, must have seemed like the destruction of this dream:

> Do you think He did not see what the empire that *He* could found without the cross might do for the kingdom of God in the world? And did it never occur to Him as a possibility that the cross might hinder that kingdom, or nip it in the bud? Was it never suggested

---

61. Forsyth saw that Jesus "regarded the mission of His life as confined to Israel—at least till near its close." The direct concern of the large part of his ministry was not the Gentile world: *Preaching of Jesus*, 5.

62. *Recent Art*, 205. See also *Ethic*, 151.

63. *Recent Art*, 197–98.

64. *Missions*, 5–6.

to Him that His cross might prevent God's throne, which a forward policy would establish on the earth?⁶⁵

The temptation Jesus faced, therefore, was that of preferring an obvious way of achieving God's purposes over (what were to him) the far more mysterious and uncertain methods of God's.⁶⁶ How much easier it would have been to ensure God's rule over the kingdoms of the world if Christ was there physically holding the reigns of power! It was therefore a temptation which, in some ways, was far more challenging to meet than the mere inducement to do evil *simpliciter*. Forsyth saw that Jesus, after a long struggle through prayer, eventually laid down his self-will in obedience to the Father's direction for his life.⁶⁷ Jesus, like all of us, had to "[die] to the natural man," and ultimately find his life by losing it.⁶⁸ This surely does not come about without pain: "A world was before Him, His foot was on the frontier—and He must turn away to die. How like was the Moses of the new Israel to the Moses of the old! It was bitter."⁶⁹ Yet another aspect of Jesus' suffering described by Forsyth is the tremendous sadness he felt when he realised that his impending death would result in Israel's destruction. Being a first-century Jew, Jesus' "conceptual world was that of Israel," and his concerns were overwhelmingly for that nation and its people.⁷⁰ He therefore experienced "the grief of the spiritual patriot at the loss and guilt of His land," one akin to the "agony" a man feels when he has "to do for conscience what he knows may ruin his family." This grief was aggravated by his realisation of the irony that it was precisely his love for Israel that resulted in her doom.⁷¹

In summary, then, God's calling of Jesus to the Cross, once perceived clearly, seemed to Jesus "the end and ruin of the Messiah's work . . . the failure of all on which He had spent His life in the hope of saving at least the better Israel from its hard taskmasters."⁷² Against tremendous temptations and difficulties, Jesus submitted to this call of God. This was not a one-off decision, but a submission which gradually deepened as Jesus

65. "Disappointment of the Cross," 138 (emphasis in original).
66. Pitt shares this observation in *Church, Ministry and Sacraments*, 25.
67. *Recent Art*, 197–98; *Missions*, 8.
68. *Recent Art*, 261–62.
69. *Missions*, 6.
70. *Preaching of Jesus*, 5–6.
71. Ibid., 6; *Ethic*, 151; *Missions*, 6–8.
72. *Ethic*, 152–53.

overcame one moral crisis after another, and learnt obedience through the things he suffered. Jesus' life was therefore the furthest thing from a pain-free existence. It was rather "a process of disillusioned love, whose reality he came to find but in service, suffering, and death, and not in the enjoyment of success."[73] Forsyth realises that his stress upon these ideas constitutes his point of departure from Schweitzer, whose thesis he finds otherwise convincing. Rather than seeing Jesus sacrifice his life primarily to a "historic necessity" of bearing the tribulations of the end times on behalf of the nation (as Schweitzer does), Forsyth understands Jesus giving up his life ultimately in obedience to God's will,[74] even when it went against his own and even when he was not completely clear why this had to be. It was not an impersonal process, but a personal God, to whom Jesus finally yielded his spirit.[75]

The Suffering of Christ on the Cross

In discussing the moment when Christ hung on the Cross, we arrive at what Forsyth calls "the nadir of that self-limitation which flowed from the supramundane self-emptying of the Son."[76] While Jesus' entire earthly life was, as we have seen, characterised by intense moral struggle and suffering, it was at the Cross that such suffering reached its climax. This is so because Christ was "made sin" on the Cross. We have already (in chapter 2) argued that Forsyth tried to convey, by this cryptic phrase, the notion that Christ assumed the personality of sin, that arch-enemy of God. Being "made sin" therefore represents the nadir of Christ's progressive self-limitation that was first manifested at the incarnation, because it was here that the Son's self-emptying reached the point where "he could identify himself

---

73. Ibid., 151.

74. *Preaching of Jesus*, 50.

75. Forsyth's ability to appropriate Schweitzer's *Quest of the Historical Jesus* is all the more remarkable given its powerful effect in Britain at that time in widening the perceived divide between the historical Jesus and the Christ of faith (see Pals, *Victorian "Lives" of Jesus*, 179–82, for a description of this). In a manner similar to his treatment of Hegel, Forsyth utilises Schweitzer's thought, but in the context of a framework (Forsyth's kenotic Christology) alien to his. This enables Forsyth to ultimately subvert Schweitzer's portrayal of Jesus by utilising key aspects of it to bolster confidence in the Christ of faith. We can therefore say that, just as he "corrected [the Logic of Hegel] by the theology of Paul" (*Positive Preaching*, 195), Forsyth also corrected the findings of Schweitzer by the Gospels and their portrayal of the Christ of Faith. See Forsyth's comments in "Faith and Mind," 633 on the utility of the Gospels in any reconstruction of the historical Jesus.

76. *Person*, 232.

with sin and death, his absolute antitheses."[77] Forsyth could consequently write that "the real Incarnation lay not in Christ being made flesh for us, but in His being made sin."[78]

It is, however, at this point of Christ's greatest suffering that Forsyth becomes the most reticent in describing his experiences. He certainly writes less about it than Christ's suffering in his journey to the Cross. One reason he gives for this is because the event of Christ being "made sin" constitutes a realm into which ordinary human experience does not enter. No human being has ever descended to the depths of suffering which Christ experienced on the Cross. Our human language therefore does not contain the categories to describe this experience adequately.[79] Forsyth himself, in his limited attempts to write on this aspect, strains at the limits of the English language to try to convey a broad sense of what he thinks Christ must have gone through.

Forsyth mentions that Christ suffered in being "made sin" on the Cross because it represents the holy one's immersion into all that contradicts him. This is not merely "the quivering of the saint's purity at the touch of evil,"[80] but the assumption of the personality of sin by the absolutely holy Son of God. Through this experience, Christ realised "how real sin was, how radical, how malignant, how deadly to the Holy One's very being."[81] He found himself, at this final stage of his life, not in a heroic struggle with a worthy foe, which would have been easier to bear. Instead, he was enveloped "in the atmosphere of base, revolting sin, of moral atheism, ashiness, mustiness, torpor, dust," one of unimaginable horror for him.[82] The closest human analogy Forsyth could find to this was "the death of an explorer, with broken nerve and evil memories, in the Arctic fog."[83]

Another significant aspect of Christ's suffering in being "made sin" has to do with his relationship to God the Father. We saw, in chapter 2, Forsyth's insistence that God never did at any time punish Christ on the Cross. We also noted, at the same time, Forsyth's affirmation that Christ's

77. *Justification*, 152–53.
78. *Positive Preaching*, 250.
79. *Recent Art*, 186–87.
80. *Work*, 183.
81. *Cruciality*, 102.
82. *Father*, 52–54.
83. Ibid., 51.

suffering on the Cross was penal, in the sense that he took the curse and the judgement of sin. We attempted to reconcile these two assertions by appealing to the different ways the same act can be perceived by different persons, depending on where they stand in relation to it. From sin's perspective, what befell Christ was indeed penal in nature, but from the Father's perspective, it was never intended as punishment for his beloved Son. Our focus shifts here to Christ's perspective. Because Christ was "made sin," in the sense that he became so closely identified with it as to become, for the purposes of judgement, the same entity, and because God did in fact "[identify] Him with sin in treatment . . . and [judge] the sin upon Him,"[84] the Father's penal treatment of sin was experienced as such by Christ in significant ways. It was not penal to his conscience, since he was sinless, and there was no basis upon which he could accuse himself of anything. But it was penal to his consciousness.[85] The Christ who was "made sin" felt the Father's "direct displeasure." The Father's face was veiled to him, and Christ felt forsaken by the one he had obeyed and served all his life. This sense of forsakenness was, to Forsyth's mind, an even worse experience than retributive suffering. If God is present, "my sense of desert may be my sanctification," and there might still be a purpose in what I go through.[86] But if God is absent, all seems lost. Christ, indeed, felt "a broken-hearted and resigned despair" on the Cross, and voiced it by his cry of forsakenness—one addressed to "My God" instead of "My Father."[87] His loneliness extended also to the experience of silence from his beloved disciples, whom at that point in time were unable to understand the nature and extent of his suffering.[88] He was the "Scapegoat," who had to walk the "lonely, dreary, and bitter" path himself, without the comfort which either the Father's presence or human companionship in suffering might bring.[89]

In the midst of such dire descriptions of the experience of Christ on the Cross, Forsyth stresses that, at the most fundamental level, the communion between the Father and the Son remained intact. The Father did withdraw the light of his communion with Christ, but never actually left

---

84. *Work*, 84.
85. "Atonement in Modern Religious Thought," 75.
86. *Work*, 243.
87. *Father*, 52; *Missions*, 30.
88. *Father*, 21.
89. *Recent Art*, 187–88; *Father*, 51.

him.[90] As a consequence, Christ lost "the Father's face," but not the Father.[91] Upon what basis does Forsyth assert this continuity of communion? One idea we find in his writings, although not fully explicated, is the notion that the forsakenness experienced by Christ was an epistemological, rather than an ontological, reality. From the perspective of the one who was "made sin," Christ indeed experienced the horror of the Father's absence. But, in reality, the Father and his love for the Son was always present. For the purposes of overcoming sin, the Father had to say, "I love you, but for the sake of all that is at issue, I may not show it."[92] The Father's still-abiding presence and love was therefore merely veiled from Christ, rather than actually removed. But Forsyth also makes the more profound claim that the Father's turning away of his face was itself an act of grace towards Christ. To comprehend this, we need to recall Forsyth's contention that a process of *plerosis* was taking place in parallel with that of *kenosis* throughout Christ's earthly life. This *plerosis* finds its peak, as the *kenosis* its depth, at the point of the Cross. Hence, the culmination of Christ's growth took place at Calvary, represented by his submission to the Father's will in spite of the fact that he was at the height of his suffering, a significant part of which was caused by his perception of his Father's abandonment. The Father's withdrawing of his face, therefore, was the final essential step in creating the conditions necessary for the perfecting of Christ in the obedience of faith. It was done for the sake of Christ as much as for us, the recipients of God's salvation. Hence, Forsyth could write, "The face was withdrawn, but never the grace . . . This bitter, dismal taste of death, it was God's grace to Christ."[93]

Some of Forsyth's statements allude (again, in inchoate form) to another source of unity between the Father and the Son at the point of dereliction. They put stress on the idea that the Cross ultimately represents a coincidence in the wills of the Father and the Son. The pre-incarnate eternal Son freely consented to empty himself to live under the human mode of being, and subsequently to undergo the Cross. This is as significant a basis for the event at Calvary as the Father's decision to send the Son to die as an atoning sacrifice. The will of one is "as original and spontaneous

---

90. *Work*, 243.
91. *Preaching of Jesus*, 20.
92. *Positive Preaching*, 249.
93. *Father*, 64. See also *Missions*, 28.

as the other," and neither should overshadow the other.[94] Moreover, the will of the incarnate Christ, after a long struggle with temptation, eventually arrived at this same point also.[95] We can therefore say (although Forsyth does not explicitly) that at the end of his process of *plerosis*, the will of the incarnate Christ became one with that of the eternal Son in consenting to the Cross. And both these wills are in line with the Father's. All went towards the "complete fulfilment of their common task."[96] There are definitely hints here of the idea, more fully expounded by Moltmann and the other exponents of (what Fiddes calls) *Kreuzestheologie*, that it is precisely at the point of the Cross, where the greatest differentiation between the Father and the Son occurs, that they are paradoxically most united, since they demonstrate there a commonality of will in mutual loving surrender.[97] Given Forsyth's voluntarism and his consequent stress upon the coincidence of wills as the basis for true unity (as we see, for example, in his description of the final unity between God and humans at the *eschaton*), we see that Forsyth would have readily embraced this idea, although in his writings he might not have made more than a suggestion towards it.

Forsyth, in addition, implies a third aspect in which the Father and the Son were united at the Cross. There was a unity in suffering – both these members of the Trinity suffered as a result what happened to the Son. Christ's perception that he was suffering alone in Godforsakenness did not reflect the reality that the Father was in fact his companion in suffering. We will discuss the nature of the Father's suffering in a later section. We will now make some comments about the relationship Forsyth envisages between Christ's journey to the Cross and his experiences on the Cross itself, and highlight the connection between the suffering of Christ in these two aspects of his life.

---

94. *Person*, 287; "Faith, Metaphysic, and Incarnation," 713.

95. This point about the unity of wills between the Father and the incarnate Christ is also made in McCurdy, *Attributes and Atonement*, 199.

96. *Positive Preaching*, 249.

97. Fiddes, *Creative Suffering of God*, 201–2; Moltmann, *Crucified God*, 243–44 and *Trinity and Kingdom*, 81–82. Unlike the exponents of *Kreuzestheologie*, however, Forsyth does not seem to have envisaged a role for the Holy Spirit as the bond of love between the Father and the Son at their moment of "separation."

atonement be achieved on its strength alone? There are two issues of interest to us here. Firstly, what is Forsyth's motivation in going down this treacherous route? Forsyth hints at the answer when he cites examples of human acts of heroism which are so out of character that they can be dismissed as "one-off" events, what he calls (after the controversial American author) the "Bret Harte type." Such acts are of far less value than those which arise from the context of a developed personality.[107] This assertion is made in pursuit of Forsyth's attempt to shift our understanding of the atonement away from "juridical" to "moral" categories. Applying it to the case of Jesus, Forsyth contends that his sacrifice on the Cross should not be viewed as an act in isolation from the rest of his life. This was precisely what "juridical" theories of the atonement, with their understanding of Christ as a "heavenly functionary," tend to do.[108] The truth, rather, is that "the work could only be done by the native action of a personality moral in its nature and methods, moral to the pitch of the Holy."[109] Christ's confession on the Cross was therefore efficacious because it arose from a person possessing a developed character of holiness, attained through difficult moral struggles throughout his life. Only in this sense did it constitute an adequate answering holiness to that of God's. Forsyth adds, moreover, that only a confession issuing from such a developed moral personality contains the power to realise the "regenerative" aspect of the atonement. Christ could proleptically represent the new penitent humanity on the Cross before God because of the moral victories he won throughout his life. His act has subjective transformative power on humanity because he had subjectively conquered in his own life. So, "every step of the moral victory in His life was a step also in the Redemption of the whole human conscience."[110] This "moral" view of the atonement is, for Forsyth, a far more accurate depiction of what happened at the Cross than those which understand it as a mere juridical transaction. The Cross arises from

107. *Work*, 26.
108. Ibid., 185; *Recent Art*, 260.
109. *Work*, 184.

110. Ibid., 185. In this sense, Forsyth, while criticising the "juridical" models of the atonement, which to his mind includes the penal substitutionary theories developed by Protestant Orthodoxy, actually comes quite close to the Reformed notion that the righteousness that is made ours in justification is that which Christ had acquired as a result of his life of obedience to the Father. There are also echoes here of Irenaeus' doctrine of recapitulation—adding to the variety of views integrated under Forsyth's exposition of the atonement.

a context of moral overcoming and is therefore efficacious in solving "the moral problem of the race," both in the objective and subjective senses.[111]

The second question we have to consider is whether Forsyth's "tuning up" of Jesus' life has, in fact, fatally undermined the centrality of the event of the Cross to his theology. Some of his language, as we have seen, does not aid our attempt to portray him as consistent in this regard. If we make allowance for Forsyth's occasional tendency to engage in hyperbole, however, we do find sufficient resources within his writings to defend his claim that he is able to "tune up" Jesus' life without a corresponding "tuning down" of his death. We recall, for a start, Forsyth's insistence that the satisfactory aspect of the Cross was realised not because Christ suffered in order to "exhaust" the wrathful judgement of God. Rather, the sufferings of Christ were significant as the context in which his confession of God's rightful judgement was made. This confession was satisfying to the Father because it was made with an obedience of faith which persists "amidst conditions of pain, death and judgement."[112] If this is the case, the first thing we can say is that it would indeed be artificial if Christ's other acts of obedience throughout his life, exercised also amidst difficult situations, had no impact upon the Father whatsoever. They must have brought satisfaction to him, though of course to a far lesser degree than Christ's confession on the Cross. Forsyth is therefore being consistent in seeing these acts of obedience as "small Passions" and "deaths manifold," which have expiatory effects in and of themselves. This, however, need not undermine the "cruciality" of the event of the Cross because of Forsyth's insistence that it was that act on Calvary which constitutes the "consummate action" which gives value and meaning to all these other acts of obedience.[113] In response to Robert Mackintosh's query as to why Gethsemane was not adequate as atonement if it was simply a matter of Christ yielding to his Father's will, Forsyth answers that it was only at the Cross that Christ exhibited a perfect intensity of the obedience of faith, one perfectly able to atone:

---

111. *Work*, 185. A. S. Peake's critique of Forsyth (in *Recollections and Appreciations*, 193) that he failed to appreciate the need to see the life and death of Christ as "all of a piece" is therefore misplaced.

112. *Work*, 205–6.

113. *Preaching of Jesus*, 24; *Cruciality*, 101.

> Gethsemane was not wholly adequate because there the nadir was not touched. The real nadir—the hinge of all—was in the dereliction . . . I would say the recognition of God's holiness was not uttermost, was not complete, till the last extremity of suffering experience for a holy soul was reached the sense of forsakenness. The oblation to God was not complete.[114]

All of Jesus' other acts of obedience, because they were not performed at the deepest depths of his *kenosis*, were therefore on their own unable to completely fulfil the satisfactory aspect of the atonement. The chief value of these other acts thus lay in building Jesus up to that crucial confession, and all that is significant about them would have been lost if the Passion had not followed.[115] We arrive at the same conclusion if we look at the issue from the perspectives of the "victorious" and "regenerative" aspects of the Cross. While the sinless Christ wrestled with sin and its effects throughout his life, the culmination of sin and its rage against the holy took place only at Calvary, and hence it was only there that it could be dealt with "as a unity" and killed in one fell swoop. Also, while Jesus' journey to the Cross was significant as an integral component of the process of *plerosis*, if this process had failed to reach its completion at the Cross, it is questionable whether Christ could have represented the "new, penitent humanity" before God and brought about its regenerative effects. All that had gone on before would then have been worthless. Finally, from the perspective of God's self-justification in the second sense, Forsyth writes that Christ's confession of God's goodness and righteousness needs to take place in the deepest agony of his death, so that "the tragedy of the universal conscience" can rise "to be become the theodicy of God."[116] The point seems to be that Christ's confession of God's righteousness must take place while he experiences the epitome of human suffering, otherwise there remains depths of suffering not covered by his confession. Persons who undergo these depths beyond the experience of Christ can then legitimately seek to be exempted from his confession, thus frustrating the completion of theodicy.

We conclude this section by reiterating Forsyth's view that Christ's journey to the Cross and his experiences on the Cross itself form parts of an "indivisible continuity," one which began not in world history, but

---

114. Forsyth's annotations in Mackintosh, "Authority of the Cross," 217.
115. "Christ's Person and His Cross," 18.
116. "Regeneration, Creation, and Miracle," 632.

in the premundane act of the Son's self-emptying. These two aspects of Christ's life are so integrally linked that each without the other would have fatally compromised the efficacy of his atoning work. As Forsyth himself puts it, his project seeks both "to find the Person in the Cross, and the Cross in the Person."[117] Bradley was therefore right in seeing that, for Forsyth, "the Cross represents the highest point in a manifestation of grace which was being worked out and exhibited throughout the lifespan of Jesus." It follows from this that Christ's suffering in these two aspects of his life are also organically connected. His suffering in his journey to the Cross serves primarily as the context of his training in obedience, culminating in his perfectly efficacious confession of obedience on the Cross in the midst of his greatest suffering.

THE SUFFERING OF THE FATHER

Forsyth postulates that the event of the Cross brings satisfaction to God the Father. He also asserts, somewhat paradoxically, that this same event leads to immense suffering for the same member of the Godhead. There is, Forsyth confidently states, a "true patripassianism."[118] In saying this, Forsyth might have been less careful with his language than someone like Moltmann, who explicitly dissociates his idea of the suffering Father from the term "patripassianism" because of the latter's association with the heresy of modalism.[119] But moving beyond the use of terminology, we see a fundamental similarity in the positions of these two theologians. In a manner anticipating the German thinker, Forsyth carefully avoids crashing on the rocks of the ancient heresy by postulating that the Father suffers in a different manner from that of the Son: "The Father did not suffer as the Son (that were too Sabellian), but He suffered with the Son."[120]

What then was the nature of the Father's suffering "with the Son"? Forsyth does not write very much about this. He does insist, however, in opposition to the liberal tendency to over-emphasise the loving father-

---

117. "Christ's Person and His Cross," 3.

118. *Revelation*, 90. In what follows, Forsyth could have been inspired by the writings of A. M. Fairbairn on the subject of the Father's suffering on the Cross (see the latter's *Place of Christ in Modern Theology*, 484–85). There are certainly key similarities between the assertions of Fairbairn and Forsyth in this matter.

119. Moltmann, *Crucified God*, 243. See Sarot, "Patripassianism, Theopaschitism, and the Suffering of God," 369–70 for a good summary of the nature of this heresy.

120. *Missions*, 29.

hood of God to human creatures, that the first member of the Trinity is Father most and foremost to his Son Jesus Christ, and then only derivatively to us. As he writes, "He is father of pity to human weakness, still more father of grace to human sin, but chiefly father of holy joy to our Lord Jesus Christ. The New Testament name and idea of God is not simply 'Our Father,' but 'the God and Father of our Lord and Saviour Jesus Christ.'"[121] This most intimate of relationships between the Father and the Son is the basis for the Father's suffering at Calvary. Forsyth's idea here seems to be that the Father suffered when he judged sin upon Christ because it involved the turning away of his face from Christ. We suggested earlier that this turning away of the Father was itself, at the root of it, an act of grace towards his Son. Nevertheless, it still caused the Father pain because it involved a conscious decision on his part to subject his beloved Son to the immense anguish of the experience of God-forsakenness. He had, in fact, to restrain himself from intervening to end this suffering by allowing Christ to be rescued from the Cross.[122] So, "when God spared not his own Son, and yielded not even to the prayer of Gethsemane, it was a piece of Himself that he forswore, and in the grief of Christ he cut off his own right hand for the sake of the Kingdom of His holiness."[123] One interesting issue Forsyth does not seem to have addressed is whether the suffering of the Father is restricted to Calvary and the immediate events leading up to it, or whether it extends throughout Jesus' entire life. Our suggestion is that, given Forsyth's view of how Jesus' suffering on his journey to the Cross can be characterised as "small Passions" and "deaths manifold," it should follow that the Father suffered "with the Son" throughout this journey as well. Whatever the case might be, Forsyth is quite certain that the Father's suffering exceeds that of the Son: "And the Father suffered in His Son even more than the Son did."[124] Forsyth also asserts that the Father's suffering far surpasses that experienced by the world in the entire history of its "crucial evolution" towards its appointed *telos*. So he imagines God asking the world "Do you stumble at the cost?" And God's answer is: "It has cost Me more than you . . . it has cost Me more than if the price paid were all

121. *Father*, 3.

122. Forsyth suggests that the Father was so inclined to spare Christ the suffering on the Cross that he would have taken Christ down from the Cross if the latter had asked for it then: Ibid., 65.

123. *Person*, 273.

124. *Justification*, 174. See also *Society*, 29–30; *Ethic*, 170.

Mankind. For it cost Me My only and beloved Son to justify My name of righteousness, and to realise the destiny of My creature in holy love."[125]

Forsyth lets us know that one significant reason why he postulates the suffering of the Father is, again, to undermine the "juridical" models of the atonement prevalent in his day. He disputes the depictions of the Cross as a sacrifice offered by Christ to a passive, receiving Father in order to assuage his wrath.[126] The correct picture, rather, is that "Father and Spirit were not spectators only of the Son's agony, nor only recipients of His sacrifice. They were involved in it."[127] So, to reiterate Forsyth's key phrase, "the atonement did not procure grace, it flowed from grace,"[128] and it was grace more costly to the Father than even the Son.

CONCLUSION

We have seen, in this chapter, that the second outcome of God's self-justification, for Forsyth, is that it reveals the suffering undergone by both the first and second members of the Trinity in their securing of the atonement. The Son suffers in his journey to the Cross and on the Cross itself. Forsyth sees his suffering on the Cross reaching a depth to which no human suffering has or ever will sink. The Father, on his part, undergoes even greater suffering in that act of turning his face away from his beloved Son at the point of his greatest agony. Forsyth is also insistent that the Father's suffering far exceeds even the sum of human suffering experienced in the history of our world. This notion of the incomparable suffering of God certainly has major implications for Forsyth's theodicy. We will explore these in the next chapter.

---

125. *Justification*, 169. The reference to "cost" here refers, in its context, to cost in terms of suffering.

126. "Atonement in Modern Religious Thought," 54–55.

127. *Missions*, 29. In addition to the suffering of the Father, Forsyth speaks in this passage about the Spirit experiencing grief at the Cross and being involved in the Son's agony. But he does not elaborate upon these ideas.

128. *Cruciality*, 40.

6

The Significance of the Second Outcome of God's Self-Justification

God as the Chief Sufferer and Giver and Christ as Our Model of Faith

INTRODUCTION

WE WILL, IN THIS chapter, consider the significance of the second major outcome of God's self-justification for Forsyth's theodicy. Several different aspects of Forsyth's thought have been covered in the previous chapter, most notably his Christology and his version of divine passibility. We focus here on their implications for his justification of God. The chief question we will be asking is, therefore, one put forward by Mozley (but to be read in the context of theodicy): "If God suffers . . . what exactly is secured by it?"[1] Our task, as in Chapter 4 when we last undertook a similar exercise, is not made easy by the fact that Forsyth did not systematically lay down the implications of his thoughts on God's incomparable suffering for his theodicy. We only have broad references to two areas in which these thoughts might be significant for his justification of God. We will begin with what Forsyth provides, and then attempt to supplement what he has to offer in a way which (we hope) bolsters his theodicy without detracting from the main thrust of his approach.

---

1. Mozley, *Impassibility of God*, 181.

GOD AS THE CHIEF SUFFERER AND GIVER

The Notion that God Paid the Greatest Price to Secure the Atonement

In our earlier discussion of the notion of God's secondary judgement, we mentioned that Forsyth saw the aim of such judgement in establishing in actuality God's holiness in the world as taking precedence over the extent of any creaturely suffering and death which might be needed in order to secure such holiness. We followed this up with a comment that this overtly harsh assertion should be read in the light of Forsyth's insistence that because God has graciously chosen, on the Cross, to establish his holiness in a manner which redeems us, we have the confidence that all secondary judgement is gracious and redemptive in nature. Another crucial supplement to this assertion stems from the contents of our previous chapter. While God makes very extensive demands upon his human creatures in his campaign to reassert his holiness in the face of sin's opposition, Forsyth's postulation of God's suffering tells us that this God does not sit above the fray of battle, directing his "troops" from behind to suffer and die for his cause. Instead, this God leads from the front, bearing the brunt of the fight against sin and undergoing the greatest of all suffering for the sake of the cause.[2] So God does not ask us to go where he has not already gone. We see this point clearly made in passages like the following:

> [God's] holiness takes its own consequences in an evil world. He does His own suffering and saving. He is a jealous God. None but himself shall redeem us for Himself. He is a monopolist of sacrifice. He does not part with the agony and glory of the Cross to any creature. None shall outdo Him in sacrifice.[3]

Forsyth's conclusion is that, after tallying the sums, God "took on Himself there [on the Cross] more than He ever inflicts."[4]

This image of God as one who will never be outdone in sacrifice and suffering sits well with what Forsyth sees when he attempts to peek into the Godhead via his *theologia crucis*. He sees there a God whose "Divinest

---

2. Forsyth's depiction of God therefore goes even further than Marilyn McCord Adams' analogy of "the commander who gets down in the trenches to take the fire with his soldiers" (*Horrendous Evils*, 170). Forsyth could have been inspired here by the depictions of God as the chief sufferer by both A. B. Bruce (in *Providential Order of the World*, 369) and James Baldwin Brown (see Forsyth, *Baldwin Brown*, 16–17).

3. *Revelation*, 11.

4. *Justification*, 32.

The Significance of the Second Outcome of God's Self-Justification 155

power is the power to resign, to sacrifice, to descend, to obey, to save." The forms of Christianity which view this God as "a Being whose first and Divinest work was to *receive* sacrifice instead of offering it" have therefore fallen into the most perverted of errors, having embraced such a pagan notion uncritically.[5] True Christian faith, on the contrary, tells us that:

> It is not [God's] prerogative to receive sacrifices greater than any He makes... It is no Christian God who sits steamed by the incense of heroic woe or filled with an aesthetic delight in the tragedy of men. The God of Jesus Christ is more of a giver than a receiver. When He gave His Son He gave more, and at more cost, than any but the Son could repay. His blessedness is not to be self-contained, and in Himself enough, but it is to seek and to save. It is more Godlike to give than to receive even life.[6]

Forsyth recognises that this claim of God as the chief giver and sufferer is hard to accept in times of great human suffering, like that brought about by the Great War. He knows that it sounds, frankly, like an occasion of "pulpit extravagance."[7] He insists, however, on pressing home this claim because of the implications he seeks to draw from it for his theodicy, which we will now consider.

Two Implications of this Notion

We see Forsyth alluding to three implications for his theodicy from his assertion that God gave the most in securing the atonement. Because the first two are relatively straightforward, we will deal with them together in this section. The first is the argument that, because God is the chief sufferer and giver, he is justified in using any means of secondary judgement, however costly they might be, for the purpose of "completing" his work on the Cross. Forsyth maintains that "if God spared not His Son He can bear to see, and rise to use, the most dreadful things that civilisation can produce" for his secondary judgement.[8] The idea here seems to be that God, having led from the front in the battle against sin and borne the brunt of the encounter, gains the moral authority to call us to follow him in our lesser sufferings so that his victory might be

---

5. *Father*, 43.
6. Ibid., 64.
7. "Reality of God," 615.
8. *Justification*, 180.

actualised in our world. It is interesting to note that Forsyth's assertions here go directly against the conclusions reached by many other proponents of a suffering God. Fiddes is representative of this other position when he states firmly that:

> The conviction that God suffers will forbid the structuring of any theological argument where God directly causes suffering . . . If God suffers then he too is a victim and not a torturer, not even a disciplinarian using suffering for reasons "which he knows best but which are hidden from us," as popular piety often suggests . . . Belief that God suffers forbids the thought altogether that God sends suffering, though he may allow it.[9]

Forsyth would reject the stark dichotomy Fiddes presents—either God sends suffering, or that he suffers. He would affirm both notions with equal force, and claim that the latter justifies the former in a powerful sense.

A second implication Forsyth draws is that the notion of God as the chief giver and sufferer justifies God in expecting the trust of the world that he will finally make all things well. The suffering God, on this argument, gives us a firm basis for our faith in God's goodness and power in the midst of all the convulsions of the world which tell us otherwise. (Such faith, as we have seen previously, is the key to appropriating the teleological and historical aspects of Forsyth's theodicy.) There are several sub-facets to this argument. The first is that, since God has paid such an immense cost to secure this world's salvation, we gain the assurance that he will complete this salvation, and not leave things hanging.[10] Another related idea is that, because God has undergone the greatest of tragedies and triumphed, there is nothing that has or will happen in our history that is able to frustrate God's plan to move our world towards a blessed *eschaton*. So, "if the kingdom of God not only got over the murder of Christ, but made it its great lever, there is nothing that it cannot get over, and nothing it cannot turn to eternal blessing and to the glory of the holy name."[11] Finally, the notion of God as the chief giver furnishes us with the confidence that God will not withhold any good thing from us:

---

9. Fiddes, *Creative Suffering*, 32. See Bauckham, "'Only the Suffering God Can Help,'" 11–12; and Sölle, *Suffering*, 119 for further versions of this dichotomy.

10. We see this alluded to in *Justification*, 99–100.

11. *Soul of Prayer*, 36. See also *Justification*, 99–100, 127–28, 155.

"He so spared not His Son as with Him to give us all things."[12] Forsyth's comments here go some way towards challenging the perception among some who contest the notion of divine passibility that the acceptance of the idea of a suffering God invariably leads to a corresponding affirmation of his weakness and inability to wholly eradicate evil.[13] The opposite is, in fact, true for Forsyth. It is precisely because of God's suffering and subsequent triumph in the atonement that we gain the assurance that God can and will eliminate all evil. Forsyth's position, therefore, seems to meet Fiddes' requirement that the doctrine of divine passibility must allow us to affirm "a God who can be the greatest sufferer of all and yet still be God."[14]

The Third Implication: God's Identification with our Suffering

The third implication Forsyth draws for his theodicy from his notion of God as the chief sufferer and giver is the idea that, since God has endured the height of suffering at the Cross, he is able to identify with the whole history of human suffering in its "crucial evolution" towards the *eschaton*. To understand this claim more fully, we need to examine again Forsyth's notion of divine passibility. Some of the literature on this subject, in Forsyth's day, envisage a general suffering of God in his relationship with creation throughout world history, one revealed or illustrated by the life and ministry of the incarnate Christ, especially his death on Calvary. As early as 1866, Horace Bushnell puts forth this idea in his oft-quoted words: "It is as if there were a cross unseen, standing on its undiscovered hill, far back in the ages, out of which were sounding always, just the same deep voice of suffering love and patience, that was heard by mortal ears from the sacred hill of Calvary."[15] C. A. Dinsmore was another who took this path, expressing it in equally poetic language: "There was a cross in the heart of God before there was one planted on the green hill outside of Jerusalem. And now that the cross of wood has been taken down, the one in the heart of God abides, and it will remain so long as there is one

---

12. *Justification*, 125.

13. See, e.g., Weinandy, *Does God Suffer?* 157, 214; and Goetz, "Suffering God," 388. These authors seem to assume that all theologies which affirm divine passibility invariably adhere to the tenets of process theology and its affirmation of a God who is unable to finally eliminate evil.

14. Fiddes, *Creative Suffering*, 2.

15. Bushnell, *Vicarious Sacrifice*, 23, quoted in Mozley, *Impassibility of God*, 143.

sinful soul for whom to suffer."[16] As Bauckham points out, even those who were hesitant to assert Christ's divinity could affirm a similar idea. H. R. Rashdall, in his Bampton Lectures of 1915 (subsequently published as *The Idea of the Atonement in Christian Theology*), argues that we have no greater revelation of the "suffering with humanity" which the God of love constantly experiences than the Christ who voluntarily underwent suffering and death out of love for his brothers.[17]

We find little in Forsyth's writings indicating that he is open to such a position. Indeed, his regular diatribes against a solely exemplary view of the Cross[18] must surely repel him from such a conclusion. It is true that Forsyth makes reference occasionally to the notion of an "eternal cross" within God, one that formed the basis for the historic event at Calvary. So, for example, he writes, "The Cross came first from the Father, in whom it is eternal. It is no temporary expedient, no historic accident."[19] Or, "the cross was in God before sin was in man, and it will be our central and vital principle still when sin has been clean destroyed."[20] And drawing inspiration from the portrayal in the Book of Revelation of the slain lamb, Forsyth asserts that Christ's "sacrifice began before He came into the world, and his cross was that of a lamb slain before the world's foundation. There was a Calvary above all which was the mother of it all."[21] Our contention, however, is that passages such as these do not lead Forsyth to the position that there exists a general mode of suffering embedded within the Godhead, one illustrated or revealed through the historic suffering of God at Calvary. This is because, when we read these passages in their context, we find that Forsyth's use of the *theologia crucis* leads him to trace, *not suffering, but the capacity for obedience, self-limitation and sacrifice*, from the historic Cross back into God's nature. So, Forsyth explains:

---

16. Dinsmore, *Atonement in Literature and Life*, 229–33, quoted in Mozley, *Impassibility of God*, 148.

17. Rashdall, *Idea of the Atonement in Christian Theology*, 435; Bauckham, "Suffering God," 11. Bauckham names Frances Young as a contemporary theologian who holds a similar position to that of Rashdall (see Young, "Cloud of Witnesses," 36–37). These thinkers are able to see the life of Jesus as revelatory of the person of God in spite of their "low" Christology.

18. E.g., *Work*, 100–102; *Preaching of Jesus*, 111–12.

19. *Missions*, 28.

20. *Pulpit and the Age*, 8–9.

21. *Person*, 271.

> The one thing which it is the business of Revelation to let us know about the depths of eternal Godhead is this, that its Divinest power is the power to resign, to sacrifice, to descend, to obey, to save. The key to the prehistoric Godhead is the historic Jesus, and His historic obedience, even to the historic cross.[22]

We might also, in support of our view, point to our earlier assertion of (to use Bradley's phrase again) "the indivisible continuity of Christ's work," beginning from the premundane decision of the Son to empty himself up to his suffering and death on the Cross. We saw there that Forsyth envisages the basis of this continuity to lie not in the idea of suffering, but in that of submission to the Father's will. We would add that we find no suggestion in Forsyth that the Father or the Son underwent any suffering in the latter's premundane act of self-emptying. The suffering began, so to speak, when the Son assumed the human mode of existence, and is solely the result of this mode of existence, in which the Son needed to "learn obedience by the things he suffered." Self-limitation in itself, therefore, does not bring pain. It is the manifestation of such self-limitation in the human mode of existence that led to the suffering of both the Father and the Son. As for the passage referring to the "eternal" Cross within the Father, it refers quite clearly to the Father's premundane willingness to sacrifice his Son for the redemption of the world—his own eternal *kenosis*, so to speak. The emphasis is again not on any notion of eternal suffering. We reiterate, moreover, that, for Forsyth, the forsakenness which Jesus experienced at the Cross was more an epistemological than an ontological reality. There is therefore nothing here which parallels the notion, advanced by Moltmann, of a rupture on the Cross in the relations between the members of the Trinity, one which goes into the very heart of the Godhead and which constitutes the being of God as suffering love.[23]

---

22. *Father*, 43.

23. Moltmann, *Crucified God*, 244 and *Trinity and the Kingdom*, 81. We should also point out, in fairness, that Forsyth's insistence on the idea of God's immutability (as seen earlier) does not sit well with his refusal to embrace the presence of an "eternal" suffering within God. If the Father did in fact suffer at the Cross, and did so while subsisting in the divine mode of existence, it is difficult to see how Forsyth can hold on to his relatively traditional understanding of immutability while postulating a unique event of God's suffering in the life and ministry of Jesus. We suggest that it would be more consistent on Forsyth's part to admit that any assertion of God's immutability must be qualified by the Cross. Forsyth might, in fact, be acknowledging such a qualification when he makes statements like "The Cross meant more change in God than in man" (*Justification*, 32).

We can therefore conclude that the references in Forsyth to the idea of the "eternal cross" are chiefly intended to point to how the obedience, self-limitation and sacrifice one sees on the part of God on the Cross are all attributable to his eternal nature. These, rather than suffering, are the very essence of who God is.[24]

This being the case, how does Forsyth envisage the relationship between God's suffering in the event of the Cross[25] and our suffering in the course of the world's "crucial evolution"? We formulate our answer by first looking at Bauckham's careful analysis of the various senses in which God can be said to identify with our suffering. Among these senses, Bauckham suggests two which are of particular relevance to Forsyth's theodicy. He writes:

> The kinds of suffering which are involved in human personal relations include compassion, in which the lover suffers sympathetically with the beloved who is suffering, and it is the divine sympathy which comes to the fore especially in discussions which focus on the problem of human suffering. A stronger form of sympathy is active solidarity with the suffering person, where the lover actually shares the situation from which the beloved is suffering. The cross has often been understood along these lines.[26]

We may, for ease of reference, call these two forms of identification "empathy" and "solidarity."[27] Now Forsyth, in some parts of his writings, clearly sees an *empathy* which God feels towards humanity and the suffering we experience in the course of our "crucial evolution" towards his goal. So, for example:

---

24. Forsyth might have played a part in influencing J. K. Mozley to also reject the notion of an "eternal cross" within God in terms of an eternal suffering revealed on Calvary. Mozley's position on this is well-summarised in Smoot, "Does God Suffer?" 253–56. It is surprising, however, that Mozley does not mention Forsyth in his magisterial survey *The Impassibility of God*.

25. In the light of our discussion in the previous chapter, whenever a reference is made here to God suffering at the event of the Cross, it should be understood as including all the suffering experienced in Jesus' journey to this Cross, since both the journey and its destination are, for Forsyth, inseparable from each other.

26. Bauckham, "Suffering God," 10. Bauckham mentions, in addition, the "suffering of rejected love, and the pain involved in forgiveness and reconciliation."

27. Bauckham uses the term "sympathy" instead of "empathy" in the above quotation, but he uses "empathy" elsewhere to convey the same meaning (*Theology of Jürgen Moltmann*, 67).

The Significance of the Second Outcome of God's Self-Justification 161

> There is an Eye, a Mind, a Heart, before Whom the whole bloody and tortured stream of evolutionary growth has flowed. We are horrified, beyond word or conception, by the agony and devilry of war, but, after all, it only discharges upon us, as it were from a nozzle, a far raster accumulation of such things, permeating the total career of history since ever a sensitive organism and a heartless egoism appeared. This misery of the ages, I have said, vanishes from human thought or feeling, till some experience like war carries some idea of it home. But there is a consciousness to which it is all and always present. And in the full view of it He has spoken. As it might be thus: Do you stumble at the cost? It has cost Me more than you—Me who see and feel it all more than you who feel it but as atoms might. "Groanings all and moanings, none of it I lose."[28]

The passage speaks of God being conscious of "the whole bloody and tortured stream of evolutionary growth" and of his seeing and feeling creaturely suffering more acutely than those who actually undergo it. This is radical empathy with creaturely suffering. The question arises, however, regarding the basis upon which such empathy rests. We could try to base it upon an abstract notion of God's omniscience—because God is all-knowing, he understands fully our experiences and is therefore able to empathise with us. This, however, runs into Marilyn McCord Adams's powerful objection that "the Divine mind is at once too vast and too stable to experience our participation in horrors in anything like the way we do."[29] Forsyth, on his part, founds God's empathy upon a particular event in world history. This he makes clear in the passage immediately following the previous. God does not lose any of the "groanings and moanings" of his creatures because:

> Yea, it has cost Me more than if the price paid were all Mankind. For it cost Me My only and beloved Son to justify My name of righteousness, and to realise the destiny of My creature in holy love. And all mankind is not so great and dear as He. Nor is its suffering the enormity in a moral world that His Cross is. I am no spectator of the course of things, and no speculator on the result.

---

28. *Justification*, 169. See *Justification*, 99–100 for another passage which might allude to such empathy.

29. Adams, *Horrendous Evils*, 174. See also Henry Simoni's elaboration on the "problem of radical particularity" which arises when we assert that God suffers in exactly the same way we do (apart from the incarnation) ("Divine Passibility and the Problem of Radical Particularity," 331–37).

I spared not My own Son. We carried the load that crushed you. It bowed Him into the ground.[30]

From the tenor of the passage, it is the event of incomparable suffering at the Cross which attunes God's consciousness and sensitivity to all human suffering throughout world history. Forsyth's point is therefore that God is able to empathise with all human suffering because he has, in the event of the Cross, experienced the height of suffering.

We suggest that Forsyth's position can be bolstered if he had more expressly appropriated the other manner of God's identification with creaturely suffering, i.e., *solidarity*, where (in Bauckham's phrase) "the lover actually shares the situation from which the beloved is suffering." Forsyth's description of the life and death of the incarnate Christ surely points to the utterly human nature of God's suffering there. In his journey to the Cross, the Son underwent a struggle which was entirely human in nature. He had to learn obedience through the things he suffered, give up his life that he might find it, and undergo various other painful experiences arising from the human mode of existence he had assumed. Even on the Cross, where he was "made sin" and lost the Father's face, it is possible to argue that Christ's experience of these conditions stemmed entirely from his human mode of existence, and were therefore essentially human in nature. We did mention that the experiences the suffering Christ went through when he was "made sin" were those which no other human being could understand or describe fully. But this, we suggest, is because our involvement in sin disqualifies us from comprehending what it would mean for the perfectly holy to be immersed into that which contradicts him. It is not our humanity, but our sinfulness, which render Christ's experience here unique. We find support for this view in one of the points Forsyth offers in defence of Christ's true humanity in the face of his insistence on the *non posse peccare*: "What is truly human is not sin. Sin is no factor of the true humanity, but only a feature of empirical humanity which is absolutely fatal to the true."[31] Christ could therefore have undergone his "immersion" into sin entirely in his capacity as a true human, one totally holy because completely free from sin. This is, in fact, the only interpretation of this experience consistent with Forsyth's Christology, since while on the Cross the *kenosis* was still ongoing (in

---

30. *Justification*, 169.
31. *Person*, 302.

fact it reaches its nadir there), and the Son must have undergone all his experiences on Calvary in the human, rather than the divine, mode of existence. The same line of reasoning could be used to assert the Son's entirely human experience of losing the Father's face. In fact, if we are right in seeing this particular experience as essentially epistemological rather than ontological in nature, the Son's perception here shows itself to be fully human as it effectively misinterprets the deeper reality of the Father's abiding presence due to the finite conditions of comprehension he was then under. We see, therefore, adequate resources in Forsyth's writings to enable him to successfully evade the trap which Bauckham warns that a doctrine of divine passibility could easily fall into. This is to subscribe to a subtle form of docetism by viewing Jesus' suffering as "the kind of suffering which we suppose to be attributable to God," and therefore compromising its fully human character. The doctrine of the incarnation, as Bauckham reminds us, dictates that God's suffering in Christ must be utterly human and distinguished clearly from all other instances of divine suffering, including the suffering of the Father at the Cross.[32]

Forsyth could have, we think, relied more upon such assertions of the utterly human nature of the Son's suffering to reinforce his assertions of God's empathy with human suffering. He could have been more explicit in founding such *empathy* upon the total *solidarity* which God experienced with human suffering once and for all on the Cross. As it is, he tends to locate such empathy in the divine suffering of the Father at Calvary.[33] This is a far weaker basis because the type of experience underwent by the Father was not strictly the same as that undergone by the world. We should, however, still credit Forsyth with the basic insight that all of God's empathy with the world's suffering must be founded upon the event of the Cross. It is constitutive, rather than illustrative, of God's suffering. Such an exclusive focus on the Cross has, perhaps quite expectedly, drawn criticism. Fiddes, for example, insists that "we must speak of a God who suffers universally, since a God who suffered only in the particular historical context of Jesus of Nazareth would seem to have a restricted range of empathy, at least in

---

32. Bauckham, *Theology of Jürgen Moltmann*, 64, 66. Weinandy makes the same point about the incarnation mandating the utterly human nature of Jesus' suffering, although he would deny that this suffering touches the divinity of the Son (*Does God Suffer?*, 199–206).

33. E.g., in *Justification*, 169–70.

the view of the contemporary sufferer."[34] We might respond by querying the nature of the relationship between this alleged universal suffering of God and God's suffering in Christ. Fiddes' likely reply would be that God suffers in the same way in both instances, i.e., via empathetic suffering (although with vastly different intensities).[35] The problem with this assertion, in our view, is that once we deny that the suffering of God in Christ is totally unique in the sense that it was utterly human suffering, we lose the only firm basis for claiming that God truly empathises with our suffering. The true foundation for empathy, in other words, is not ever-widening or deepening attempts at empathy, but complete solidarity. It is certainly true that God in Christ, because he was confined by time and space and existed in a particular context, has not experienced every conceivable kind of human suffering. We would, however, echo Forsyth in saying that Christ, in being "made sin" and experiencing the Father's abandonment, underwent the epitome of all human suffering. Because he has plunged to the depths of this experience, it is possible to envisage him being able to empathise with all other incidents of human suffering.[36]

In saying this, we do not deny the likelihood that the empathy of God which we see flowing from his solidarity with human suffering on the Cross might in its turn lead to new experiences of suffering for God. There are, as far as we can tell, various degrees of empathy. If the relationship in question is a detached one, like that involving a doctor and his patient, the former might be able to "empathise" with the pains of the latter without this leading to any significant suffering on his part. On the other hand, in the setting of a much more intimate relationship, e.g., that between a parent and his child or between spouses, it is quite difficult to

---

34. Fiddes, *Creative Suffering*, 32. Fiddes is not specifically contesting Forsyth's position here.

35. Ibid., 8–10, 168, 260. Here we concur here with Bauckham's interpretation of Fiddes' view of the relationship between God's universal suffering and his suffering in Christ (Bauckham, *Theology of Jürgen Moltmann*, 57). Fiddes, in his later work *Participating in God*, 185–86, refines his position to say that there is a sense in which God suffers *as* humans do. This form of suffering is experienced by God in the "movement of sonship" within the Trinity. But the Cross is still not constitutive of this form of suffering for God. It merely deepens the experience of such suffering on God's part. The fundamental way in which God identifies with our suffering is still sympathy.

36. This also goes further than Adams' suggestion that one way for Christ's suffering to have emphatic value for all the world's suffering is to postulate that he, "in His human nature, participates in a representative sample of horrors sufficient to guarantee His appreciation of the depth of their ruinous potential" (*Horrendous Evils*, 174).

envisage genuine empathy without considerable suffering on the part of the one who understands what his loved one is going through. It is clear that the Biblical metaphors of God's relationship to his covenant people, both in the Old and New Testaments, belong more to the latter category. Even God's relationship with the world as a whole invokes the language of profound sacrificial love (e.g., John 3:16). It is therefore likely that God's empathy with the suffering of the world in its "crucial evolution" towards the *telos* results in fresh suffering on his part. Forsyth himself seems to accept this in the passage from *The Justification of God* we quoted above, which speaks of God seeing and *feeling* all that his creatures go through. In another part of the same work, Forsyth speaks of the War being "a greater cross to God than to us" and that "it is but a part of the tragic and bloody course of history whose sword has pierced through His own heart also."[37] Hence Forsyth himself is likely to have asserted an empathic co-suffering of God with his creatures throughout world history. The key point of difference between his position and that of Fiddes, Bushnell and the others we have cited is his insistence (partly reconstructed by us) that such empathic co-suffering must arise from and be founded upon Christ's utterly human suffering on the Cross. The Cross therefore functions not merely as the illustration, revelation, or even climax, but the effective source and ground of all God's suffering.[38]

We move now to consider the more general question of how God's identification with human suffering (in terms of both solidarity and empathy) is relevant for theodicy. The effect of such identification is not easily describable, but most of us would certainly derive a sense of psychological comfort from the idea that God understands our situations of pain in a very intimate fashion. We can do no better here than quote Fiddes:

> At the most basic level it is a consolation to those who suffer to know that God suffers too, and understands their situation from within. The psychological effect upon a sufferer of being aware of a suffering God who understands his predicament may be below the

---

37. *Justification*, 99–100.

38. The issue of how God can then empathise with human suffering prior in time to the event at Calvary can, we suggest, be resolved according to the idea we proposed earlier—which is to see the Cross both as an event in time and eternity, with repercussions throughout the entire length of world history.

level of theological argument, but it may in the end soar on wings far higher than any formal theodicy can.[39]

We also refer to Moltmann's suggestion that God's identification with our suffering (especially in terms of his solidarity) overcomes the "suffering in suffering"—the sense of Godforsakenness all those in agony invariably feel.[40] In fact, Forsyth's picture of Christ on the Cross as one who undergoes the experience of total abandonment by both God and human beings makes him a perfect companion for others who feel likewise. The thrust of explanations such as these is that God's identification with our suffering has the capability to alleviate this very suffering by depicting a God who is with us in our suffering and understands what we go through. Forsyth alludes to these ideas when he writes simply, "He can bear his sorrow easily who sees his God sorrow with him."[41]

One possible additional significance the idea of God's identification with our suffering holds for Forsyth is the assurance this gives that God carries out his acts of secondary judgement with an understanding of what we humans have to undergo as a result of them. If God is a God of mercy, this must impact his decisions as to what type of judgement to inflict and for how long, although (as we have seen) Forsyth would disagree with the idea that God, as the chief sufferer and giver, is in principle morally constrained by the extent of human suffering his judgements might bring. Perhaps more profoundly, Forsyth's openness to the idea of God's empathic co-suffering with his creatures means that God adds to his suffering whenever he ordains secondary judgement. The closest human analogy to this might be that of a parent disciplining his child—it might not be too facetious to attribute to God's experience the well-used phrase that "this will hurt me more than it hurts you." Acts of secondary judgement, therefore, not only incur a cost, in terms of suffering, for their human recipients. They bring pain to God as well—greater, in fact, than that we bear. This should bolster our faith that God would only carry out such acts if they are necessary and appropriate to the situation in question. It might also comfort the sufferer (especially the "innocent") to know that God bears the cost of these acts with us, even though he was not responsible for the sins which led up to them.

39. Fiddes, *Creative Suffering*, 32.
40. Bauckham, *Theology of Jürgen Moltmann*, 12–23.
41. "Strength of Weakness," 87.

Finally, we should also note, as some have pointed out, that an *exclusive* emphasis on God's identification with our suffering can be counterproductive for the exercise of theodicy. Thomas Weinandy's warning is salutary:

> Many contemporary theologians, who posit suffering within God's divine nature, give the impression that once they have demonstrated this, they have done all that is required and significant. The soteriological import of divine suffering remains barren. It does not achieve any end other than to register that God does indeed suffer in solidarity with humankind, and so comfort can be taken from this. Why we should be comforted by a suffering God remains unclear, especially if he, like us, can now do little to alleviate it and is rendered helpless in vanquishing its actual causes.[42]

Richard Harries gives an analogy which drives home the point:

> We would not think much of a surgeon who undertook an operation without any thought about whether the outcome was likely to be successful and who then in the middle of the operation cut himself open as an act of solidarity with the patient. No more is it possible to trust a God whose sole quality is sharing our suffering.[43]

For the idea of God's identification with our suffering to be serviceable for theodicy, therefore, it must be accompanied by the assertion that such identification is the basis for the eventual abolition of sin and suffering. This we happily find in Forsyth. For him, God identifies with our suffering, in terms of both solidarity and empathy, not chiefly for its own sake. It serves rather the end of the defeat of sin, the establishment of God's holiness in actuality and the moving of the world towards a blessed *eschaton* where suffering will be abolished.

CHRIST AS OUR MODEL OF FAITH

Faith as the Means by which Christ Conquered

We move on now to explore the second major significance the revelation of the incomparable suffering of God has for Forsyth's theodicy. We have explored Forsyth's assertion of the incarnate Christ's full humanity, and

---

42. Weinandy, *Does God Suffer?* 214.

43. Harries, "Ivan Karamazov's Argument," 110. This comment was made in the context of his critique of Sölle's position as set out in her book *Suffering*.

the utterly human nature of his experiences, including suffering. Forsyth goes on to say that the way in which this Christ triumphed over his suffering and completed his redemptive work was via an utterly human means as well:

> He [Christ on the Cross] parted with what men call "soul," or fine insight, and took the state of the commonest, dreariest man or woman who has been robbed of everything—fortune, faculty, and feeling—except faith . . . And He survived this world of death, and He conquered for every man by nothing imaginative, but by the quenchless power and vitality of the one thing left Him—of His faith in God.[44]

In chapter 3, we had described Forsyth's understanding of "faith" as an exercise of trust in a personal God. Forsyth often contrasts such faith with "sight," in which we act because we know all the reasons why. This was precisely the type of faith Christ demonstrated on the Cross when he was "made sin." There, Forsyth postulates, everything that could have provided "sight" to Jesus was taken away. His hopes for the Kingdom of God to come through "its one organ on earth," ethnic Israel, were dashed.[45] He was deserted by all he considered his brothers.[46] He was not given there the opportunity to enter into a conscious heroic struggle with a majestic foe, but was instead, as we saw, helplessly immersed into the "Arctic fog" of sin's suffocating atmosphere.[47] Even his experience of the Father was taken away, as the Father hid his face.[48] This utterly bleak situation was, however, the perfect opportunity for faith, and the faith of Christ seized and clung on to it. He exercised there a "fixed obedience of His will" which endured no matter what the circumstances were. In doing so, he achieved "a Protestant salvation—by faith alone."[49] Consistent with Forsyth's assertion that faith is a "life act" rather than a one-off decision of committal, he traces this demonstration of the epitome of faith on the Cross to the "moral habit" of obedience Jesus had cultivated throughout his life.[50]

---

44. *Father*, 58.
45. "Faith of Jesus," 9.
46. *Father*, 64–65.
47. Ibid., 51, 55.
48. "Faith of Jesus," 9.
49. *Father*, 55, 65.
50. Ibid., 55.

Christ's Faith as a Model for Us

We stated at the close of chapter 4 that Forsyth sees faith as that which enables us to appropriate both the teleological and historical aspects of his theodicy. Throughout his writings, Forsyth cites the faith Christ exercised on the Cross as the model for us in this regard. For example, when he calls the people of his day to cultivate an "immoderate, absolute trust" in God, one able to meet the challenge of an extraordinary tragedy like the War, he points to "the kind of belief in which Christ conquered the whole crisis of the world not to say of Eternity" as the model to emulate.[51] In a similar vein, Forsyth wrote that "if the unspared Son neither complained nor challenged, but praised and hallowed the Father's name, we may worship and bow the head" amidst our own tribulations.[52] More strikingly, Forsyth cites with high praise specific examples of persons who exercised faith in like manner to that of Christ. He mentions a "Dr. Moon" who trusted in God's grace even though he had become blind, and in doing so followed the example of Christ, the "captain of all those that have the grace of dying."[53] A second example is provided by that missionary to the North American Indians (to whom we have already been introduced) who "justified God" in spite of having seen his wife and children killed before him and being himself "harried in bonds across the prairie." Forsyth interprets his response in the following manner:

> I do not know a sublimer order of experience than from the heart to bless and praise a good and holy God in despairs like these. It is to this order of experience that the work, the blood, of Christ belongs . . . Never is man so just with God as when his broken, holy heart calls just the judgment of God which he feels but has not himself earned . . .[54]

The missionary's response to judgement was in the same "order of experience" as that of Christ. Like Christ, he confessed God's holiness and goodness in spite of his conviction that he was not morally deserving of the sufferings he was undergoing, and is thus to be commended. This, therefore, constitutes the basic idea behind the second significance of the revelation of the incomparable suffering of God for Forsyth's theodicy—

51. *Justification*, 128.
52. Ibid., 203.
53. *Father*, 64–65.
54. *Cruciality*, 102.

in the midst of Forsyth's constant call for us to exercise faith as the means by which we would be enabled to appropriate the key aspects of his theodicy, he gives a concrete example of such faith for our emulation: that of Christ on the Cross.[55]

As is often the case with Forsyth's writings, however, things are not so straightforward. A difficulty arises because we also see other passages in which he appears to postulate a deep chasm between the type of "faith" Jesus exercised and that which we are called to manifest, with the implication that we are not at all to try to emulate Jesus in this regard. In a short article entitled "The Faith of Jesus," just after a passage in which Forsyth movingly expounds the complete trust Jesus had to put in his Father when everything he had hoped for with regards to Israel failed to materialise, he draws a stark distinction between such faith and that which we should possess. He cites with approval the findings of German biblical scholar Adolf Schlatter to the effect that the New Testament never calls us to have faith in God in the same way Jesus had. There is, Forsyth postulates, a material difference between the relationship Jesus had with God and the one we have with God. Because of this, "in our faith we have to make our way over a kind of moral difficulty which for Jesus did not exist."[56] One basis of this assertion seems sound—Jesus, unlike us, was sinless, so the elements of repentance and confession of sin were absent from his faith. He "never quailed before that [Holiness] which humbles us to the dust" because he himself was always perfectly holy. But we think Forsyth is unduly obscure when he writes that "where we believe, [Jesus] knew. Ours is the confidence of faith, His of vision. Where we believe with effort and godly fear, He knew and rejoiced in spirit (Mt 11:25–27)."[57] It is likely that Forsyth is referring here to the unique communion Jesus enjoyed with his Father, and how it is far more intimate than what any of us can aspire to, because he had "a spiritual continuity with [God] which for us does not exist."[58] Such a claim is unobjectionable, but here is a case where Forsyth could have dispensed with his favoured device of the epigram in expressing it, because of its potential to confuse. As Forsyth's own tendency to contrast faith with sight dictates, to "know" and to "see" is to

55. Walter Adeney also points his readers to Christ's faith as our model in the midst of the War (*Faith-To-Day*, 60–62).

56. "Faith of Jesus," 9.

57. Ibid.

58. Ibid. See also *Person*, 133.

obviate the need for faith. Therefore, the bald assertion that Jesus "knew" rather than "believed" and "had the confidence of vision" rather than that of "faith" could potentially undermine the genuineness of any faith Jesus might have exercised. This threatens, at one level, to dilute the reality of the *kenosis* undergone by the Son and his consequent limitation in knowledge, which Forsyth contends for so strongly elsewhere. More vitally, it might compromise the very efficacy of Christ's confession on the Cross, which was satisfying to God because it was made without knowledge of the full significance of his sacrifice, and therefore in the obedience of faith. None of these consequences are, of course, intended by Forsyth, but his antithetical mode of expression does not help him here.[59] Moreover, looking at the issue at a more fundamental level, even if we accept (and we do) Forsyth's contention that we find it far more difficult to exercise faith in God than Jesus did because, unlike him, we are not sinless and divine, it does not necessarily follow that Jesus is disqualified from being our model of faith. We might never attain to his level of trust in God, but there is no reason why we should not aim for it. The question we have to ask again is, what is Forsyth seeking to achieve here by taking the arduous path of insisting on such an untraversable chasm between the faith of Jesus and ours?

Forsyth tells us explicitly that he is fighting here against the trend in the theology of his time to see Christ's relevance for us mainly in terms of his example.[60] In one of his more generous moods, Forsyth is willing to concede that "it is better, of course, to imitate the example of Christ than to be conformed to the world."[61] But, in his more usual fiery style, he castigates the view that Christianity consists merely of the *imitatio Christi* as "an apostacy more serious than anything that has occurred in the Church's history since Gnosticism was overcome."[62] Such a harsh assessment stems from Forsyth's conviction that an exclusive focus on the

---

59. We echo Sell's comment that there are many occasions on which "Forsyth is needlessly disjunctive" ("What Has P. T. Forsyth to Do with Mercersburg?" 183).

60. Forsyth mentions in his writings three significant movements in his day which tended to place undue emphasis on the *imitatio Christi*. The first was that of theological liberalism: *Person*, 189–92. The next was the Anglican Church, which, in Forsyth's view, had retained significant elements of the Roman Catholic teaching on the subject: *Rome, Reform and Reaction*, 137. The third was the pacifist movement which opposed Britain's involvement in the Great War: *Ethic*, 136.

61. *Father*, 131.

62. *Person*, 52.

imitatio Christi would be fatal to the Gospel he was trying to preach: "To imitate the religion of Jesus is to cultivate an order of piety absolutely different from the entire tradition of the Christendom created by the Gospel of Christ, a tradition which became most explicit in evangelical Protestantism."[63] This tradition teaches us that "we do not believe *with* [Christ], or by his help, but *in* him."[64] Once we do that, we find ourselves in a completely different realm from one in which Christ serves merely as our example. We are incorporated into Christ, and consequently enter the blessed communion between the Father and the Son. There, we "hide with [Christ] in God," and are given the marvellous privilege of "[partaking] of His Eternal Love to His Eternal Son."[65]

Is there then a way to reconcile Forsyth's apparently contradictory statements on the appropriateness of Christ's faith as a model for us?[66] The previous paragraph in which we noted Forsyth's emphasis on our incorporation into Christ gives us a starting point to do so. This notion of *en Christo* recalls Forsyth's writings on the regenerative aspect of the atonement. We saw, in chapter 2, how Forsyth views Christ's confession on the Cross as a proleptic one by the "new penitent Humanity" whom Christ both creates and represents before God. The completion of this aspect of the atonement will take place when all of humanity is incorporated into Christ through faith and actually come to confess likewise. This, we suggest, is the context in which Forsyth's writings on the appropriateness of Christ's faith as our example should be understood. Christ and his faith can legitimately serve as an example for us, but only if our attempt to imitate him is firmly based upon the work of Christ on the Cross in regenerating us. Therefore, we imitate the faith of Christ, not as an end in itself and not doing so in reliance upon our own strength, but as the subjective fulfilment of the Christ's crucial confession and being dependent upon its nature as a proleptic act to empower us to carry out such emulation. This, we think, is the idea behind Forsyth's explanation that Christ's obedience was one:

---

63. Ibid., 51.

64. Ibid., 56 (emphasis in original).

65. Ibid., 58; *Missions*, 206.

66. A. E. Garvie confesses himself "quite unable to follow Dr. Forsyth in his too subtle distinction between the trust of Jesus in God and the faith which man is called to exercise" (*Christian Certainty Amid the Modern Perplexity*, 188).

> ... which makes ours possible; it was inimitable, but reproducible. It cannot be emulated, it can but be repeated by Himself in the members whose life and whole it is. Our great act of obedience is to give up the hope of any similar and rival obedience, of any obedience so comparable or parallel to His that we could harbour the jealous complaint that He had an advantage. He who so complains is outside Christ. Our one obedience is to welcome His obedience as the gift of God, which we must accept, enter, and share as a new and saving obedience.[67]

So, "the faith *of* Christ is beyond us, and anything in its nature can only come by faith *in* Christ."[68] Our faith in Christ leads to our incorporation into Christ, and from that position we can appropriately look to the faith of Christ as our example. The *imitatio Christi* is legitimate only in the context of us being *en Christo*. The notion of Christ as our model of faith, therefore, functions thus not only an aid to theodicy, in the sense that it gives us a concrete example to emulate in our times of suffering. It leads also, on a more profound level, to the fulfilment of theodicy, as we seek to participate ever more completely in Christ's confession by undergoing our sufferings in a faith of the same "order" as his, anticipating the day when, by God's enabling, all creation will perfectly join this chorus of praise to a holy and good God.

A Place for Protest?

Our final observations in this section have to do with Forsyth's interpretation of Jesus' attitude as he suffered on the Cross. Forsyth, as we have seen, does portray realistically the struggles and suffering of the "historical Jesus" in his journey towards the Cross. There were times of serious doubt concerning God's call for his life, and Jesus had to undergo the painful process of dying to himself and his own ambitions for God's kingdom. Such struggle continued even to Gethsemane, where Jesus begged the Father for an alternative to the Cross. When we come to the event of the crucifixion itself, however, we notice a discernable change in the tenor of Forsyth's descriptions. He makes little mention now of Jesus' doubts and struggles. The emphasis is rather on his perfect submissive faith. This comes across most clearly in a passage we have already cited in chapter 4:

67. "Revelation and the Person of Christ," 128.
68. "Faith of Jesus," 9 (emphasis in original).

> Christ stills all challenge since He made none, but, in an utter darkness beyond all our eclipse, perfectly glorified the Holy Father. If He, the great one conscience of the world, who had the best right and the most occasion in all the world to complain of God for the world's treatment of Him—if He hallowed and glorified God's name with joy instead (Matt. xi. 25–27; Luke xxiii. 46), there is no moral anomaly that cannot be turned, and is not by long orbits being turned, to the honour of God's holy love, and the joy of His crushed and common millions.[69]

When Forsyth writes about the type of faith Christ models for us, he frequently refers to this form of submissive faith, where one responds to God's acts of judgement with the blessing and praise of God. Forsyth's approach does make sense in the scheme of his thought, since the event at Calvary represents for him both the nadir of the *kenosis* and the climax of the *plerosis* undergone by the incarnate Christ. It is at that point where Christ exercised the greatest of faiths—so it is proper for us to focus on it as our model for emulation. We suggest, however, that Forsyth's description of Jesus' posture on the Cross is rather one-sided. He seems to have pictured Jesus at Calvary as having resolved all his doubts and struggles, and so was in a position where he no longer made any "challenge" to the Father's will, but humbly and quietly submitted himself to it. Moltmann would, however, point out that Jesus was not silent on the Cross—he let out there his "death cry" of forsakenness. Forsyth does refer to this "death cry" as evidence of Jesus' experience of the Father's abandonment upon being "made sin," but he fails to go on to see it, as Moltmann does, as an act of protest against the God who willed the Cross for him.[70]

Such an act of protest, as many have pointed out, need not be inimical to true faith. There is a long Jewish tradition of seeing such protest as integral to the exercise of faith, as evidenced by the actions of major Biblical figures like Abraham, Moses, Jeremiah, and Job, and also the writings of the Psalmists.[71] The protests of these figures were "lifted up not as rejections of faith and hope, but because God is encountered as one whose good promises can be real."[72] Many of us would concur with John

---

69. *Justification*, 127–28.

70. Moltmann, *Crucified God*, 252–53.

71. Fretheim, "To Say Something—About God, Evil, and Suffering," 348; Gordis, "Cruel God or None," 279–80; Roth, "Theodicy of Protest," 21.

72. Roth, "Theodicy of Protest," 15.

Roth's observation that there are indeed times when no theodicy succeeds in stilling our anger, hostility and sadness over a tragedy. In such times, the act of protest can be the only way we remain honest to God and keep utter despair at bay.[73] Looking at it from another perspective, Forsyth's failure to articulate a role for protest in his theodicy leads him to the danger that he might (to use Alan Lewis' terms) be moving too quickly from Good Friday to Easter Sunday, without giving due regard to the reality of Holy Saturday. This, according to Lewis, is "a day of waiting, a hiatus and a barrier which prevents a knowing, onward rush to victory and joy by interjecting a painful pause, empty of hope and filled instead with death and grief, with memories of failure and betrayal, of abandonment and anguish." This "painful pause" is necessary because in Christian history:

> Too often has the prospect of heaven served to dull the sense of the poor, oppressed, and suffering to their grievous, earthly burdens—future beatitude offered as recompense or anaesthetic for present misery. Therefore must Sunday's life and hope always leave us with one foot still in Sabbath suffering and death.[74]

Although Lewis himself does not seem to have particularly approved of the act of protest,[75] as far as Forsyth is concerned, such an act could "put the brakes" on his tendency to swing too quickly from our present sufferings to the glory that is to be revealed in us, and represent the needed hiatus where these sufferings are appreciated for the "enormity in the moral world"[76] they truly constitute. Protest, in other words, articulates the reality that we do not always receive God's acts of secondary judgement with joy and thanksgiving, and allows us to recognise (what Timothy Wengret has called) the essential nature of suffering as a "curse," even that sent by God for his redemptive purposes.[77]

---

73. Ibid., 15–56, 20–21.

74. Lewis, *Between Cross and Resurrection*, 412, 433. We should note that Forsyth's approach to evil differs in fundamental ways from Lewis'—e.g., there is not the stress in Forsyth that Holy Saturday is an experience of God himself, and there is absent in Lewis the notion that God could be the author of suffering.

75. Ibid., 426.

76. *Justification*, 169.

77. Wengert, "'Peace, Peace... Cross, Cross,'" 200–202. Wengret's point is that Luther's classification of suffering and death as God's *opus alienum* carries the implication that they are essentially "curses"—no doubt, curses that God can transform to his use in his proper work of redemption, but curses nonetheless.

Although Forsyth did not specifically cite protest as a valid response of faith in suffering, there are certainly resources within his thought which would have enabled him to do so quite easily. Firstly, we have seen in chapter 4 that Forsyth's writings on prayer teach the paradoxical notion that it can be God's will that we resist this same will in particular matters, especially in situations of suffering.[78] This can easily be expanded to legitimatise acts of protest on our part. Secondly, the whole point of Forsyth's reliance on the *theologia crucis* is to say that there will be many times when we fail to see the whole point (or, perhaps, any point at all) to our suffering. This was even the case with the incarnate Christ. It is surely legitimate at these times to approach God honestly and express the way things look from our perspective, rather than try to suppress our true feelings by imaging various hypothetical purposes God might have. All this can be done without giving up our trust in God. Forsyth at one point describes Christ's experience of dereliction as his "sense of the certainty but the elusiveness of the Holy Love."[79] That expresses well the attitude we might adopt in our protest. Finally, while Forsyth the prophet might have exhorted the people to receive their purifying judgements with joyful submission, Forsyth the pastor demonstrates emphatic awareness when he openly acknowledges that his theocentric theodicy might seem "heartless" to those "who cannot see for tears, cannot think for heartbreak, and cannot believe for shock." His approach when speaking to such is not to berate them for their failure in their time of sorrow to transcend their anthropocentric perspective and go beyond merely viewing God as one who must always be "for us" in clearly visible ways. Instead, he praises such perspective as "the first stage of sainthood."[80] This demonstrates a sense of realism in Forsyth's writings that takes people where they are, and might indicate his receptiveness to the ideas proposed there.[81]

---

78. Roth expresses a similar idea when he writes that "it remains possible to be for God by being against God" ("Theodicy of Protest," 19).

79. *Preaching of Jesus*, 308.

80. *Justification*, 20–21.

81. For the rest of Forsyth's theodicy to retain their integrity, however, he would have to deny some of the conclusions proposed by the proponents of "protest theodicy," like the idea that it functions ultimately as an "anti-theodicy" leading to the undermining of all attempts to justify God (Roth, "Theodicy of Protest," 19).

CONCLUSION

We have, in this chapter, considered what we see to be the two main significances of the second outcome of God's self-justification for Forsyth's theodicy. The first is that it introduces the picture of God as the chief sufferer and giver, one who has paid the greatest price to secure the atonement. Such a picture carries three main implications. God gains, firstly, the moral authority to use any means of secondary judgement, whatever their cost in terms of human suffering and death, to realise in actuality what was secured at the Cross. God is, secondly, justified in expecting the world to take the difficult step of trusting him, in the midst of all the convulsions of history, to complete his task of bringing all of creation to a blessed *eschaton*. Finally, the complete solidarity with human suffering that God underwent in Christ enables him to empathise completely with all human suffering in our evolution towards this end. This gives us the comfort that God is with us, in a very real sense, in our suffering, and also inculcates the confidence that he would not demand any suffering on our part which is unnecessary to move the world towards its goal. The second significance of the revelation on the Cross of God's incomparable suffering is that it provides us with a concrete model of faith to emulate in our times of suffering: that of the crucified Christ. Such emulation is to be done not apart from, but in conjunction with, our faith in the same Christ, and leads to the very fulfilment of the theodicy Forsyth seeks to expound.

The type of evil Forsyth seeks to address here is, as in chapter 4, that of human suffering. Whereas, in that previous chapter, Forsyth focuses on the manner in which God relates *ad extra* to the world, here Forsyth concentrates on how such a relation to the world affects God *ad intra*. This picture of a God who has invested himself so completely into the situation of our evil world is pivotal to Forsyth's theodicy. Forsyth recognises that a different picture of God might render our attempts to justify him impossible:

> A God that merely hides Himself may, as Bacon says, be but playing hide-and-seek with His children, and longing to be found. He is more tolerable than one who is indifferent—much more tolerable than one who seems to withdraw offended to His heavenly tent when His creatures most need Him in their battle; or who even from His invisible retreat shoots casual darts upon them, or wraps them in a blight without sympathy or justice.

We close, as we did chapter 4, with Camus' observations, this time on what the "metaphysical rebel" seeks to do to God:

> [The metaphysical rebel] draws this superior power [i.e. God] into the same humiliating adventure as himself—the power being equally as ineffectual as our condition. He subjects it to the power of our refusal, bends it to the unbending part of human nature, forcibly integrates it into an existence which we render absurd, and finally drags it from its refuge outside time and involves it in history—very far from the eternal stability that it can only find in the unanimous consent of all men . . . His insurrection against his condition is transformed into an unlimited campaign against the heavens for the purpose of capturing a king who will first be dethroned and finally condemned to death.[82]

Forsyth's message is that our God has voluntarily done all that the metaphysical rebel demands of him, and far more besides. This must surely have the effect of subverting the rebel's view of what God is like, and jolt him into rethinking who and what he is rebelling against.[83] The Christian God is not the detached being who "withdraws to his heavenly tent" and from there "shoots casual darts" at his creatures. He is the God in Christ who is the chief sufferer and giver in our common cause against sin. Forsyth's likely answer to this rebel comes close to Aloysha's response to his brother Ivan's incessant challenge to his faith based on the spectre of innocent suffering. There is a being upon which the edifice of the world's future happiness is founded. It is not the "small, tortured child" or any of the innocent sufferers whom Ivan cites, but the one who "gave Its innocent blood for all things and all men." Because of what this person has done, all creation can and will justify the goodness of God.[84] Forsyth's thought, as described in this chapter and the previous one, can be seen as an exposition of this reply of Aloysha's.

---

82. Camus, *Rebel*, 30–31.

83. Moltmann, in *Crucified God*, 221, makes a similar point: "But if metaphysical theism disappears, can protest atheism still remain alive?"

84. Dostoyevsky, *Brothers Karamazov*, 321. We follow Bauckham's interpretation of the passage here: "Alyosha . . . does not recognise the God against whom Ivan directs his protest as the Christian God, since he is not the crucified God" (*Theology of Jürgen Moltmann*, 80).

7

Forsyth's View on the Origin of Evil

INTRODUCTION

Having looked at the two main outcomes of God's self-justification and their significance for Forsyth's theodicy, we turn now to examine Forsyth's view on the origin of evil, i.e., *how* and *why* sin and suffering came into our world. These are issues which Forsyth seems to have addressed in an even more indirect manner than the previous ones. We shall certainly not expect to find any systematic treatment of them, such as a chapter in *The Justification of God* neatly entitled "The Origin of Evil." In fact, as we shall see, some of Forsyth's writings suggest that he is not inclined to venture at all into this aspect of theodicy. Why then are we addressing it in our study?

We offer two justifications for our decision. Firstly, it is our conviction that, for a theodicy to be complete, it has to address, no matter how tangentially, this difficult issue of the origin of evil. It has become common, especially after Auschwitz, for writers on theodicy to claim that they are approaching their subject matter from a "practical" rather than a "theoretical" angle.[1] What this means, as Surin explains, is that theodicy should seek to answer the question of what God and his human creatures have done and are doing to overcome evil in our world, rather than questions concerning the nature of evil and the compatibility of its existence with that of an all good and powerful God.[2] This "practical" approach would imply, amongst other things, that discussions concerning the "how" and the "why" of the origin of evil remain strictly out of bounds. Surin identi-

---

1. See, e.g., Surin, *Problem of Evil*, chap. 2; Trakakis, "Theodicy," 183–88.
2. Surin, *Problem of Evil*, 59–60.

fies Forsyth as a proponent of such a "practical" approach to theodicy.[3] There are certainly grounds for such a categorisation. Forsyth himself writes in *The Justification of God*:

> No doubt insoluble problems remain. Why in His creation must the way upward lie through suffering? Why, on this hard hill road, should we be met by sin descending upon us, seized, and flung into the abyss? . . . These questions are quite unanswerable. That is why a book on such a subject is at a disadvantage. We can but fall back on the last choice and committal which we call faith. And that seems to suggest a sermon rather than a discussion. Yet when God came to deal with the position practically and finally it was by the folly of preaching. He took the dogmatic note and not the dialectic. He did not put thought on a new line, but the thinker in a new life. The situation is insolubly irrational, so far as we are concerned. The solution is in action, as Carlyle said,—but in God's, as he did not say.[4]

This tells us that Forsyth sees the problems concerning the origin of evil to be essentially insoluble from an intellectual or theoretical perspective.[5] He therefore prefers to approach the whole exercise of theodicy from what he himself calls a "practical" or "historic" angle. What this means, as he explains in the passage above and reiterates in others, is that he chooses to treat the existence of evil in our world as a given reality, and direct his focus on God's practical overcoming of it through his act on the Cross and its effect on world history.[6] This is, in fact, how Forsyth sees God presenting his own theodicy to the world, suggesting therefore that it is the only one we have: "The Christian message is that the answer is there, and is the gift of God. It is provided. And it is practical. It is done more than spoken, and done to our hand . . . The solution is practical, not philosophical. It is not really an answer to a riddle, but a victory in battle."[7]

We would argue, however, *contra* both Surin and Forsyth, that the distinction between "theoretical" and "practical" theodicy is not as water-

---

3. Ibid., 132–36.

4. *Justification*, 139.

5. Forsyth's view on the insolubility of the problem of the origin of evil stretches back to his early, pre-"conversion" days: "'Milton's Paradise Lost,'" 4.

6. *Justification*, v–vi, 98.

7. Ibid., 220. Forsyth makes a similar point in "Revelation and the Person of Christ," 104.

tight as they might suggest. All "practical" theodicists have to work with the fundamental assumption that the true account of the origin of evil is not one which ultimately destroys the thrust of their theodicies.[8] For example, "practical" theodicies which focus on the suffering God as our companion in pain must surely hold the assumption that God did not, in a manner akin to masochism, initially send evil into our world just so that he can suffer with us. Certain accounts of the origin of evil, therefore, have to be eliminated, and other accounts preferred, for any "practical" theodicy to make sense. Forsyth, in fairness to him, does seem to recognise this need for consistency between one's understanding of the origin of evil and one's "practical" theodicy. He provides, for example, the accounts of the origin of evil which must be rejected in the light of his "practical" theodicy, ones we will examine subsequently.

The distinction between "theoretical" and "practical" theodicy also breaks down in another area. The "practical" question of what we can do to eliminate evil is, on occasions, best answered by the call for us to engage in "theoretical" theodicy. Marilyn McCord Adams gives a fine exposition of the need to undertake "theoretical" theodicy in order to be truly "victim-centred" and to alleviate suffering:

> My point is that many (though, to be sure not all) participants in horrors, sooner or later, not at every stage but eventually, over and over, raise questions of meaning: of why God allowed it, of whether and how God could redeem it, of whether or how their lives could now be worth living, of what reason there is to go on? They demand of us, their friends and counsellors, not only that we sit *shiva* with them, but also that we help them try to make sense of their experience. They look to us for hints, beg for coaching as they embrace, struggle to sustain the spiritually difficult assignment of integrating their experiences of the Goodness of God and horrendous evil into the whole of a meaningful life. Delicate and perilous as this assignment is, participants in horrors themselves often thrust it upon us.[9]

---

8. David Fergusson makes a similar comment in *Cosmos and the Creator*, 84.

9. Adams, *Horrendous Evils*, 187–88. See also the similar arguments made by Cobb, "Problem of Evil and the Task of Ministry," 167 and Sponheim, "To Say Something—About God, Evil, and Suffering," 341. This serves as a necessary corrective to the assumption sometimes held by those who reject the "theoretical" approach to theodicy that those who suffer seek only alleviation of their pain or an understanding of their immediate situation, and not answers to the larger question of why evil exists (see, e.g., Surin, *Problem of Evil*, 64, 145–46). This, we submit, represents a reductionist and even patronising view

Our first justification, then, for addressing this issue of the origin of evil is that it is necessary to complete our study of Forsyth's theodicy, "practical" as it might be. This leads us to our second (related) justification, one we have already alluded to when we mentioned that Forsyth does outline the accounts of the origin of evil he rejects. In spite of his purported "practical" emphasis, Forsyth has important things to say on this subject of origins, fragmentary and incomplete as they stand. Moreover, there are aspects of his theology, though not directly related to this topic, which carry weighty implications as to how and why evil came into the world. All these features of Forsyth's writings bring forth important facets of his theodicy we have not yet considered. It would indeed be a pity if these features were excluded from our study as a result of an all-too ready acceptance of the assumption that Forsyth does not venture into "theoretical" theodicy at all. A more refined approach is necessary—one which acknowledges that Forsyth chooses to leave some aspects of the origin of evil a mystery, yet attempts to shed light on others in ways illuminating for his justification of God. In this task we are inspired by the example of George Hall, who in his article "Tragedy in the Theology of P. T. Forsyth" both recognises the essentially "practical" nature of Forsyth's theodicy and yet ventures, albeit briefly, into inferring Forsyth's view of how and why evil entered this world.[10] We will make reference to Hall's observations at the appropriate junctures in what follows.

HOW EVIL CAME INTO OUR WORLD

Introduction

Our discussion in this section will focus on *how* Forsyth envisages evil (i.e., sin and suffering) to have come into our world. It is not our intention to deal here with suggestions as to *why* this might have happened, although some aspects of that will arise, since issues relating to the *how* cannot be entirely separated from the *why*. The main discussion on the

---

of the sufferer because it assumes that he is so overcome by his circumstances that he becomes totally absorbed into his own suffering and is unable to contemplate and seek answers to larger questions.

10. Hall, "Tragedy in the Theology of P. T. Forsyth," 94–98. This is a section of Hall's article for which, unfortunately for our purposes, he has provided very scanty reference to his sources. He does, however, use many of Forsyth's own phrases and sentences in his description of Forsyth's position, giving us a fair degree of confidence that we know the passages to which he refers.

latter is, however, reserved for the following section. We should say at the outset that Forsyth's view of how sin entered this world is very different from how suffering made its appearance. We will focus our discussion here on the entry of sin, as Forsyth writes far more about this than the advent of suffering. The latter will, however, be touched upon in the course of our section.

One of the most striking aspects of Forsyth's theodicy is his allusion to the idea that the entry of sin into our world was inevitable. His statements "man is born to be redeemed. The final key to the first creation is the second; and the first was done with the second in view"[11] and "the key of creation is its redemption. It can come to itself only by being redeemed"[12] speak of the inevitability of redemption and therefore, by extension, of sin.[13] Why is this the case? Let us look first at the options for understanding this inevitable entry of sin which Forsyth rejects.

The Options which Forsyth Rejects

Forsyth, in *The Justification of God*, launches a fierce attack on "philosophical theodicies," which are what he sees as purely rational attempts to explicate sin. Such theodicies are doomed to failure because they approach what is essentially irrational in nature using reasonable means.[14] All "philosophical theodicies," according to Forsyth, inevitably proffer one of two unsatisfactory outcomes. They either "[postulate] a limitation on the power of God other than He imposes on Himself (which is to reduce His deity)," or "[deny] the fundamental principle of the conscience, which is the radical and eternal antagonism of good and bad."[15] "Philosophical theodicies," in other words, lead inescapably to the diametrically opposing alternatives of what we often call "dualism" and "monism."[16] It is clear that Forsyth is against the first of these alternatives, i.e., the idea of an absolute dualism between God and sin. Such dualism postulates the existence of "two Gods, neither of them the Almighty; and so there is no God, as the

---

11. *Justification*, 126.

12. *Parnassus*, 262–63. See also "Veracity, Reality, and Regeneration," 207–10.

13. Hall also notes this sense of inevitability ("Tragedy in the Theology of P. T. Forsyth," 97).

14. Forsyth states his conviction of sin's irrationality in "Reality of God," 610.

15. *Justification*, 140.

16. See Hick's concise descriptions of these two alternatives in *Evil and the God of Love*, 15–16.

word has been, and craves to be, understood."[17] It follows that Forsyth would reject any account of the entry of sin into our world which rests on such absolute dualism, such as the notion that sin constitutes an eternal principle forever contesting for supremacy with the good.[18]

While Forsyth makes clear his aversion to absolute dualism, he reserves the bulk of his criticism for the opposing notion of a "monistic" universe, in which the utter incompatibility between God and sin is not taken seriously. This imbalance in the distribution of his criticism can be accounted for by the specific context in which he was writing—Forsyth sees the "philosophical theodicies" he encounters in his day as tending far more significantly towards such "monism" than dualism. These theodicies seek "to graft the untoward into the general good in some rational way" because of the drive in the field of philosophy to subsume everything into "the ordered course and content of the world."[19] There are two methods with which these theodicies have sought to undermine the severity of sin vis-à-vis God. Some of them utilise the mechanism of the "buffer." They seek to lessen the impact of sin (and also suffering) by holding on to the optimistic belief that, from God's perspective, ours is indeed "the best of worlds." All the evils we experience are inevitable aspects of such a best possible world, the shades of dark which must necessarily exist in a beautiful picture.[20] Forsyth's specific targets here are obviously Gottfried Leibniz and Alexander Pope. He might also have intended the larger task of undermining the particular strand of the Augustinian heritage of theodicy in which they stand.[21] Forsyth would certainly have taken issue with these famous lines of Pope:

> All Nature is but Art, unknown to thee;
> All Chance, Direction, which thou canst not see;
> All Discord, Harmony, not understood;

17. *Father*, 34.

18. Forsyth mentions the need to reject a "Persian" form of dualism in *Authority*, 206.

19. *Justification*, 143.

20. Ibid., 144.

21. Both Leibniz's *Essais de Théodicée* and Pope's *Essay on Man* are cited in the bibliography of *Justification*. For the relationship between Leibniz's thought and the Augustinian heritage of theodicy, see Hick, *Evil and the God of Love*, 146–47; and Peterson, *God and Evil*, 93–94. The possibility, raised by some commentators, of classifying Leibniz's theodicy under the "dualistic" rather than "monistic" category will be discussed in the following chapter.

All partial Evil, universal Good:
And, spite of Pride, in erring Reason's spite,
One truth is clear, "Whatever is, is RIGHT."[22]

The second method "philosophical theodicies" use to cope with the troublesome phenomenon of sin is that of the "shunt." Here, "the grievance is turned into a loop line, which further on restores it, after some delay, to the main line of harmony." Both the main line and loop lines are actually within the "whole," so that, in the larger scheme of things, "evil is but good in the making." If we could only attain to "the right sense of the blessed whole," we would understand the evils we experience to contribute in the end to a larger good, and this might enable us to bear them in the right spirit.[23] Forsyth's likely target here is Hegel and those successors of his who see human sin as a necessary stage in the evolution of the world towards the perfection of the whole.[24]

Besides seeing these two classes of "philosophical theodicies" as fatally flawed because they are incompatible with his notion of sin and its severity vis-à-vis God, Forsyth, driven surely by a deep pastoral concern, castigates them for "[reducing] the individual . . . to a resolute subordination." These theodicies demand that we stifle our feelings of shock and outrage against sin because it ultimately constitutes a necessary part of a larger and better whole. But this will not work, because we cannot hope to suppress completely the dictates of our conscience, which tell us that sin is something which should not be. In the end, Forsyth predicts that many who are offered such theodicies will sink into the deadly depths of pessimism, where they will be left to languish with no hope that things will get better. Some might then even go to the extreme of preferring a return to the "unconscious chaos" from which our sensible world emerged.[25]

---

22. Pope, *Essay on Man*, 50–51. See Fraser, *Philosophy of Theism*, 189 for a similar critique against the Leibnizian approach to theodicy.

23. *Justification*, 145.

24. Forsyth elaborates upon his critique of this aspect of Hegel's thought in *Positive Preaching*, 161–62. Summaries of Hegel's view of evil can be found in Reardon, *Hegel's Philosophy of Religion*, 68–70, 114; and Galloway, *Philosophy of Religion*, 528–29. Galloway also names F. H. Bradley and Bernard Bosanquet as two English writers who have appropriated Hegel's view of evil. Another English disciple of Hegel which might have been in Forsyth's sight is R. J. Campbell (see Forsyth, "God, Sin, and the Atonement," 670). Campbell's view of the "Fall" is described in his *The New Theology*, 66–67.

25. *Justification*, 144–46.

Forsyth's strong and unwavering insistence on the utter malignity of sin vis-à-vis God therefore leads him to reject explanations of its inevitable entry premised upon the notion of an absolute monism. For him, God did not (and could not have) ordained[26] or even permitted sin, either as a means towards a greater end (i.e., the "shunt" approach), or as the necessary condition of a superior objective (i.e., the "buffer" approach).[27] Forsyth essentially sees that sin cannot be used as a sort of "bargaining chip," one which can be traded off for something else of higher value. There is, from God's perspective, no worse state of affairs than the presence of sin in his good creation. We see this to be the crux of Forsyth's critique against Leibniz and Hegel (and their followers). They have placed something else at a higher value to God than the maintenance of his holiness, whether it be metaphysical richness[28] or his self-realisation through his other. This recalls the point we made in our opening chapter about how Forsyth's voluntarism is strictly bounded by the notion of God's essential being as holy. A holy God could never have intentionally used that which is diametrically opposed to his holiness (and which therefore threatens his very life) to arrive at a goal of greater significance to him.

Forsyth's Account of the Origin of Evil

Forsyth therefore rejects accounts of the origin of sin bound up with either the notions of an absolute dualism or monism. How then does he explain the inevitable entry of sin into our world? His key move is to

---

26. The explanation that God ordained the entry of sin would have been one readily available to Forsyth as a Congregationalist standing in the Reformed tradition—since John Calvin was one of the foremost advocates of this idea (Calvin's view is well summarised in Hick, *Evil and the God of Love*, 117–21). We have already seen, in Chapter 2, Forsyth's creative revision of the Calvinistic notion of predestination, to eradicate the idea that God actively effects the reprobation of a class of humanity. He rejects similarly Calvin's idea that the Fall was willed by God.

27. *Justification*, 138–39, 159; *Work*, 242; *Ethic*, 30; *Christian Aspects of Evolution*, 29. Liebniz prefers to speak of God "permitting" rather than "willing" evil (esp. moral evil) in his scheme of theodicy—see his *Theodicy*, 61, 136–37.

28. J. S. Feinburg points out that, for Liebniz, "good" and "evil" are to be understood primarily in a metaphysical sense. It is always "good" for the world to be metaphysically richer in terms of the plenitude of being. Therefore, under this system of values, God is ethically justified in creating a world which is the "best" metaphysically, even though this carries with it the presence of sin ("Theodicy," in *Evangelical Dictionary of Theology*, 1185). Leibniz himself agrees that God "could have avoided all these evils" if he had chosen to create a different type of world (*Theodicy*, 61).

locate this entry of sin in the wrong exercise of the free will given to human creatures.[29] Forsyth views the bestowal of such creaturely freedom as another act of *kenosis* on God's part:

> In love we were created and endowed with freedom by an act of God wherein he limited his own freedom by the area of ours. His omnipotence received a restriction—but it was from an exercise of His own loving power and freedom; and an exercise of it greater than could be rivalled by all the freedom man received.[30]

This freedom graciously granted to human creatures included the freedom to sin,[31] a power which we did in fact choose to exercise, ushering in the rebellion against God's holiness that brought Christ to the Cross. But why did Forsyth perceive this abuse of moral freedom on our part to be inevitable? What was it about the world in which the first human inhabitants dwelled which made it so?

The starting point for an answer is given by Forsyth's general acceptance of the notion of biological evolution. He mentions that it "has a place and value in science that can never be lost."[32] There is, for him, nothing in this theory of Darwin's which is detrimental to Christian thought. There is therefore no need for Christianity to contest its validity in any way.[33] So, for Forsyth, "man is a close for all the evolution that preceded him in nature."[34] There was a point in world history "when man first appeared, dimly self-conscious, on the earth."[35] This probably happened when "a creature of the wild" rose to "psychological freedom over the necessities of natural force."[36] This newly evolved human being lived in a world already

---

29. In this, Forsyth follows the approach to the origin of sin taken by many of his contemporaries. See, e.g., Martineau, *Study of Religion*, 57, 107; Pfleiderer, *Philosophy of Religion on the Basis of Its History*, 38–39; Bruce, *Moral Order of the World*, 344–45; Galloway, *Philosophy of Religion*, 540; Griffith-Jones, *Challenge of Christianity to a World at War*, 12; Adeney, *Faith-to-Day*, 30–32.

30. *Person*, 314.

31. *Ethic*, 175; *Authority*, 204–5.

32. *Christian Aspects of Evolution*, 6

33. Ibid., 7, 13–14. The real problems, for Forsyth, arise when we magnify the evolutionary idea beyond the realm of biology into a fundamental philosophy governing all other aspects of life. Evolution is then distorted to become a form of rival "religion" to Christianity: ibid., 33.

34. *Person*, 146.

35. *Missions*, 179.

36. *Authority*, 412.

filled with suffering and death, caused by, amongst other things, predation, hunger, illness and accidents. "Suffering," Forsyth asserts, "abounded in the animal world before man appeared with the moral freedom that makes sin possible. Pain came before sin, and, as it has no connection with freedom, it is non-moral."[37] The newly evolved human creature was, of course, not exempt from such suffering and death. This forms, we suggest, the context for Forsyth's discussion of the *divided human consciousness*. In his passages describing such consciousness, Forsyth does not explicitly say that they apply to the first human beings who lived at the time before sin made its appearance (what we shall call "pre-Fall humanity"). From the language he uses, however, it seems clear that Forsyth is, in these passages, describing something fundamental to the human consciousness, which we expect would have applied even to pre-Fall humanity. Moreover, as we shall see, Forsyth cites the neo-Kantian thinker Wilhelm Windelband as his philosophical authority here, and Windelband's writings on the divided human consciousness were certainly intended to describe humanity at its most basic. We further suggest that Forsyth's rejection of the "Augustinian" view of creation in favour of a more "Irenaean" one (a point we will also consider below) would dictate that there exists a large measure of continuity between pre and post-Fall humanity, such that the passages under consideration in this section should be read as applying equally to both.[38]

---

37. *Justification*, 138. See also *Soul of Prayer*, 88–90 which similarly affirms that disease and death were the lot of animals before sin arose.

38. In saying this, we are consciously departing from McCurdy's conclusion that, for Forsyth, "there is no way back to some past Eden, and no hope for the theologian of rediscovering an unfallen conscience created in the image of God" (*Attributes and Atonement*, 60). McCurdy cites a passage from "Cross as the Final Seat of Authority," 173 as his authority for his assertion. A careful reading of this passage, however, reveals that the thrust of Forsyth's argument there has to do with his rejection of "natural ethics" in favour of a "theological" one (i.e., one based upon God's redeeming act in the Cross). The latter must "take man in his actual historical situation" and work from there. The passage does not claim the impossibility of inquiring into the state of the "unfallen" conscience. Another passage by Forsyth, also cited by McCurdy in a further argument (pp. 61–62), states that "the natural conscience, were it accessible, would certainly be an object of scientific interest. But, strictly speaking . . . in civilized communities today it does not exists. It is a mere abstraction of thought" (*Authority*, 403). Forsyth refers here, as McCurdy rightly points out, to the impossibility of finding an actual conscience in the Western society of his time that has not been "moulded by the Christian ethic of sin and redemption, which for two thousand years has been shaping European morals" (*Authority*, 304). He is therefore also not claiming here that we are unable to discover what a "pre-Fall" human conscience would be like.

Examining the basic state of the human moral consciousness, one "anterior to its branches as theoretic, aesthetic, or ethical," Forsyth notes that "it is not, like the philosophic, single, simple and harmonious, but double, divided, and even rent. It is not monistic but dualistic." Why is this so? There exists a "fundamental antimony of the conscience which emerges in the conflict of 'must' and 'ought,' of instinct and obligation, of natural law and moral norm." Why does this conflict arise? Forsyth does not give a straightforward answer, but points to a "deep distinction between . . . the make up of our natural constitution and the state of our moral will."[39] The context for this distinction is, we suggest, the world in which humans dwelled from the very first—one "abounding" with suffering and death. This results in the need for humans to struggle against the demands of nature in order to survive and thrive.[40] Forsyth describes this struggle as essentially one to subdue the earth:

> What man has to do is to secure his place in the world, in the vast and mighty evolutionary process. That world is at first in a conspiracy against him. The human infant has more against it than the young of any other creature. Man has to secure a footing in the world. But this can only be done by overcoming the world. The only place he can keep in the face of nature is the place of nature's master. He can exist only as a ruler. He must harness nature. He cannot run in the team, he must drive from the box. He can endure only by overcoming the world.[41]

Our suggestion here is that, given this context in which the first human creatures equipped with moral consciousness found themselves, Forsyth saw that they soon faced a contradiction between "the make up of [their] natural constitution and the state of [their] moral will." The "natural law" which dictates what they "must" do in order to survive and thrive seems at many junctures to conflict with what they perceive the "moral norm" to be telling them they "ought" to do.[42] There is a "collision of life with ethic . . .

39. *Authority*, 5.
40. *Justification*, 9; *Person*, 339.
41. *Authority*, 194–95.
42. Hall seems to read Forsyth in a similar way. He writes, "From the moment of their appearance, human beings are engaged in a battle for existence that necessarily involves collision and conflict. To struggle for life is natural and he even suggests that we begin as 'warring atoms' and that it is as natural to destroy as it is to help. The picture here is one in which the natural conditions of human existence are, at the same time, conditions conducive to, but not the cause of, sin" ("Tragedy in the Theology of P. T. Forsyth," 96–97).

of morality with happiness."[43] To give a hypothetical example of our own, these first humans might reason that they could prosper more efficiently if they stole the possessions of their peers, but something within their moral consciousness told them this was something they should not do. The result of this is "a civil war . . . waged within the unity of the person," because "the defiance of the moral norm seems to be as much bound up with our nature as obedience is."[44] These first human creatures, we presume, more often than not chose to give in to the dictates of natural law rather than the requirements of the moral norm, leading to a profound sense of what Forsyth calls "accusation"—"we do not only desire [the moral ideal], we dread it. Its very grandeur fills us with a sense of weakness, nay, of blame, shame, and despair."[45]

Forsyth goes on to observe that, in spite of experiencing this conflict between natural law and moral norm at such a fundamental level, human beings have not generally been led to embrace a belief in an absolute dualism. Instead, we hold on to an idea of the primacy of the moral. This can be seen in how we tend to identify the moral norm with the holiness of an absolute God, a holiness which is "the ideal good, fair, and true." Whenever we encounter this holiness, we honour it as "the one thing in the world valuable in itself and making a world."[46] Forsyth, as we might expect after our discussion of his view of reality in chapter 1, approves of such an identification of the moral norm with "the ultimate reality of the world."[47] This, however, "creates a problem quite insoluble for any philosophy," because:

> . . . it seems to involve (what is a moral impossibility condemning any theory) that all reality, even that of evil, should be a part of the absolute moral normality. It seems to require that the norm of all reality should cover what is contrary to a moral norm, that absolute reality, ruled by a moral norm, should yet have the morally abnormal among its appearances or products.[48]

---

43. "Veracity, Reality, and Regeneration," 208.
44. *Authority*, 5.
45. Ibid., 7.
46. Ibid., 5–6.
47. Ibid., 6.
48. Ibid., 5–6.

The point Forsyth seems to be making here is that philosophy, as he understands it, with the stark distinction it draws between monism and dualism, is unable to explain the situation just described. The most fundamental reality of our world is the holiness of God, as represented to us by the moral norm which tells us through our conscience what we "ought" to do. Yet, at the same time, there exists a real conflict between this norm and our sense of necessity. So everything does not dissolve into a simple monism. But there is also no ultimate dualism—the greater reality beyond this conflict is that represented by the moral norm. For Forsyth, this situation, as Rodgers accurately concludes, "is not thinkable." It is, however, "knowable,"[49] and here we see Forsyth's *theologia crucis* in action again. All our vague hopes that the moral norm (and, by extension, the holiness of God) does indeed represent the ultimate reality and will one day establish itself in our sin-ravaged world with a corresponding absoluteness are transformed into an unqualified certainty by the act of the Cross. The "Revelation of the Holy" and its triumph over sin comes through (and only through) the crucial act of "Redemption by the Holy."[50] This act of redemption re-creates our human conscience over time, such that the dualism which human beings have experienced from the first will ultimately be ended.[51] So, in the *eschaton*, "the moral world and its conflict with nature" will be overcome, and not in a way which results in the "beating down" of nature, but rather her full involvement "in the grand co-operation of all things in the everlasting kingdom."[52]

Those familiar with the works of neo-Kantian philosopher Wilhelm Windelband will recognise much in the preceding paragraphs which have been derived from his thought. Forsyth, in a rare footnote, acknowledges Windelband's essay "Das Heilige" as the philosophical inspiration for his own comments on the divided human consciousness.[53] Philip Swoboda provides a fine summary of the relevant section of this essay:

49. Rodgers, *Theology of P. T. Forsyth*, 273.
50. *Authority*, 7.
51. Ibid., 388–89, 404–5; *Justification*, 110–11.
52. *Authority*, 206; "Regeneration, Creation, and Miracle," 95–96.
53. *Authority*, 5. Forsyth is referring here to the essay as it appears in a collection of Windelband's articles entitled *Präludien*. It is interesting that Rodgers sees the writings of Kant and those of the neo-Kantians of the Baden School (for whom Windelband was a primary figure) as constituting "one of the most decisive of the philosophical influences upon Forsyth" (*Theology of P. T. Forsyth*, 369–70).

> The need for such a principle [of "the Holy"] emerges from a consideration of the fundamental "*antinomy of consciousness*" which comes to light in the examination of human psychic life. Human consciousness is placed under two different legislative instances—while it acknowledges the "ideal necessity" of norms, of the ideal, of the eternally valid, it is subject in its natural functioning to causal laws which, more often that not, issue in results which are contrary to norms (*normwidrig*). We embrace error rather than truth: we choose wrongdoing over virtue. "This natural necessity of that which is contrary to norms (*das Normwidrig*)" is the "primordial fact" (*Urtatsache*) which lies at the base of all the problems with which critical philosophy is concerned.[54]

Windelband himself adds, in another work, that this distinction between the "ought" and the "must" is in fact essential to the whole exercise of human "valuation." We would be unable to employ our judgement in favour of the true, the good and the beautiful, if what we "ought" to do is completely identical to what we "must" do. This tells us that the dualism we perceive subjectively is in fact embedded in reality.[55] Windelband sees one implication of this "objective dualism" as the rendering insoluble of the problem of theodicy:

> Besides the values which are realised in it there is a dark power of something indifferent to or opposed to value. If we mean by God a single principle in which all that can be experienced has a common being and a common origin, we can never understand how it divides into a duality that contradicts itself... We cannot get over the contradiction. The dualism is the most certain of all facts, yet Henism [i.e., monism] is the most solid of all assumptions of our philosophy of reality... From the very nature of the case this final problem [of theodicy] is insoluble."[56]

This, as Forsyth himself tells us, is one significant basis for his rejection of "philosophical theodicies." All purely rational attempts to explain the origin of evil are doomed to over-emphasise either the fact of dualism or the reality of monism at the expense of the other. This releases the tension

---

54. Swoboda, "Windelband's Influence on S. L. Frank," 265–66. His page references to *Präludien* appearing within the quoted passage have been left out.

55. Windelband, *Introduction to Philosophy*, 351–52.

56. Ibid., 358.

which must be held for a truly Christian account of God and sin to be maintained.[57]

For Forsyth, therefore, there is, in the end, no satisfactory philosophical or intellectual explanation of the origin of sin. The element of mystery cannot be done away with. But what about responsibility for sin's entry into the world? On one level, Forsyth insists that, although it was to be expected that the first human creatures would choose to violate the moral norms which govern them because of the situation in which they were placed, these acts of violation were committed "chiefly by our fault, crime and sin."[58] Hall shares this observation of Forsyth's position:

> It almost seems as though these conditions and forces are such that, given human free will, sin is irresistible. And, yet, God could not ordain sin, and since sin is a primarily a matter of the will, we are wholly responsible for the infection that has time and again poisoned whatever progress humankind has made in the actualisation of unity, harmony, and reconciliation. We are responsible because the alternative of not sinning is a possibility, if only in principle. Hence sin is inevitable, though not necessary.[59]

From another perspective, as we shall see subsequently, God takes responsibility for the situation which arises due to his decision to create. But we focus here on Forsyth's determination to expel any notion that God is

---

57. Another source of influence on Forsyth on this issue is possibly Galloway, whose theodicy bears many striking resemblances to Forsyth's position (see Galloway, *Philosophy of Religion*, 517, 519–20, 540). Forsyth, would, however, have disagreed with Galloway's anthropocentric characterisation of moral norms as nothing more than standards set by human communities, which are subsequently projected to be the will of a divine power.

58. *Authority*, 7.

59. Hall, "Tragedy in the Theology of P. T. Forsyth," 97. In this, Forsyth's position can be seen as prefiguring key aspects of Reinhold Niebuhr's account of the origin of sin given in his Gifford Lectures: *The Nature and Destiny of Man*, vol. 1: Human Nature, chap. IX. Like Forsyth, Niebuhr would like to maintain "the seemingly absurd position that man sins inevitably and by a fateful necessity, but that he is nevertheless to be held responsible for actions which are prompted by an ineluctable fate" (256). Moreover, Niebuhr takes a similar route to Forsyth in locating the temptation to sin "in the contingencies and necessities of the natural process" in which humans live, leading to "anxiety" on our part, which we seek to overcome by illegitimately attempting a "qualitative" leap into infinity on our own ability (266–67). Fiddes approves of the "paradox" which writers like Niebuhr seek to hold, as this does "equal justice to various features that [Christian theology] sees as givens in the human situation, among them the feeling of man's moral freedom, the observation that mankind has an inherent tendency to decline from the good, and an underlying belief in the goodness of God" (*Creative Suffering*, 214).

responsible as the author of sin—as one who actively wills or permits sin's intrusion into his good creation for a purpose.

Concerning the origin of suffering, on the other hand, we do not see an equal eagerness on Forsyth's part to dissociate it so completely from the will of God. Suffering was an aspect of the good creation from its very beginning, and in this sense can be seen as something which God intends for his creatures, at least until the *eschaton* when we can look forward to "the end of pain."[60] Such a view is entirely consistent with what we saw in Chapter 1 concerning Forsyth's insistence that a clear distinction must be drawn in a truly Christian theodicy between evil as sin and evil as suffering. As shown most clearly in the Cross, suffering is not incompatible with God's holiness, and can be made to serve his purposes. Sin, however, is the irreconcilable antagonist of God which is only to be destroyed.[61] This mention of the idea of "God's purposes" leads us conveniently to our next section, where we endeavour to press even further and ask if Forsyth held a view of *why* evil originated and what it might be.

WHY EVIL CAME INTO OUR WORLD

Introduction

"These questions are quite unanswerable"[62]—Forsyth's firm response to the question of why evil came into our world seems to preclude our attempt to write this section. We soldier on, however, in the belief that there exists much room for manoeuvre in spite of the seemingly dismissive tone of Forsyth's response. This belief finds two sources of support. We note, firstly, that Forsyth's response was given as a prelude to his discussion of the failures of "philosophical theodicies" (which we have outlined above).[63] Therefore, we suggest, when Forsyth points to the "unanswerable" nature of the question "why," he is referring specifically to the impossibility of a philosophical approach to theodicy to explain the fine interplay between monism and dualism described in the previous section. This still leaves the door open for us to probe the possible reasons for the origin of suffering, since that does not seem to have been the primary issue involved

---

60. *Justification*, 140.
61. Ibid., 138–39.
62. Ibid., 139.
63. Both are contained in chapter VIII of *Justification*, entitled "Philosophical Theodicies."

in Forsyth's rejection of "philosophical theodicies." Secondly, although Forsyth seems here to have firmly prohibited any inquiry into the reasons for the entry of sin into our world, there are other parts of his writings which suggest that he might not always have been consistent on this issue. It behoves us to examine these passages carefully to determine Forsyth's final position on the matter.

The "Irenaean" Nature of Forsyth's View of Creation

John Hick, in his seminal work *Evil and the God of Love*, promotes what he terms as an "Irenaean" theodicy.[64] He bases it on the depiction of creation he finds in the writings of the early Church Father Irenaeus of Lyons. This contrasts with the more established "Augustinian" view of creation:

> Instead of the doctrine that man was created finitely perfect and then incomprehensibly destroyed his own perfection and plunged into sin and misery, Irenaeus suggests that man was created as an imperfect, immature creature who was to undergo moral development and growth and finally be brought to the perfection intended for him by his Maker.[65]

There is much in this passage we believe Forsyth would agree with. His acceptance of the general tenets of biological evolution would lead him to affirm the statement that "man was created as an imperfect, immature creature." The notion that this creature was intended by God from the very first "to undergo moral development and growth and finally be brought to the perfection intended for him" would also be consistent with Forsyth's position.[66] We say this because of Forsyth's constant insistence that (what he calls) the "first creation" was never intended to serve statically as an end in itself.[67] The goal of creation, rather, is the complete establishment of divine holiness within the human race, "on a plane which by the first

---

64. Hick's characterisation of his theodicy as "Irenaean" has attracted criticism on historical grounds, leading him to issue the qualification that he merely sees Irenaeus as the "father figure" for "a family of responses" to the problem of evil (*Evil and the God of Love*, 372). This debate has no bearing on our discussion, as the historical accuracy of the attribution of aspects of Hick's theodicy to Irenaeus is not relevant to our point here.

65. Ibid., 214.

66. Although he would have his own unique definition of what "perfection" for humans consists of—something we would consider later.

67. See, e.g., *Justification*, 126, 160; "Regeneration, Creation, and Miracle: Second Article," 92, 99.

creation was only prefigured and prophesied."[68] Consequently, on the level of the human being, Forsyth sees the process of natural evolution producing only "the elemental instinctive individual," who then has to grow his personality "through the exercise and discipline of moral freedom, judgment, and responsibility."[69] He also conceptualises the *imago Dei* not as something fully bestowed upon humans at the onset of their appearance, but our "ear-mark and far destiny, slowly to be won."[70] Further, Forsyth's assertion that suffering and death "abounded" before humans (and their sin) appeared would also lead him to affirm another central tenet of this "Irenaean" view of creation, which is that humans never did live in a paradisal pre-Fall environment, one in which suffering and death followed the first human sin.[71] Forsyth disputes the existence of a "primeval perfection which never was real,"[72] and, in the context of an argument against polygamy, observes with approval that the notion of evolution has undermined "those social theories which began by imagining an aboriginal state of nature and went on striving back to it, either as it was in Eden or anywhere else."[73]

We can therefore say, broadly, that Forsyth affirms an "Irenaean" view of creation, one in which (in Gunton's words) "nothing is complete in the beginning."[74] God's purpose for his creation is hence to be viewed teleologically—it is the end of creation which represents its goal, rather than the beginning.[75] We have already, in Chapter 3, described what Forsyth

68. "Regeneration, Creation, and Miracle," 639.
69. *Authority*, 289.
70. Ibid., 160. See also *Sacraments*, 87; *Justification*, 127; *Ethic*, 174.
71. Hick, *Evil and the God of Love*, 256–58.
72. *Positive Preaching*, 40.
73. *Marriage*, 30.
74. Gunton, *Actuality of the Atonement*, 153.

75. In this, Forsyth follows the trend established by the British theodicies of his time: Hick, *Evil and the God of Love*, 1st ed., 242. This is not to say, however, that Forsyth would have agreed with every aspect of Hick's description of the "Irenaean" view of creation. He would, for example, have demurred when Hick rejects the characterisation of the first human sin as "an utterly malignant and catastrophic event" (214). For Forsyth, the entry of sin is "malignant and catastrophic," not so much because of its effect on the outward state of creation, but its effect on the Creator himself. Something insidious appeared then which sought to undermine God's holiness and ultimately to kill him. Surely nothing is more "malignant and catastrophic" than that, both for God and the world. There is a real sense in which Hick's theodicy, in the end, underestimates the antagonism between God and sin in much the same way as the "monistic" theodicies did in Forsyth's day. See

envisages to be the end-state of creation intended by God. Human beings are to be perfected in holiness, in terms of perfect communion with the holy God and with one another. The rest of creation is to be gloriously renewed and invited to participate, with humanity, in the final self-justification of God. This description of the end-state in terms of "communion" implies that it involves a moral response to God on our part. As mentioned in chapter 2, Forsyth conceptualises this response as our subjective participation in the "obedience of faith" Christ showed towards his Father as he hung upon the Cross. It is therefore not surprising to see Forsyth repeatedly characterising faith as the highest possible moral response we human beings can ever make to God.[76] It is, in fact, only faith which constitutes a sufficiently holy answer to God, being our response "in kind" to the revelation of a God of holy love.[77] But what about the other human moral responses, such as love (which, according to Paul in 1 Cor 13:13, is the greatest virtue)? Are they not crucial as well? Forsyth answers in the affirmative, but adds that they are ultimately rooted in faith. "All morality is folded up in [faith] and expands from it,"[78] even love, which is but "the impassioned expression on the face of faith."[79] The primacy which Forsyth allocates to faith leads him ultimately to see it not as a means, but an end. Faith is not something which brings salvation. It is, rather, salvation itself, the very goal of redemption.[80] The person of faith has attained to Christian perfection *coram Deo*, whatever the state of his life might be at that point in time.[81] Hunter has a good exposition of Forsyth's position on the matter (one which also dispels the fear that it might contain an insidious antinomianism):

> What Christ demanded of those who came to Him was not character, not achievement, but faith, faith in Himself as God's Grace. That was the one demand of God, and to answer it is perfection ... All other excellence flows from that. All ideal perfection is latent in that ... The man of faith is perfect before God because his will

---

Trethowan, "Dr. Hick and the Problem of Evil," 411, for a critique of Hick's instrumental view of sin.

76. *Person*, 332; *Authority*, 67; *Sacraments*, 189.
77. *Justification*, 109; *Ethic*, 174.
78. *Rome, Reform and Reaction*, 153.
79. *Father*, 100.
80. *Authority*, 43, 345; *Sacraments*, 199; *Preaching of Jesus*, 80.
81. *Father*, 124.

> and person is in the relation to God which is God's will for him. And he has the germ and the conditions which will work out in sanctifying time to ethical perfection as well.[82]

Our reading of Forsyth suggests that he sees certain basic conditions as essential to facilitate our moral response of faith. We will examine what these conditions are in what follows.

The Conditions Necessary for Our Moral Response of Faith

Let us look first at a passage:

> Moralisation is possible only in accordance with the nature of morality, i.e., in the exercise of freedom, through struggle, effort, experience, all demanding time as an indispensable condition, even for the sanctification of the individual, still more for the humanisation of the community, or the race.

These are not Forsyth's words, but those of his Victorian contemporary A. B. Bruce.[83] They are quoted here because they summarise very handily the three basic conditions which Forsyth sees must exist if we are to make our moral response of faith. Humans beings must, firstly, be given the ability to exercise freedom (as mentioned previously, "freedom" for Forsyth is generally meant in a "libertarian" sense, i.e., the ability to choose which is not wholly determined by prior causes). At the most basic level, according to Forsyth, it is such freedom which renders our actions moral.[84] The abstract concept of humans being "good without choice" is, at the end of the day, "neither goodness nor freedom."[85] We can infer from this that, *a fortiori*, human freedom is necessary for the exercise of faith. In arguing against the traditional Calvinistic view of faith as God's gift (in the sense that it is allocated by divine decree to the elect), Forsyth writes that such "faith" "would be no answer to grace, whose freedom must be answered with ours." It is, in fact, not faith at all, since faith, at the root of it, "is not a

---

82. Hunter, "P. T. Forsyth Neutestamentler," 105.

83. Bruce, *Providential Order of the World*, 137. Other thinkers of that time postulating similar conditions include Martineau, *Study of Religion*, 99–104, 107–10; Flint, *Theism*, 245–51, 257–58; Fairbairn, *Philosophy of the Christian Religion*, 254–55; Ward, *Realm of Ends*, 372–75; Galloway, *Philosophy of Religion*, 542.

84. "Immanence and Incarnation," 51.

85. *Positive Preaching*, 44.

thing but a freedom."[86] All these sit well with what we have seen in chapter 1 concerning Forsyth's voluntarism, one which leads him to understand morality (on one level) simply as the right exercise of the will.[87]

The second condition which enables our response of faith is brought forth by the words "struggle, effort, experience" in the above quotation. In our earlier discussion of Windelband's notion of the divided conscience, we noted how he perceives the distinction between the "ought" and the "must" as essential to the whole exercise of human valuation. This implies that morality can only exist in a situation where we have, at least at times, to sacrifice something beneficial to our survival and thriving in order to choose the good. In other words, for our decision in favour of the moral to be meaningful, it must sometimes be made through struggle, as only this demonstrates the binding effect of morality upon us beyond all considerations of self-interest. (Kant's tendency to define "duty" as that which must be carried out in opposition to all motivations to self-benefit is a palpable influence here.) Forsyth hints at his concurrence with this line of thinking when he writes, in an essay against the monism of the "New Theology" of R. J. Campbell, that "for moral life we must have a dualism and a reconciliation, not a monism with a mere identity and continuity."[88] Since struggle is necessary for moral decisions, it can be no less essential for the ultimate

---

86. *Authority*, 356, 158.

87. There is one aspect of Forsyth's theology which does not appear to sit well with his emphasis here on the need for human freedom. This is his adherence to the doctrine of *non posse peccare*—the belief that Christ had a "foregone immunity" to sin (see our discussion in chapter 5). This necessarily implies that Christ did not possess freedom in the "libertarian" sense, which seems to be main aspect of freedom Forsyth refers to here. We have therefore to ask, "Was Christ in a position to make a genuine moral response to God?" One way for Forsyth to defend himself here is to say that all he is claiming when he asserts *non posse peccare* is that it was "practically" impossible, given who Christ was, for him to do wrong. There are aspects of his writings which suggest this, such as when he compares the impossibility of Christ sinning with the impossibility that some of us would "steal some article from a shop on [our] way home" (*Person*, 301). But this, as Trevor Hart points out, entails a substantial weakening of the *non posse peccare*, rendering it to mean only that it was "supremely unlikely" that Christ would ever sin (Hart, "Sinlessness and Moral Responsibility," 53). It is not clear if this reformulation of *non posse peccare* would be acceptable to Forsyth—his phrases such as "foregone immunity" seem to suggest a more absolute conception of the doctrine. Forsyth's fellow Nonconformist Walter Adeney was perhaps more consistent in asserting that the *non posse peccare* has to go when one relies upon the free-will defence to account for the entry of sin into our world (*Faith-to-Day*, 32–33).

88. "Immanence and Incarnation," 50.

moral act of faith. We have noted earlier Forsyth's tendency to contrast faith with sight. This generates a dualism not dissimilar to that between the "must" and the "ought." The dichotomy between faith and sight implies the need to struggle in order to trust, since faith often goes against that which is evidently the case. So Forsyth castigates those who regard faith as "a rest–and–be–thankful spot, which we attain at last, occupy, and even fortify." The truth is rather that "faith can only exists as an inner warfare," and has to "fight its way in every age," because of the fundamental reality of a conflict between the world and the Word.[89] The organic relationship between faith and struggle is also brought forth when we recall Forsyth's depiction in chapter 5 of the incarnate Son's growth in his "obedience of faith." This growth was attained through "the things he suffered," including his soul's painful struggle with the temptation to defy his Father's will. Moreover, Forsyth sees Christ's greatest confession of faith as one made in (and facilitated by) the depths of his most intense suffering, when he was "made sin" and perceived the Father's abandonment.

The first two conditions of freedom and struggle necessarily imply the third which Bruce mentions, which is the provision of time. To the charge that God is responsible for the lack of faith on the part of humans beings because he did not create faith in them, Forsyth replies that it is wrongly based on a "magical" (as opposed to "moral") concept of creation, which imagines that God could immediately make faith appear like a magician who "[brings] out blossoms with a wave of his hand." But, in reality, "there is no such thing as a faith which could be created and inserted in a soul."[90] Time for development is therefore an indispensable condition for true faith to arise.

It is clear from a quick recollection that all these three conditions of human freedom, struggle and time were present in what Forsyth sees as the context in which the first human beings found themselves. They were given the autonomy to decide in favour of either the "must" or the "ought," but had to make their decisions in the face of a world which strongly encouraged them to go against the dictates of their conscience. They existed firmly in time and space, as did the creatures preceding them in the evolutionary process. It is this situation, then, rather than the paradisal state of existence envisaged by the "Augustinian" view, that proves condu-

---

89. *Authority*, 30–32.
90. Ibid., 15.

cive for the development of creation towards its *telos*. Such an observation contains important implications as to why God could have allowed evil to enter his creation. It is to these implications we turn next.

Why God Could Have Allowed Evil

Why God Could Have Allowed Suffering

Forsyth, to the best of our knowledge, never attempted to draw a link between the conditions he postulates as essential for human faith to arise and those he saw existed at the emergence of the human race in the evolutionary process. We propose here to draw such a link, and suggest that Forsyth's theodicy would have been rendered more complete if he had expressly stated the likelihood that God might have allowed suffering to constitute an integral aspect of his creation in order to establish the conditions fertile for human faith to develop. Suffering, therefore, can be seen as that which God permits as a means to the end of the eventual perfection of the world. The specific pre-condition of faith which suffering facilitates is, as we have seen, that of the need for struggle. The presence of suffering, distributed in such a way that it often accompanies the choice in favour of the moral, sets a cost humans frequently have to incur in order to do what is right. It therefore helps to maintain the differential between the "must" and the "ought," which Windelband sees as essential for true morality. Suffering also serves to augment the tension between "faith" and "sight," in that it defeats any attempt on our part to gain evidential assurance from observing the ways of the world that the moral is indeed the real and will finally triumph over the dualism we now experience. This brings us near to Hick's notion of the "epistemic distance" God deliberately places between him and his human creatures in order to facilitate our "faith-response" to him. Hick suggests that:

> The reality and presence of God must not be borne in upon men in the coercive way in which their natural environment forces itself upon their attention. The world must be to man, to some extent at least, *etsi deus non daretur*, "as if there were no God." God must be a hidden deity, veiled by His creation.[91]

Hick's implicit appropriation here of Luther's idea of the "hidden deity" leads us to observe that our suggestion of how Forsyth could have

---

91. Hick, *Evil and the God of Love*, 281.

understood the reasons for the entry of suffering into our world is quite consistent with his general appropriation of the *theologia crucis*. The reasoning goes like this: Because God intends suffering as a foil to "sight," and it "abounds" in our world, we can never gain true knowledge of God and the world from the mere observation of creation as it stands.[92] It is only by looking at the Cross, which reveals (to the eyes of faith) the *telos*, that we truly come to know God and the nature and purpose of the world. There is much in Forsyth's writings which suggests that creation can only be properly understood from the perspective of the end, as revealed in the Cross. He insists, for example, that "we must begin with the end, taken as a gift. We must carry it back to the beginning."[93] This is the methodology we have consciously tried to follow in seeking to derive the possible reasons for the entry of suffering. The beginning must be seen to serve the end, so we understand God to have allowed suffering into the world in order to facilitate his goal of "faith-production."[94] Such a conclusion is, we submit, demanded by Forsyth's appropriation of the *theologia crucis*, and there does not seem to be anything in his writings which detracts from it.

This way of extrapolating Forsyth's theodicy has another benefit of offering a satisfactory explanation for his conviction (mentioned in chapter 3) that suffering will cease, together with sin, in the *eschaton*. Forsyth does not seem to have given any explicit grounds for our confidence that this would happen. Why, indeed, should suffering cease with the final destruction of sin, when it arose prior to and independently of the latter? The answer suggested by our conclusion is that suffering will cease at the *eschaton* because it will then have exhausted its purpose. When all human creatures have arrived at the goal of perfect faith, there will be no further reason for struggle, and suffering can therefore come to an end. This also reinforces the point that, for Forsyth, suffering is strictly a means and never an end in itself. There is nothing worthwhile in suffering for the sake of suffering. Also, Forsyth does not adopt the view that suffering is inherently embedded in creation because of its finitude or physicality.[95]

---

92. Steven Paulson elaborates on this notion of the "hidden God" in "Luther on the Hidden God," 366–67.

93. *Justification*, 54. See also "Our Experience of a Triune God," 244; "Regeneration, Creation, and Miracle," 91–92.

94. The phrase "faith-production" is described by Forsyth as the goal of redemption in *Preaching of Jesus*, 80.

95. See Hick, *Evil and the God of Love*, 187–91 for a discussion of "metaphysical evil."

There is therefore nothing metaphysically inevitable about creaturely suffering that prevents it from being completely done away with when God so wills.

Why God Could Have Allowed Sin

We turn now to the second type of evil Forsyth deals with in his theodicy—sin. Do Forsyth's writings suggest that he sees God allowing sin into our world for a similar reason as he did suffering? There are two sets of passages which, on an initial reading, might suggest this to be the case. In the first (which we have already seen), Forsyth asserts unambiguously that the goal of creation is redemption. The first creation was plainly done "with the second in view."[96] We stated earlier that this speaks of the inevitability of sin, since redemption here must mean our redemption from sin. But it might also suggest the purposefulness of sin, because the idea that we were created to be redeemed seems to allocate to sin the status of an indispensable condition for the realisation of the stated goal of redemption. The second set of passages alludes to the idea that sin functions as an impetus towards our attainment of higher levels of faith. Human faith in the context where sin exists is of a far richer quality than even sinless obedience. The following sections from Forsyth's writings bring forth this idea clearly:

> And God, though He wills that we be perfect, has not appointed sinlessness as His object with us in the world. His object is communion with us through faith. And sin must abide, even while it is being conquered, as an occasion for faith. Every defect of us is a motive for faith. To cease to feel defect is to cease to trust. To cease to feel the root of sin would be to have one motive the less to cast us on God for keeping. Every need is there in order to rouse the need for God.[97]

> It has pleased God to leave us *in* our sin (though not *to* our sin) that we may be driven to seek more than His help, namely Himself . . . We are compelled by cleaving sin to press on into close and permanent communion . . . All life, it has been said, is the holding down of a dark, wild, elemental nature at our base, which is most

---

Austin Farrer is a prominent example of a theologian who has linked suffering with the physical nature of creation (see his *Love Almighty and Ills Unlimited*, chap. 4).

96. *Justification*, 126.
97. *Father*, 102.

> useful, like steam, under due pressure. So with sin and its mastery by faith. The pressure from below drives us to God, and the communion with God by faith keeps it always below.[98]
>
> Faith is not a second best; as if the absolute best would have been sinless obedience to instructions, correct attention to orders, or even full trust in a lovable person, who yet might not have power in His love to redeem. There are moral resources in God and His holiness which nothing but our sin and Redemption draw out. So far, *O felix culpa* . . . The trust of Grace is greater than the obedience that never strayed from Love and knows no repentance. It is a greater God that redeems than just blesses; and to trust Him as Saviour is therefore the greatest work possible to the soul. The praise of men is greater than that of angels.[99]

The emphasis in these passages is clearly on the profound utility of sin for the development of faith. They seem to suggest two reasons for this. The first is that the presence of sin dramatically intensifies the struggle we have to undergo in order to exercise our faith. It exerts a strong "pressure from below" which drives us to cling to God in a deeper trust than if such pressure was absent. The second reason Forsyth gives is that sin (and the redemption which follows) enhances faith because our perception of faith's object goes far deeper in its wake. Perhaps inspired by that part of the traditional Easter liturgy which follows upon the "*O felix culpa*" with the exclamation that our sin has gained for us "so great a Redeemer," Forsyth suggests in the third passage quoted above that the challenge posed by sin brought forth the full display of God's "moral resources." In the light of the Cross, therefore, we do not merely commit ourselves to a "loveable person," but a "Saviour." This radically enhances the quality of our faith, possibly because we are now able to put our trust, not merely in a vague deity who created us, but a God who has demonstrated concretely that he possesses both the love and the power to redeem us from sin at a tremendous personal cost. It is also noteworthy that Forsyth appears to contrast "faith" with both "sinlessness" and "sinless obedience" in the above passages, possibly going so far as to suggest that our response of "faith" is only possible in the context of sin, and that even our complete obedience in a sin-free situation belongs to an altogether different moral category from that of "faith."

98. Ibid., 103.
99. *Ethic*, 175.

In the light of these two sets of passages, can we safely conclude that Forsyth holds the implicit view that God allowed sin to enter this world for the same reason as he did suffering—to facilitate the realisation of his goal for creation? The answer must clearly be no, if we have taken to heart our earlier description of Forsyth's disavowal of "philosophical theodicies" and the ways in which they minimise the absolute antagonism between God and sin. Forsyth, as we have seen, rules out the possibility that God could have ordained or even permitted sin, either as a means towards a greater end (i.e., the "shunt" approach), or as the necessary condition of a superior objective (i.e., the "buffer" approach). Sin, unlike suffering, has nothing in it "which can be preserved and utilized for the divine purpose." Any compromise in this regard will make a mockery of the conflict between God and sin that brought "death to God in the Son of God" on the Cross.[100] Therefore, while it was through the application of Forsyth's *theologia crucis* that we came to our earlier conclusion that suffering was possibly permitted by God in order to bring this world to its intended *eschaton*, the same methodology prevents us from coming to the same conclusion with regard to sin.

How then are we to reconcile these seemingly conflicting statements? The following admonition from Henri Blocher might help us navigate the impasse (if we take his term "evil" to refer to sin, which is its primary intended meaning). After giving some Biblical examples of how God can use "evil" for his purposes, he continues:

> It would, however, be exceeding the teaching of the texts to think that there we have the final explanation of evil. In all the cases considered, evil was *already* in the world. God channelled it, directed it and broke down its outworkings so that these might serve his purposes. The decision to permit evil, which is rationally justified by the end in view, concerns only particular crystallizations, transgressions and misfortunes, and the pattern that God imposes on them. But it would be an undue extrapolation to suppose a decision with a like purpose for the first permission of evil *itself*. The import is no longer the same. When evil is already present, if God makes use of that hostile reality as an opportunity to act, and even as a means to punish and to warn, the fact in no measure lessens the malignity of evil, and in no way allows for any insinuation that God might be its accomplice. Rather, it is the victory of God over evil that is proclaimed. If, on the contrary, God had permitted evil

---

100. *Positive Preaching*, 162.

itself for the sake of the use he was going to make of it, then *evil itself*, the counterpart of something good, *would be explained and excused*, at least to some extent; instead of holding it in horror, we would have to understand that everything is for the best in the best of all possible worlds. Holy Scripture, if our reading of it is correct, never takes that path; it asserts that God, whose competence infinitely transcends the devilry of his adversaries, is well able to play off evil against evil, and overturns the stratagems of the enemy for his own glory; but that is always, once evil has come in, by way of a counterstroke.[101]

We can, therefore, reconcile Forsyth's seemingly opposing statements by focusing on what God's intention was in creating the world. At the risk of being overly speculative and anthropomorphic about what was in God's mind when he created, we set out the following position which we think sits well with Forsyth's apparently contrasting assertions on this topic. If Forsyth is to be true to his rejection of "philosophical theodicies," he must postulate that God had no intention whatsoever to use sin as a means towards his end when he created the world. His plan for the development of human creatures towards perfection must therefore have been formulated without the involvement of sin—we could, in other words, have arrived at the intended *eschaton* even if sin never made its appearance. But God, being almighty, foresaw the inevitable entry of sin given the conditions in which we were placed. He persisted, however, in creating because he knew he possessed the resources within himself to overcome sin and bring about an even "more perfect" end[102] with the destruction of sin. Forsyth's exclamation of "*O felix culpa!*" (see above) must therefore be understood as one which accurately describes both the human and divine perspectives on the appearance of sin. The fall can properly be termed "fortunate," even from God's viewpoint, because it was never intended.[103] As Hall points out, it was inevitable, but not necessary,[104] and any benefits

---

101. Blocher, *Evil and the Cross*, 89–90 (emphasis in original). A similar point is made by Trethowan, "Dr. Hick and the Problem of Evil," 412.

102. I am using the term "perfect" in the way suggested by Fiddes, "Creation out of Love," 173–74, which allows for an increase in "perfection."

103. There are other ways of interpreting the significance of the "*O felix culpa*" exclamation. Arthur Lovejoy suggests that some in the Christian tradition have interpreted the phrase to imply that God willed the Fall in order to bring about the greater good: "Milton and the Paradox of the Fortunate Fall," 289–94.

104. Hall, "Tragedy in the Theology of P. T. Forsyth," 97.

which accrue from its appearance have an accidental quality about them. Moreover, these benefits, if we recall our discussion in chapter 3 concerning God's use of a lesser sin in his secondary judgement to destroy a greater, are acquired not through friendly cooperation between God and sin in furtherance of a common cause. They arise rather through the deception of sin—God inducing it to act towards its destruction while it labours under the belief that it was doing so in its own interest and against God's. Forsyth can therefore rightly claim that "doubtless [sin] must be made to minister to God's greater glory, but never by any kind of exploitation; and only by entire destruction."[105]

How then should we understand the passages cited above which seem to promote the idea that sin was intended by God as a means to his end? The first set of passages postulating redemption as the goal of creation should, we suggest, be read as an affirmation of God's foreknowledge of sin's entry, rather than any intention on his part to will such entry for his purposes.[106] Because God foreknew the entry of sin, the end of creation for him, practically speaking, was always redemption. But this does not necessarily imply that God's intended goal for creation was, from the first, redemption, with the entry of sin a necessary aspect of this goal. Our interpretation of these passages is supported by Forsyth's frequent reference, within them, of the notion that God knew he possessed the resources "in reserve" to "remedy" or "recover" the situation arising from the inevitable "abuse" of the freedom he granted to his human creatures. So, for example, he writes:

> It is no light problem that faces the Creator in His world. There was never such a fateful experiment as when God trusted man with freedom. But our Christian faith is that He well knew what He was about. He did not do that as a mere adventure, not without knowing that He had the power to remedy any abuse of it that might occur, and to do this by a new creation more mighty, marvellous, and mysterious than the first.[107]

105. *Positive Preaching*, 162.

106. This also seems to be how Rodgers, *The Theology of P. T. Forsyth*, 190; and Bradley, *Man and His Work*, 142 read these passages.

107. *Justification*, 125. This passage might have been intended as an implicit contrast to R. J. Campbell's assertion (in *New Theology*, 24) that creation was "a divine experiment without the risk of failure." Forsyth asserts, like Campbell, that God will have his way in the end, but it will be through an intense moral struggle leading to a new creation, rather than a non-moral metaphysical reconciliation between the finite and the infinite. Other

This idea of God "remedying" a situation involving the "abuse" of his good gift surely suggests God's response to a state of affairs he did not intentionally bring about.

As for the second set of passages emphasising the utility of sin towards the development of faith, our response is to suggest that the issue here is one of a difference in degree rather than type. While, hypothetically speaking, we might not have been able to respond to God in as holy a manner if sin and our redemption from it had not occurred, because the vital conditions of free will, struggle and time were present, we would still be in a position to render some sort of moral response to God. The invariable dichotomy between the "must" and the "ought" should ensure that this "lower" moral response involves a degree of trust in God, as doing what is morally right (and therefore what pleases him) would frequently incur a cost on our part. While Forsyth might have been ambiguous about whether this "lower" form of moral response can properly be called "faith," we see no fundamental reason why it cannot. It is, to be sure, "faith" of a far lower quality than the trust we exercise in the context of sin and redemption, but in so far as it is genuine trust in the holy God, it should not be relegated to an altogether distinct category of moral response. Some observations from Forsyth's Christology might also be relevant here. He understands Christ to have demonstrated the perfect "obedience of faith," one which in fact provides the basis for all our individual responses of faith. While the presence of sin surely augmented the struggle Christ had to undergo in order to trust the Father (especially when he was "made sin"), Forsyth affirmed in the strongest possible terms Christ's absolute sinlessness. Christ therefore never related to his Father in terms of a sinner to his Redeemer. If, in spite of this, he can be said to exercise faith, one which constitutes a model for us (see our discussion on this in Chapter 6), it must follow that human faith is possible outside of our relating to God as Redeemer. We reiterate Forsyth's defence of his *non posse peccare* formula: "What is truly human is not sin. Sin is no factor of the true humanity, but only a feature of empirical humanity which is absolutely fatal to the true."[108] To see sin and redemption as indispensable to God's initial goal of the development of a humanity who is able to respond to him with the holiness of faith does seem to detract from the main thrust of

passages which go along similar lines include *Authority*, 184; *Life*, 99; "Regeneration, Creation, and Miracle: Second Article," 99.

108. *Person*, 302.

this statement. Our suggestion here is therefore to read this second set of passages as merely saying that the entry of sin and the redemption which followed facilitated the development of a richer faith, and therefore a "more perfect" end. Sin and redemption, however, were not themselves necessary for the development of a more basic level of faith, and were therefore not indispensable aspects of God's initial goal for his creation.[109]

This attempt to reconcile Forsyth's writings on this issue has been so challenging that we should end this section by acknowledging the possibility that Forsyth was simply inconsistent, and that he sought "to have his cake and eat it" by affirming both the absolute antagonism between God and sin and the idea that God might somehow have willed sin into the world in order to achieve his goals. As Arthur Lovejoy points out, such inconsistency might be justified as a kind of literary device. While the notion of *felix culpa* must not be allowed to intrude into the part of the narrative dealing with the Fall, it is a valid exclamation when we arrive at the conclusion, "where it could heighten the happy final consummation by making the earlier and unhappy episode in the story appear as instrumental to that consummation, and, indeed, as its necessary conditions."[110] Forsyth might, after all, have intended his statements to be understood in such a fashion. The other possibility is that his battle against the movement of evolutionary idealism, so influential in his day, was so fierce that he went overboard in some of his statements asserting the primacy of the new creation over the old, of crisis over process. Whatever Forsyth's motivations were, the danger, of which he does not always seem to have appreciated, is that this way of writing might compromise the theme of sin's utter malignity for God—one so fundamental to the rest of his theology. Our reconstruction of Forsyth's view of the origin of sin has sought to protect this theme from a fatal dilution, while preserving the basic import of his writings.

Conclusion

We conclude this section by summarising our main proposals. We have suggested that Forsyth's statements on suffering, when read together with his "Irenaean" view of creation, tell us that he might well have held the

---

109. See Galloway, *Philosophy of Religion*, 541 for another attempt to assert both that great good comes forth from "moral evil," and yet that it cannot properly be termed a necessary instrument of good.

110. Lovejoy, "Milton and the Paradox of the Fortunate Fall," 295.

implicit view that God permitted suffering to constitute an integral aspect of his creation in order to establish one of the necessary conditions for the development of human faith ("struggle"). But when it comes to sin's entry into creation, we do not associate it with the notion of God's purposes. Despite some statements which appear to assert the contrary, we see Forsyth ultimately holding fast to his insistence that, fundamentally, with sin God "can make neither use nor terms."[111] In doing so, he heeds the warning issued by Blocher (and others) that giving a reason for the entry of sin would be to "explain and excuse" it, at least to some extent. Such a justification of sin, for Forsyth, would seriously undermine his justification of God, which has thus far proceeded on the assumption of the utter malignity of sin for both God and human beings.

THE LARGER CONTEXT: FORSYTH'S VIEW OF THE GOD-WORLD RELATIONSHIP

There is one other aspect of Forsyth's theology we need to mention briefly before we close our description of his likely position on the origin of evil and move on to consider its implications for his theodicy. It concerns Forsyth's view of how God and the world are related. Our discussion of Forsyth's theodicy so far should lead us to see that his view of the God-world relationship differs quite significantly from that of much traditional Christian theism, which sees God and his creatures existing in distinct ontological orders, with the result that God remains largely unaffected by what goes on in the world.[112] Our description, for example, of Forsyth's view of sin and how it represented a real threat to the very life of God tells us that, for him, God is profoundly impacted by what goes on in his world.[113] This impression is reinforced when we remember Forsyth's description of the intense suffering undergone by both the Father and the Son at the historic event of the Cross, and also his insistence that God's self-justification finally depends upon creation's eschatological justification of God for having made it. This way of envisaging the God-world

---

111. *Justification*, 139.

112. The traditional position is well expounded by Weinandy, *Does God Suffer?* 153–57.

113. Corresponding to this is Forsyth's bold insistence that God "needs" the atonement ("Inner Life," 161–62), and that it represents "final salvation both for man and God" (*Justification*, 152).

relationship has significant implications on one's beliefs concerning why God created.

Forsyth seems to have addressed this issue of God's reasons for creating only on rare occasions. In a key passage from his article entitled "Regeneration, Creation, and Miracle," Forsyth writes that the notion of "creation" has become unreal to many in his day. He attributes this to two prevailing beliefs, both of which he disputes—the notion that creation arose *ex nihilo*, and that it was an arbitrary act on the part of God, who could just as easily have refrained from creating.[114] Utilising his *theologia crucis* once again, Forsyth claims that, according to what Christ reveals of God, we can be certain that he had to create. This necessity was, however, a moral one, arising not from any external pressure or internal lack, but God's own character. Because God, as told to us by Christ, is "Holy Love," he was inexorably moved to create personalities who would manifest this same characteristic and who could therefore answer him like with like.[115] This statement seems to be based upon Forsyth's insistence elsewhere that God's "love" is to be understood primarily as the "outgoing" of his holiness, one which involves the "brimming and overflowing" of it to that which is not God.[116] Forsyth goes on to say that this "love" is such an integral aspect of holiness that without it God cannot truly be called holy. It is, in other words, the very nature of holiness to spread itself: "But if the holiness do not go out to cover, imbue, conquer, and sanctify all things, if it do not give itself in love, it is the less holy . . . As holy he must subdue all and bless all."[117] Herein lies the necessity for creation—God's holy love determined that it "would not only be perfectly met in his Uncreated Son, but really multiplied in his sons create."[118]

Forsyth, in the same passage, further seeks to defend the freedom of God in creation from external compulsion by contesting the traditional notion of *creatio ex nihilo*. It was impossible for God to have created out of nothing, because "if God is in any sense all in all, there never was a nothing out of which the creature should rise."[119] Because creation came out,

---

114. "Regeneration, Creation, and Miracle," 640.
115. Ibid., 641–43.
116. *Society*, 12, 30; *Positive Preaching*, 145.
117. *Life*, 33.
118. "Regeneration, Creation, and Miracle," 642–43.
119. Ibid., 640. See also "Things New and Old," 276. This misunderstands in some ways the central thrust of the doctrine of *creatio ex nihilo* as it was traditionally understood—it

so to speak, from within God, "the other that [God] needed and created in his world was still within himself," constituting his "own Other," therefore further dispelling the notion that God was determined by something outside of himself. Forsyth does not say very much more about how we are to conceive of the world arising from and existing within God. He does suggest, when discussing his Christology, that creation can be conceived of as being always in the Son, so that the Father's relationship with creation is subsumed under his relationship with the Son.[120] Elsewhere, Forsyth proposes a different imagery, and suggests that we can think of the world belonging to God in a similar way as a body belongs to its soul.[121] As a result, the life of the world is "the immanence of the Transcendent," and "the infinite is the content of a finite which holds of the eternal."[122] This profound immanence of God in creation, however, faces a limit. God cannot be understood as being immanent in the will of the human creatures he made, thus ensuring that these creatures possess genuine freedom. Reinforcing what we have seen earlier concerning the necessity of freedom for the moral response of faith, Forsyth adds that it is only the moral soul owning a conferred freedom who can "realise God in his free transcendence," because "only freedom can understand freedom."[123]

Our brief foray into how Forsyth views God's relationship with creation reveals a large degree of sympathy on his part for that view of the God-world relationship commonly known as "panentheism."[124] Now "panentheism" is a slippery term that has been used to depict movements

---

does not affirm that there ever was a "nothing" out of which God created. Its purpose was rather to exclude both the ideas that God used pre-existing matter to fashion the world and that the world was an emanation from God's own being. This is well explained in Fergusson, *Cosmos and the Creator*, 23–31.

120. *Person*, 342–43. This point is made in the context of Forsyth's discussion on God's changelessness. Such changelessness "has in it the power and secret of all change, all outgoing, without going out of himself." This on its own, however, cannot explain God's relationship to human beings, since they are not eternally within God's self. Forsyth's solution is: "But he went out always to His increate Son, in whom and through whom all creation is and all Humanity . . ."

121. Forsyth adds, in *Authority*, 158, that this imagery has the added benefit of precluding the idea that God enters into a substantive union with the world, something we have seen Forsyth rejecting in chapter 3.

122. *Justification*, 73.

123. "Regeneration, Creation, and Miracle," 643.

124. A similar observation has been made by Russell, "Spoiling the Egyptians," 233.

as diverse as process theism and the idealism of George Berkeley.[125] We do not intend to enter here into a technical exposition of the term, but merely to observe that Forsyth holds on to two tenets commonly associated with this position. The first is the idea that the world is, in some sense or other, to be conceived of as arising from and existing within God. The second is the affirmation that God, again in some sense or other, fulfils a need of his through the world.[126] These two tenets certainly have an impact on Forsyth's theodicy, especially in relation to his position on the origin of evil. In the next chapter, we will examine the main criticisms to which Forsyth opens himself, and how he might defend the viability of his position.

CONCLUSION

We have examined, in this chapter, Forsyth's likely position on the origin of evil, i.e., *how* and *why* sin and suffering came into our world. We have adopted what we hope to be a sufficiently refined approach to this exercise, one which draws out the implications of Forsyth's thought where appropriate, but refrains from dispelling the aspects of mystery he clearly wishes to retain. We gain, in the end, some answers as to how Forsyth understood sin and suffering to have come into our world. We also suggested a justification which Forsyth might implicitly have held for the advent of suffering. This, however, does not apply to the entry of sin, which remains, in Forsyth's view, a historical occurrence to which no higher purpose can be ascribed. This does not prevent Forsyth from uttering that ancient exclamation "*O felix culpa!*" All has turned out well—in fact, even better than first intended, because God had the resources within himself to turn what was literally a "life-threatening" situation (to both himself and the world) to his advantage. What these resources are have been described in our earlier chapters dealing with the "practical" aspect of Forsyth's theodicy. We looked finally at Forsyth's view of the God-world relationship and noted his embrace of some of the tenets of panentheism. In the next chapter, we will offer some reflections on the significance for Forsyth's theodicy of what we have covered here.

125. See, e.g., Beck, "Panentheism," in *New Dictionary of Theology*, 486.

126. These two characteristics of "panentheism" are mentioned in Leftow, "God, Concepts Of," in *Routledge Encyclopedia of Philosophy*, online: http://www.rep.routledge.com/article/K030SECT8.

8

The Significance of Forsyth's View on the Origin of Evil

IMPLICATIONS OF FORSYTH'S VIEW OF THE GOD-WORLD RELATIONSHIP

Two Possible Objections to Forsyth's Theodicy

A GOOD STARTING POINT for our reflection is Forsyth's view of the God-world relationship. His affinity to certain aspects of panentheism implies that some of the critiques levelled by classical theists against this position might potentially apply to his thought. We see two objections to panentheism which have a particular bearing on the subject of theodicy. They are the arguments that panentheism renders evil meaningful and that it compromises the notion of God's love for the world. David Bentley Hart has perhaps stated the first most sharply (in the context of his critique of Moltmann and Jüngel):

> A God who can by nature experience finite affects and so be determined by them is a God whose identity is established through a commerce with evil; if the nature of God's love can be in any sense positively shaped by sin, suffering, and death, then sin, suffering, and death will always be in some sense features of who he is . . . And so, if one pursues the logic of divine becoming to its proper end, one will find that all things are necessary aspects of God's odyssey towards himself; every painful death of a child, every casual act of brutality, all war, famine, pestilence, disease, murder . . . all will turn out to be moments in the identity of God, resonances within the event of his being, aspects of the occurrence of his essence: all evil will become meaningful—speculatively meaningful and so necessary—as the crucible in which God is forged . . . And

> so [God] may include us in his story, but his story will remain both good and evil even if it ends in an ultimate triumph over evil. After all, how can we tell the dancer from the dance? . . . And this is a fearful thought, especially if, like Moltmann one seeks in the passions of the divine an explanation for the suffering of creatures: what a monstrous irony it would be if, in our eagerness to find a way of believing in God's love in the age of Auschwitz, we should in fact succeed only in describing a God who is the metaphysical ground of Auschwitz.[1]

The point then is that panentheism[2] renders evil meaningful because it treats evil as a means towards God's end of establishing his own identity. More fundamentally, Hart mentions that the claim that "the nature of God's love can be in any sense positively shaped by sin, suffering, and death" leads inevitably to the idea that "sin, suffering and death will always be in some sense features of who [God] is." This suggests that panentheism leads finally to the notion that evil is rooted within God himself. After all, the "dancer" cannot be separated from the "dance," and therefore, God (under this scheme) must constitute "the metaphysical ground of Auschwitz."

The second relevant objection to panentheism has already been hinted at in the quotation above. Because God fulfils a need of his through the world, it follows that his acts of creation and redemption are not thoroughly altruistic in nature. God's love for the world is therefore severely compromised, in that there exists a significant element of the self-seeking in such "love."[3] This objection can be reinforced by incorporating Hart's point that, in order to fulfil his need through creation, God has allowed (and is continuing to allow) it to be subjected to immense suffering, especially that caused by the wickedness of humans. We can therefore question not only God's love, but his morality. Related to this is the critique that, under a panentheistic scheme, God's acts of creation and redemption were not performed out of love because they were not truly free. If God could not have done otherwise than to create and redeem, this makes it dubious to call them acts of love. Clifford Pitt makes these points against Forsyth's position:

---

1. Hart, "No Shadow of Turning," 191–92.
2. This is not a term Hart uses, but it is implied that he is speaking against the major features of this position.
3. Weinandy, *Does God Suffer?* 226–27.

> If redemption was required by [God's] holiness, it could not have been withheld. It could not then be voluntary action. In what sense then is grace a gift? The God presented by this picture seems more concerned about himself and his infrangible holiness, than with the plight of the miserable sinner. He becomes a selfish God and his purpose in "creation" is called into question. It is the question of whether man was made for God's gratification, or as an expression of love.[4]

Forsyth's Likely Response to the First Objection

It should not surprise us to find that Forsyth did not deal with these two objections in a systematic fashion. Nevertheless, we find portions of his writings, especially those which recognise and warn against the dangers of a Hegelian "monism," containing important resources for developing a response to these objections. Let us first consider the critique that panentheism treats evil as a means to God's end, and, more fundamentally, that it roots evil within the being of God. As far as evil as sin is concerned, we must say that Forsyth's insistence on the absolute antagonism between God and sin makes it highly unlikely that his theodicy concludes (whether wittingly or not) with the idea that sin is "in some sense [a feature] of who God is." Echoing the words of 1 John 1:5, Forsyth asserts that there is "no darkness . . . in [God] at all,"[5] and we see no reason to doubt his statement. We have argued in the previous chapter that Forsyth should be interpreted as precluding the notion that God ordained sin into the world as a means to his end. If a more perfect *eschaton* results from the entry of sin into the world (and Forsyth asserts it does), it arises through the destruction of sin rather than its incorporation into a higher synthesis. In Forsyth's scheme, therefore, sin does not have the status of a *conditio sine qua non* of God's plan for the world (and for himself), nor does it have any role at all in the glorious *eschaton*. Whatever else it might allow, Forsyth's version of panentheism does not leave room for the integration of God and sin.

Regarding evil as suffering, the issue is less clear-cut. There can be no doubt that Forsyth sees God using suffering as a means to his end. This was so at the point in biological evolution when humans first emerged.

---

4. Pitt, *Church, Ministry and Sacraments*, 41.
5. "Regeneration, Creation, and Miracle: Second Article," 87.

This was so in the earthly career and death of Christ. This continues to be so in the secondary judgement we experience in the light of the Cross. Since such suffering is necessary for the fulfilment of God's holiness, does this not make it an integral aspect of who God is? Moreover, if suffering, and the struggle it gives rise to, is a prerequisite of morality, and morality is derived from God's holiness, is there not an inevitable eternal suffering within the holy God? We answer these questions in the negative, because of what we see to be Forsyth's successful attempt to distinguish his position from that of full-fledged Hegelian panentheism. Forsyth denies that God's "need" for the world should be understood in terms like "self-completion," "self-realisation" or "perfecting."[6] God is not in a process of "becoming" together with the world, because "He is the ever holy, the morally self-sufficient and self-complete."[7] Forsyth, in fact, denigrates the Hegelian notion of a God who needs to realise himself through creation. Such a God "might end anywhere, even in an ethic that reversed all his past" and cannot therefore be a person who merits our trust.[8] How then does Forsyth understand God to "need" the world? Inferring from what he has written, it seems that, for him, God "needs" the world in two related senses. Firstly, God "needs" the world in the very limited sense that God's holiness generates a moral necessity for him to create an "other" whom he can shape into his holy likeness. God "needs," in other words, a recipient outside of the Trinity for his holy love to flow into.[9] Secondly, once this world has come into being, God "needs" it to fulfil the purpose for which it was created, for his fate is now inextricably tied up with it. We suggest that this "need" is best understood as a moral one—God "needs" the world to arrive at the *telos* he has appointed for it because he, as the Creator, holds ultimate responsibility for how the world turns out. As we have seen earlier, Forsyth understands God to have created the world in spite of foreseeing the inevitable intrusion of sin, because God knew he possessed the resources within himself to remedy the undesirable state of affairs that would result. For God to be justified in this decision, therefore, the world must reach its intended goal.[10] Otherwise he would be proved

6. Ibid.
7. Ibid., 90.
8. Ibid., 89–90.
9. This has some resonances with Moltmann's postulation of God's need for the world (*Trinity and the Kingdom*, 58–59).
10. Hall also sees the notion of God's responsibility arising from Forsyth's writings on the origin of evil ("Tragedy in the Theology of P. T. Forsyth," 97).

wrong, and that must mean he ceases to be God in any meaningful sense of the term. Now these two senses of "need" do not imply any lack in God. It represents, on the contrary, overflowing fullness on God's part, one that brims over into that which is not God, and which possesses immense confidence in its own ability to achieve its purposes in spite of the intrusion of its antithesis. For Forsyth, therefore, God did not create with the aim of completing or realising himself, but rather in selfless love for his creatures[11]—because his sole motivation was to share his holiness with them. This point is perhaps brought forth most clearly in a rather surprising source. In his book of stories addressed to children entitled *Pulpit Parables for Young Hearers*, Forsyth recounts a tale about a boy and a Christmas tree his parents had set up for him:

> Now, what did they do it all for? Not to find their way about; they had gas for that. Not because they were obliged to do it; nobody is obliged by the laws to have a Christmas-tree, with candles or presents or anything else. They did it to make delight; they did it for the joy of seeing you joyful and sharing your joy; they did it out of the full kindness of their good fatherly and motherly hearts; they did it to make more happiness in the world than there was before; they did it to help make home more of home and more of heaven. Now we have the answer to our puzzle. That is also the reason why God made this huge Christmas-tree of a world, and lighted it up with innumerable living souls as candles of the Lord, and gave gifts unto men. It was out of the fullness of His great, great heart. It was because He wanted to have you, and you, and you, shining spirits, to share His ever-shining joy. From His own light He lighted up millions of lights more that He might rejoice in them, and they rejoice in Him. You, with your minds and souls—candles of the Lord—were set by Him for His joy and yours, that joy might be full.[12]

Keeping in mind the danger of drawing theological inferences too readily from a story meant for children, the point seems to be clearly brought forth that God created the world for the sole purpose of sharing his joy with his creatures. After the world came into existence, there does arise a mutuality whereby both God and the world rejoice in each other. God's joy then becomes very much dependent upon how the world turns out. This, however, does not affect the point that God's act of creation was, fun-

---

11. "Regeneration, Creation, and Miracle," 641–42; *Person*, 353–54.
12. *Pulpit Parables for Young Hearers*, 113–14.

damentally, not self-seeking. What started off as perfect self-giving love ends up in a vulnerable dependence on the object of love. This, we suggest, is also reflected in our human experience of love, and we should have little difficulty comprehending it.[13] So, in response to the first objection, Forsyth would, we think, say that since God does not need "sin, suffering, and death" to complete himself, none of these constitute "a [feature] of who God is." He would also, we suggest, have reiterated the point we saw him making in chapter 5, that struggle, and therefore suffering, is a prerequisite for holiness only for human creatures (and, we should add, the incarnate Son) who exist in the context of time and space. "What is of Godhead," Forsyth asserts, "does not grow,"[14] and that includes God's holiness. This holiness does find a satisfaction in obtaining the holy response of God's creatures, but this response does not add to God's holiness in any way—it does not render God more holy than before.[15] We may therefore state here the same conclusion we had arrived at (on a different basis) in chapter 5: there is, for Forsyth, no "eternal cross" within God in the sense that suffering forms an integral part of his being. Forsyth, as we mentioned earlier, sees suffering strictly as a means to an end. Where there is no necessity to utilise such means, it does not enter the picture at all.

Forsyth's Likely Response to the Second Objection

Turning now to the second objection, we find that we have already answered it in part. Contrary to Pitt's observation, there is no "selfish God" in Forsyth's theology. God created purely out of grace and not self-interest. In any case, the decisive objection to Pitt's criticism is that he draws a stark dichotomy between God's interest and ours, one alien to Forsyth's thought. We have already made this point in our evaluation of Forsyth's notion of God's secondary judgement in chapter 4. For Forsyth, human

---

13. If we might be allowed a human analogy of our own, when a set of "perfect" parents decide to adopt a child, they do not do so with the aim of deriving anything from him, whether it be tangible returns like material support in their old age, or intangible ones like joy and companionship. They do it out of a sole desire for his well-being and happiness. However, after the child becomes part of the family, the parents find their joy intrinsically bound up with his. They will only find joy if he does. So, what started off as perfect self-giving love ends up in a vulnerable dependence on the object of love. This might also serve to illustrate the principle that we do not find true joy if we seek it specifically—it has to be the by-product of a quest for something else.

14. *Person*, 284.

15. *Monism*, 9.

welfare is best secured by our concern with the satisfaction of God's holiness. Whether (in Pitt's words) "man was made for God's gratification, or as an expression of love" is, at a deeper level, irrelevant, for God's gratification is derived from the success of his love's mission to bring creation to its glorious end. God's joy, as Forsyth's parable suggests, is found in ours. Anders Nygren's proposal for distinguishing love into the mutually exclusive categories of "agape" and "eros" has received its share of criticism.[16] Forsyth would, we think, propose the total abolition of the dichotomy in God's case. God's "eros" is best attained by his "agape," and vice versa.

On the point of God's freedom, Forsyth, as we have seen, is not afraid to say that God was bound by a "real necessity" to create our world.[17] In doing so, he rejects the avenues taken by some in their bid to preserve the notion of God's freedom in creation. He would definitely have denied Barth's insistence on God's unfettered freedom vis-à-vis his creation, one in which God could theoretically not have created.[18] "The freedom of God," Forsyth maintains, "was not a freedom to create or not create. That were a freedom very elementary, arbitrary, and for him unreal. It were to introduce something accidental into him."[19] We suggest that Forsyth would also have rejected Keith Ward's more limited attempt to preserve God's freedom by arguing that, although God's "outward-directed love and creativity *must* be actualised at some particular place and time," God can choose the "particular world in which to actualise this potential for relationship with created beings."[20] Forsyth, in a passage probably directed against Leibniz, expressly precludes this possibility:

> And the relation between [God] and his world is not accidental. His world is not merely the best possible, perhaps but a second best. He did not deliberate, pick, and choose among possible worlds, and then decide on the fittest. That were too anthropomorphic. Within a created world indeed diverse possibilities might be

16. See, e.g., Badcock, "Concept of Love," 40–46; Fiddes, *Creative Suffering*, 169–73 and "Creation out of Love," 168–75.

17. "Regeneration, Creation, and Miracle," 641.

18. Barth, *Church Dogmatics* II/1, 280–81. See Fiddes, *Creative Suffering*, 71; Moltmann, *Trinity and the Kingdom*, 52–55; Lewis, *Between Cross and Resurrection*, 209–12 for criticisms of Barth's position.

19. "Regeneration, Creation, and Miracle," 642.

20. This description of Ward's position is derived from Fiddes, "Creation out of Love," 180 (emphasis in original). Ward's views are expressed in his works *Rational Theology and the Creativity of God*, 140–46 and *Religion and Creation*, 175, 225–27.

presented to him by himself as means to an end, means contingent on the free behavior of the creature; but he could not present to himself worlds good and less good for his own selection as ends. If he could but choose the best, he could but think the best.[21]

Forsyth would, we think, even have rejected Fiddes' attempt to modify Barth's position and suggest the integration of "will and desire." Fiddes' view is well summed up in the following:

> Understanding God's will as desire indicates that there can be no "otherwise" in the love of God for mankind. Because he thirsts and longs for fellowship with his creatures it makes no sense to say that he need not do so. But if we ask why he so thirsts, we cannot get back behind the choice of God. Each aspect, will and desire, defines the other.[22]

We suggest that Forsyth would try to break the tension so carefully preserved in the above passage, and insist that God's choice is fully determined by God's nature. As Forsyth himself puts it, if he retains the language of God's "will and choice," it is merely to signify that creation was done not from "external coercion, internal poverty, or blind instinct."[23] It is not to give a primacy to choice in the sense that it can be conceived of as somehow prior or even parallel to God's nature. To use Fiddes' phrase, "the furthest frontier of our knowledge of God" is, for Forsyth, not "God's choice of his creation,"[24] but God's being as holy love.

In spite of all these, Forsyth insists as strongly as those surveyed above on the reality of God's freedom in creation. He does so by appealing to the idea that it is true freedom to act in accordance with who one is. Because the necessity which God faced was solely that "of his personal spiritual nature," it is "a necessity whose action is perfect freedom."[25] We see in

21. "Regeneration, Creation, and Miracle," 642. A similar point in made in "Christ's Person and His Cross," 8.

22. Fiddes, *Creative Suffering*, 74. See also his "Creation out of Love," 181–84.

23. "Regeneration, Creation, and Miracle," 642. This binding effect of God's nature upon God's will, and how it does not violate the requirement that God be omnipotent, have been asserted by prominent Christian philosophers of Forsyth's time. See, e.g., Rashdall, "Problem of Evil," 96; and Pringle-Pattison, *Idea of God in the Light of Recent Philosophy*, 404.

24. Fiddes, *Creative Suffering*, 74.

25. "Regeneration, Creation, and Miracle," 641. The contemporary theologian whom Forsyth comes closest to in his view of God's freedom in creation is probably Moltmann: see, e.g., his *Trinity and the Kingdom*, 53–55, 105–8 and *God in Creation*, 76, 80–83.

statements like this the possible influence again of George Galloway. In a discussion on human freedom, Galloway advances the view that humans possess a real power to choose between alternatives because a distinction exists between our self and character:

> The motives with which this basal self identifies itself are those which issue from the character that has been formed, and it is by realising one motive or another that the act of will becomes bad or good. But the character through which the self expresses itself is not something fixed and immutable: it is more or less plastic and growing. And so long as it is not a perfectly unified and consistent whole, it contains within it certain open possibilities, which may lead to different courses of action . . . It is these open possibilities which make the act of choice a real choice, and explain the agent's conviction that he could have done otherwise.[26]

Galloway follows through with the proposition that "the less plastic character becomes, the greater internal unity and coherency it achieves, the fewer are the variations which it admits, and the smaller the likelihood of new beginnings. The ideal is perfect self-determinism under the dominance of the good will." Under his scheme, therefore, a personality whose self and character are perfectly united, like God, does not possess choice in the libertarian sense. Yet he exercises a "freedom of [a] higher kind" than the mere freedom to do otherwise.[27] This differentiating of freedom into two kinds might be behind Forsyth's statement that human beings were given "moral freedom" (i.e., libertarian freedom) at creation in order to realise a higher "spiritual freedom" at the *eschaton*.[28]

In response, then, to the objection that God's acts of creation and redemption were not done out of love because they were not truly free, Forsyth would, we think, have disputed the point that these were not free. They represent, on the contrary, the acme of freedom, which is the unity of nature and will, such that the latter flows perfectly in conformity with the former. It is a freedom, in fact, which we humans with our power to choose between alternatives are still to strive for. Forsyth might also point to the absurdity inherent within the objection. If God, as he understands it, is holy love, and love is to be primarily understood as the "outgoing"

---

26. Galloway, *Philosophy of Religion*, 538–39.

27. Ibid., 539.

28. *Justification*, 125–26. This might be related to Forsyth's assertion that the conflict we face between the "must" and the "ought" will cease at the *eschaton*.

of his holiness, resulting in creation and redemption, it does not make sense to say that these acts were not done out of love. The sole motivation behind these acts, and the only reason why they were carried out, is love.[29] Therefore, according to Forsyth's scheme of thought, which includes the way he utilises terms and concepts, the objection that God did not create out of love because that act was necessitated can be quite easily refuted.

A DUALISM IN FORSYTH'S THEODICY?

While we are on the topic of God's freedom, we should add that Forsyth's insistence on the "moral necessity" God faced to create *this* world (and not another) must mean that our world, at its point of creation and before the intrusion of sin, was indeed "the best of all possible worlds" God could have created. Forsyth acknowledges as much.[30] This evaluation should, we suggest, be made according to Forsyth's "Irenaean" view of creation, i.e., that this world was, at the point of its coming into being, in the best possible state for its development towards its intended *telos*. Both the presence of suffering within creation and the subsequent entry of sin which results from the wrong exercise of human freedom do not detract from this conclusion, because suffering and human free will are, as we have seen, two essential conditions for the development of a human moral response to God. These observations lead us to consider George Hall's suggestion that, for Forsyth, there is a "surd element" in creation in the sense that "sin and evil are always 'already there.'" Let us see his full comment:

> Forsyth's reticence to speak of the origin of sin and his silence on the myth of the Garden of Eden, taken together with what he says about collision, struggle, and the fall of the will, is indicative not only of the ambiguity of human freedom and the inevitability of sin, but also, by implication only, the possibility that here we speak of a surd element in things—wherever we look, sin and evil are already there. While it is not said explicitly, the message seems to be that "sin posits itself"—Forsyth says nothing that would contradict it and much that he does say implies it. If sin and evil are always "already there" this only reinforces Forsyth's conviction that the battle between "eternal sin" and "eternal Saviour" is of such magnitude that only God's tragic self-negation could gain the victory.[31]

29. "Regeneration, Creation, and Miracle," 642.
30. Ibid.
31. Hall, "Tragedy in the Theology of P. T. Forsyth," 98.

Hall is possibly suggesting here that Forsyth comes near to a dualism in his theology—not a final dualism in which God and sin forever co-exist in opposition, but at least a provisional one whereby an "eternal sin" which is "always already there" mysteriously manifests itself in God's good creation. While we ultimately disagree with the way Hall characterises Forsyth's position, we acknowledge his insightful remark that there might be something tending towards a dualism in Forsyth's thought. This "dualism" is, however, not founded upon an "eternal sin" which was "always already there," but Forsyth's redefinition of the notion of God's "omnipotence."[32]

Forsyth boldly states that "in the natural, arbitrary, and unregenerate sense in which we understand the word, God is not omnipotent."[33] What he rejects here is the idea that the omnipotence of God means that God can do everything imaginable. Rather, we learn from "the God incarnate in Christ" that "He can do only the things that are congruous with His moral, His holy nature and purpose."[34] It follows from this, we suggest, that for God to establish a holy creation, he *must* do it in the particular way dictated by the demand of holiness. This means that God *must* utilise the elements of human free will, struggle and time. There is no way, even for God, to short-circuit the process. Now this potent mix of free will, struggle and time leads, as we have seen, inevitably to sin (although, as we have argued, this was not actively intended by God). It would therefore not be inaccurate to say that, for Forsyth, God is bound to have to work through the conditions of suffering and sin in order to arrive at his goal for his creation. There is, in other words, no other way to creaturely holiness except through the path of evil. Now this way of "limiting" God's omnipotence has been termed "dualistic" by some writers. This is seen perhaps most clearly when they apply this label to Leibniz's theodicy. As the argument goes, Leibniz's idea that God was unable to create "the best of all possible worlds" without positing evil (i.e., both sin and suffering) as the *conditio sine qua non* of such a world[35] places such a

---

32. The phrase "eternal sin" is used by Forsyth in his writings, but he makes it clear that he derives it from Mark 3:29 (*Person*, 54, 94). Robert A. Guelich, in his *Word Biblical Commentary*, vol. 34a, *Mark 1—8:26*, 179, suggests that this Bible passage speaks about the "eternal" consequence of sin rather than the "eternal" nature of sin. There is nothing in Forsyth's use of the phrase which suggests that he departs from this understanding.

33. *Person*, 227.

34. Ibid., 227–28.

35. Leibniz, *Theodicy*, 270, 335.

severe limitation on God's power that the theodicy should ultimately be seen as dualistic in nature.[36] Forsyth would have been familiar with this argument, since John Stuart Mill made it as far back as 1874 in his *Essays on Religion*, a work familiar to Forsyth.[37] It is interesting, therefore, that Forsyth should still choose (as we have seen earlier) to classify Leibniz's theodicy under the "monistic" category (and attack it on that basis) rather than the "dualistic" one. We suggest that this could be because Forsyth did not consider Leibniz's limitation on the notion of God's omnipotence a dualistic manoeuvre. It is, after all, a move which Forsyth himself makes, with the crucial difference that God permitted only suffering (and not sin) to be the *conditio sine qua non* of this, "the best of all possible worlds." Sin is therefore removed from both necessity and God's intention under Forsyth's approach, a distinction which allows him to turn and criticise Leibniz's system for its "monism."[38]

So, is Forsyth's theodicy ultimately dualistic? We suggest not, for the reason that Forsyth sees the limitation on God's power described above

---

36. See, e.g., Hick, *Evil and the God of Love*, 151, 156, 165–66; Walker, *Decline of Hell*, 57.

37. In Mill, *Essays on Ethics, Religion and Society*, 390. Mill's *Essays on Religion* is cited in the bibliography of *Justification*.

38. Forsyth, we suggest, might have directed a similar criticism towards Barth if he had read the section entitled "Creation as Justification" of *Church Dogmatics* III/I (hereafter "*CD* III/I"). This section develops Barth's argument that our world is indeed the best of all possible. Barth's basis for saying so is that both the "positive" and "negative" aspects of this world were "created for Jesus Christ and His death and resurrection" and its effect in lifting humans up to fellowship with God (375–76). Forsyth would, we think, deny that the death and resurrection of Christ was purposed by God at the outset of creation, for that would render the entry of sin necessary. He has, in combating the Hegelian notion that the synthesis of God and human beings was necessitated by the dialectical process, contested the speculation that the incarnation would have taken place had sin not entered creation (*Justification*, 148–49). It is interesting that Barth characterises his writings on the subject as the theological "counterpart" to the philosophical approach of Leibniz and his disciples (*CD* III/I, 388). Barth, for sure, goes on to subject the optimistic theodicies of the eighteenth century to a searching criticism and distinguish his position from theirs. But while an aspect of Barth's critique is that "Leibnizian optimism passes too lightly over the problem of evil, sin and death" (407), there is finally no objection to the notion of sin as a *conditio sine qua non* of the best of all possible worlds. It is also interesting to note that while Barth's approach is clearly Christocentric and depends to a large extent on the *theologia crucis*, Forsyth's is no less so. For the latter, the life and death struggle between God and sin in the life of Christ and, most supremely, on the Cross, tells him that God could never have intended sin as a necessary condition for any higher goal.

as one solely generated by God's own nature as holy. It is a self-limitation and not one imposed upon God by an alien power or principle. Forsyth would, in fact, say that such self-limitation represents the height of omnipotence. In a telling statement, Forsyth writes that "God's method with evil is not prevention but cure."[39] In overcoming and "curing" evil, God demonstrates a greater omnipotence than if he had merely "prevented" it. Let us leave the last word in this section to Forsyth's eloquent tribute to God's conquering omnipotence:

> "How awful goodness is." The more we know about cosmic forces, antres vast, deserts horrible, Alps of thick ribbed ice, seas, continents, vastitudes of every kind; of geological ages, stellar spaces, solar storms; of creature agonies, of social miseries, devilish wickedness, civilised triumphs, historic heroisms, the grandeur of genius and unquenchable love; of all the passion, for evil on the one hand, or, on the other, for the Eternal, Immortal, and Invisible good so much the more we must feel how awful is the holy love of God, that has secured the grand issue for ever, that surmounts all principalities and powers, things past, present, and to come, every other omnipotence; surmounts, nay exploits, them all. In the Holy One of God, who by His cross is the same world-conqueror yesterday, to-day, and for ever.[40]

ANOTHER SOURCE OF THE EVILS WE EXPERIENCE?

While Forsyth makes extensive references to God's acts of secondary judgement as the source of much of the suffering we experience in this world, we have noted in chapter 3 that nowhere does he assert that all of our suffering can be explained on this basis. Indeed, his statement that "all sin is an ill, but all ill is not sin, nor is it caused by it"[41] indicates his understanding that suffering can occur apart from sin and the purpose of its overcoming. One clear example of such suffering can be seen in our earlier description of Forsyth's view of the origins of the human race. Because of his acceptance of the theory of biological evolution, Forsyth saw that "suffering abounded in the animal world before man appeared with the moral freedom that makes sin possible."[42] Such pre-human suf-

39. *Justification*, 14.
40. *Person*, 228–29.
41. *Justification*, 138.
42. Ibid.

fering cannot conceivably be justified according to the principles of secondary judgement. We suggest that, for Forsyth, this severance between suffering and sin applies as a general principle throughout the history of this world, and not merely in the period before (sinful) humanity makes its appearance. So, while some of this world's suffering can indeed be attributed to the aims of secondary judgement, there remains suffering which does not arise on that basis. One possibility which readily comes to mind is the suffering that results from the occurrence of natural disasters. It is true that nothing in Forsyth's writings precludes the possibility that these disasters could be the result of God's judgement—God is able to use even "nature" to shatter our self-confidence and turn us to him. But given Forsyth's postulation of an "Irenaean view" of creation, where such disasters arise from the fundamental way the world was constituted (rather than from the Fall), the possibility must surely remain that the disasters we experience in the here and now can be attributable to this basis rather than God's judgement of sin. As for the suffering which arises due to human sin, while Forsyth sees God's sovereignty extending to the point where he can use sin against sin (see chapter 3), he does not seem to have extended this to an absolute principle accounting for all occurrences of sin. It is also doubtful if he could have done so, since the primacy Forsyth allocates to the functioning of creaturely free will might dictate that he cannot also affirm that God is able to render purposive every single act of sin. Michael Smith points out the "difficulty in reconciling an account of evil in which God is respecting our free choices with one in which he is using these evils as goads or cures."[43] While we wish to affirm that God, in his wisdom and power, is certainly able to subvert sin in order to fulfil his purposes in many instances, it might be stretching the notion of God's sovereignty too far for Forsyth's comfort to say that this is always the case. We therefore suggest that Forsyth probably sees some of the suffering caused by sin as having no deeper source or purpose than simply the result of evil acts willed by human beings.

If our analysis of Forsyth's position is accurate, we can say that at least some of the evil (i.e., sin and suffering) humankind has experienced throughout world history finds its source not in God's secondary judgement, but the conditions in which the first human beings found themselves. The same types of suffering which "abounded" then in order for

---

43. Smith, "What's So Good About Feeling Bad?" 424. The specific target of Smith's comment is Eleonore Stump's theodicy.

"faith-production" to be possible still afflict us now. And the sin which arose inevitably due to the conflict the first human beings faced between the "must" and the "ought" still plagues us today—we who continue to experience that same enduring conflict, whose resolution will only take place in the *eschaton*.

Two questions arise from this. Firstly, how are we to tell whether a particular instance of suffering is the result of God's secondary judgement or that of the conditions of our origin? Some situations are more obvious than others—if the tragedy that strikes us is the "expected" moral consequence of our sinful acts (e.g., someone who contracts a venereal disease after numerous encounters with prostitutes), we can perhaps say with some certainty that God's secondary judgement is operative here. This idea of the "expected" moral consequence extends beyond an individual level, as Forsyth's analysis of the situation leading up to the Great War tells us. Outside of this, Forsyth does not offer much guidance, and perhaps there is no way to tell conclusively based on our limited human perspective. In keeping with the spirit of Forsyth's constant exhortation for his readers to undergo ruthless self-examination, however, perhaps the key attitude we can adopt in this matter is that of a constant openness to the possibility of secondary judgement whenever tragedy strikes us. We should examine our lives, both individually and corporately, to see if this tragedy speaks to our situation in any meaningful sense. For tragedy falling upon others, we should perhaps be less quick to attribute it to God's judgement. Even if we eventually do so, we should try to imbibe Forsyth's extreme aversion to any form of triumphalism, and ask if we ourselves are not guilty of the same sins we ascribe to others, and then inquire fearfully if greater judgement is not being stored up for us who escape it this time around.

The second question which arises is the impact this other source of suffering has on Forsyth's theodicy. We have seen how Forsyth has tried to justify the suffering which arises from God's acts of secondary judgement on the bases of its necessity for the attainment of the glorious end and the notion of God as the chief sufferer and giver. Our response is to say that all these arguments should apply with equal force to the suffering which arises from the conditions of our origin. Because these conditions are essential to the development of human faith (which is *the* key component of the glorious *eschaton*), the suffering to which they lead can be justified on the same teleological basis. To the objection that these conditions are too harsh and lead to suffering which cannot be accounted for on the basis of "faith-production" alone, Forsyth would likely point again to the need on our part to trust God and commit the issues of necessity and appropriateness into his hands. The arguments in chapter 6 concerning how God's suffering speaks to ours are also applicable here—the most significant cost of our "crucial evolution" towards the *telos* is actually borne by God himself, and his identification with all our suffering transforms the perspective with which we view them.

We should add, however, that in the light of our discussion here, Forsyth's refusal (or, more properly, inability) to postulate universalism without qualifications incurs a greater cost for his theodicy. There are, as we have seen, parts of his writing where he suggests that the inevitable entry of sin into our world does not significantly diminish the human responsibility for sin. But surely the larger perspective must be that God retains ultimate responsibility for how the world and its creatures turn out. A. M. Fairbairn's comment seems a reasonable one:

> . . . although it be granted that man is responsible for the introduction of moral evil (and we here recognize the fact that many would refuse to grant so much), yet we must conceive the Creator as responsible for the system under which it was introduced, which made it possible, which allowed it to become actual, and which now follows it with moral penalties and physical sufferings. We ought not to shrink from affirming what we have called the responsibility of God . . .[44]

We have seen that Forsyth implicitly affirms this notion of God's ultimate responsibility for the world. Indeed, under the "Irenaean view" of creation, God holds a far greater responsibility for the entry of both sin and suffering into the world than he would under the "Augustinian" scheme, which at least envisages the possibility that the first human beings might have refrained from sin altogether, with the implication that suffering would also not have made an appearance. For the "Irenaean view," however, suffering was ordained in the first instance by God, and sin follows as an inevitable consequence of this context of suffering. The justification for this entire scheme is found in the *telos*, when "the end will justify the means." But what if some (or even just one) human soul fails to arrive at this intended *telos*? Can God be said to have fulfilled his responsibility to

---

44. Fairbairn, *Philosophy of the Christian Religion*, 132–33.

his creatures, who never had the real opportunity to avoid the advent of suffering and (consequently) sin? John Hick, the foremost contemporary proponent of a theodicy based upon the "Irenaean view" of creation, gives a clear negative answer:

> If the justification of evil within the creative process lies in the limitless and eternal good of the end-state to which it leads, then the completeness of the justification must depend upon the completeness, or universality, of the salvation achieved. Only if it includes the entire human race can it justify the sins and sufferings of the entire human race throughout all history.[45]

This reasoning seems incontestable. We note, with some irony, that the early Forsyth (prior to his evangelical "conversion") might have been more consistent on this matter than the mature thinker. As he preached in his early sermon "Mercy the True and Only Justice":

> Can it be just that God should bring beings into the world unprotected by an infinite armour of foresight against the infinite chances and temptations to wrong, and yet hold them liable to infinite punishment when they had gone wrong? Could he have sent the first man here with faculties limited, and experience nothing, and then fix eternal torment as the penalty of his slightest sin? Could that be just? No.[46]

Forsyth's theodicy, therefore, can be said to fall into the conundrum which afflicts most other theodicies relying upon an "Irenaean view" of creation. Because of the strong notion of God's responsibility that comes with it, they are compelled to postulate universal salvation as the logical completion of their schemes, but find it difficult to state with certainty such an outcome because of the premium these schemes invariably place on the human free will.[47] This reinforces the criticisms we have made of Forsyth's position on this matter in chapter 4.

---

45. Hick, "Irenaean Theodicy," 52.

46. *Mercy the True and Only Justice*, 9. Forsyth's contemporary James Orr has made a similar point: "How can man be held responsible for acts which the constitution of his nature and his environment—without the intervention of moral causes of any kind, such as is involved in the idea of a 'Fall'—make inevitable?" (*Christian View of God*, 209). See also A. B. Bruce's argument (in *Apologetics*, 61–63) that sin should not be viewed as inevitable.

47. See Hick, *Death and Eternal Life*, 250–59 for a comprehensive attempt to resolve this conundrum. For the reasons given earlier, this remains an unsatisfactory solution for us.

CONCLUSION

We have considered, in this chapter, the implications for Forsyth's theodicy of his views on the origin of evil and the God-world relationship. We arrived at the conclusion that nothing Forsyth asserts compromises his beliefs that evil is not ultimately rooted in God and that God has perfect love for the world. We then considered and rejected the possibility that Forsyth's theodicy can properly be termed "dualistic," as the "thing" which determines God's freedom is God's holiness, the most fundamental aspect of who he is. We finally suggested that Forsyth's theodicy allows for sources of suffering other than God's acts of secondary judgement. These are founded upon the conditions in which the first human beings existed, and can be justified on the same bases as those which arise from God's secondary judgement. We hope to have shown, through this chapter and the previous one, that a consideration of Forsyth's view on the origin of evil is critical for a complete understanding of Forsyth's theodicy. Although necessarily speculative in nature, because of Forsyth's failure (or refusal) to write comprehensively on the subject, these chapters have brought forth important facets of Forsyth's theodicy which were not apparent from our earlier discussion. With this, we complete our description of Forsyth's theodicy, and proceed now to make some concluding remarks for our study.

9

Conclusion

> To vindicate Eternal Providence,
> And justify the ways of God to man.

WE HAVE, IN THIS study, sought to describe P. T. Forsyth's attempt to do the above. We began by making some preliminary comments concerning Forsyth's understanding of "the moral as the real" and his view of evil. We examined next his methodology of the *theologia crucis* and his understanding of that crucial phrase "the self-justification of God," one which forms the basis for all human attempts to justify God. We then looked at the first outcome of such self-justification, which is that God moves the world inexorably towards his glorious *telos*, and proceeded to consider the significance of this for Forsyth's theodicy. We discussed here the teleological and historical natures of this theodicy, and proposed the possible responses Forsyth could have made to the objections that have been raised against attempts to justify God based upon the notion that "the ends shall justify the means." We then considered the second outcome of God's self-justification, which is the revelation that God suffered incomparably in the event of the Cross. This provides the basis for God's emphatic co-suffering with his creatures in the "crucial evolution" of the world towards its *telos*. Following this, we drew out two major implications of this second outcome for Forsyth's theodicy, based upon the idea that God is the chief sufferer and giver in our battle against sin, and the possibility that Christ might serve as a model of faith for us in our times of suffering. We turned, finally, to look at Forsyth's view of the origin of both sin and suffering, and his position on the God-world relationship. We considered the significance of these for Forsyth's theodicy, concluding that Forsyth's understanding of the God-world relationship does not undermine his theodicy, and that there is no insidious dualism lurking in Forsyth's thought. We also examined another source of evil Forsyth might have postulated based upon his view on the origin of evil, and suggested that the arguments raised in the earlier chapters apply with equal force to the evils arising from this other source, thus rendering his theodicy a fairly comprehensive one.

What, then, is the heart of Forsyth's response to evil? For evil as suffering, Forsyth suggests that many instances of such evil can be explained as the result of God's acts of secondary judgement. These follow the pattern of that primary act of God's judgement on the Cross and constitute God's chief strategy for moving the world towards its *telos*. Forsyth's key argument here is that "the end will justify the means"—when we reach the *eschaton*, both God and his creatures will acknowledge that all these acts of secondary judgement and the suffering they produced were worth the attainment of the glorious end. Forsyth complements this by introducing the notion of God as the one who suffers the most in the battle against sin, thus conferring upon this God profound moral authority to use any means necessary to complete the victory in this battle, and justifying our trust that he can and will make all things well in the end. God's identification with our suffering also promises to significantly affect our response to the tragedies which strike us, and the faith of Christ as he hung on the Cross serves as a concrete model for our emulation in our times of suffering, provided we do so after we have first been incorporated into him through trust in his saving work. We also suggested that Forsyth's writings allow for instances of suffering which do not result from God's acts of secondary judgement. These arise rather from the conditions which existed in the beginning when the world was created, and which will persist until the *eschaton*. Since these conditions are essential for "faith-production" in human beings, and faith is our response to God that, in a sense, constitutes the *telos*, we have argued that God can be justified with regard to these instances of suffering on the same bases as those which arise from his secondary judgement.

For evil as sin, Forsyth does not, as we have argued, seek to justify this on instrumental grounds. God did not, in the beginning, ordain or permit the entry of sin into our world in order to fulfil his purposes. Following this pattern, we suggested that Forsyth does not see God ordaining any acts of sin in the history of our world. God can indeed make use of the sin which has come about through human willing to achieve his goals—as he sometimes does in his acts of secondary judgement. Moreover, Forsyth is able to joyously participate in the ancient exclamation of "*O felix culpa!*" The entry of sin into the world has made possible, through God's redeeming action, a more glorious *eschaton*. All these, however, arise not through the reconciliation of sin into a higher synthesis, but its complete destruction and disappearance from the *eschaton*. Forsyth's main justification of God vis-à-vis sin is to argue that it arises from human free will, and that such free will is an essential condition again of "faith-production." The path to the *eschaton*, therefore, has to lie through sin (since its occurrence was inevitable, given the conditions necessary for faith to arise). God, in spite of knowing this, proceeded with creation because he was confident that he possessed the resources within himself to "remedy" the situation and still bring the world to its *telos*. This means, in the context of Forsyth's scheme, that God knew he had the ability to undergo the experience of the Cross, that act which overcame sin and provides the irreversible impetus for the "crucial evolution" of the world. Forsyth's justification of God with regard to sin is therefore also an essentially teleological one—its main difference from suffering is that sin is seen as a by-product (although a catastrophic one) of the essential conditions for "faith-production," rather than a *conditio sine qua non* in itself. The portions on God's suffering are also relevant here, for they tell us that, in deciding to proceed with creation in spite of knowing the inevitable entry of sin, God knew he had to bear the brunt of the fight against sin. He is himself therefore the primary "victim" of his decision to create, and we are called merely to follow in his wake as he leads the charge. This must surely augment the justification of God and his decision to create such a world as ours.

We might pause here a little to consider how Forsyth's approach to the problem of evil compares with those suggested by his contemporaries, both prior to and during the Great War. As the relevant footnotes throughout our study indicate, there is very little that is truly new in the major features of Forsyth's theodicy, if they are taken on their own. The teleological approach to theodicy, the notion that suffering can be ordained for God's purposes, the view that God deals with the world in terms of judgement, the idea that God as chief sufferer identifies with our suffering, the insistence on the absolute antagonism between God and sin such that only a sort of free-will defence is viable as the explanation for sin's entry—all these have been promoted by other thinkers of that era. Forsyth's distinctive contribution, we suggest, has been to bring together all these strands of thought and weave them according to the pattern of the Cross. The event which provides both the epistemological and effective bases for all these assertions is that which took place two millennia ago at Calvary. The Cross, moreover, does not merely serve as a unifying theme for all these features of theodicy—it in turn affects how these features are to be understood and appropriated. So, for example, while Forsyth shares a belief in the evolutionary progress of this world towards its *telos* with many of his contemporaries, the fact that he founds this belief on the Cross allows him to postulate a "crucial" evolution of the world, one which goes far deeper than the naïve belief held then by some that evolutionary progress would be evident to all if we were to study the facts carefully. Also, while the eminent Victorian theologian A. B. Bruce had, prior to Forsyth, suggested the idea that God should be viewed as the chief sufferer, all he did was to base it upon a vague notion of God's immanence in the world, one illustrated by the Cross.[1] It was only with Forsyth that God's paramount suffering was truly founded upon the Cross, with that event having a real impact on the very life of God itself, rather than being a mere illustration of eternal truths about God. Forsyth's theodicy therefore reinforces what we have mentioned in chapter 2 concerning the Cross-centred nature of all of Forsyth's thought. This Cross-centredness gives this theodicy a unity, cohesion and groundedness in the historical reality of this world—rendering Forsyth's justification of God one which, in our judgement, far surpasses the other writings on this issue during that era.

We have expressed in our introduction the hope that our study will advance the state of research into Forsyth's theology. Besides setting out Forsyth's theodicy in what we hope has been a systematic and comprehensive manner, we have tried to describe systematically other areas of Forsyth's thought which have not yet been so dealt with, like his epistemology, Christology, and understanding of the atonement. We have also attempted to outline aspects of his theology of which not very much has been written about, like his doctrine of sin, his understanding of providence and divine passibility, his view of the origin of humankind, and his conceptualisation of the God-world relationship. We hope that this will spur further research into these areas, so that the basic presentation offered here can be augmented and refined.

---

1. *Providential Order of the World*, 369.

We have also stated the hope that our study might make some contribution to the task of Christian theodicy, given the state of the discipline today. As described earlier, Forsyth's theodicy was unique in its time for being so thoroughly founded upon the Cross. This Cross-centredness has imparted to this theodicy an ability to integrate insights from different approaches that have been suggested to the issue, such that they cohere into a whole whose parts mutually reinforce one another. Indeed, Forsyth's theodicy reconciles what many today consider to be diametrically opposing notions in the field. So, amongst other things, Forsyth's theodicy integrates:

a) Atonement and theodicy: The Cross is both God's answer to the problem of human sinfulness and human doubt of God's goodness;

b) The exercise of theodicy (both in the academic sense of formulating justifications of God and the practical sense of trusting in God's righteousness when we undergo suffering) and the fulfilment of theodicy: What we do now to justify God is based upon God's self-justification and in turn contributes towards the realisation of such self-justification;

c) God's interest and ours: The best way to secure human welfare is to be concerned with the realisation of God's holiness, since it is because of and for his holiness that we are saved;

d) The notions of the suffering God and the God who sends suffering: Forsyth would deny they are mutually contradictory, and insist that the former justifies the latter;

e) The idea of God as the greatest sufferer of all and a belief in his power to realise his goal for the world: These are, again, not opposing ideas for Forsyth, since the former provides the basis for the latter;

f) The notions that God takes a personal hand in the events of this world and that he allows the conditions he instituted upon the creation of this world to function in an "autonomous" fashion: We have argued that suffering, for Forsyth, can arise from both these sources. Forsyth's view therefore departs both from traditional Calvinism which insists on God's ordination in all things, and from

Deism which loses altogether the idea of God's active interest and intervention in our world;

g) "Victim-centred" and "theocentric" approaches to theodicy: There is ultimately no dichotomy between the two because the greatest victim of evil is the incarnate Son. There is also no divergence between Christ's confession of God's goodness at the Cross and our confession at the *eschaton*. As the one true human being, Christ proleptically announces our verdict on God's ways with the world;

h) "Practical" and "theoretical" approaches to theodicy: There is, in the end, no conflict between these two for Forsyth. Each go towards supporting the other.

We have, in addition, proposed modifications to Forsyth's approach which allow it to integrate both retributive and reformative elements into God's secondary judgement, as well as to view both quiet trust and angry protest as legitimate expressions of a true faith. We have also suggested that the notions of solidarity and empathy, when applied accurately, helps to bring together in a satisfactory way God's particular suffering in Christ and his general suffering with the world. All these integrations should be seen as a part of Forsyth's larger project to bring together what theologians have frequently rent asunder, as evidenced by his attempts to integrate, for example, the theories of the atonement, and Christ's life with his death on the Cross. This integrating tendency might be attributable to the Hegelian influence Forsyth had imbibed. But the one key area where he resists such integration represents his decisive break from the control of the German philosopher: God and sin cannot, in the end, be integrated into any sort of higher synthesis. "Die sin must or God."

There remain, at the close of our study, questions left unanswered by Forsyth's theodicy. Perhaps because he was addressing his theodicy primarily to the situation arising from the Great War, he did not grapple with the thorny issue of animal suffering. Here, our sympathies lie with Forsyth's old rival R. J. Campbell when he writes that the failure to address this issue in one's theodicy "omits something of considerable importance to a thorough and consistent worldview."[2] This is especially so in light of Forsyth's acceptance of the theory of biological evolution, which stretches animal suffering "over millions and millions of years and millions of

2. Campbell, *New Theology*, 47.

species, most of them now extinct."³ But perhaps the most significant omission has to do with the two aspects of Forsyth's theology which he fails (or, more properly, refuses) to integrate: the salvation of the entire human race and the integrity of the human free will, which leaves open the possibility that persons might indefinitely reject God's salvation. As mentioned in the previous chapter, this seems to be a problem afflicting most other theodicies relying upon an "Irenaean view" of creation. Unless this conundrum can be satisfactorily resolved one way or another, such theodicies will be in a consistently disadvantaged position compared with those whose starting point adheres to the "Augustinian" scheme.⁴

Some might also be left unsatisfied with his constant appeals to faith whenever we fail to explain how a particular instance of evil fits within his scheme. But perhaps we should not begrudge Forsyth his extravagant reliance upon faith. It is not something he adds on to his theodicy in order to plaster over the cracks. It is, rather, the crux of his theodicy, since it is the means by which we are enabled to appropriate his justification of God, as well as the goal of such justification. Forsyth mentions that his greatest hope for himself is to end his life with his faith intact:

> And I should count a life well spent, and the world well lost, if, after tasting all its experiences, and facing all its problems, I had no more to show at its close, or carry with me to another life, than the acquisition of a real, sure, humble, and grateful faith in the Eternal and Incarnate Son of God. All is still well if the decay of everything else but fertilise the knowledge of him (Phil. iii. 8).⁵

William Robertson Nicoll, in a tribute to Forsyth after his death, reports that this hope was fulfilled: "Of the end we will only say that we have never known a Christian die with a more absolute trust in the all-suffi-

---

3. The phrase is taken from Southgate, *Groaning of Creation*, 2. Contemporaries of Forsyth who have tried to address the issue of animal suffering in the light of biological evolution include Martineau, *Study of Religion*, 61–97; Flint, *Theism*, 245–51; and, of course, Campbell, *New Theology*, 47–48.

4. According to Hick, one major advantage the "Irenaean view" has over the "Augustinian" one is its supposed compatibility with the theory of biological evolution, with its notion that suffering existed in the world before the advent of sin ("Irenaean Theodicy," 40–41). But there have been attempts (admittedly speculative in nature) to preserve the key tenets of the "Augustinian view" while affirming such evolution: e.g., Lewis, *Problem of Pain*, 71–81; Van Inwagen, "Argument from Evil," 68–72.

5. *Person*, 255.

cient Atonement of the Eternal Christ."[6] Forsyth therefore not only wrote about his theodicy. He lived it out through his life of faith. This is perhaps the most important aspect of his integrative approach to the subject—the way he lived his life coheres with his justification of God. His theodicy, after all, is not one meant for detached intellectual satisfaction. It seeks to change lives in order for this theodicy to find fulfilment. If any of us find our faith strengthened upon reading it, he would definitely have said that his efforts in justifying the ways of God to man have been worthwhile.

---

6. Nicholl, "Principal Forsyth," 146.

Bibliography

WORKS BY P. T. FORSYTH

If an edition other than the first is shown, the date of first publication of the work is given in square brackets at the end. If no date of publication is given in the material itself, the likely date of publication (if known) is stated in these square brackets. All these dates are derived from Leslie McCurdy's bibliography in *Attributes and Atonement*.

Books

The Charter of the Church: Six Lectures on the Spiritual Principle of Nonconformity. London: Alexander & Shepheard, 1896.
The Church and the Sacraments. London: Independent Press, 1947.
The Cruciality of the Cross. 2nd ed. London: Independent Press, 1948.
Christ on Parnassus: Lectures on Art, Ethic, and Theology. London: Independent Press, 1911.
The Christian Ethic of War. London: Longmans, Green, 1916.
Faith, Freedom and the Future. New ed. London: Independent Press, 1955.
Intercessory Services for Aid in Public Worship. Manchester: John Heywood, n.d.
The Justification of God: Lectures for War-Time on a Christian Theodicy. London: Duckworth, 1916.
Marriage: Its Ethic and Religion. Australia: New Creation, 1999.
Missions in State and Church: Sermons and Addresses. London: Hodder & Stoughton, 1908.
The Person and Place of Jesus Christ. The Congregational Union Lecture for 1909. London: Independent Press, 1909.
Positive Preaching and Modern Mind: The Lyman Beecher Lecture on Preaching, Yale University, 1907. London: Hodder & Stoughton, 1907.
The Power of Prayer. With Dora Greenwell. Little Books on Religion. London: Hodder & Stoughton, n.d.
The Principle of Authority in Relation to Certainty, Sanctity and Society: An Essay in the Philosophy of Experimental Religion. 2nd ed. London: Independent Press, 1952.
Pulpit Parables for Young Hearers. With J. A. Hamilton. Manchester: Brook & Chrystal, n.d.
Religion in Recent Art: Expository Lectures on Rossetti, Burne Jones, Watts, Holman Hunt and Wagner. 2nd ed. London: Hodder & Stoughton, 1901.

Rome, Reform and Reaction: Four Lectures on the Religious Situation. London: Hodder & Stoughton, 1899.
Socialism, the Church and the Poor. London: Hodder & Stoughton, 1908.
The Soul of Prayer. 2nd ed. London: Independent Press, 1949.
Theology in Church and State. London, New York: Hodder & Stoughton, 1915.
This Life and the Next: The Effect on This Life of Faith in Another. London: Macmillan, 1918.
The Work of Christ. New ed. London: Independent Press, 1938.

Anthologies and Collections of Forsyth's Writing

The Church, the Gospel, and Society. London: Independent Press, 1962.
Congregationalism and Reunion: Two Lectures. London: Independent Press, 1952.
The Creative Theology of P. T. Forsyth: Selections from His Works. Grand Rapids: Eerdmans, 1969.
God the Holy Father. London: Independent Press, 1957.
The Gospel and Authority: A P. T. Forsyth Reader: Eight Essays Previously Published in Journals. Minneapolis: Augsburg, 1971.
P. T. Forsyth and the Cure of Souls: An Appraisement and Anthology of His Practical Writings. Revised and enlarged ed. London: Allen & Unwin, 1970.
The Preaching of Jesus and the Gospel of Christ. Blackwood, S. Australia: New Creation, 1987.
Revelation Old and New: Sermons and Addresses. London: Independent Press, 1962.
A Sense of the Holy: An Introduction to the Thought of P.T. Forsyth through His Writings. Eugene, OR: Wipf & Stock, 1996.

Articles, Pamphlets and Letters

Annotations on a paper written in 1906 by Robert Mackintosh. "The Authority of the Cross." *Congregational Quarterly* 21 (July 1943) 209–18.
"The Argument for Immortality Drawn from the Nature of Love: A Lecture on Lord Tennyson's 'Vastness.'" *Christian World Pulpit* 28 (2 Dec 1885) 360–64.
"The Atonement in Modern Religious Thought." In *The Atonement in Modern Religious Thought: A Theological Symposium*, by Frederick Godet and 16 others, 51–78. London: Clarke, 1907.
Baldwin Brown: A Tribute, a Reminiscence, and a Study. London: Clarke, 1884.
"'The Bible Doctrine of Hell and the Unseen': Sermon by the Rev. P. T. Forsyth, Preached in the Bradford Road Congregational Church, Shipley, Nov. 23rd." *Shipley and Saltaire Times* (13 Dec 1879) 4.
"The Catholic Threat of Passive Resistance." *Contemporary Review* 89 (Apr 1906) 562–67.
"Chinese Labour in the Transvaal." Letters. *Times (London)*, 18 Jan 1906, 4; 20 Jan, 12; 25 Jan, 11; 26 Jan, 7; 29 Jan, 7.
"Christ and the Christian Principle." In *London Theological Studies*, by members of the Faculty of Theology in the University of London, 133–66. London: University of London Press, 1911.
"Christ at the Gate." *Christian World Pulpit* 73 (18 Mar 1908) 177–82.
"Christ Our Sanctification." *Wesleyan Methodist Magazine* 134 (1911) 732–34.
"Christ's Person and His Cross." *Methodist Review* 66 (Jan 1917) 3–22.

Christian Aspects of Evolution. London: Epworth, 1950.
"Christian Evidence Society." Letter. From Forsyth and 7 others. *Times (London)*, 10 May 1918, 11.
"Christianity and Nationality." *British Weekly* (9 July 1914) 385–86.
"The Christianity of Christ and Christ Our Christianity." *Review and Expositor* 15 (July 1918) 249–65.
"The Church and Society—Alien or Allied." *British Weekly* (9 Oct 1913) 43.
"The Church and the Children." Letter. *British Weekly* (15 May 1913) 169.
"Churches, Sects and Wars." *Contemporary Review* 107 (May 1915) 618–26.
"The Church's One Foundation." *London Quarterly Review* 106 (Oct 1906) 193–202.
"Congregationalism and the Principle of Liberty." *Constructive Quarterly* 1 (Sept 1913) 498–521.
"The Conversion of Faith by Love." *British Weekly* (28 October 1897) 22.
"The Conversion of the 'Good.'" *Contemporary Review* 109 (June 1916) 760–71.
The Courage of Faith. Glasgow: William Asher, 1903.
"The Cross of Christ as the Moral Principle of Society." *Methodist Review* 99 (Jan 1917) 9–21.
"The Cruciality of the Cross." Letter. *British Weekly* (12 July 1906) 344.
"The Disappointment of the Cross." *Puritan* 3 (1900) 135–39.
"Does the Church Prolong the Incarnation?" *London Quarterly Review* 133 (Jan and Apr 1920) 1–12, 204–12.
"Dr. Dale." Review of *The Life of R. W. Dale*, by A. W. W. Dale. *London Quarterly Review* 91 (Apr 1899) 193–222.
"Dr. Martineau." *London Quarterly Review* 93 (Apr 1900) 214–50.
"The Efficiency and Sufficiency of the Bible." *Biblical Review* 2 (Jan 1917) 10–30.
"The Evangelical Churches and Higher Criticism." *Contemporary Review* 88 (Oct 1905) 574–99.
"Evangelicals and Home Reunion." *Churchman* 32 (Sept 1918) 528–36.
"Faith and Experience." *Wesleyan Methodist Magazine* 123 (1900) 415–17.
"Faith and Mind." *Methodist Review Quarterly* 61 (Oct 1912) 627–43.
"The Faith of Jesus." *Expository Times* 21 (Oct 1909) 8–9.
"Faith, Metaphysic, and Incarnation." *Methodist Review* 97 (Sept 1915) 696–719.
"The Foolishness of Preaching." *Expository Times* 30 (Jan 1919) 153–54.
Freedom. An Ode for Baritone Solo, Chorus, and Orchestra. The Words written by the Rev. P. T. Forsyth, M.A. The Music Composed by Ebenezer Prout (Op. 20). [Score.] London: Novello, Ewer, 1885.
"A German Theologian." Review of *The Ritschlian Theology*, by Alfred E. Garvie. *Speaker (London)*, 23 December 1899, 317–19.
The Glorious Gospel. 1975–1945 Triple Jubliee Papers. London: Livingstone, n.d.
"God, Sin, and the Atonement." *British Weekly* (28 March 1907) 669–70.
"God Takes a Text and Preaches." *British Weekly* (14 April 1910) 36.
The Grace of the Gospel as the Moral Authority in the Church. Pamphlet. London: Congregational Union of England and Wales, n.d.
The Happy Warrior: A Sermon on the Death of Mr. Gladstone (May 22, 1898). London: Allenson, 1898.
Holy Christian Empire. London: Clarke, n.d.
"Ibsen's Treatment of Guilt." *Hibbert Journal* 14 (Oct 1915) 105–22.

"Immanence and Incarnation." In *The Old Faith and the New Theology*, edited by C. H. Vine, 47–61. London: Sampson Low Marston, 1907.
"The Inner Life of Christ." *Constructive Quarterly* 7 (Mar 1919) 149–62.
"Intellectualism and Faith." *Hibbert Journal* 11 (Jan 1913) 311–28.
"Jubilee of the London Biblewomen and Nurses' Mission (Founded 1857)." Letter. From Forsyth and 16 others. *Times (London)*, 26 April 1906, 4.
Letter. From Forsyth and others to Adolf Von Harnack. *British Weekly* (3 September 1914) 557.
"The Love of Liberty and the Love of Truth." *Contemporary Review* 93 (Feb 1908) 158–70.
"Majesty and Mercy." *Christian World Pulpit* 79 (17 May 1911) 305–7.
"The Man and the Message." *London Quarterly Review* 121 (Jan 1914) 1–11.
Mercy the True and Only Justice. A Sermon Preached in Shipley Congregational Church, on Missionary Sunday, September 30, 1877. Bradford: T. Brear, n.d.
"Milton's God and Milton's Satan." *Contemporary Review* 95 (Apr 1909) 450–65.
"'Milton's Paradise Lost': Lecture by the Rev. P. T. Forsyth, M.A." *Shipley and Saltaire Times* (22 March 1879) 4.
Monism: A Paper Read before the London Society for the Study of Religion. Letchworth: Garden City, n.d.
"The Moralisation of Religion." *London Quarterly Review* 128 (Oct 1917) 161–74.
"Mystics and Saints." *Expository Times* 5 (June 1894) 401–4.
"The Need for a Positive Gospel." *London Quarterly Review* 101 (Jan 1904) 64–99.
"A Nonconformist on the Enabling Bill." Letters. *Times (London)*, 28 May, 6 and 16 June 1919, all 8.
The Old Faith and the New. Leicester, Birmingham and Leamington: Midland Educational Company; Manchester: Brook & Chrystal, 1891.
"One Step to Reunion: Interchange of Pulpits." Letter. From Forsyth and 6 others. *Times (London)* (30 August 1919) 6.
"Orthodoxy, Heterodoxy, Heresy and Freedom." *Hibbert Journal* 8 (Jan 1910) 321–29.
"Our Experience of a Triune God." *Cambridge Christian Life* 1 (June 1914) 240–46.
"The Paradox of Christ." *London Quarterly Review* 102 (June 1904) 111–38.
"Pessimism." *Christian World Pulpit* 25 (16 January 1884) 42–44.
Pfleiderer's View of St Paul's Doctrine. Review of *Paulinism: A Contribution to the History of Primitive Christian Theology*, by Otto Pfleiderer. London: W. Speaght, n.d.
"The Preacher and the Publicist." *London Quarterly Review* 127 (Jan 1917) 1–18.
"The Preaching of Jesus and the Gospel of Christ. [VII:] the Meaning of a Sinless Christ." *Expositor* 25 (Apr 1923) 288–312.
"The Problem of Forgiveness in the Lord's Prayer." In *The Sermon on the Mount: A Practical Exposition of the Lord's Prayer*, edited by E. Griffith-Jones et al., 181–92, 193–207. Manchester: Robinson, 1903.
The Pulpit and the Age. Manchester: Brook & Chrystal, 1885.
"The Reality of God: A War Time Question." *Hibbert Journal* 16 (July 1918) 608–19.
"Reconstruction and Religion." In *Problems of Tomorrow: Social, Moral and Religious*, edited by Fred A. Rees, 15–23. London: Clark, 1918.
"Regeneration, Creation, and Miracle." *Methodist Review Quarterly* 63 (Oct 1914) 627–43.
"Regeneration, Creation, and Miracle: Second Article." *Methodist Review Quarterly* 64 (Jan 1915) 89–103.

"The Relation of the Church to the Poor." *Congregational Monthly* 1 (Mar 1888) 64.
"Religion and Reality." *Contemporary Review* 115 (May 1919) 548–54.
"Religion, Private and Public." *London Quarterly Review* 131 (Jan 1919) 19–32.
"Revelation and the Person of Christ." In *Faith and Criticism: Essays by Congregationalists*, 95–144. London: Sampson Low Marston, 1893.
"Ritschl on Justification." Review of *The Christian Doctrine of Justification and Reconciliation*, vol. 3, by Albrecht Ritschl, translated by H. R. Mackintosh and A. B. Macauley. *Speaker (London)*, 16 February, 9 March 1901, 549–51, 629–31.
The Roots of a World-Commonwealth. 1918. Reprint, London: Independent, 1952.
"Self-Denial and Self-Committal." *Expositor* 4 (July 1912) 32–43.
"Slavery and Contempt." *Times (London)* (25 January 1906) 11.
"The Slowness of God." *Expository Times* 11 (Feb 1900) 218–22.
Socialism and Christianity in Some of Their Deeper Aspects. Manchester: Brook & Chrystal, 1886.
"Some Christian Aspects of Evolution." *London Quarterly Review* 104 (Oct 1905) 209–39.
"Some Effects of the War on Belief." *Holborn Review* 9 (Jan 1918) 16–26.
"The Spiritual Needs in the Churches." *Christian World Pulpit* 89 (3 May 1916) 251–55.
"The Strength of Weakness." *Christian World Pulpit* 13 (6 Feb 1878) 85–87.
"Sunday Schools and Modern Theology." *Christian World Pulpit* 31 (23 Feb 1887) 123–27.
"Testamentary Ethics." *London Quarterly Review* 129 (Apr 1918) 169–79.
"Theological Liberalism v. Liberal Theology." *British Weekly* (17 February 1910) 557–58.
"Things New and Old." *Christian World Pulpit* 84 (29 Oct 1913) 273–76.
"The Turkish Atrocities: Sermon by the Rev. P. T. Forsyth." *Shipley and Saltaire Times* (23 September 1876) 4.
"Unity and Theology: A Liberal Evangelicalism the True Catholicism." In *Towards Reunion: Being Contributions to Mutual Understanding by Church of England and Free Church Writers*, edited by J. Scott Lidgett et al., 51–81. London: Macmillan, 1919.
"Veracity, Reality, and Regeneration." *London Quarterly Review* 123 (Apr 1915) 193–216.
"The Village Churches and the War." Letter. *British Weekly* (29 March 1917) 496.
"The Way of Life." *Wesleyan Methodist Magazine* 120 (London, Feb 1897) 83–88.
The Weariness in Modern Life. No publication data.
"The Word and the World." Letter. *British Weekly* (10 February 1910) 533–34.

WORKS ON P.T. FORSYTH

This section consists of materials whose main focus (or one of whose primary foci) is the life and thought of the Scottish theologian. Some of the materials in the next section entitled "Other Works" might also make reference to Forsyth, but they do so within the context of a wider discussion.

Anderson, Marvin W. "P. T. Forsyth: Prophet of the Cross." *Evangelical Quarterly* 47 (1975) 146–61.
Barth, Markus. "P. T. Forsyth: The Theologian for the Practical Man." *Congregational Quarterly* 17 (1939) 436–42.

Begbie, Jeremy. "The Ambivalent Rainbow: Forsyth, Art and Creation," in *Justice the True and Only Mercy: Essays on the Life and Theology of Peter Taylor Forsyth*, edited by Trevor A. Hart, 197–219. Edinburgh: T. & T. Clark, 1995.

Benedetto, Robert. *P. T. Forsyth Bibliography and Index*. Bibliographies and Indexes in Religious Studies 27. Westport, CT: Greenwood, 1993.

Binfield, Clyde. "Peter Taylor Forsyth: Pastor as Principal." In *P. T. Forsyth: Theologian for a New Millennium*, edited by Alan Sell, 7–40. London: United Reformed Church, 2000.

———. "Principal When Pastor: P. T. Forsyth, 1876–1901." In *The Ministry: Clerical and Lay*, edited by W. J. Sheils and Diana Wood, 397–414. Oxford: Blackwell, 1989.

Bishop, John. "P. T. Forsyth: 'Preaching and the Modern Mind.'" *Religion in Life* 48 (1979) 303–8.

Bradley, William Lee. "Forsyth's Contributions to Pastoral Theology." *Religion in Life* 28 (1959) 546–56.

———. *P. T. Forsyth: The Man and His Work*. London: Independent Press, 1952.

Brake, George Thompson. *Peter Taylor Forsyth: An Introduction*. Theology Starters 2. Ilford, Essex: Odcombe, [1990].

Brown, Robert McAfee. "The 'Conversion' of P. T. Forsyth." *Congregational Quarterly* 30 (1952) 236–44.

———. "P. T. Forsyth." In *A Handbook of Christian Theologians*, edited by Martin E. Marty and Dean G. Peerman, 144–65. Cambridge: Lutterworth, 1984.

———. *P. T. Forsyth: Prophet for Today*. Philadelphia: Westminster, 1952.

Camfield, F. W. "Peter Taylor Forsyth." *Presbyter* 6.2 (1948) 3–10.

Cave, Sydney. "Dr P. T. Forsyth: The Man and His Writings." *Congregational Quarterly* 26 (1948) 107–19.

Cocks, H. F. Lovell. "Books on the Person of Christ, Pt 7: P. T. Forsyth's *The Person and Place of Jesus Christ*." *Expository Times* 64.7 (1953) 195–98.

———. "The Message of P. T. Forsyth." *Congregational Quarterly* 26 (1948) 214–21.

Coggan, Donald. "Under-Estimated Theological Books: P. T. Forsyth's *Positive Preaching and the Modern Mind*." *Expository Times* 72 (1961) 324–26.

Cook, E. Albert. "The Defence of God and Other Problems." [Review of *The Justification of God*.] *American Journal of Theology* 22 (1918) 303–5.

Craston, R. C. "The Grace of a Holy God: P. T. Forsyth and the Contemporary Church." In *Authority in the Anglican Communion: Essays Presented to Bishop John Howe*, edited by Stephen S. Sykes, 47–64. Toronto: Anglican Book Centre, 1987.

Cuncliffe-Jones, H. "P. T. Forsyth: Reactionary or Prophet?" *Congregational Quarterly* 27 (1950) 344–56.

Davis, D. A. "On Re-Reading T. P. [sic] Forsyth's *Justification of God*." *British Weekly* (19 October 1939) 31.

Dillistone, F. W. Review of *The Justification of God*. *Anglican Theological Review* 35 (1953) 63–64.

Duthie, Charles S. "The Faith of P. T. Forsyth, 'Fireworks in a Fog'?" *British Weekly* (17 December 1964) 9.

Floyd, Richard L. "The Cross and the Church: The Soteriology and Ecclesiology of P. T. Forsyth." *Andover Newton Review* 3 (1992) 1–16.

Gardner, J. Review of *The Justification of God*. *Journal of Bible and Religion* 20 (1952) 44–45.

Gardom, James T. D. "The Cross in Time and the Hidden Hand of God: Theology and the Problem of Evil with Reference to the Work of Peter Taylor Forsyth and Austin Farrer." University of London, 1992.
Garrett, John. "Forsyth, Forsooth." In *Studies of the Church in History: Essays Honoring Robert S. Paul on His Sixty-Fifth Birthday*, edited by Horton Davis, 243–52. Pittsburgh Theological Monographs 5. Allison Park, PA: Pickwick, 1983.
Garvie, A. E. "A Cross-Centred Theology." *Congregational Quarterly* 22 (1944) 324–30.
———. "P. T. Forsyth and Reunion." Letter to the Editor. *Congregational Quarterly* 23 (1945) 96.
———. "Placarding the Cross. The Theology of P. T. Forsyth." *Congregational Quarterly* 21 (1943) 343–52.
Goroncy, Jason. "Bitter Tonic for Our Time—Why the Church Needs the World: Peter Taylor Forsyth on Henrik Ibsen." *European Journal of Theology* 15.2 (2006) 105–18.
———. "The Elusiveness, Loss and Cruciality of Recovered Holiness: Some Biblical and Theological Observations." *International Journal of Systematic Theology* 10.2 (2008) 195–209.
———. "Fighting Troll-Demons in Vaults of the Mind and Heart—Art, Tragedy, and Sacramentality: Some Observations from Ibsen, Forsyth, and Dostoevsky." *Princeton Theological Review* 36 (2007): Online: http://www.princetontheologicalreview.org/issues_web/36_text.html#article6.
Griffith, Gwilym O. *The Theology of P. T. Forsyth*. London: Lutterworth, 1948.
Griffith-Jones, E. "Dr Forsyth on the Atonement." *Expositor* 9 (1910) 307–19.
Gummer, Selwyn. "Peter Taylor Forsyth: A Contemporary Theologian." *London Quarterly and Holborn Review* 173 (1948) 349–53.
Gunton, Colin. "Foreword." In *Justice the True and Only Mercy: Essays on the Life and Theology of Peter Taylor Forsyth*, edited by Trevor A. Hart, xiii–xv. Edinburgh: T. & T. Clark, 1995.
———. "The Real as the Redemptive: Forsyth on Authority and Freedom." In *Justice the True and Only Mercy: Essays on the Life and Theology of Peter Taylor Forsyth*, edited by Trevor A. Hart, 37–58. Edinburgh: T. & T. Clark, 1995.
Hall, George. "Tragedy in the Theology of P. T. Forsyth." In *Justice the True and Only Mercy: Essays on the Life and Theology of Peter Taylor Forsyth*, edited by Trevor A. Hart, 77–104. Edinburgh: T. & T. Clark, 1995.
Hamilton, Kenneth. "Love or Holy Love? Nels Ferré Versus P. T. Forsyth." *Canadian Journal of Theology* 8 (1962) 229–36.
Hart, Trevor A. "Morality, Atonement and the Death of Jesus: The Crucial Focus of Forsyth's Theology." In *Justice the True and Only Mercy: Essays on the Life and Theology of Peter Taylor Forsyth*, edited by Trevor A. Hart, 16–36. Edinburgh: T. & T. Clark, 1995.
Hibbs, John. "Forsyth, Hayek and the Remoralisation of Society: Or Church, Life and Economics." Text of the author's Dr Shergold Memorial Lecture, 1992.
Hughes, T. Hywel. "A Barthian before Barth?" *Congregational Quarterly* 12 (1934) 308–15.
———. "Dr. Forsyth's View of the Atonement." *Congregational Quarterly* 18 (1940) 30–37.
Hunter, A. M. *P. T. Forsyth: Per Crucem Ad Lucem*. London: SCM, 1974.
———. "P. T. Forsyth Neutestamentler." *Expository Times* 73 (1962) 100–106.
———. "The Theology of P. T. Forsyth." In *Teaching and Preaching the New Testament*, 129–87. London: SCM, 1963.

Huxtable, W. J. F. "National Recognition of Religion." *Congregational* Quarterly (1957) 297–310.

———. "P. T. Forsyth: 1848–1921." *Journal of the United Reformed Church History Society* 4 (1987) 72–78.

Jackson, George D. "The Interpreter at Work: XIV. P. T. Forsyth's Use of the Bible." *Interpretation* 7 (1953) 323–37.

Justice and Mercy: A Review of a Sermon Published by Rev. P. T. Forsyth, M.A. By a Curious Reader. Bradford: M. Field, n.d. [likely 1878]

Lambert, D. W. "A Great Theologian and His Greatest Book: *The Work of Christ*." *London Quarterly and Holborn Review* 173 (1948) 244–47.

———. "The Missionary Message of P. T. Forsyth." *Evangelical Quarterly* 21 (1949) 203–8.

———. "The Theology of Missions: The Contribution of P. T. Forsyth." *London Quarterly and Holborn Review* 176 (1951) 114–17.

Lawler, Howard. "The Universalism of P. T. Forsyth: An Exposition to Indicate Particular Problems." MA thesis, Wheaton College, 1987.

Leow, Theng Huat. "The 'Cruciality of the Cross': P. T. Forsyth's Understanding of the Atonement." *International Journal of Systematic Theology* 11.2 (2009) 190–207.

Logan, Alastair H. B. "Peter Taylor Forsyth: Review Article." *Expository Times* 107 (1996) 115–16.

MacKinnon, Donald M. "Teleology and Redemption." In *Justice the True and Only Mercy: Essays on the Life and Theology of Peter Taylor Forsyth*, edited by Trevor A. Hart, 105–9. Edinburgh: T. & T. Clark, 1995.

Mackintosh, Robert. "The Authority of the Cross." *Congregational Quarterly* 21 (1943) 209–18.

McCurdy, Leslie. *Attributes and Atonement: The Holy Love of God in the Theology of P. T. Forsyth.* Paternoster Biblical and Theological Monographs. Carlisle, UK: Paternoster, 1998.

Meadly, Thomas D. "Great Church, P. T. Forsyth, and Christian Unity." *London Quarterly and Holborn Review* 190 (1965) 225–33.

———. "The 'Obscurity' of P.T. Forsyth." *Congregational Quarterly* 24 (1946) 308–17.

Mews, Stuart. "Neo-Orthodoxy, Liberalism and War: Karl Barth, P. T. Forsyth, and John Oman 1914–1918." In *Renaissance and Renewal in Church History*, edited by Derek Baker, 361–75. Studies in Church History, vol. 14. Oxford: Basil Blackwell, 1977.

Mikolaski, Samuel J. "P.T. Forsyth." In *Creative Minds in Contemporary Theology*, edited by P. E. Hughes, 307–39. 2nd ed. Grand Rapids: Eerdmans, 1969.

———. "P. T. Forsyth on the Atonement." *Evangelical Quarterly* 36 (1964) 78–91.

———. "The Theology of P. T. Forsyth." *Evangelical Quarterly* 36 (1964) 27–41.

Miller, Donald G. "P. T. Forsyth: The Man," in *P. T. Forsyth—The Man, The Preacher's Theologian, Prophet for the Twentieth Century: A Contemporary Assessment*, by Donald G. Miller, Browne Barr, and Robert S. Paul, 1–30. Pittsburgh: Pickwick, 1981.

"Ministerial Libraries: V. Principal Forsyth's Library at Hackney College." *British Monthly* 4 (1904) 267–70.

Mozley, J. K. "Forsyth—the Theologian." *British Weekly* (21 Nov 1946) 110.

Nicholl, W. R. "Principal Forsyth." *British Weekly* (17 Nov 1921) 145–46.

Paddison, Angus. "P. T. Forsyth, Scripture, and the Crisis of the Gospel." *Journal of Theological Interpretation* 1.2 (2007) 129–45.

Pitt, Clifford S. *Church, Ministry and Sacraments: A Critical Evaluation of the Thought of Peter Taylor Forsyth.* Washington, DC: University Press of America, 1983.

Porritt, Arthur. "Leading Churches and Preachers: VI—Emmanuel Church, Cambridge, and Dr. P.T. Forsyth." *Puritan* 1 (1899) 713–19.
Reviews of *The Justification of God* (Anonymous). Found in *Times Literary Supplement* (23 November 1916) 564; *Expository Times* 28 (1917) 177; *London Quarterly and Holborn Review* 173 (1948) 280.
Robinson, N. H. G. "The Importance of P. T. Forsyth." *Expository Times* 64 (1952) 76–79.
Rochelle, Gabriel C. "Apophatic Preaching and the Postmodern Mind." *St Vladimir's Theological Quarterly* 50.4 (2006) 397–419.
Rodgers, John H. *The Theology of P. T. Forsyth: The Cross of Christ and the Revelation of God*. London: Independent Press, 1965.
Russell, Stanley. "Spoiling the Egyptians: P. T. Forsyth and Hegel." In *Justice the True and Only Mercy: Essays on the Life and Theology of Peter Taylor Forsyth*, edited by Trevor A. Hart, 220–36. Edinburgh: T. & T. Clark, 1995.
Sell, Alan P. F. "P. T. Forsyth as Unsystematic Systematician." In *Justice the True and Only Mercy: Essays on the Life and Theology of Peter Taylor Forsyth*, edited by Trevor A. Hart, 110–45. Edinburgh: T. & T. Clark, 1995.
———. "Telling the Story: Then and Now." In *Story Lines: Chapters on the Thought, Word, and Deed: For Gabriel Fackre*, edited by Skye Fackre Gibson, 146–56. Grand Rapids: Eerdmans, 2002.
———. "What Has P. T. Forsyth to Do with Mercersburg?" In *Testimony and Tradition: Studies in Reformed and Dissenting Thought*, edited by Alan P. F. Sell, 171–210. Aldershot: Ashgate, 2005.
Shaw, J. M. "The Theology of P. T. Forsyth." *Theology Today* 3 (1946) 358–70.
Simpson, A. F. "P. T. Forsyth: The Prophet of Judgement." *Scottish Journal of Theology* 4 (1951) 148–56.
Sykes, Stephen. "P. T. Forsyth on the Church," in *Justice the True and Only Mercy: Essays on the Life and Theology of Peter Taylor Forsyth*, edited by Trevor A. Hart, 1–15. Edinburgh: T. & T. Clark, 1995.
Thompson, John. "Was Forsyth Really A Barthian Before Barth?" In *Justice the True and Only Mercy: Essays on the Life and Theology of Peter Taylor Forsyth*, edited by Trevor A. Hart, 237–55. Edinburgh: T. & T. Clark, 1995.
Torrance, Iain R. "Dominated by His Own Illustrations? P. T. Forsyth on the Lord's Supper." In *Justice the True and Only Mercy: Essays on the Life and Theology of Peter Taylor Forsyth*, edited by Trevor A. Hart, 59–66. Edinburgh: T. & T. Clark, 1995.
Vicchio, Stephen J. "The Problem of Evil with Special Reference to P. T. Forsyth, John Wisdom, and Ludwig Wittgenstein." University of St Andrews, 1985.
———. *The Voice from the Whirlwind: The Problem of Evil and the Modern World*. Westminster, MD: Christian Classics, 1989.
Waddell, H. C. "Is P. T. Forsyth Coming to His Own?" *Biblical Theology* 7 (1957) 35–39.
Warschauer, J. "'Liberty, Limited': A Rejoinder to Dr Forsyth." *Contemporary Review* 101 (1912) 831–39.
Webster, Douglas. "P. T. Forsyth's Theology of Missions." *International Review of Missions* 44 (1955) 175–81.
Widdicombe, D. W. "Theology and Experience: Methodological Issues in the Theology of P. T. Forsyth." PhD thesis, Oxford University, 2000.
Wilkinson, David. "'We Preach Jesus Christ and Him Crucified': A Comparison and Contrast of P. T. Forsyth and James Denney's Understanding of the Atonement and of How They Preached It." MPhil thesis, King's College, London, 1995.

Williams, W. Bryn. "P. T. Forsyth: Holy Love and the Cross of Christ." In *P. T. Forsyth: Theologian for a New Millennium*, edited by Alan Sell, 107–29. London: United Reformed Church, 2000.

Wood, Ralph C. "Christ on Parnassus: P. T. Forsyth among the Liberals." *Literature and Theology* 2 (1988) 83–95.

Worrall, B. G. "The Authority of Grace in the Theology of P. T. Forsyth." *Scottish Journal of Theology* 25 (1972) 58–74.

OTHER WORKS

Adams, Marilyn McCord. *Horrendous Evils and the Goodness of God*. Ithaca, NY: Cornell University Press, 1999.

Adams, Marilyn McCord, and Robert Merrihew Adams. "Introduction." In *The Problem of Evil*, edited by Marilyn McCord Adams and Robert Merrihew Adams, 1–24. Oxford: Oxford University Press, 1990.

Adams, Robert Merrihew. "Middle Knowledge and the Problem of Evil." In *The Problem of Evil*, edited by Marilyn McCord Adams and Robert Merrihew Adams, 110–25. Oxford: Oxford University Press, 1990.

Adeney, Walter F. *Faith-to-Day*. London: Clark, 1915.

Almond, Philip. "Rudolf Otto: The Context of His Thought." *Scottish Journal of Theology* 36.3 (1983) 347–62.

Althaus, Paul. *The Theology of Martin Luther*. Translated by Robert C. Schultz. Philadelphia, PA: Fortress, 1966.

Badcock, Gary. "The Concept of Love: Divine and Human." In *Nothing Greater, Nothing Better: Theological Essays on the Love of God*, edited by Kevin J. Vanhoozer, 30–46. Grand Rapids: Eerdmans, 2001.

Badham, Roger A. "Redeeming the Fall: Hick's Schleiermacher versus Niebuhr's Kierkegaard." *Journal of Religion* 78.4 (1998) 547–70.

Baillie, Donald M. *God Was in Christ: An Essay on Incarnation and Atonement*. 2nd ed. London: Faber & Faber, 1961.

Baldwin Brown, James. *The Divine Treatment of Sin*. London: Jackson, Walford & Hodder, 1864.

———. *The Doctrine of Annihilation in the Light of the Gospel of Love*. London: Henry S. King, 1875.

———. *First Principles of Ecclesiastical Truth: Essays on the Church and Society*. London: Hodder & Stoughton, 1871.

Barber, Bruce L., and David Neville, editors. *Theodicy and Eschatology*. Adelaide: ATF, 2005.

Barth, Karl. *Church Dogmatics*. Vol. II, *The Doctrine of God, First Half Volume*. Edited by G. W. Bromiley, and T. F. Torrance. Translated by T. H. L. Parker, W. B. Johnston, Harold Knight, and J. L. M Haire. Edinburgh: T. & T. Clark, 1957.

———. *Church Dogmatics*. Vol. III, *The Doctrine of Creation, Part I*. Edited by G. W. Bromiley, and T. F. Torrance. Translated by J. W. Edwards, O. Bussey, and Harold Knight. Edinburgh: T. & T. Clark, 1958.

———. *Protestant Theology in the Nineteen Century: Its Background and History*. New Edition. Grand Rapids: Eerdmans, 2002.

Bauckham, Richard. "'Only the Suffering God Can Help': Divine Passibility in Modern Theology." *Themelios* 9.3 (1984) 6–12.

———. "Theology after Hiroshima." *Scottish Journal of Theology* 38.4 (1985) 583–601.

———. *The Theology of Jürgen Moltmann*. Edinburgh: T. & T. Clark, 1995.

———. "Universalism: A Historical Survey." *Evangelical Review of Theology* 15 (1991) 22–35.

Bauer, Yehuda, editor. *Remembering for the Future*. Vol. I, *Jews and Christians During and After the Holocaust*. Oxford: Pergamon, 1989.

Beck, W. D. "Panentheism." In *New Dictionary of Theology*, edited by Sinclair B. Ferguson and J. I. Packer, 486–87. Downers Grove, IL: InterVarsity, 1998.

Blocher, Henri. *Evil and the Cross: Christian Thought and the Problem of Evil*. Translated by David G. Preston. Leicester: Apollos, 1994.

Boyd, Gregory A. *Satan and the Problem of Evil: Constructing a Trinitarian Warfare Theodicy*. Downers Grove, IL: InterVarsity, 2001.

Braaten, Carl E., and Robert W. Jenson, editors. *Sin, Death and the Devil*. Grand Rapids: Eerdmans, 2000.

Breslauer, S. Daniel. "Theodicy and Ethics: Post-Holocaust Reflections." *American Journal of Theology & Philosophy* 8.3 (1987) 137–49.

Brown, Kenneth D. *A Social History of the Nonconformist Ministry in England and Wales 1800–1930*. Oxford: Clarendon, 1988.

Brown, Stuart C., editor. *Reason and Religion*. Ithaca: Cornell University Press, 1977.

Bruce, Alexander Balmain. *Apologetics; or, Christianity Defensively Stated*. 3rd ed. The International Theological Library. Edinburgh: T. & T. Clark, 1895.

———. *The Humiliation of Christ: In Its Physical, Ethical, and Official Aspects*. 2nd ed. Edinburgh: T. & T. Clark, 1881.

———. *The Moral Order of the World in Ancient and Modern Thought*. London: Hodder & Stoughton, 1899.

———. *The Providential Order of the World*. London: Hodder & Stoughton, 1897.

Butler, Joseph. *The Analogy of Religion to the Constitution and Course of Nature*. London: Tegg, 1867.

Burnley, William F. E. "Impassibility of God." *Expository Times* 67 (1955) 90–91.

Burns, R. M. "The Origins of Human Evil." *Scottish Journal of Theology* 53.3 (2000) 292–315.

Cairns, David S. *The Reasonableness of Christianity*. London: Hodder & Stoughton, 1918.

Camus, Albert. *The Plague*. Translated by Stuart Gilbert. Harmondsworth: Penguin, 1960.

———. *The Rebel*. Translated by Anthony Bower. Penguin Modern Classics. Middlesex: Penguin, 1953.

Cameron, Nigel M. De S., editor. *The Power and Weakness of God: Impassibility and Orthodoxy*. Papers presented at the Third Edinburgh Conference in Christian Dogmatics, 1989. Edinburgh: Rutherford House, 1990.

Campbell, R. J. *The New Theology*. London: Chapman & Hall, 1907.

Carson, Donald A. *How Long, O Lord? Reflections on Suffering and Evil*. Grand Rapids: Baker, 1990.

Chadwick, Owen. *The Secularization of the European Mind in the Nineteen Century*. Cambridge: Cambridge University Press, 1975.

Clark, Kelly James. "Hold Not Thy Peace at My Tears: Methodological Reflections on Divine Impassibility." In *Our Knowledge of God: Essays on Natural and Philosophical Theology*, edited by Kelly James Clark, 167–93. Dordrecht, Netherlands: Kluwer, 1992.

Clements, Keith. *Lovers of Discord: Twentieth Century Theological Controversies in England*. London: SPCK, 1988.

Cobb, John B., Jr. "The Problem of Evil and the Task of Ministry." In *Encountering Evil: Live Options in Theodicy*, edited by Stephen T. Davis, 167–76. Edinburgh: T. & T. Clark, 1981.

Constantine, Stephen, Maurice W. Kirby, and Mary B. Rose, editors. *The First World War in British History*. London: Arnold, 1995.

Conyers, A. J. "Teaching the Holocaust: The Role of Theology." *Perspectives in Religious Studies* 8.2 (1981) 128–42.

Cook, R. R. "Is Universalism an Implication of the Notion of Post-Mortem Evangelism?" *Tyndale Bulletin* 45.2 (1994) 395–409.

Corner, Mark A. "'The Umbilical Cord': A View of Man and Nature in the Light of Darwin." *Scottish Journal of Religious Studies* 4 (1983) 121–37.

Cox, Samuel. *Salvator Mundi or Is Christ the Saviour of All Men*. 12th ed. London: Kegan Paul, 1888.

Davis, Philip. *The Victorians*. The Oxford English Literary History, vol. 8: 1830–1880. Oxford: Oxford University Press, 2001.

Davis, Rupert E. *Religious Authority in an Age of Doubt*. London: Epworth, 1968.

Davis, Stephen. "Introduction." In *Encountering Evil: Live Options in Theodicy*, edited by Stephen T. Davis, 1–6. Edinburgh: T. & T. Clark, 1981.

———. "Universalism, Hell, and the Fate of the Ignorant." *Modern Theology* 6.2 (1990) 173–86.

Dawe, Donald. *The Form of a Servant: A Historical Analysis of the Kenotic Motif*. Philadelphia: Westminster, 1963.

De Maistre, Joseph Marie. *St Petersburg Dialogues: Or Conversations on the Temporal Government of Providence*. Translated by Richard A. Lebrun. Montreal; London: McGill-Queen's University Press, 1993.

Dillistone, F. W. *The Significance of the Cross*. Philadelphia: Westminster, 1944.

Dostoyevsky, Fyodor. *The Brothers Karamazov*. Translated by David McDuff. Strand: Penguin, 1993.

Drummond, Henry. *The Lowell Lectures on the Ascent of Man*. London: Hodder & Stoughton, 1894.

Eckardt, Alice L. "The Holocaust: Christian and Jewish Responses." *Journal of the American Academy of Religion* 42 (1974) 453–69.

Eckardt, A. R. "Jürgen Moltmann, the Jewish People, and the Holocaust." *Journal of the American Academy of Religion* 44.4 (1976) 675–91.

Elliott-Binns, L. E. *English Thought 1860–1900: The Theological Aspect*. London: Longmans, Green, 1956.

Escott, Harry. *A History of Scottish Congregationalism*. Glasgow: Congregational Union of Scotland, 1960.

Fairbairn, Andrew Martin. *The Philosophy of the Christian Religion*. London: Hodder & Stoughton, 1902.

———. *The Place of Christ in Modern Theology*. 2nd ed. London: Hodder & Stoughton, 1983.

Farley, Wendy. *Tragic Vision and Divine Compassion*. Louisville: Westminster / John Knox, 1990.

Farrer, Austin. *Love Almighty and Ills Unlimited: An Essay on Providence and Evil, Containing the Nathaniel Taylor Lectures for 1961*. London: Collins, 1962.

Feinburg, J. S. "Theodicy." In *Evangelical Dictionary of Theology*, edited by Walter A. Elwell, 1184–87. Grand Rapids: Baker Academic, 2001.

Fergusson, David A. S. *The Cosmos and the Creator: An Introduction to the Theology of Creation.* London: SPCK, 1998.

———. "Will the Love of God Finally Triumph?" In *Nothing Greater, Nothing Better: Theological Essays on the Love of God,* edited by Kevin J. Vanhoozer, 186–202. Grand Rapids: Eerdmans, 2001.

Fiddes, Paul S. "Creation out of Love." In *The Work of Love: Creation as Kenosis,* edited by John Polkinghorne, 167–91. Grand Rapids: Eerdmans, 2001.

———. *The Creative Suffering of God.* Oxford: Clarendon, 1988.

———. *Participating in God: A Pastoral Doctrine of the Trinity.* London: Dartman, Longman & Todd, 2000.

———. *Past Event and Present Salvation: The Christian Idea of Atonement.* London: Darton, Longman & Todd, 1989.

Fiorenza, Elisabeth Schüssler, and David Tracy, editors. *The Holocaust as Interruption.* Concilium 175. Edinburgh: T. & T. Clark, 1984.

Flint, Robert. *Anti-Theistic Theories: Being the Baird Lecture for 1877.* 4th ed. Edinburgh and London: Blackwood and Sons, 1889.

———. *Theism; Being the Baird Lectures for 1876.* 8th revised ed. Edinburgh and London: Blackwood & Sons, 1891.

Floyd, Richard L. *When I Survey the Wondrous Cross: Reflections on the Atonement.* Acton, MA: Confessing Christ, 2000.

Fontinell, Eugene. "John Hick's 'After-Life': A Critical Comment." *Cross Currents* 28.3 (1978) 310–17, 324.

Ford, David. *Theology: A Very Short Introduction.* Oxford: Oxford University Press, 1999.

Foyle, Anastasia. "Human and Divine Suffering: The Relation between Human Suffering and the Rise of Passibilist Theology." *Ars disputandi* 5 (2005). Online: http://www.arsdisputandi.org (accessed: 26 Mar 2008).

Fraser, Alexander Campbell. *Philosophy of Theism.* Second Series. London: Blackwood & Sons, 1896.

Fretheim, Terence E. "To Say Something—About God, Evil, and Suffering." *Word & World* 19.4 (1999) 339, 346–50.

Friedman, M. *Problematic Rebel: Melville, Dostoievsky, Kafka, Camus.* Chicago, London: University of Chicago Press, 1970.

Froude, James Anthony. "The Book of Job." In *Short Studies on Great Subjects,* vol. 1, 281–338. London: Longmans, Green, 1890.

Galloway, George. *The Philosophy of Religion.* Edinburgh: T. & T. Clark, 1914.

Garvie, A. E. *The Christian Certainty amid the Modern Perplexity: Essays, Constructive and Critical, Towards the Solution of Some Current Theological Problems.* London: Hodder & Stoughton, 1910.

Geivett, R. Douglas. *Evil and the Evidence for God: The Challenge of John Hick's Theodicy.* Philadelphia: Temple University Press, 1993.

Glover, Willis B. *Evangelical Nonconformists and Higher Criticism in the Nineteenth Century.* London: Independent Press, 1954.

Goetz, Ronald. "The Suffering God: The Rise of a New Orthodoxy." *Christian Century* 103 (1986) 385–89.

Gordis, Robert. "Cruel God or None: Is There No Other Choice?" *Judaism* 21 (1972) 277–84.

Gore, Charles. *Dissertations on Subjects Connected with the Incarnation.* 2nd ed. London: Murray, 1896.

Gottschalk, Stephen. "Theodicy after Auschwitz and the Reality of God." *Union Seminary Quarterly Review* 41.3–4 (1987) 77–91.

Grant, John W. *Free Churchmanship in England 1870–1940: With Special Reference to Congregationalism*. London: Independent Press, n.d. [pre-1957]

Graves, Thomas H. "A Critique of John Hick's Theodicy from an African Perspective." *Perspectives in Religious Studies* 18.2 (1991) 23–37.

Greenberg, Irving. "Cloud of Smoke, Pillar of Fire: Judaism, Christianity, and Modernity after the Holocaust." In *Auschwitz: Beginning of a New Era? Reflections on the Holocaust*, edited by Eva Fleischner, 7–55. New York: KTAV, 1977.

———. "Judaism and Christianity after the Holocaust." *Journal of Ecumenical Studies* 12.4 (1975) 521–51.

Gregersen, Niels Henrik. "The Cross of Christ in an Evolutionary World." *Dialog* 40.3 (2001) 192–207.

Griffith-Jones, E. *The Challenge of Christianity to a World at War*. London: Duckworth, 1915.

Guelich, Robert A. *Word Biblical Commentary*, vol. 34a, *Mark 1–8:26*. Dallas: Word, 2002.

Gunton, Colin E. *The Actuality of the Atonement: A Study of Metaphor, Rationality and the Christian Tradition*. Edinburgh: T. & T. Clark, 1988.

———. "The Church on Earth: The Roots of Community." In *On Being the Church: Essays on the Christian Community*, edited by Colin E. Gunton and Daniel W. Hardy, 48–80. Edinburgh: T. & T. Clark, 1989.

———. *Yesterday and Today: A Study of Continuities in Christology*. London: Darton, Longman & Todd, 1983.

Haar, Murray. "God, the Bible, and Evil after the Holocaust." *Word & World* 19.4 (1999) 372–80.

Hall, Douglas J. *God and Human Suffering: An Exercise in the Theology of the Cross*. Minneapolis: Augsburg, 1986.

Hamilton, Kenneth. "Created Soul—Eternal Spirit: A Continuing Theological Thorn." *Scottish Journal of Theology* 19.1 (1966) 23–34.

Hanratty, Gerald. "Divine Immutability and Impassibility Revisited." In *At the Heart of the Real: Philosophical Essays in Honour of the Most Reverend Desmond Connell, Archbishop of Dublin*, edited by Fran O'Rourke, 137–62. Dublin: Irish Academic, 1992.

Hardy, Daniel W. "Created and Redeemed Sociality." In *On Being the Church: Essays on the Christian Community*, edited by Colin E. Gunton and Daniel W. Hardy, 21–47. Edinburgh: T. & T. Clark, 1989.

Harries, Richard. "Ivan Karamazov's Argument." *Theology* 81 (1978) 104–11.

Hart, David Bentley. *The Doors of the Sea: Where Was God in the Tsunami?* Grand Rapids; Eerdmans, 2005.

———. "No Shadow of Turning: On Divine Impassibility." *Pro Ecclesia* 11.2 (2002) 184–206.

Hart, Trevor A. "Sinlessness and Moral Responsibility: A Problem in Christology." *Scottish Journal of Theology* 48 (1995) 37–54.

———. "Universalism: Two Distinct Types." In *Universalism and the Doctrine of Hell*, edited by Nigel M. De S. Cameron, 1–34. Grand Rapids: Baker Book House; Carlisle: Paternoster, 1993.

Hart, Trevor A., and Daniel P. Thimell, editors. *Christ in Our Place: The Humanity of God in Christ for the Reconciliation of the World: Essays Presented to James Torrance*. Allison Park, PA: Pickwick, 1989.
Hastings, Adrian. *A History of English Christianity 1920–1990*. 3rd ed. London: SCM, 1991.
Hegel, Georg W. F. *Lectures on the Philosophy of Religion*. 3 vols. Translated by E. B. Speirs and J. B. Sanderson. London: Kegan Paul, 1895.
———. *Lectures on the Philosophy of Religion*. 3 vols. Edited by Peter C. Hodgson. Translated by R. F. Brown, P. C. Hodgson and J. M. Steward. Berkeley: University of California Press, 1987.
———. *Vorlesungen über die Philosophie der Religion: Nebst Einer Schrift über die Beweise vom Dasen Gottes*. 2 vols. 2nd ed. Berlin: Duncker u. Humblot, 1840.
Helmstadter, Richard, and Bernard Lightman, editors. *Victorian Faith in Crisis: Essays on Continuity and Change in Nineteen-Century Religious Belief*. London: Macmillian, 1990.
Hermann, Wilhelm. *The Communion of the Christian with God: Described on the Basis of Luther's Statements*. 2nd English ed. London: Williams & Norgate, 1906.
Hick, John. "Coherence and the God of Love Again." *Journal of Theological Studies* 24 (1973) 522–28.
———. *Death and Eternal Life*. London: Collins, 1976.
———. "Evil and Incarnation." In *Incarnation and Myth: The Debate Continued*, edited by Michael Goulder, 77–84. London: SCM, 1979.
———. *Evil and the God of Love*. Fontana Library. London: Collins, 1966.
———. *Evil and the God of Love*. 2nd ed. London: Macmillian, 1977.
———. "Freedom and the Irenaean Theodicy Again." *Journal of Theological Studies* 21 (1970) 419–22.
———, editor. "God, Evil, and Mystery." In *God and the Universe of Faiths*, 53–61. London: Macmillan, 1973.
———. "The Problem of Evil in the First and Last Things." *Journal of Theological Studies* 14.2 (1968) 591–602.
Highfield, Ron. "The Problem with *The Problem of Evil*: A Response to Gregory Boyd's Open Theist Solution." *Restoration Quarterly* 45.3 (2003) 165–80.
Holmes, Steve. "Can Punishment Bring Peace? Penal Substitution Revisited." *Scottish Journal of Theology* 58 (2005) 104–23.
Hopko, Thomas. "On Good and Evil." In *Abba: The tradition of Orthodoxy in the West; Festschrift for Bishop Kallistos (Ware) of Diokleia*, edited by John Behr, Andrew Louth, and Dimitri Conomos, 179–92. Crestwood, NY: St. Vladimir's Seminary Press, 2003.
Horrocks, Don. *Laws of the Spiritual Order: Innovation and Reconstruction in the Soteriology of Thomas Erskine of Linlathen*. Studies in Evangelical History and Thought. Milton Keynes: Paternoster, 2004.
House, Francis H. "The Barrier of Impassibility." *Theology* 83 (1980) 409–15.
Indinopulos, Thomas A. "Christianity and the Holocaust." *Cross Currents* 28.3 (1978) 257–67.
Iverach, James. *Evolution and Christianity*. London: Hodder & Stoughton, 1894.
Jantzen, Grace. "Do We Need Immortality?" *Modern Theology* 1 (1984) 33–44.
Jenkins, Philip. *The Next Christendom: The Coming of Global Christianity*. Oxford: Oxford University Press, 2002.
Johnson, John J. "Should the Holocaust Force Us to Rethink Our View of God and Evil?" *Tyndale Bulletin* 52 (2001) 117–28.

Johnson, Mark D. *The Dissolution of Dissent, 1850–1918*. New York: Garland, 1987.
Johnson, Robert Clyde. *Authority in Protestant Theology*. Philadelphia: Westminster, 1959.
Jones, Peter d'A. *The Christian Socialist Revival 1877–1914: Religion, Class, and Social Concern in Late-Victorian England*. Princeton: Princeton University Press, 1968.
Kane, Stanley G. "The Failure of Soul-Making Theodicy." *International Journal for Philosophy of Religion* 6 (1975) 1–22.
———. "Soul-Making Theodicy and Eschatology." *Sophia* 14.2 (1975).
Kant, Immanuel. "On the Failure of All Attempted Philosophical Theodicies." In *Kant on History and Religion*, edited by Michel Despland, 283–98. Montreal: McGill—Queen's University Press, 1973.
Kärkkäinen, Veli-Matti. "'Evil, Love and the Left Hand of God': The Contribution of Luther's Theology of the Cross to an Evangelical Theology of Evil." *Evangelical Quarterly* 74.3 (2002) 215–34.
King-Farlow, John, and Niall Shanks. "Theodicy: Two Moral Extremes." *Scottish Journal of Theology* 41.2 (1988) 153–76.
Langford, T. A. *In Search of Foundations: English Theology 1900–1920*. Nashville: Abingdon, 1969.
Leibniz, Gottfried Wilhelm. *Theodicy: Essays on the Goodness of God, the Freedom of Man and the Origin of Evil*. Edited with an Introduction by Austin Farrrer. Translated by E. M. Huggard. London: Routledge & Kegan Paul, 1951.
Leftow, Brian. "God, Concepts Of," in *Routledge Encyclopedia of Philosophy*, edited by E. Craig. London: Routledge, 1998. Online: http://www.rep.routledge.com/article/K030SECT8.
Lerner, Berel Dov. "Interfering with Divinely Imposed Suffering." *Religious Studies* 36 (2000) 95–102.
Lewis, Alan E. *Between Cross and Resurrection: A Theology of Holy Saturday*. Grand Rapids: Eerdmans, 2001.
Lewis, C. S. *The Problem of Pain*. Reprint ed. San Francisco: HarperSanFrancisco, 1996.
Loades, Ann. "Kant's Concern with Theodicy." *Journal of Theological Studies* 26 (1975) 361–76.
Lovejoy, Arthur O. "Milton and the Paradox of the Fortunate Fall." In *Essays in the History of Ideas*, 277–95. New York: Capricon, 1960.
Lyonnet, Stanislas, and Léopold Sabourin. *Sin, Redemption, and Sacrifice: A Biblical and Patristic Study*. Rome: Biblical Institute Press, 1970.
MacKinnon, Donald M. "Aspects of Kant's Influence on British Theology." In *Kant and His Influences*, edited by George MacDonald Ross and Tony McWalter, 348–66. Bristol: Thoemmes, 1990.
———. "Some Aspects of the Treatment of Christianity by the British Idealists." *Religious Studies* 20 (1984) 133–44.
Mackintosh, H. R. *The Doctrine of the Person of Jesus Christ*. Edinburgh: T. & T. Clark, 1912.
MacKintosh, Robert. *Christianity and Sin*. London: Duckworth, 1913.
Marshall, I. Howard. "The Theology of the Atonement." In *The Atonement Debate: Papers from the London Symposium on the Theology of the Atonement*, edited by Derek Tidball, David Hilborn, and Justin Thacker, 49–68. Grand Rapids: Zondervan, 2008.
Martineau, James. *A Study of Religion: Its Sources and Contents*. Vol. 2. Oxford: Clarendon, 1888.

Marty, Martin E., and Dean G. Peerman, editors. *A Handbook of Christian Theologians.* Cambridge: Lutterworth, 1984.

Maxwell, Jack M. "A Conversation with Robert Paul." In *Studies of the Church in History: Essays Honoring Robert S. Paul on His Sixty-Fifth Birthday,* edited by Horton Davis, 3–26. Pittsburgh Theological Monographs 5. Allison Park, PA: Pickwick, 1983.

McCabe, Hebert. "The Involvement of God." *New Blackfriars* 66 (1985) 464–76.

McCormack, Bruce L. *For Us and for Our Salvation: Incarnation and Atonement in the Reformed Tradition.* Studies in Reformed Theology and History 1.2. Edited by David Willis-Watkins. Princeton: Princeton Theological Seminary, 1993.

McGrath, Alister E. *Bridge-Building: Communicating Christianity Effectively.* Leicester: InterVarsity, 1992.

———. *Christian Theology: An Introduction.* 3rd ed. Oxford: Blackwell, 2001.

———. *The Enigma of the Cross.* 2nd ed. London: Hodder & Stoughton, 1996.

———. *Luther's Theology of the Cross: Martin Luther's Theological Breakthrough.* Oxford: Backwell, 1985.

McKenzie, David. "A Kantian Theodicy." *Faith and Philosophy* 1 (1984) 236–47.

McWilliams, Warren. "Divine Suffering in Contemporary Theology." *Scottish Journal of Theology* 33 (1980) 35–53.

———. "Only the Triune God Can Help: The Relation of the Trinity to Theodicy." *Perspectives in Religious Studies* 33.3 (2006) 345–59.

Meeks, M. Douglas. "God's Suffering Power and Liberation." *Journal of Religious Thought* 33 (1976) 44–54.

Mesle, C. Robert. "Does God Hide from Us: John Hick and Process Theology on Faith, Freedom and Theodicy." *International Journal for Philosophy of Religion* 24.1–2 (1988) 93–111.

———. "The Problem of Genuine Evil: A Critique of John Hick's Theodicy." *Journal of Religion* 66.4 (1986) 412–30.

Mill, John Stuart. *Essays on Ethics, Religion and Society.* Collected Works of John Stuart Mill. Edited by J. M. Robson. Toronto: University of Toronto Press, 1969.

Milton, John. *Paradise Lost.* New York: Longman, 1998.

Moltmann, Jürgen. *The Crucified God: The Cross of Christ as the Foundation and Criticism of Christian Theology.* Translated by R. A. Wilson and John Bowden. Reprint ed. Minneapolis: Fortress, 1993.

———. *God in Creation: A New Theology of Creation and the Spirit of God.* Translated by Margaret Kohl. New York: Fortress, 1993.

———. "Theodicy." In *A New Dictionary of Christian Theology,* edited by A. Richardson and J. Bowden, 564–66. London: SCM, 1983.

———. *The Trinity and the Kingdom: The Doctrine of God.* Translated by Margaret Kohl. San Francisco: Harper & Row, 1981.

Moorhead, J. H. "'As Though Nothing at All Happened': Death and Afterlife in Protestant Thought, 1840–1925." *Soundings* 67 (1984) 453–71.

Mozley, J. K. *The Doctrine of the Atonement.* London: Duckworth, 1915.

———. *The Heart of the Gospel.* London: SPCK, 1925.

———. *The Impassibility of God: A Survey of Christian Thought.* Cambridge: Cambridge University Press, 1926.

Müller, Julius. *The Christian Doctrine of Sin.* Translated by William Urwick from the German of the Fifth Edition. 2 vols. Edinburgh: T. & T. Clark, 1868.

Newbigin, Lesslie. *The Gospel in a Pluralist Society.* Grand Rapids: Eerdmans, 1989.

Ngien, Dennis. *The Suffering of God According to Martin Luther's Theologia Crucis*. New York: P. Lang, 1995.

———. "Trinity and Divine Passibility in Martin Luther's 'Theologia Crucis.'" *Scottish Bulletin of Evangelical Theology* 19 (2001) 31–64.

Niebuhr, Reinhold. *The Nature and Destiny of Man: A Christian Interpretation*. Vol. 1, *Human Nature*. London: Nisbet, 1941.

Orr, James. *The Christian View of God and the World as Centring in the Incarnation: Being the Kerr Lectures for 1890–1891*. Edinburgh: Elliot, 1893.

Packer, J. I. "What Did the Cross Achieve? The Logic of Penal Substitution." *Tyndale Bulletin* 25 (1974) 3–45.

Padgett, Alan G. "Crucified Creator: The God of Evolution and Luther's Theology of the Cross." *Dialog* 42.3 (2003) 300–304.

Pals, Daniel L. *The Victorian "Lives" Of Jesus*. San Antonio: Trinity University Press, 1982.

Pannenberg, Wolfhart. "A Theology of the Cross." *Word & World* 8.2 (1988) 162–72.

Paterson-Smyth, John. *God and the War*. London: Hodder & Stoughton, 1915.

Paulson, Steven D. "Luther on the Hidden God." *Word & World* 19.4 (1999) 363–71.

Peake, A. S. *Recollections and Appreciations*. London: Epworth, 1938.

Peel, Albert. *These Hundred Years: A History of the Congregational Union of England and Wales 1831–1931*. London: Congregational Union of England and Wales, 1931.

Perry, Michael, editor. *Deliverance: Psychic Disturbances and Occult Involvement*. London: SPCK, 1987.

———. "Taking Satan Seriously." *Expository Times* 101.4 (1990) 105–12.

Peters, Ted. "Grace, Doubt, and Evil: The Constructive Task of Reformation Theology." *Dialog* 41.4 (2002) 273–84.

Peterson, Michael L. *God and Evil: An Introduction to the Issues*. Boulder, CO: Westview, 1998.

Pfleiderer, Otto. *The Philosophy of Religion on the Basis of Its History*. Vol. 4. Translated by Allan Menzies. London & Edinburgh: Williams and Norgate, 1888.

Phillips, D. Z. *The Concept of Prayer*. London: Routledge and Kegan Paul, 1965.

———. *The Problem of Evil and the Problem of God*. London: SCM, 2004.

Pollard, T. Evan. "Impassibility of God." *Scottish Journal of Theology* 8 (1955) 353–64.

Pope, Alexander. *An Essay on Man*. Edited by Maynard Mack. London: Methuen, 1947.

Powys, David J. "The Nineteenth and Twentieth Century Debates about Hell and Universalism." In *Universalism and the Doctrine of Hell*, edited by Nigel M. De S. Cameron, 93–138. Grand Rapids: Baker Book House, 1993.

Pringle-Pattison, Andrew Seth. *The Idea of God in the Light of Recent Philosophy*. Oxford: Clarendon, 1917.

Puccetti, Roland. "Loving God: Some Observations on John Hick's Evil and the God of Love." *Religious Studies* 2 (1967) 255–68.

Quanbeck, Warren. "Divine Sovereignty and Human Freedom—a Perennial Problem." *Word & World* 19.4 (1999) 401–9.

Quinn, Philip L. "Original Sin, Radical Evil and Moral Identity." *Faith and Philosophy* 1.2 (1984) 188–202.

Rahner, Karl. "Why Does God Allow Us to Suffer?" In *Theological Investigations* 19, 194–208. New York: Crossroad, 1983.

Ramsey, Arthur Michael. *From Gore to Temple: The Development of Anglican Theology between Lux Mundi and the Second World War 1889–1939*. London: Longmans, 1960.

Rashdall, H. R. *The Idea of the Atonement in Christian Theology*. London: Macmillan, 1919.

———. "The Problem of Evil." In *The Faith and the War: A Series of Essays by Members of the Churchmen's Union and Others on the Religious Difficulties Aroused by the Present Condition of the World*, edited by F. J. Foakes-Jackson, 77–100. London: Macmillan, 1916.

Reardon, Bernard M. G. *Hegel's Philosophy of Religion*. London: Macmillian, 1977.

———. *Kant as Philosophical Theologian*. Basingstoke: Macmillian, 1988.

———. *Religious Thought in the Victorian Age: A Survey from Coleridge to Gore*. London: Longman, 1980.

Reichenbach, Bruce R. "Evil and a Reformed View of God." *International Journal for Philosophy of Religion* 24.1–2 (1988) 67–85.

Richard, Lucien. *What Are They Saying About the Theology of Suffering?* New York: Paulist, 1992.

Ricoeur, Paul. "Evil, a Challenge to Philosophy and Theology." *Journal of the American Academy of Religion* 53.4 (1985) 635–48.

Rist, John M. "Coherence and the God of Love." *Journal of Theological Studies* 23 (1972) 95–105.

Robbins, Jerry. "The Mystery of Evil." *Word & World* 19.4 (1999) 381–88.

Robinson, N. H. G. *Christ and Conscience*. London: Nisbet, 1956.

Roth, John K. *A Consuming Fire: Encounters with Elie Wiesel and the Holocaust*. Atlanta: John Knox, 1979.

———. "The Silence of God." *Faith and Philosophy* 1 (1984) 407–20.

———. "A Theodicy of Protest." In *Encountering Evil: Live Options in Theodicy*, edited by Stephen T. Davis, 7–22. Edinburgh: T. & T. Clark, 1981.

Routley, Erik. *The Story of Congregationalism*. London: Independent Press, 1961.

Rowell, Geoffrey. *Hell and the Victorians: A Study of the Nineteen-Century Theological Controversies Concerning Eternal Punishment and the Future Life*. Oxford: Clarendon, 1974.

Russell, Jeffrey Burton. *Mephistopheles: The Devil in the Modern World*. Ithaca and London: Cornell University Press, 1986.

Sarot, Marcel. "Auschwitz, Morality and the Suffering of God." *Modern Theology* 7 (1991) 135–52.

———. "Patripassianism, Theopaschitism and the Suffering of God. Some Historical and Systematic Considerations." *Religious Studies* 26 (1990) 262–375.

Scaer, David P. "The Concept of Anfechtung in Luther's Thought." *Concordia Theological Quarterly* 47 (1983) 15–30.

Schweitzer, Albert. *The Quest of the Historical Jesus: A Critical Study of Its Progress from Reimarus to Wrede*. Translated by W. Montgomery. London: A. & C. Black, 1910.

Sell, Alan P. F. "Anabaptist-Congregational Relations and Current Mennonite-Reformed Dialogue." *Mennonite Quarterly Review* 61.3 (1987) 321–34.

———. *Nonconformist Theology in the Twentieth Century*. The Didsbury Lectures; 2006. Bletchley, Milton Keynes: Paternoster, 2006.

———. *Philosophical Idealism and Christian Belief*. New York: St. Martin's Press, 1995.

———. *Theology in Turmoil: The Roots, Course, and Significance of the Conservative-Liberal Debate in Modern Theology*. Grand Rapids: Baker, 1986.

Simmons, Ernest L. "Creation in Luther's Theology of the Cross." *Dialog* 30 (1991) 50–58.

Simoni, Henry. "Divine Passibility and the Problem of Radical Particularity: Does God Feel Your Pain?" *Religious Studies* 33.3 (1997) 327–47.

Smail, Thomas A. *Once and for All: A Confession of the Cross*. London: Darton, Longman & Todd, 1998.

Smith, Michael P. "What's So Good About Feeling Bad?" *Faith and Philosophy* 2.4 (1985) 424–29.

Smoot, J. F. "Does God Suffer? Divine Passibility in Anglican Theology from Lux Mundi to the Second World War: With Particular Reference to the Thought of William Temple and John Kenneth Mozley." PhD thesis, University of Aberdeen, 1996.

Sölle, Dorothee. *Suffering*. London: Darton, Longman & Todd, 1975.

Southgate, Christopher. *The Groaning of Creation: God, Evolution, and the Problem of Evil*. Louisville: Westminster John Knox, 2008.

Sponheim, Paul R. "To Say Something—About God, Evil, and Suffering." *Word & World* 19.4 (1999) 338, 340–45.

Strohl, Jane E. "Suffering as Redemptive: A Comparison of Christian Experience in the Sixteenth and Twentieth Centuries." In *Revisioning the Past: Prospects in Historical Theology*, edited by Mary Potter Engel and Walter E. Wyman Jr., 95–111. Minneapolis: Fortress, 1992.

Stump, Eleonore. "Faith and the Problem of Evil." In *Seeking Understanding: The Stob Lectures, 1986–1998*, 491–550. Grand Rapids; Eerdmans, 2001.

———. "The Problem of Evil." *Faith and Philosophy* 2.4 (1985) 392–423.

———. "Second-Person Accounts and the Problem of Evil." In *Faith and Narrative*, edited by Keith E. Yandell, 86–103. Oxford: Oxford University Press, 2001.

———. "Suffering for Redemption: A Reply to Smith." *Faith and Philosophy* 2.4 (1985) 430–36.

Sundberg, Walter. "Satan the Enemy." *Word & World* 28 (2008) 29–37.

Surin, Kenneth. "The Impassibility of God and the Problem of Evil." *Scottish Journal of Theology* 35 (1982) 97–115.

———. "Theodicy?" *Harvard Theological Review* 76 (1983) 225–47.

———. *Theology and the Problem of Evil*. Signposts in Theology. Oxford: Blackwell, 1986.

Sutherland, Steward. *Atheism and the Rejection of God: Contemporary Philosophy and "The Brothers Karamazov."* Oxford: Blackwell, 1977.

Swanton, R. "Scottish Theology and Karl Barth." *Reformed Theological Review* 33 (1974) 17–25.

Swoboda, Philip J. "Windelband's Influence on S. L. Frank." *Studies in East European Thought* 47.3–4 (1995) 259–90.

Sykes, Stephen S. "Theology through History." In *The Modern Theologians: An Introduction to Christian Theology in the Twentieth Century*, edited by David F. Ford, 229–35. Oxford: Blackwell, 1997.

Taliaferro, Charles. "The Passibility of God." *Religious Studies* 25 (1989) 217–24.

Temple, William. *Mens Creatrix: An Essay*. London: Macmillan, 1935.

Terry, Justyn Charles. *The Justifying Judgement of God: A Reassessment of the Place of Judgement in the Saving Work of Christ*. Paternoster Theological Monographs. Milton Keynes: Paternoster, 2007.

Thompson, Thomas R. "Nineteenth-Century Kenotic Christology: The Waxing, Waning, and Weighing of a Quest for a Coherent Orthodoxy." In *Exploring Kenotic*

Christology: The Self-Emptying of God, edited by C. Stephen Evans, 74–111. Oxford: Oxford University Press, 2006.

Tilley, Terrence W. "The Use and Abuse of Theodicy." *Horizons* 11 (1984) 304–19.

Tinder, Galen. "Luther's Theology of Christian Suffering and Its Implications for Pastoral Care." *Dialog* 25 (1986) 108–13.

Tomlin, Graham. "The Theology of the Cross: Subversive Theology for a Postmodern World?" *Themelios* 23 (1997) 59–73.

Torrance, Thomas F. "The Atonement. The Singularity of Christ and the Finality of the Cross: The Atonement and the Moral Order." In *Universalism and the Doctrine of Hell*, edited by Nigel M. De S. Cameron, 223–54. Grand Rapids: Baker, 1993.

Trakakis, Nick. "Theodicy: The Solution to the Problem of Evil, or Part of the Problem?" *Sophia* 47 (2008) 161–91.

Travis, Stephen H. *Christ and the Judgement of God: Divine Retribution in the New Testament*. Basingstoke: Marshall Morgan & Scott, 1986.

———. "Christ as Bearer of Divine Judgement in Paul's Thought About the Atonement." In *Jesus of Nazareth: Lord and Christ: Essays on the Historical Jesus and New Testament Christology*, edited by Joel B. Green and Max Turner, 332–45. Grand Rapids: Eerdmans, 1994.

Trethowan, Illtyd. "Dr. Hick and the Problem of Evil." *Journal of Theological Studies* 18 (1967) 407–16.

Tulloch, John. *The Christian Doctrine of Sin*. Croall Lectures, 1876. Edinburgh: Blackwood & Sons, 1876.

Van Inwagen, Peter. "The Argument from Evil." In *Christian Faith and the Problem of Evil*, edited by Peter van Inwagen, 55–73. Grand Rapids: Eerdmans, 2004.

———. *The Problem of Evil*. Oxford: Clarendon, 2006.

Volf, Miroslav. "I Protest, Therefore I Believe." *Christian Century* 122.3 (2005) 39.

Voltaire. *Candide, or Optimism*. Translated by Norman Cameron. London: Hamish Hamilton, 1947.

von Loewenich, Walther. *Luther's Theology of the Cross*. Translated by Herbert J. A. Bouman. Belfast: Christian Journals, 1976.

Walker, D. P. *The Decline of Hell*. Chicago: University of Chicago Press, 1964.

Ward, James. *The Realm of Ends; or Pluralism and Theism: The Gifford Lectures Delivered in the University of St Andrews in the Years 1907–1910*. Cambridge: Cambridge University Press, 1911.

Ward, Keith. "Freedom and the Irenaean Theodicy." *Journal of Theological Studies* 20 (1969) 249–54.

———. *Rational Theology and the Creativity of God*. Oxford: Blackwell, 1982.

———. *Religion and Creation*. Oxford: Clarendon, 1996.

Weinandy, Thomas G. *Does God Suffer?* Notre Dame: University of Notre Dame, 2000.

———. *In the Likeness of Sinful Flesh: An Essay on the Humanity of Christ*. Edinburgh: T. & T. Clark, 1993.

Wengert, Timothy J. "'Peace, Peace . . . Cross, Cross': Reflections on How Martin Luther Relates the Theology of the Cross to Suffering." *Theology Today* 59.2 (2002) 190–205.

Wetzel, James. "Can Theodicy Be Avoided? The Claim of Unredeemed Evil." *Religious Studies* 25 (1989) 1–13.

Wheeler, Michael. *Heaven, Hell, and the Victorians*. Cambridge: Cambridge University Press, 1994.

Whitaker, W. "Is Our Faith Shaken?" In *Ethical and Religious Problems of the War: Fourteen Addresses*, edited by J. Estlin Carpenter, 134–46. London: Lindsey, 1916.
Whitney, Barry L. *What Are They Saying About God and Evil?* New York: Paulist, 1989.
Wiesel, Elie. *The Night Trilogy*. [Consisting of the Three Stories: *Night, Dawn*, and *The Accident*.] New York: Hill & Wang, 1990.
Wickham, E. R. *Church and People in an Industrial City*. London: Lutterworth, 1957.
Williams, Rowan. "Redeeming Sorrows." In *Religion and Morality*, edited by D. Z. Phillips, 132–48. London: Macmillan, 1996.
Willis, Robert E. "Christian Theology after Auschwitz." *Journal of Ecumenical Studies* 12.4 (1975) 493–519.
———. "Confessing God after Auschwitz: A Challenge for Christianity." *Cross Currents* 28.3 (1978) 269–87.
Williams, Robert R. "Theodicy, Tragedy, and Soteriology: The Legacy of Schleiermacher." *Harvard Theological Review* 77.3–4 (1984) 395–412.
Windelband, Wilhelm. *An Introduction to Philosophy*. Translated by Joseph McCabe. London: Unwin, 1921.
———. *Präludien*. Tübingen: Mohr, 1907.
Wollaston, Isabel. "The Possibility and Plausibility of Divine Abusiveness or Sadism as the Premise for a Religious Response to the Holocaust." *Journal of Religion & Society* 2 (2000). Online: http://moses.creighton.edu/JRS/2000/2000-1.html.
———. "'Starting All over Again': The Criteria for a Christian Response to the Holocaust." *Theology* 93 (1990) 456–62.
Wolterstorff, Nicholas. "If God Is Good and Sovereign, Why Lament?" *Calvin Theological Journal* 36 (2001) 42–52.
Young, Frances. "A Cloud of Witnesses." In *The Myth of God Incarnate*, edited by John Hick, 13–47. London: SCM, 1977.

Index

Adams, Marilyn McCord, 154n2, 161, 164n36, 181
Adeney, Walter, 170n55, 199n87
Anglo-Afghan War (1878–1880), 116
atonement
    Christ "made sin" in, 18, 37, 41–47, 57, 140–43, 162–63
    critiques of Forsyth's understanding of, 35, 41
    integrative nature of, 53–54
    "juridical" models of, 147, 152
    mode of Christ's death, 24–25
    need for, 12–13
    penal element in, 40–47, 141–42
    as regeneration, 48–52, 147, 149, 172
    relation to the resurrection, 36, 39–40, 48, 52
    as satisfaction, 37–40, 147, 149
    sin dealt with as a unity in, 24–25, 43–44, 47
    substitutionary nature of, 47–49
    as victory, 40–48, 149
Augustine of Hippo, 103
Auschwitz. *See* Second World War

Baldwin Brown, James, 18n80, 66n33, 71n58, 154n2
Barth, Karl, x, 8, 73, 220–21, 225n38
Bauckham, Richard, 5, 101–2, 105, 107n35, 124, 158, 160, 162–64, 178n84
Begbie, Jeremy, 62
Bergson, Henri, 22

Blocher, Henri, 205–6, 210
Bradley, William Lee, 145, 150, 159
Brothers Karamazov, The. See Fyodor Dostoyevsky
Bruce, A. B., 154n2, 198, 200, 235
Bulgarian uprising (1876), 109–10, 116
Bushnell, Horace, 157, 165

Calvin, John, and Calvinism, 31–33, 186n26, 198
Campbell, R. J., 118, 199, 207n107, 237
Camus, Albert, 5, 102n16, 127, 178
Cave, Sydney, 35
Christ
    affirmation of his humanity and divinity, 37, 54
    faith of Jesus: as our model, 169–73; exercised on the cross, 168, 173–74
    growth of Jesus, 131–40
    "historical Jesus," 135–40
    kenosis. See under kenosis of God
    non posse peccare, 134, 162, 199n87, 208
    obedience of Jesus, 38, 53, 66, 133–34, 138–40, 143–50, 158–60, 171
    suffering of. *See under* suffering of God
Cook, R. R., 72
conscience
    as a corporate entity, 102–3

conscience (*cont.*)
   as point of contact with the moral, 13–14
   as source of the sense of guilt, 92–93
Cox, Samuel, 120–22
creation
   "Augustinian" view of, 195, 200, 229, 238
   "best of all possible worlds," 206, 223–25
   ex nihilo, 211–12
   God's relationship with: evil as a feature of God, 214–19; God's "necessity" to create, 215–16, 220–23; God's "need" for the world, 217–19; God's love for creation, 215–16, 218–23; panentheism, 210–13
   "Irenaean" view of, 195–96, 223, 227, 229–30, 238
cross
   as centre of Forsyth's theodicy, x–xi, 4–5, 29, 234–36
   "eternal" cross within God, 158–60
   Forsyth's understanding of, 30
   as God's "self-justification" (atonement), 34–54. See also atonement
   as God's "self-justification" (theodicy), 55–58, 64–65, 149
   as revelation of God and his ways (*theologia crucis*), 7, 30–31: "crucial" evolution of the world, 74–82; election, 30–33; "eternal" *kenosis* of God, 158–60; faith as protest, 176; God as chief sufferer, 154–55; God's "self-justification," 34; human involvement in sin, 103; Jesus' "inner life," 134n41; kenotic Christology, 130; moral as the real, 31, 191; necessity of creation, 211; reasons for entry of sin, 205, 225n38; reasons for entry of suffering, 201–2; response to "victim-centred" theodicy, 110–14; "secondary acts of judgement," 83–86, 91, 93; work of the Holy Spirit, 51n113
   as revelation of sin, 23–26
   relationship to God's suffering, 157–60
   relationship to Jesus' life, 145–50
   where Christ was forsaken, 142–44

Dale, R. W., 66, 93
Dinsmore, C. A., 157
divine passibility. *See* suffering of God.
Dostoyevsky, Fyodor, 5, 101–2, 105–6, 113n56, 120, 123, 178
dualism, possibility of. *See* omnipotence of God

election of God, 31–33, 69–71
eschatology, personal. *See under* evolution, "crucial": goal of humanity
evil
   Forsyth's understanding of, 15–16, 27–28
   as "sin" and "suffering," 14–15. *See also* sin; suffering
evolution, "crucial"
   goal of humanity, 60–61: annihilation, 66–67; personal eschatology, 69–72, 96–97, 124n92; universalism, 65–73, 104, 117–19
   goal of the rest of creation, 62–65
   need for faith to grasp, 80–82, 106, 127
   progress, modern notions of, 75–78

evolution, Darwinian, 27, 73–74, 77, 187–88, 195–96, 226–27, 237–38

Fairbairn, A. M., 150n118, 229
faith
  conditions necessary for, 198–200
  as the crux of Forsyth's theodicy, 238–39
  Forsyth's understanding of, 79–80
  as the highest moral response to God, 197
  as protest, 174–76
  relationship with sin, 203–4, 208–9
  to appropriate "secondary acts of judgement," 96, 106, 127
  to grasp "crucial evolution," 80–82, 106, 127.
  See also Christ: faith of Jesus
Fergusson, David, 72
Fiddes, Paul, 144, 156–57, 163–66, 193n59, 221
First World War
  fate of non-Christian soldiers who died, 70
  as God's "secondary act of judgement," 82–86, 94–95, 97, 100–101, 228
  impact on Christianity, x, 2, 27, 73–75, 124–25
  response of pacifism, 91, 94
Floyd, Richard, 19
Forsyth, Peter Taylor
  his life, ix, 8
  need to quote him liberally, 5–6
  significance of his theodicy, xi, 3–4
  significance of his work in general, ix–x, 3n13
  theocentric approach, 32, 67, 94–95, 111–13, 116–17
  unsystematic nature of his writings, 4–5.
  See also theodicy (Forsyth's)
free will, human
  cause of entry of sin, 186–87
  as a condition of faith, 198–99
  relation to "secondary acts of judgement," 85, 100–101, 227
  relation to God's will, 114–15, 212
  relation to morality, 11
  relation to *non posse peccare*, 199n87
  relation to sin as personality, 21
  relation to universalism, 68–73, 117, 230, 238
  understood in "libertarian" sense, 11

Galloway, James, 21, 193n57, 209n109, 222
Gore, Charles, 130
Great War. *See* First World War
Greenberg, Irving, 107–8
Gunton, Colin, 3, 31, 63–64, 88, 145, 196

Hall, George, 44, 182, 189n42, 193, 206, 223–24
Harries, Richard, 167
Hart, David Bentley, 214–15
Hart, Trevor, 4, 8, 10, 14, 29, 46, 50, 199n87
Hegel, G. W. F., and Heglianism, 41–44, 77–79, 86–87, 90, 125, 130, 185–86, 216–17, 237
Hick, John, 3, 71, 195–96, 201, 230, 238n4
Holman Hunt, William, 104
Holocaust. *See* Second World War
Holy Spirit, 51, 59–60, 98, 144n97, 152
Hughes, T. Hywel, 40–41, 112
Hunter, A. M., 35, 197–98

Index

Immutability, God's, 131–32, 159n23, 212n120
Irenaeus of Lyons, 53n120, 147n110, 195

Jantzen, Grace, 72
judgement, God's
   primary act of, 82
   "secondary acts of": effected by human agency, 89–92, 115–17; certainty of, 95–97; First World War as an event of (*see under* First World War); how they arise, 86–88; how to identify, 228; likely recipients of, 88–89; nature of, 85–86; purpose of, 83–86; relation to primary act, 83; retributive aspects of, 121–23; what they encompass, 92–95
Justification of God, The, x, 1, 6–7, 9, 26, 179

Kant, Immanuel, 10, 31, 39n50, 105n32, 125, 199
Karamazov, Ivan. *See* Fyodor Dostoyevsky
kenosis of God
   in the act of creation, 187
   of the Father, 159
   of the Son, 20, 38, 128–31, 134, 143, 149, 162–63, 171

Lawler, Howard, 6, 68, 119n78
Leibniz, Gottfried, 184, 186, 220, 224–25
Lewis, Alan, 20, 175
Lewis, C. S., 111n50, 119n77
Lovejoy, Arthur, 209
Luther, Martin, 7, 30, 79, 81, 201

Mackintosh, Robert, 148
McCurdy, Leslie, 8, 13n55, 188n38, 241

McGrath, Alister, 113–14
Mill, John Stuart, 225
Milton, John, 2
Moltmann, Jürgen, x–xi, 5, 55n126, 125, 144, 150, 159, 166, 174
morality
   conscience as point of contact, 13–14
   source and nature of, 10–13
   as ultimate reality, 10
Mozley, J. K., 5–6, 11, 29, 41, 50, 55–56, 153, 160n24

"New Theology." *See* Campbell, R. J.
Nicoll, William Roberston, 238
Niebuhr, Reinhold, 193n59
Nygren, Anders, 220

"*O felix culpa*," 204, 206, 209, 213, 234
omnipotence of God, 224–26

panentheism. *See under* creation: God's relationship with
Pitt, Clifford, 215–16, 219–20
Pope, Alexander, 184
post-death existence. *See under* evolution, "crucial": goal of humanity
predestination. *See* election of God

Rashdall, H. R., 158
Reardon, Bernard, 42–43
resurrection. *See* atonement: relation to the resurrection
Ritschl, Albrecht, ix, 23, 51
Rodgers, John H., 62, 75, 191
Roth, John, 174–75
Russell, Stanley, 41, 51n111, 60
Satan, 18–20, 26, 36, 91, 119, 122. *See also* sin: relation to Satan
Schlatter, Adolf, 170
Schweitzer, Albert, 135–36, 140
Second World War, 4, 107–11

"self-justification" of God. *See under* cross
Sell, Alan, 30, 41
Simpson, A. F., 82
sin
  antagonism towards God (*see* sin: nature and severity of)
  as an aspect of evil, 15–16
  entry of: as inevitable, 183; Forsyth's account of, 187–93; God's foreknowledge of, 207–8; reasons for, 203–9; rejection of "dualism," 183–84; 190–93; rejection of "monism," 184–86; 190–93; responsibility for, 193–94, 229–30
  God's use of, 90–91, 207, 227
  knowledge of, 23–26
  nature and severity of, 16–17, 44, 185–86, 205, 209, 216
  our resulting guilt, 21, 103
  as a personality, 18–23
  relation to Satan, 18–20
  summary of Forsyth's response to, 233–34
Smail, Thomas, 20, 54, 55n126, 99, 128
Smith, Michael, 227
Sölle, Dorothy, 107
Stump, Eleonore, 108–9
suffering
  of animals, 26, 188, 237–238
  as an aspect of evil, 15–16
  arising from "acts of secondary judgement" (*see* judgement, God's: "secondary acts of")
  arising from the conditions surrounding the origin of humanity, 226–30
  cessation of, 202–3
  due to natural disasters, 227
  entry of: reasons for, 201–3, 224–25; responsibility for, 194, 229–30
  experienced by "pre-Fall humanity," 187–89
  of God. *See* suffering of God
  nature of, 26–28
  summary of Forsyth's response to, 233
suffering of God
  implications for theodicy: Christ as our model for faith, 167–76; God as the greatest sufferer, 155–67
  incomparable nature of, 128, 154–55, 162
  relationship to the Cross, 157–60
  relationship to the suffering of the world, 160–65
  suffering of Christ: as the epitome of human suffering, 57, 83, 149, 164; in the process of growth, 133–40; on the cross, 140–44, 162–63; purpose in the atonement, 38
  suffering of the Father, 150–52, 163
Surin, Kenneth, 3, 107–11, 179–80
Swoboda, Philip, 191–92

Terry, Justyn, 46n84 and 87, 53n120, 60
theocentric approach. *See under* Forsyth, Peter Taylor
theodicy (Forsyth's)
  his description of "philosophical theodicies," 183–86
  his understanding of, 2, 57–58
  historical nature of, 123–26
  integrative nature of, 236–237, 239
  in relation to his contemporaries, 234–35

theodicy (Forsyth's) (cont.)
   response to "victim-centred" approach, 107–11
   significance of, xi, 3–4
   teleological nature of, 98–99: necessity and appropriateness of the means, 100–6; need for universal salvation, 117–19, 229–30; place of retributive judgement, 120–23; possibility of leading to greater suffering, 114–17; possibility of means justifying the end, 106–14
   See also theodicy (general); suffering of God: implications for theodicy
theodicy (general)
   definitions, 1
   distinction between "defences" and "theodicy" proper, 1–2
   distinction between "practical" and "theoretical," 1–2, 179–82
   ways of classification, 1–2
theologia crucis. See cross: as revelation of God and his ways
Torrance, T. F., 118
Trakakis, Nick, 104n25, 105n32
Travis, Stephen, 122

universalism. See under evolution, "crucial": goal of humanity

Ward, Keith, 220
Weinandy, Thomas, 167
Wengret, Timothy, 175
White, Edward, 66
Windelband, Wihelm, 188, 191–92, 199, 201
Wood, Ralph, 78
Wundt, Wihelm, 22

www.ingramcontent.com/pod-product-compliance
Lightning Source LLC
Chambersburg PA
CBHW071242230426
43668CB00011B/1549